"This remarkably comprehensive textbook shaped by contributions from international experts in online group psychotherapy, advances the field in a clear, valuable and absolutely necessary fashion. In presenting the state of the art of online group therapy—research, theory, accrued wisdom and technique—across modalities, and across ages, this textbook responds effectively to a major paradigm shift in contemporary practice. The authors address the implementation gap that exists between what our clients seek and need, and what practitioners must understand to embrace this evolution in our field. It is an essential guide for group therapy clinicians, supervisors, and educators."

Molyn Leszcz, M.D. *Past-President, The American Group Psychotherapy Association. Professor of Psychiatry, University of Toronto*

"This is an illuminating volume that arrives at a perfect time in our post-pandemic world. *The Virtual Group Therapy Circle* is a comprehensive compendium of up-to-date information, perspectives, and instruction about online group therapy, a burgeoning field that many professionals believed could not work. How does one build an alliance and create cohesion? Don't we need to need to be able to see the body? To feel the other's presence? To experience the visceral intensity of the moment? This volume candidly tackles such questions focusing on how different models of group therapy (including Interpersonal, Modern Analytic, Psychodramatic, CBT, Systems-Centered, and more) can achieve successful outcomes balanced by addressing drawbacks to online intervention. The Virtual Group Therapy Circle will undoubtedly be viewed as the essential reference book on the subject on online group therapy."

Joseph Shay, Ph.D. *co-author of Psychodynamic Group Psychotherapy and co-editor of Odysseys in Psychotherapy and Complex Dilemmas in Group Therapy*

"Some might consider 'remote group psychotherapy' an oxymoron. Is it possible that the highly interactive and relational form of psychotherapy practiced in a group format can be effective in a remote situation? There are certainly advantages to remote therapy. It makes therapy available to some who would otherwise be unable to access it. It can be cost-efficient since it reduces office costs, travel expense, etc. It is convenient. There are also obvious disadvantages. It is not the same as sitting together. There are some who do not have the technical skills to properly use remote sessions. Some cannot afford the technology required to participate in remote psychotherapy. Some people's living situations do not allow sufficient privacy to participate online. Indeed, there is a question as to whether online group therapy can guarantee confidentiality. Nonetheless, prompted by Covid-19, group therapy now is being practiced remotely. Some therapists have found it so convenient that they have decided to offer only remote group therapy henceforth. Haim Weinberg, Arnon Rolnick, and Adam Leighton present us a comprehensive text to examine this new world of group psychotherapy. They have brought together a stellar cast of authors who examine various aspects of remote group psychotherapy. The group begins by examining some of the challenges of doing group therapy remotely. The next section focuses on various group process approaches and how they are impacted by being online. The book then examines some specific approaches: Psychodrama and Person-Centered groups online. The book concludes with the important topic of training, teaching and supervising online groups. This is an important book that focuses on an extremely important topic in the practice of group psychotherapy today."

J. Scott Rutan, Ph.D. *Founder, Center for Group Psychotherapy, Massachusetts General Hospital/Harvard Medical School. Past President, American Group Psychotherapy Association*

The Virtual Group Therapy Circle

This book provides group therapists and counselors with the necessary knowledge and help to develop their skills in effectively conducting online groups.

Group therapy represents the most efficient utilization of the scarce resource of mental health interventions. Online settings dramatically increase the dissemination of this approach. This book identifies the diverse challenges and suggests solutions in remote group therapy for specific therapeutic approaches such as psychodynamic, relational, psychodrama, CBT, ACT, and group supervision. The contributing authors explore specific issues that anyone who conducts groups online should be aware of.

Using a group therapy lens, this book develops further the ideas and areas explored in the authors' previous books *Theory and Practice of Online Therapy* and *Advances in Online Therapy*.

Haim Weinberg, PhD, is a clinical psychologist, group analyst, and certified group psychotherapist based in California, USA.

Arnon Rolnick, PhD, is a licensed clinical psychologist with a special interest in the usage of technology in psychotherapy. Based in Tel Aviv, Israel, he is a certified supervisor in CBT and biofeedback.

Adam Leighton is a counselor, group facilitator, wilderness therapy facilitator, and lecturer at the Ruppin Academic Centre, Israel.

The Library of Technology and Mental Health

Series Editor: Jill Savege Scharff, M.D.

This series, established in 2011, features authors from various parts of the global economy discuss the effects of technology on our growth and development, our relationships, our society in general, and the relevance of communication by telephone and internet to the spread of psychoanalysis. They discuss the impact of internet addiction including pornography, the effects of screen time and social media, and the value of telepsychotherapy, telepsychoanalysis, and telesupervision, all illustrated with clinical examples, ethical considerations, and personal reflections. The series editor is Jill Savege Scharff.

Screen Relations
Gillian Russell

Psychoanalysis Online 2
Impact of Technology on Development, Training and Therapy
Jill Savege Scharff

Psychoanalysis, Identity and the Internet
Explorations into Cyberspace
Andrea Marzi

Psychoanalysis Online 3
The Teleanalytic Setting
Jill Savege Scharff

Psychoanalysis Online 4
Teleanalytic Practice, Teaching, and Clinical Research
Jill Savege Scharff

Advances in Online Therapy
Emergence of a New Paradigm
Haim Weinberg, Arnon Rolnick, and Adam Leighton

The Virtual Group Therapy Circle
Advances in Online Group Theory and Practice
Haim Weinberg, Arnon Rolnick, and Adam Leighton

The Virtual Group Therapy Circle

Advances in Online Group Theory
and Practice

Edited by
Haim Weinberg, Arnon Rolnick and
Adam Leighton

Routledge
Taylor & Francis Group

NEW YORK AND LONDON

Cover image: © Getty Images

First published 2024
by Routledge
605 Third Avenue, New York, NY 10158

and by Routledge
4 Park Square, Milton Park, Abingdon, Oxon OX14 4RN

Routledge is an imprint of the Taylor & Francis Group, an informa business

Library of Congress Cataloging-in-Publication Data
A catalog record for this title has been requested

ISBN: 978-1-032-16446-5 (hbk)
ISBN: 978-1-032-16445-8 (pbk)
ISBN: 978-1-003-24860-6 (ebk)

DOI: 10.4324/9781003248606

Typeset in Times New Roman
by Taylor & Francis Books

Contents

Illustrations

Figures

Tables

About the Contributors

Deniz Altinay, MA, is a psychodrama trainer and psychotherapist. He gained his Master's degree in Psychological Counseling in Ankara, Türkiye (Turkey). He is the former General Secretary of the Turkish Group Psychotherapy Association and the founder and President of the Istanbul Psychodrama Institute, the Turkish Union of Psychodrama Institutes, and the Istanbul Playback Theatre. He is the founder of Child Psychodrama, School and Company Educations Section. His published seven books include *Psychodrama 450 Warm-Up Games, Handbook of Psychodrama, Group Psychotherapy, and Spontaneity Theatre, Child Psychodrama, Selected Issues in Psychodrama, Contemporary Applications of Psychodrama, and The Moment*. He is the Managing Editor of the *IGPP E-Journal*. Deniz is a board member of the International Association for Group Psychotherapy and Group Processes (IAGP) and a member of the Federation of European Psychodrama Training Organization (FEPTO) and European Association for Psychotherapy (EAP).

Rachel Arnold, MS, is a graduate student in the Clinical Psychology doctoral program at Brigham Young University. Her research focuses on therapy effectiveness and factors that make therapy work, with group psychotherapy being a specific theme throughout the majority of her research.

Aaron E. Black is a clinical psychologist in full-time private practice in Rochester, NY, where he treats individuals, couples, and groups, and provides clinical consultation. Additionally, he leads training groups and workshops nationally and writes about attachment theory, psychological trauma, and group psychotherapy. He is a Fellow and a past Board member of the American Group Psychotherapy Association (AGPA) and he is on the faculty at the Center for Group Studies in New York City.

Cliff Briggie, MBA, PsyD, LCSW, spent more than 45 years providing leadership, consultation, supervision, and direct clinical care in a variety of behavioral health organizations, most recently working at Community Health Center in Connecticut. He has authored numerous publications and presentations on many topics in the fields of Clinical and Organizational Psychology. He had expertise in the areas of trauma, addiction, and group therapy; and was passionate about providing training and supervision to future generations of psychotherapists to come.

Nina W. Brown, EdD, LPC, NCC, Distinguished Fellow of the AGPA and an American Psychological Association (APA) Fellow, is a professor and eminent scholar at Old Dominion University in Norfolk, VA. She received her doctorate from the College of William and Mary, and has served as President of the Mid-AGPA, Secretary of the AGPA, President of APA Division 49, President of the Group Council, and other positions. She has written and published more than 40 books on group psychotherapy and narcissism, some of which have been translated into other languages.

Gary M. Burlingame, PhD, is Professor and Chair of the Brigham Young University Psychology Department, and he is affiliated with the clinical psychology doctoral program. His scholarly work is focused on factors that lead to effective small group treatments for mental/medical illness and measurement. He has contributed over 60 books, technical manuals, and chapters, and more than 150 peer-reviewed articles.

Carlos Canales, PsyD, CGP, FAGPA, SEP^{TM}, is a bilingual licensed clinical psychologist, a certified group psychotherapist, and a Somatic Experiencing® practitioner. He specializes in working with affect, the body, and relationships. He leads training groups and workshops emphasizing attachment and Somatic Experiencing principles. He is the founder of Vida Psychotherapy, an outpatient clinic in Des Moines, IA.

Katherine S. Chapman, MA, is a current doctoral student in clinical psychology at Fielding Graduate University, based in Houston, TX. She has experience working in private practice and medical school settings with individuals across the lifespan in both digital and in-person formats.

Stavros Charalambides is a relational analyst and group psychotherapist, and an elected member of the International Association for Relational Psychoanalysis and Psychotherapy (IARPP) Board of Directors since 2018. He co-chairs the IARPP special interest group focusing on couples, families, and groups. In 2016, he founded and is Director of the Greek Institute for Relational and Group Psychotherapy. His latest book, *The Envy Executioner*, has been published in Greek (Disigma Publications, 2021). His main interests are in sibling dynamics, envy, and mourning in the transference and countertransference.

Hanan El-Mazahy, MD, PhD, ABMPP, is a child and adolescent mental health consultant. She is Triple Board certified in Psychiatry, Pediatrics, and Mental Health, and practices in Alexandria, Egypt. Her psychotherapeutic interests include psychodrama, EMDR, and DBT.

Shelley Firestone, MD, F-AGPA, PAT, CGP, has been in private practice for 30 years treating adults, adolescents, and children with individual, couple, and group psychotherapy and psychodrama. She is an active contributor to the AGPA and the American Society for Group Psychotherapy and Psychodrama (ASGPP), and the founder of the Jacob and Zerka Moreno Foundation for Psychodrama, Sociometry and Group Psychotherapy (MZF); she is also a member of the American Society of Marriage and Family Therapy (AAMFT) and the American Society of Addiction Medicine (ASAM). She is the winner of the Zerka T. Moreno Award (2016). Her contributions to multiple journals reflect her passion for psychodrama, group psychotherapy, and writing.

Robi Friedman, PhD, is a clinical psychologist and past President of the International Group Analytic Society. His combined small/large groups model, called the Sandwich Model, is applied in many present conflict dialogue meetings. He writes on dreaming and dreamtelling, on interpersonal pathology known as Relation Disorders, and on the habitus of societies under threat or glory which he calls the "Soldier's Matrix."

Susan P. Gantt, PhD, ABPP, CGP, AGPA-DF, FAPA, has coordinated group psychotherapy training in psychiatry at Emory University for 29 years. She chairs the Systems-Centered Training (SCT) and Research Institute; teaches SCT in the US, Europe, China; and trains groups in Atlanta, San Francisco, and the Netherlands. Susan has co-authored four books with Yvonne Agazarian, and she co-edited *The Interpersonal Neurobiology of Group Psychotherapy and Group Process* with Bonnie Badenoch. She received the 2011 Alonso Award for Excellence in Psychodynamic Group Psychotherapy. Her most recent book is *Systems-Centered Training: An Illustrated Guide for Applying a Theory of Living Human Systems* (Agazarian, Gantt, & Carter, 2021).

Kimberly B. Harrison, PhD, is a clinical psychologist based in Houston, TX. She has a robust private practice which incorporates both virtual and in-person sessions for groups and individuals. Kimberly also is the founder of the Conative Group, PLLC, a collective of mental health practitioners serving a variety of needs in local and virtual communities.

Ruthellen Josselson, PhD, ABPP, is Professor of Clinical Psychology at the Fielding Graduate University and a psychotherapist in practice. She is Co-director of the Irvin D. Yalom Institute of Psychotherapy and has led, taught, and supervised group therapy for many years. Her most recent book is *Narrative and Cultural Humility: Reflections from "The Good Witch" Teaching Psychotherapy in China.*

Iris Lachnit is a trainee in clinical psychology based in Berlin, Germany. She obtained her Master's degree in Clinical Psychology and Psychotherapy in 2018, and trained at Dresden University of Technology (Germany), the University of Turku (Finland), and the University of Connecticut (US). As part of her training, she has worked in a psychosomatic-focused clinic and now focuses on outpatient systemic therapy. In 2021, she returned to the US in order to work with Dr. Meera Rastogi on online art therapy groups at the University of Cincinnati.

Anat Laronne, PhD, is a medical psychologist and head of the medical psychology service at Assuta Medical Centers in Israel. Anat is a lecturer in the fields of medical and health psychology in several colleges in the country. She has specialized in psycho-oncology and in CBT treatment for the last 12 years, working in a variety of health care services. She has served as a member of the medical psychology consultant community for the Israeli Ministry of Health since 2018.

Enav Karniel Lauer, PhD, is a licensed clinical social worker, a psychotherapist, and a group analyst. She currently works as a lecturer at the Bar-Ilan University's School of Social Work and as a Coordinator of the Therapy Rehabilitation and Health Supplementary Study Program. She is also a lecturer at the Training Program at the Israeli Institute of Group Analysis. Enav serves as a supervisor of group and individual therapists and works with individuals and groups in her private practice. Her fields of expertise include Holocaust trauma, trauma loss and dissociation, and analytical group therapy.

Adam Leighton is a counselor, group facilitator, and wilderness therapy facilitator. He specializes in experiential therapy, merging technology, outdoor activities, and Acceptance and Commitment Therapy. Adam created and instructs the CBT-based Group Facilitation with Outdoor Experiential Work course at Ruppin Academic Center. He is also the co-founder of Digi Card Therapy, a virtual therapy card platform for online therapy.

Uri Levin is a clinical psychologist, group analyst, and organizational consultant. He is a member of the IIGA, GASi, and IAGP, and chairs the Groups section of the EFPP. He teaches at Tel Aviv University and supervises individual and group settings. He works mainly at his private practice in Tel Aviv with adults, adolescents, couples, and groups. His book (co-edited with Anna Zajenkowska) *Europe on the Couch* was published in 2020 (Routledge).

Cheri L. Marmarosh, PhD, is a Professor of Clinical Psychology at the George Washington University, and has published over 50 empirical and theoretical articles that focus on how group and individual psychotherapy facilitate change. She authored *Attachment in Group Psychotherapy and Groups: Fostering a Culture of Change*. She is the incoming editor of the *International Journal of Group Psychotherapy*. She is a Fellow of the AGPA and APA. Cheri is a certified group therapist, past President of APA Division 49, and is Board certified (ABPP). She has a private practice and works with individuals, couples, and groups.

Gila Ofer, PhD, is a clinical psychologist, training psychoanalyst, and group analyst. The co-founder and past President of the Tel Aviv Institute of Contemporary Psychoanalysis and a founding member of the Israeli Institute of Group Analysis, she serves on the faculty of both institutes and at the Post-Graduate School for Psychoanalytic Psychotherapy, Tel Aviv University. She is the editor of the *EFPP Psychoanalytic Psychotherapy Review*. She has published articles in leading journals and has presented her work and taught in Israel, Europe, East Asia, and the US. Her edited book *A Bridge over Troubled Water: Conflicts and Reconciliation in Group and Society* was published in 2017.

Tate Paxton is a clinical psychology graduate student under Dr. Gary Burlingame's mentorship. His research focuses on measurement of group therapeutic relationships, group therapy outcomes, and group therapy process.

Darryl L. Pure, PhD, ABPP, FAGPA, CGP, is a clinical psychologist with 38 years of experience facilitating groups in many different settings both clinically and in training group formats. Formerly on the faculty of the Feinberg School of Medicine, Northwestern University, where he coordinated group training in the Department of Psychiatry, he is now Clinical Associate Professor of Leadership at the University of Chicago Booth School of Business. Darryl also maintains a private practice in which he conducts six groups weekly.

Aileen Rands, MS, is a doctoral student at Brigham Young University. Her ongoing research work with Dr. Gary Burlingame focuses on the study of group psychotherapy outcomes.

Meera Rastogi, PhD, MAAT, ATR-BC, CGP, is a licensed psychologist, board certified art therapist, certified group psychotherapist, and psychology professor at the University of Cincinnati, Clermont College. She teaches in the psychology program and directs the University's Pre-Art Therapy Certificate Program. In addition to teaching, Meera runs an art therapy group at the University of Cincinnati Gardner Neuroscience Institute and has a small practice where she sees individual clients. She recently co-edited *Foundations of Art Therapy: Theory and Applications* (2023).

Alexandra Robelo, MPsy, is a third-year doctoral candidate in the George Washington University Professional Psychology Program. Alexandra has an interest in conducting research around the various factors that contribute to the efficacy of group therapy. With the changing landscape of online healthcare following the outbreak of the COVID-19 pandemic, that interest has expanded to understanding how the shift to more online work will impact clinicians and patients.

Arnon Rolnick, PhD, is a clinical psychologist and is certified as a supervisor in CBT and biofeedback. He has authored works focusing on the integration of interpersonal neurobiology with technological innovations. Arnon advises different organizations on transitioning to online training and supervision. Additionally, he is the director of a clinic in Tel Aviv, Israel, where he fosters the integration of various psychotherapeutic approaches among the clinic's team of therapists.

Reut Ron, MSc, is a research analyst at the Assuta Health Services Research Institute and a lecturer in the fields of epidemiology and research at several colleges in Israel. Reut holds a degree in Epidemiology from Tel Aviv University, and she has experience in promoting, designing, and conducting research. Before taking up her position at Assuta, Reut was a research coordinator in the Department of Child and Women's Health at the Gertner Institute for Epidemiology and Health Policy Research.

Judith Schoenholtz-Read, EdD, is Professor Emeritus and a former Director of Clinical Training, Doctoral Program in Clinical Psychology, Fielding Graduate University. She is a Fellow of the AGPA and the Canadian Group Psychotherapy Association. Her book *Handbook of Online Learning in Higher Education* was co-edited with Kjell Rudestam and Monique Snowden (Fielding Graduate University Press,

2021). She is a registered psychologist living and practicing in Vancouver, BC, Canada.

Dana Shor, MAAT, is an art therapist, a cognitive behavioral psychotherapist instructor at ITA, and an expert in ACT therapy through experience. She manages the CBT unit in a public mental health institute and works as a therapist in a private clinic.

Ingrid Söchting, PhD, RPsych, is the Director of the UBC Psychology Clinic and a Clinical Professor in the Department of Psychiatry at UBC. Over the past 25 years, she has specialized in treatment for mood and anxiety disorders including groups for depression, anxiety disorders, OCD, and trauma. She teaches courses in psychotherapy and ethics in the clinical psychology program at UBC and supervises psychology and psychiatry residents in CBT and Interpersonal Psychotherapy. She is involved in psychotherapy research and has published over 30 peer-reviewed articles on psychotherapy program evaluations, outcomes, and process variables such as expectations for therapy, perceptions of treatment credibility, and dropout prevention. She has given over 50 invited lectures and workshops in Canada and abroad. Her *Cognitive Behavioral Group Therapy: Challenges and Opportunities* (Wiley Blackwell, 2014) is a complete guide to group therapy across mental health problems. Ingrid is a Canadian-certified CBT therapist and a certified group therapist of the AGPA.

Alicia Solorio, MPsy, is a current student in the Professional Psychology Program at George Washington University. Alicia practices from an integrative lens, using Psychodynamic and Cognitive-Behavioral Therapy techniques in her work with patients. Her research interests include online group therapy, the juxtaposition of religion and psychotherapy, and forensic populations within correctional settings.

Lisa Stefanac, MBA, is Clinical Professor of Leadership at the University of Chicago Booth School of Business. Lisa is also co-founder and partner of KSE Leadership, a privately held leadership consulting firm, and co-founder and partner of Assessing in Action, a leadership and team effectiveness tools business. Lisa has deep experience and proven results in team coaching, interpersonal and team dynamics, leadership development, and organizational change.

Ella Stolper, MA, is a psychoanalytic psychotherapist and training group analyst, a supervisor and teacher at the Institute of Group Analysis in Israel and at the Group Facilitation Programs at Tel Aviv University. She founded and manages an institute for group analysis in the Russian Federation (Stavropol), is a member of the board of directors of an Israeli association for group therapy, a consultant for organizations, and has a private practice.

Barney Straus, MSW, MA, is an adventure-based therapist in private practice in Chicago, IL, where he works with individuals and groups to treat people recovering from addictions and compulsive behaviors. Barney has created programming for many treatment centers in the US. He is a part-time faculty member at Loyola University Chicago, School of Social Work, Roosevelt University, Department of Psychology, and New Mexico Highlands University, School of Social Work. Barney is the founder of Adventure Forward Therapy, a practice dedicated to integrating adventure into the therapeutic process. He is the author of the 2018 book *Healing in Action: Adventure-Based Counseling with Therapy Groups*. He is also the co-author of the fourth edition of *Group Psychotherapy with Addicted Populations* (Routledge, 2023).

Nikolaos Takis, PhD, is a clinical psychologist, an individual and group psychotherapist, and a psychodrama trainer. He is Associate Professor and Director of the counselling centre of the American College of Greece. He is a full member of the French and Hellenic Society of Psychoanalytic Group Psychotherapy and past president of FEPTO. He is also a candidate psychoanalyst at the Hellenic Psychoanalytical Society.

Haim Weinberg, PhD, is a clinical psychologist, group analyst, and certified group psychotherapist based in California, USA. He served as the Director of International Programs at the Professional School of Psychology where he created and coordinated an online doctoral program in group psychotherapy. He co-edited a series of books about the social unconscious and wrote a book on Internet groups. He developed group therapy training groups in Asia, and is leading online training process groups for therapists around the world.

Darrah Westrup, PhD, is a licensed clinical psychologist with a private practice in Durango, CO. She is a recognized ACT expert and has authored or co-authored four books on ACT, including *Learning ACT in Groups: An Acceptance and Commitment Therapy Skills Training Manual for Therapists* and *Advanced ACT: An Experienced Practitioner's Guide to Optimizing Delivery*. Darrah is an ACBS Fellow and a peer-reviewed ACT trainer, providing supervision, consultation, and training to individuals and institutions worldwide.

Ellen L. Wright, PhD, is a licensed psychologist and psychoanalyst in private practice in Philadelphia. She is a founder and faculty member at the Center for Group Studies in New York City and a supervising and training analyst at the Philadelphia School of Psychoanalysis and the Institute of Contemporary Psychoanalysis in Los Angeles. Ellen lectures nationally and internationally and has authored papers on innovative applications of psychoanalytic techniques. Her recent book chapter, "Redefining Female Power: The Myth of the Selfless Therapist," can be found in *Women, Intersectionality, and Power in Group Psychotherapy Leadership* (Routledge, 2022).

Feng Xing is a doctoral student in the Professional Psychology Program at George Washington University. He is currently training at Georgetown University, providing short-term psychotherapy and group therapy. His research interests focus on group therapy, supervision, and training models for international trainees.

Efrat Zigenlaub, PhD, is an expert organizational social psychologist and group facilitator. She is a graduate of the Israeli Institute for Group Analysis and leads an analytical therapeutic group in her private clinic. She serves as a senior lecturer at Ono Academic College, a lecturer at Haifa University, School of Social Work and Tel Aviv Jaffa Academic College, and is a faculty member of the Tel Aviv University group mentoring program. Efrat is also a consultant and group facilitator in public and business organizations.

Chapter 1

Introduction

Haim Weinberg, Arnon Rolnick and Adam Leighton

In the virtual world we meet,
Strangers bound by common need,
To heal our wounds and mend our hearts,
Online group therapy starts.
Through screens we share our deepest fears,
And shed our doubts and tears,
With others who understand,
The struggles of a helping hand.
We find solace in the words,
Of those who've been there, heard,
The same stories, felt the same,
And found a way to make a change.
Though miles apart, we're not alone,
In this digital therapy home,
We find strength in one another,
To face our fears and heal our cover.
So let us come together,
In this virtual space forever,
To heal and grow, to be set free,
In online group therapy.

The above poem was authored by ChatGPT, an interactive model designed to generate text based on provided instructions. We requested the model to create a poem about online group therapy, and this was the output it produced. Is this the future of online group therapy?

Preface

This is the third book we have co-edited about remote therapy (Weinberg & Rolnick, 2020; Weinberg et al., 2023). It will certainly not surprise readers to hear our main message: that this is a new paradigm with advantages and disadvantages. Specifically regarding group therapy we expect that the

DOI: 10.4324/9781003248606-1

transition to remote therapy is likely to lead to a significant leap in the use of this format. We argue that remote therapy enables a significant increase in the accessibility and prevalence of group therapy.

In 1968, Carl Rogers said that groups will be "the most significant social invention of the century" (p. 16). Research (Burlingame et al., 2021) shows that group therapy outcomes are equivalent to individual therapy. Groups have many benefits both in terms of the processes that take place in them and in the practical and cost-effective context. Many individual therapists as well as group therapists emphasize that participation in courses and experiences of group therapy was very important to their professional development (Hahn at al., 2022). Despite this, there is a concerning trend of a decrease in the number of training programs offering group therapy (Yalom & Leszcz, 2020).

In the latest (sixth) edition of *The Theory and Practice of Group Psychotherapy*, Yalom and Leszcz (2020) write:

> Paradoxically, however, professional training for group therapists has failed to keep pace with the widespread clinical application of the group therapies. Fewer and fewer training programs—whether in psychology, social work, counseling, or psychiatry—provide the depth of training and supervision that future practitioners require.
>
> (p. 2)

In sum, there is a huge gap between the growing need for group psychotherapeutic interventions and the relative lack of use of groups.

Amid a shortage in mental health professionals and an increasing demand due to the COVID-19 pandemic, the United States is currently facing a mental health crisis (White House, 2023). Whittingham et al. (2023) conducted a statistical analysis of publicly available data sets and other resources to assess the utilization of unmet therapy needs across the United States. Their findings were remarkable; if 10% of unmet needs for therapy were fulfilled through group therapy rather than individual therapy, the impact would be threefold: (1) mental health treatment would be accessible to an additional 3.5 million people; (2) the need for 34,473 new therapists would be reduced; and (3) the United States would save more than $5.6 billion. Utilizing online groups could play a significant role in increasing the prevalence of group therapy and achieving these positive outcomes.

Recruiting and selecting participants for group therapy can be a challenging task, particularly when therapists choose participants from their existing pool of individual patients, which may raise ethical conflicts of interest. However, we believe that online group therapy offers a simpler and more efficient recruitment process. Patients can now participate in groups from remote geographical areas, and the selection process can be expedited since we can conduct intake meetings with group candidates online, thereby saving time.

Online groups can also mitigate issues such as high dropout rates and inconsistent meeting attendance. The ease of connecting from home and the elimination of the commute and associated stress can lead to increased attendance. In in-person groups, a patient's inability to attend physically can lead to dissatisfaction among group members and decreased group cohesion. Remote group therapy can effectively minimize such situations. We anticipate that this book, along with other publications, will encourage therapists to offer more group therapy sessions.

The Mystery of Online Groups

A mysterious gap exists between our intuition regarding online therapy and our experience while treating people online (at least for the editors of this book and for many of our colleagues): On the one hand, our common sense and our bodily experience clearly tell us that the presence of the body is crucial in order to create the trust, safety, and intimacy necessary for a therapeutic encounter. This is not just a matter of intellectual understanding or theoretical arguments: We all "know" that smell, physical proximity, and eye-to-eye contact are essential elements in creating "moments of meetings" (Stern et al., 1998), and we find it hard to believe that without them we can still create an authentic intimate connection, or establish a therapeutic alliance. From a theoretical point of view, the Interpersonal Neurobiology (IPNB) approach emphasizes the importance of mutual regulation based on physical presence. Schore (2003), Siegel (1999), Cozolino (2013) and others claim that what works in therapy is not just the words but the mutual regulation of brain-to-brain, body-to-body. Shifting to online therapy is perceived by many as a relational impoverishment. The missing elements are obvious. But how much do they really matter? We discuss this in depth in our previous books (see the Introduction in Weinberg et al., 2023).

This seems even truer in groups. Mark-Goldstein and Ogden (2013) describe this eloquently:

> For example, when conflict arises in the group, there may be multiple reactions: some group members are on the edge of their chairs ready to fight, some want to get out of the room, and some just freeze or shut down and seem to disappear into the couch.

They suggest that participants should:

> notice what's going on in our bodies with this conflict ... the sensations in our chest, our breath (shallow or deep), the rhythm of our breathing, the changes in posture, tilt of the head, angle of the shoulders, muscular tension, and so forth.

(p. 135)

All these changes are harder to see in online group therapy: In-person, the leader and the group act as a container and help to regulate the emotional and physiological reaction of the group members. But can it happen in online groups?

Most of our colleagues who were forced to treat patients online during the COVID-19 pandemic were surprised not only that it works well, but also about the strong intimate connection that they were able to create with many of their patients in the online world. Having learned how to address the challenges of ensuring a private and confidential space (as discussed in our previous books: Weinberg and Rolnick, 2020; Weinberg et al., 2023), therapists have found that they can establish a warm holding environment in online therapy. Patients are often able to share deep and emotionally charged material, including traumatic or shameful feelings, while still sensing the empathy, acceptance, and presence of their therapists through the screen. As we discussed in our previous book on online individual and couple therapy (Weinberg et al., 2023) there is ample research indicating that a strong therapeutic alliance can be established online (Kaiser et al., 2021) and that the outcome of online therapy is comparable to in-person meeting (Fernandez et al., 2021).

This gap, between our "common sense" and our online experience and research evidence, is even more remarkable in group psychotherapy, since one of the main healing factors in groups is the group cohesion (Burlingame et al., 2018), the group is the vehicle of change. Can we create the same group cohesion online? Can a deep and authentic relationship, similar to that which we observe in in-person groups, be achieved in online groups?

Again, our clinical/human intuition tells us that the answer to these questions is negative. People perceive technology as creating a barrier and the computer screen as hindering intimacy. Indeed, any technological mediation seems to block the ability to be present, which is one of the goals we try to achieve in our groups. However, those of us who have conducted groups online for years, and those who joined this venture during the pandemic, found out that those magical moments of connection that are part of our group tradition can also occur online. People express strong emotions in our online groups: joy, sadness, excitement, yearning, anger—the entire range of human feelings. They cry, they laugh, they mourn, they regress, they raise their voice, they connect on a deep level. Moments of meeting that we see in our "traditional" groups repeat themselves online. The online group can be inspirational, full of transforming moments that can energize therapists and make them feel alive at the end of the session, despite any tiredness or fatigue.

Here is a short group vignette:

> A woman in an online group went through a very difficult period due to family and work stress. She described her suffering in the group,

shed some tears and expressed the lack of support. In fact, she felt very lonely and isolated in her surrounding environment. Group members were very supportive, encouraged and empowered her with warm words, and one female member said: "You see the couch in your room behind you? Imagine that we sit together on that couch, and that I hold you in my arms, wrapping my body around you, allowing you to feel safe and calm." This strong image made a huge impact not only on the distressed member but also created deep intimate feelings for all group members.

Some Possible Explanations

We might have some theoretical explanations for the above mystery. For example, we can look at the different aspects of presence (Lombard & Ditton, 1997) and notice that they lead to a definition of presence as "the perceptual illusion of non-mediation," which can be achieved online (see Weinberg, 2014 for a detailed discussion). Geller (2020, 2023) argues that cultivating and training therapeutic presence in tele-therapy can help therapists to explicitly express presence, enabling clients to experience emotional and psychological safety, and allowing a shared experience, even from a distance. However, this does not explain how *group members* learn to stay present and connect authentically online. In a way, this book tries to unravel this mystery and explain how the here-and-now experience is created in our online groups.

One of the important factors contributing to the success of the online group is the group therapist's *secure presence* (Neeman-Kantor, 2013). This secure presence can compensate for fuzzy conditions, loose boundaries, and leaking containers. The presence of the therapist involves his/her immersion, passion, attention, emotional involvement, reverie, and a readiness to be drawn into enactments (Grossmark, 2007). However, there is something beyond those features, which is how the group therapist holds the group in his/her mind. We assume that the mere fact that the therapist perceives the group as an entity beyond its individual members, addresses some of the interpretations to the group-as-a-whole, and fantasizes the group's matrix, the group as a gestalt, has an impact on the group's cohesion.

The group therapist does not act in void, and it is important to consider the contribution of the group members as they find a way to overcome the limitations of a leaking container (Weinberg, 2016). The participants can imagine the group as a good-enough holding environment despite its problematic "real" qualities. The function of the group depends not on the real properties of the setting, but more on the imagined ones: those that we keep in our mind. Nery (2021, p. 107) calls this experience "the imaginary together." Perhaps this is the "invisible group" that Agazarian (1989) mentioned: "It is important to understand that this ... has absolutely nothing to do with the real, visible people in the real, visible groups" (p. 357).

The capacity of groups and their members to overcome the challenges of online therapy may also be attributed to our innate human urge and longing for social connection. Systems-Centered Therapy, as outlined in Chapter 10, describes the inherent driving forces of groups and systems. We suggest that this driving force is part of what enables successful online group therapy. As group therapists, we believe it is part of our duty to preserve and harness the group's driving force.

The Scope of This Book

As the title of this book clarifies, it is about online *group* therapy. To determine the chapters to be included in this edited volume, we needed to establish the extent of group psychotherapy we wished to cover. The American Group Psychotherapy Association (AGPA) defines group psychotherapy thus:

> Group psychotherapy is an effective form of therapy in which a small number of people meet together under the guidance of a profession-ally trained therapist to help themselves and one another. There are many different approaches to group therapy, but they share in common creating a safe, supportive, and cohesive space to address personal, relationship and societal issues.[1]

As this definition mentions that there are different approaches to group therapy, we had to decide which of these approaches to include in our book. The AGPA website also clarifies that there is a difference between therapy groups, support groups, and self-help groups:

> Group therapy is different from support and self-help groups in that it not only helps people cope with their problems but also provides opportunities for change and growth. Group therapy focuses on relationships, helping you learn how to get along better with other people under the guidance of a trained professional. In contrast, support groups, which may or may not have professional leadership, help people cope with difficult situations but are usually geared toward alleviating symptoms, rather than addressing underlying patterns.

Kivlighan & Kivlighan (2014) identified four clusters of groups, based on the relative ranking of perceived therapeutic factors:

a   Affective insight groups where acceptance, catharsis, interpersonal learning, and self-understanding are viewed as most important (e.g., psychodynamic therapy group).
b   Affective support groups where acceptance, instillation of hope, and universality are perceived as most important (e.g., trauma group).
c   Cognitive support groups where vicarious learning and guidance are ranked most important (e.g., 12-step support groups).
d   Cognitive insight groups where interpersonal learning, self-understanding, and vicarious learning are most important (e.g., cognitive behavioral therapy, or CBT group).

In this book, we focus on groups that are clustered under category (a) and (d) although some authors mention social traumatic situations in online groups.

Burlingame et al. (2021, p. 585) suggest classifying therapeutic groups according to the following breakdown:

- Leaderless groups e.g.,
  - Support
  - 12-step
  - Self-help
- Psychoeducational groups e.g.,
  - Bipolar disorder
  - Cancer
- Psychotherapy groups
  - Manual and time limited
  - Model- and principle-based

Manualized group treatments are typically time-limited upon a specific theoretical orientation (e.g., CBT). Model-based group treatments are less structured than manualized protocols with principle-based interventions that are tailored to individual members as well as the developmental stage of the group-as-whole (for example, group analysis or other psychodynamic approaches).

For our book we decided to include all psychotherapy and psychoeducational groups in the above classification, we do not include leaderless groups, such as the 12 Steps of Alcoholics Anonymous. We focused on the processes that are universal to all groups such as cohesion. We were curious how different approaches to group therapy face and resolve the challenges we identified in our previous book (Weinberg et al., 2023). However, we also asked the authors of the chapters to relate to the specific concepts, methods, and processes that are an integral part of their group approach and to describe how they are converted when we move the group from the circle to the screen. For example, what happens to the group matrix, an important concept of the group analytic approach (Foulkes & Anthony, 1965), when we move online? (see Chapter 8). How is immediacy, a central concept in Modern Group Analysis (Ormont, 1993), affected in remote groups? (see Chapter 7). Can we create functional subgrouping online the same way that we do in-person in the Systems-Centered Therapy approach? (see Chapter 10). How do we focus on the here-and-now, a central idea of Yalom's approach, online? (see Chapter 9).

Our goal was for each author to provide the following elements in their respective chapters:

- A concise introduction to the approach for readers who may not be familiar with it.
- An examination of the benefits, drawbacks, as well as practical and theoretical considerations stemming from the shift to online therapy, with a focus on:
  - Group processes in the context of the particular modality, drawing on group process frameworks (such as Yalom, Foulkes, Bion, etc.)
  - The specific modality being discussed.

Online Interpersonal Processes

By identifying the main interpersonal processes that occur in groups, we can explore whether and how they manifest in online groups, and how group leaders can enhance them in online group settings. Interpersonal group processes lay the foundation for the effectiveness of other group processes and are thus especially important in achieving desired goals. According to Marks et al. (2001), there are three primary types of interpersonal group processes: (a) how group members deal with conflict (conflict management); (b) developing and maintaining engagement and safety; and (c) fostering a sense of togetherness, emotional balance, and effective coping with stress (cohesion and affect management). Conflict management might feel more difficult online; however, from our experience the same skills that group leaders need to manage them in their office work online as well. Safety in online groups can be achieved by wisely calculated dynamic administration (Weinberg, 2020, 2021) and is discussed in many of this book's chapters, as well as cohesion and affect management.

Greene (2019) writes:

> Typically, and most simply, three levels of analysis [in therapy groups] need to be considered:
>
> • The personality of the individual patient, and more particularly the internal world of needs, wishes, motives, anxieties, and "working models" of self and significant others,
> • The interpersonal relationship patterns and processes occurring in the group
> • The collective or shared dynamics within the group-as-a-whole, such as the "basic assumptions" of the group (Bion, 1961).
>
> (p. 60)

The first level of analysis that includes the individual personality and their internal world is not challenged when moving groups online. The question remains whether interpersonal patterns change (see the section on "Disadvantages of Online Groups") and especially whether the group-as-a-whole dynamics are different online than in-person. In this book, we focus on those two levels of analysis and wonder how they change according to each theoretical frame of reference. We were very interested whether Yalom's therapeutic factors (Yalom & Leszcz, 2020) are manifested differently online, and especially the group cohesion, since it is the main therapeutic factor correlated with the group positive outcome. Can it still be achieved online and is it the same kind of cohesion as in offline groups?

Group leaders experience difficulty with two types of behaviors among members of virtual groups (Kozlowski & Holmes, 2017): (1) distraction, mental absenteeism, and difficulty adhering to group boundaries (e.g., punctuality; see below); and (2) difficulty in expressing emotions leading to a diminished sense of intimacy (Gibbs et al., 2017; Weinberg, 2020).

The following are instances of participant behaviors that undermine group boundaries: challenging the group setting (punctuality or lack thereof, etc.); frequent participant absence; entering and exiting group space during sessions; participant exhibiting distraction (e.g., checking text messages); and participant eating during sessions.

Examples of emotional expression include participant disclosure of significant personal information; participant expression of interest in continuing group meetings near the end of the group process; and participant expression of negative emotions (sadness, anger, helplessness) near the end of the group process.

All the above are addressed in our book, taking into account that groups interact at multiple levels (Burlingame et al., 2021; Lo Coco et al., 2019): namely member-to-member, member-to-group-as-a whole, member-to-therapist.

Disadvantages of Online Groups

Groups online share the same risks and dangers as any online treatment faces: privacy and confidentiality are difficult to achieve totally in the online setting, and the fact that groups involve more than one patient only complicates these issues. Since we do not see the full body, we miss some important gestures and postures that give us a lot of information when we see people in our offices. As we have noted in our earlier publications, online platforms can provide clearer visibility of facial expressions, and greater opportunities to observe and interpret the dynamics among all members, provided that one develops the skills to read and attend to these expressions.

In moving group therapy online, there is a loss of liminal space—the time before and after the group therapy session where people have an opportunity to interact with one another. Groups that meet in-person socialize, interact with each other, and bid farewell with customary group rituals during these times.

Allied with the loss of the liminal space is a complaint that patients have about the loss of a boundary between their therapy world and their personal world and the need to create space moving from one to the other. Commuting from home or work to the group taking place in the therapist's office or agency allows for an in-between time where people slowly disconnect from the daily hassles and prepare themselves for the group meetings.

We will briefly describe further contrasts in how we encounter face-to-face groups compared to online groups, differences that may not be immediately apparent when transitioning to online work. For instance, during an in-person session, individuals can choose who they want to sit next to, maybe a person he or she feels particularly comfortable with, thus providing a sense of ease.

If a participant feels overwhelmed (or underwhelmed) during a session, they can distract themselves by dissociation, sometimes by focusing on other members of the group and using non-verbal cues, such as eye contact, to communicate. However, in online groups, available "distractions" will typically be outside the group context, such as checking emails.

Another contrast between in-person and online group therapy, which also differs from online one-on-one therapy, is the size of the faces or images that we see. In in-person meetings, although we sit farther away, we can still focus on an individual, resulting in a perceived larger image, whereas in online therapy, we are limited to viewing a small portion of a person on a computer screen. This disadvantage can be compensated by seeing the facial expressions larger and clearer.

The online group loses its classical format of people sitting in a circle: the circle is squared. The closed circular form provides an additional holding environment sensation since it conveys archaic associations to the womb. In online groups, the members are shown on the screen in boxes, one beside, above, and below the other. Although it is possible to rearrange the order of those boxes in Zoom, and even to impose it on how group members see the group on their screens, most of the group therapists do not do that or even do not know it. Usually, we do not necessarily have the same order on all the screens, as each computer is generating a different group composition, and this arrangement changes every session.

A fascinating result of the "squared circle" is the ability to observe 25 faces simultaneously. This provides a unique opportunity to perceive the group as a cohesive entity without having to shift one's gaze. This new perspective may have implications for group therapists and participants in terms of their ability to maintain a mental image of the entire group, which we previously discussed. The ability to see the entire group at once also has other potential benefits, such as the ability to consciously select which faces to focus on and an increased ease in paying attention to non-speakers. We delve further into these implications in Chapters 24 and 26.

As described above, during group sessions multiple physiological reactions occur, with our senses continuously bombarded by multisensory stimuli directly related to the session's content. Not surprisingly, online sessions may seem bland in comparison. This is akin to watching a nature movie at home versus being in a jungle with a group of people and experiencing the full sensory richness. We do not suggest that one is inherently superior to the other, but undoubtedly a wholly distinct experience.

One danger associated with offering online treatment, especially for groups, is the rapid mass entry of commercial companies. Remote treatment of mental health problems surged in the pandemic, as in-person treatment became difficult while pandemic-driven isolation increased anxiety and depression. Digital mental health companies plunged in, promising to provide millions with access to high-quality care by video, phone, and messaging. Rolfe Winkler in the *Wall Street Journal* described it (December 18, 2022) thus: "Heavy advertising and other strategies from Silicon Valley's playbook boost providers' growth but not the quality of care." This is not to say that commercial offerings are inherently low quality, but to suggest that greater regulation and supervision are required.

Issues of Privacy and Confidentiality

The protection of patients' privacy is an essential aspect of any therapeutic work, and mental health professionals receive extensive training to ensure that it becomes second nature. The concept of confidentiality is fundamental to all forms of psychotherapy. However, when working with groups, ensuring privacy becomes a considerably more complex task. Lasky and Riva (2006) write: "Confidentiality in group psychotherapy is more complicated than in individual therapy because self-disclosure is at the core of group therapy and there are numerous people hearing the disclosures" (p. 455). Unlike working with individuals, the facilitator must ensure that every group participant is behaving in a way that protects the privacy of all members. This poses a particular challenge, as group participants typically do not have the same level of training and awareness regarding privacy and confidentiality. Additionally, the facilitator must ensure that all participants are using relevant tools, such as video conferencing software, in a manner that safeguards everyone's privacy. Overall, maintaining privacy in online group therapy requires a heightened level of vigilance and attention to detail from mental health professionals.

When working with face-to-face groups, the facilitator is responsible for ensuring that the physical venue is suitable, preventing unwanted interruptions, and minimizing the risk of participants being overheard by outsiders. However, in online group therapy, the facilitator must go one step further and direct participants to ensure that they are alone and that no one can see or hear the group sessions online. With each participant a potential "breach," it is crucial to establish clear guidelines and protocols to safeguard the privacy and confidentiality of all group members.

Co-facilitation

Co-leading groups (when two therapists lead the group together) provides several advantages when leading groups, such as two different points of view, two different leading styles, and a model for couple relationship and communication (Yalom & Leszcz, 2020). To date, little has been written about the effects of online settings on co-facilitation, despite it being considered optimal in many group therapy formats (e.g., trauma groups, couples groups, etc.). Regretfully, even in this book, this aspect has been overlooked. Our anecdotal experience suggests that the primary difference is how co-facilitators communicate with each other. Eye-to-eye contact between the two co-leaders is crucial for their successful collaboration. Typically, non-verbal cues such as a nod or a gesture would convey a desire to comment, an agreement or disagreement with the other co-leader's interpretations. However, in the online setting, non-verbal cues are limited and these communication channels need to be adapted due to the limitations of the format.

One possible solution that some colleagues found helpful is to use the chat channel to communicate privately with the other co-leader. We found this solution problematic, for several reasons: (1) It distracts the group therapists from the here-and-now and the immediate communication happening in the group; (2) It carries the risk that mistakes will be made when the leader inadvertently sends the message to the entire group instead of the co-leader; and (3) It creates a "behind the group's back" communication, which is against the guidelines provided to group members. To address this difficulty, one of the authors has found it helpful to make a conscious decision to communicate verbally with his co-facilitators in front of the group. The implications of this decision extend beyond the technical aspects of coordination. It has encouraged us to be more transparent about our thoughts and concerns regarding the here-and-now of the group, and provided a model for open negotiation between couple partners. This has propelled us to shift from a secretive and distant approach to a more open, collaborative, and vulnerable stance as facilitators.

Who Might Benefit from Online Group Therapy?

One question that frequently arises when discussing online therapy, including online group therapy, is its suitability for various patients. In both our previous and current books, we indirectly addressed this question by including chapters on various patient characteristics, such as children, adults, the elderly, and the chronically ill. Our diverse group of authors come from various backgrounds, including different ethnicities, geographies, and professions. However, none have definitively stated the suitability or unsuitability of online group therapy for specific populations.

Weinberg (2020) suggests that people with intimacy problems who do not show enough improvement in the in-person group can benefit more from online groups. Some support to this argument comes from Marmarosh et al. (2013), who pointed out that individuals with a dismissive-avoidant attachment style often engage in defensive self-enhancement when in groups, resulting in less positive outcomes and more dropouts of group therapy. The online group format can help these individuals to become less defensive since they feel protected by the "screen barrier." Some group members with dissociative symptoms might also engage more in the group process. Participating in online groups allows them to lower their use of dissociative defenses while in-person groups might be emotionally overwhelming for them. The reduction in immediacy and sense of self-consciousness in online groups, which may be debilitating in in-person groups for socially anxious clients, may also improve their performance. The above does not mean that we should avoid confronting those people with their defenses in the offline groups. The best recommendation for them is to have a two-stage therapy, starting with online groups and moving later to in-person ones.

The most honest answer we can provide at this time is that there is no research that provides clear criteria to confidently predict who is suited to online group therapy. While sensory-oriented individuals may find it less suitable (see Chapter 18), there is currently no empirical evidence to support this claim.

There are certain populations, such as those with speech difficulties, or those who are visually impaired, who may find online group therapy more challenging. In contrast, those with hearing difficulties might find that they can perceive sound more effectively while utilizing earphones or headsets online. We strongly encourage research and the development of solutions to ensure that online group therapy is as inclusive as possible.

Online Large Group Interventions

Amid the pandemic, an innovative form of online group intervention, known as the Online Large Group (OLG), gained immense popularity and demonstrated the significant advantages of the online mode of therapy during periods of crisis and social upheaval. This modality became ubiquitous and rapidly disseminated, as reported in Chapters 11, 12 and Epilogue. Given the isolation and lockdowns that people experienced during the pandemic, OLGs provided crucial support, aiding individuals in combating anxiety and depression. Social trauma typically results in a disconnection from support systems, thereby diminishing one's resilience. The widespread participation in OLGs indicates their indispensability. These groups were often convened in an unstructured group analytic manner, allowing members to freely express their distress and respond with warmth and empathy towards one another. However, as stated in Chapter 12, OLGs were also guided by psychodramatic, mindfulness and CBT techniques. They proved highly effective during previous times of social crisis, such as the war in Ukraine. These groups were established to support individuals in Ukraine who had suffered the severe consequences of the Russian invasion. Participants from all over the world joined to express their solidarity and support, which greatly impacted and touched the Ukrainian people. Occasionally, even Russian colleagues participated, facilitating a difficult dialogue. Furthermore, following the earthquake in Türkiye (Turkey) and North Syria in 2023, OLGs provided mental health support to the helpers assisting individuals affected by the disaster.

Hybrid Groups

Chapter 6 provides a comprehensive overview of this modality and caution against hasty adoption without careful consideration of members' motivations. We agree with their conclusion and would like to emphasize two critical factors that influence the success of the hybrid model: group cohesion and technological quality.

We recommend against using the hybrid solution at the outset of group formation. Instead, the group should become cohesive enough to manage any potential dynamics of competition and envy between members in-person and those online. It takes a skilled group therapist to create an inclusive environment that does not exclude anyone.

Technological considerations are also crucial, as appropriate equipment can make or break the hybrid experience. High-quality audio and video solutions are necessary to enable seamless communication between members. Camera location and quality are critical factors in creating an inclusive environment. External cameras such as the OWL can capture a 360-degree view of the surroundings, enabling online members to see the entire group and identify the speaker. Placing the laptop (or screen) on a high stool and pinning the online member's picture on the screen at the same level as the in-person members' faces can create a sense of equal participation. Additionally, placing the external camera near the laptop can overcome the gap between the source of the audio and the speaker's image.

In sum, we advise against using the hybrid model unless it is the only option available. If necessary, ensure that the group is cohesive and equipped with appropriate technology to support an inclusive and effective hybrid experience.

What Technological Capabilities Might Significantly Influence Online Group Therapy?

Currently, one of the most challenging technical issues with video conferencing is the inability to discern where the speaker is directing their gaze. This is also true, but less crucial, with regards to determining who another participant is looking at when they gaze at someone other than the speaker (lack of eye-to-eye contact). While it is uncertain which specific group processes may impact, we believe that this could significantly alter the online group therapy experience and the sense of intimacy.

Although virtual reality (VR) may have the potential to tackle these concerns and also offer solutions like enabling anonymity by using avatars, current VR options are still not a practical substitute for video conferencing.

An additional important feature would be the capability to hear multiple speakers distinctly even when they are speaking at the same time. Currently, most voice conferencing applications do not offer this functionality, resulting in the loss of some participants' voices. This may especially affect individuals who speak softly or are hesitant, and their voices are the ones we often want to hear. This deficiency places added responsibility on the facilitator, who must continually scan and determine whether participants are attempting to speak.

Lower on our list of priorities would be the capability to provide a more comprehensive visual representation of the participants, and subsequently integrating other sensory experiences such as touch and smell.

The possibility of utilizing recordings is discussed in several chapters of this book and has been extensively detailed in other literature. Nevertheless, the process of recording therapy sessions still requires refinement. Video conferencing platforms must thoroughly address ethical, legal, and technological concerns regarding privacy and consent, enabling therapists and participants to record pertinent parts of therapy sessions while respecting the privacy and willingness of all participants to be recorded.

Our Vision

The field of economics concerns itself with the most efficient allocation of resources, which often catalyzes transformations in various sectors. We propose that group therapy represents a more efficient utilization of the scarce resource of mental health professionals, and that an online setting enables dramatically increased dissemination of this approach. Given that previous research has shown group therapy and online group therapy to be equally effective as individual therapy, we maintain that not informing patients about the availability of online group may be considered unethical, as it is the clinician's responsibility to assist patients in selecting the best therapeutic option among the available alternatives.

Our vision begins at a family doctor's office: after a brief conversation, the doctor and patient establish that some of the latter's problems may be linked to mental health. The doctor suggests online group therapy as an option, which is covered by the patient's basic insurance plan.

To make this scenario possible, several changes must occur. Technological platforms must address the issues raised earlier in this text. Healthcare providers need to acknowledge that online group therapy is a viable and cost-effective solution. Mental health professionals must become familiar with the potential benefits of online group therapy, and a large number of them will require training. We recommend that all mental health professionals experience both in-person and online group therapy, and that group therapists receive training in online therapy as part of their standard training (as outlined in Chapter 24).

While online therapy cannot solve all mental health problems, it may act as a catalyst for much-needed change. We hope that this book can contribute to the infrastructure necessary to support such change.

Note

1 https://www.agpa.org/home/practice-resources/what-is-group-psychotherapy-.

References

Agazarian, Y. (1989). The invisible group: An integrational theory of group-as-a-whole. *Group Analysis*, 22(4), 355–369.

Bion, W. (1961). *Experiences in groups and other papers*. Tavistock.

Burlingame, G. M., McClendon, D. T., & Yang, C. (2018). Cohesion in group therapy: A meta-analysis. *Psychotherapy*, 55(4), 384–398. https://doi.org/10.1037/pst0000173.

Burlingame, G. M., Strauss, B., & Joyce, A. (2021). Efficacy of small group treatments: Foundation for evidence-based practice. In M. Barkham, W. Lutz, & L. G. Castonguay (Eds.), *Bergin and Garfield's handbook of psychotherapy and behavior change: 50th anniversary edition* (pp. 583–624). John Wiley and Sons.

Cozolino, L. J. (2013). *The social neuroscience of education: Optimizing attachment & learning in the classroom*. W. W. Norton & Company.

Fernandez, E., Woldgabreal, Y., Day, A., Pham, T., Gleich, B., & Aboujaoude, E. (2021). Live psychotherapy by video versus in-person: A meta-analysis of efficacy and its relationship to types and targets of treatment. *Clinical Psychology & Psychotherapy*, 28(6), 1535–1549. https://doi.org/10.1002/cpp.2594.

Foulkes, S. H., & Anthony, E. J. (1965). *Group psychotherapy: The psycho-analytic approach*. Karnac Books.

Geller, S. (2020). Cultivating online therapeutic presence: Strengthening therapeutic relationships in teletherapy sessions. *Counselling Psychology Quarterly*, 1–17.

Geller, S. (2023). Being present and together while apart: Therapeutic presence in telepsychotherapy. In H. Weinberg, A. Rolnick, & A. Leighton (Eds.), *Advances in online therapy: The emergence of a new paradigm* (pp. 21–34). Routledge.

Gibbs, J. L., Sivunen, A., & Boyraz, M. (2017). Investigating the impacts of team type and design on virtual team processes. *Human Resource Management Review*, 27(4), 523–590, 603. https://doi.org/10.1016/j.hrmr.2016.12.006.

Greene, L. (2019). Group structure and levels of analysis. In F. Kaklauskas & L. Greene, *Core principles of group psychotherapy* (1st ed., pp. 58–65). Routledge.

Grossmark, R. (2007) The edge of chaos: Enactment, disruption, and emergence in group psychotherapy. *Psychoanalytic Dialogues*, 17(4), 479–499.

Hahn, A., Paquin, J. D., Glean, E., McQuillan, K., & Hamilton, D. (2022). Developing into a group therapist: An empirical investigation of expert group therapists' training experiences. *American Psychologist*, 77(5), 691–709. https://doi.org/10.1037/amp0000956.

Kaiser, J., Hanschmidt, F., & Kersting, A. (2021). The association between therapeutic alliance and outcome in internet-based psychological interventions: A meta-analysis. *Computers in Human Behavior*, 114, 106512.

Kirkman, B. L., & Mathieu, J. E. (2005). The dimensions and antecedents of team virtuality. *Journal of Management*, 31(5), 700–718. https://doi.org/10.1177/0149206305279113.

Kivlighan, D. C. M., & Kivlighan, D. M. (2014) Therapeutic factors. In J. L. DeLucia-Waack, D. A. Kalodner, & M. T. Riva (Eds.), *Handbook of group counseling and psychotherapy* (2nd ed., pp. 46–54). SAGE.

Kozlowski, K. A., & Holmes, C. M. (2017). Teaching online group counseling skills in an on-campus group counseling course. *Journal of Counselor Preparation and Supervision*, 9(1). https://doi.org/10.7729/91.1157.

Lasky, G. B., & Riva, M. T. (2006) Confidentiality and privileged communication in group psychotherapy. *International Journal of Group Psychotherapy*, 56(4), 455–476. doi:10.1521/ijgp.2006.56.4.455.

Lo Coco, G., Tasca, G. A., Hewitt, P. L., Mikail, S. F., & Kivlighan, D. M., Jr. (2019). Ruptures and repairs of group therapy alliance: An untold story in psychotherapy research. *Research in Psychotherapy: Psychopathology, Process and Outcome*, 22(1). https://doi.org/10.4081/ripppo.2019.352.

Lombard, M., & Ditton, T. (1997). At the heart of it all: The concept of presence. *Journal of Computer-Mediated Communication, 3*(2).

Mark-Goldstein, B., & Ogden, P. (2018). Sensorimotor psychotherapy as a foundation of group therapy with younger clients. In *The interpersonal neurobiology of group psychotherapy and group process* (pp. 123–145). Routledge.

Marks, M. A., Mathieu, J. E., & Zaccaro, S. J. (2001). A temporally based framework and taxonomy of team processes. *Academy of Management Review*, 26 (3), 356–376. https://doi.org/10.5465/AMR.2001.4845785.

Marmarosh, C. L., Markin, R. D., Spiegel, E. B. (2013). *Attachment in group psychotherapy*. American Psychological Association.

Neeman-Kantor, A.-K. (2013) *Secure presence* [Unpublished PsyD Dissertation]. Professional School of Psychology, Sacramento, CA.

Nery, M. P.da (2021). Online psychodrama and action methods: Theories and practices. *Revisita Brasiliera de Psicodrama*, 29(2), 107–116. https://revbrasp sicodrama.org.br/rbp/artice/view/442.

Ormont, L. R. (1993) Resolving resistances to immediacy in the group setting. *International Journal of Group Psychotherapy*, 43(4), 399–418. https://doi.org/ 10.1080/00207284.1993.11491235.

Rogers, C. R. (1968). Interpersonal relationships: U.S.A. 2000. *The Journal of Applied Behavioral Science*, 4(3), 265–280. https://doi.org/10.1177/00218863680 0400301.

Schore, A. N. (2003). *Affect dysregulation and disorders of the self*. W.W. Norton & Company.

Siegel, D. (1999). *The developing mind*. Guilford Press.

Stern, D. N., Sander, L. W., Nahum, J. P., Harrison, A. M., Lyons-Ruth, K., Morgan, A. C., Bruschweilerstern, N., & Tronick, E. Z. (1998). Non-interpretive mechanisms in psychoanalytic therapy: The "something more" than interpretation. *International Journal of Psycho-Analysis*, 79, 903–921.

Weinberg, H. (2014). *The paradox of internet groups: Alone in the presence of virtual others*. Karnac Books.

Weinberg, H. (2016). Impossible groups that flourish in leaking containers: Challenging group analytic theory. *Group Analysis*, 49(4), 330–349.

Weinberg H. (2020). Online group psychotherapy: Challenges and possibilities during COVID-19—A practice review. *Group Dynamics*, 24(3), 201–211.

Weinberg, H. (2021). Obstacles, challenges and benefits of online group psychotherapy. *American Journal of Psychotherapy*.

Weinberg, H. & Rolnick, A. (Eds.) (2020). *Theory and practice of online therapy: Internet-delivered interventions for individuals, families, groups, and organizations*. Routledge.

Weinberg, H., Rolnick, A., & Leighton, A. (Eds.) (2023). *Advances in online therapy: Emergence of a new paradigm*. Routledge.

White House (2023). *Fact Sheet: President Biden to announce strategy to address our national mental health crisis, as part of unity agenda in his first state of the union.* https://www.whitehouse.gov/ostp/news-updates/2023/02/07/white-house-report-on-mental-health-research-priorities/.

Whittingham, M., Marmarosh, C., Mallow, P., & Scherer, M. (2023). Mental health care and equity: A group therapy solution. *American Psychologist*, 78(2), 119–133. https://doi.org/10.1037/amp0001078.

Yalom, I. D., & Leszcz, M. (2020). *The theory and practice of group psychotherapy* (6th ed.). Basic Books.

Part I

Exploring the Challenges and Opportunities in Online Groups: Insights from Research and Theory

Chapter 2

Research on Online Groups

Gary M. Burlingame, Rachel Arnold, Tate Paxton and Aileen Rands

Online therapy holds exciting potential in the treatment of mental health, with research demonstrating positive outcomes for depressive symptoms (Berryhill et al., 2019), post-traumatic stress (Barak et al., 2008), body dissatisfaction (Carlbring et al., 2018), anxiety (Reger & Gahm, 2009), and more. In fact, Internet-delivered treatments may be as effective as in-person therapy for some clients (Andersson, 2016; Carlbring et al., 2018), further bolstering the argument that online therapy is a valid form of treatment. Additionally, online therapy can address barriers that may otherwise preclude clients from seeking services (e.g., cost; availability of services) (Barker & Barker, 2022). Thus, there are both empirical and practical arguments to offer online therapy. Despite this, providers have historically been hesitant to implement online services (Wind et al., 2020). The onset of the COVID-19 pandemic in early 2020 opened the doorway for the potential of online therapy to be better realized, with many clinicians shifting from in-person to remote services to prevent transmission of the virus (APA, 2020).

As part of this transition to remote services, online group therapy became increasingly prevalent (e.g., Ward et al., 2022). However, while online therapy in general had received considerable attention, research on online group therapy was limited at the start of the pandemic (Weinberg, 2020). Initial research showed positive outcomes (e.g., Lemma & Fonagy, 2013; Mariano et al., 2019) and gave evidence that outcomes may be comparable to those achieved in in-person groups (Banbury et al., 2018; Gentry et al., 2019). Yet, with relatively few studies assessing online groups, there was a clear need for further research. Fortunately, just as the use of online group therapy has grown over the last couple of years, so too has the research literature. The purpose of the present chapter is to review this recent research, with an aim to evaluate the effectiveness of online group therapy. Given that randomized controlled trials (RCTs) are considered the gold standard for effectiveness research (Hariton & Locascio, 2018), the scope of this review will be primarily limited to RCTs. This chapter will also review recent research comparing online group interventions and in-person interventions.

DOI: 10.4324/9781003248606-3

Online Group Therapy: Results from Randomized Controlled Trials

Our search of the literature identified 27 RCTs on online group therapy that have been published since 2020 (see Table 2.1). These RCTs broadly relate to medical concerns, neurodevelopmental concerns, family relations, and internalizing problems.

Medical Concerns

Of the RCTs identified in our search, the majority studied online psychological group interventions for individuals with medical conditions (e.g., cancer, aphasia, spinal cord injury, etc.). Most of these studies focused specifically on various forms of cancer with mixed results. Milbury et al. (2021) examined group-based psychosocial interventions for women with lung cancer undergoing medical treatment. Results of this feasibility study showed that regardless of group emphasis (i.e., mindfulness or psychoeducation), the majority of patients found the program to be useful and easily accessible. Penedo et al. (2021) studied a different group approach for men with advanced prostate cancer. The effects of group cognitive behavioral stress management (CBSM) were examined in comparison to an active health promotion control. Contrary to hypotheses, CBSM did not lead to significant changes in measured biomarkers (i.e., circulating inflammatory markers and cortisol) relative to health promotion. Some differences were detected in diurnal cortisol rhythm, suggesting that CBSM may lead to some unique health benefits. A few studies examined online group treatment for those who have survived cancer. Lleras de Frutos et al. (2020) compared the effectiveness of face-to-face group positive psychotherapy to online adaptations of the intervention for cancer survivors. Results showed significant treatment effects for both modalities, supporting the notion that online intervention has the potential to perform just as well as in-person therapy (see the section on 'Online Group Interventions Versus In-Person Interventions' below). Lastly, Sansom-Daly et al. (2021) studied the effects of online cognitive behavioral groups compared to peer support groups and a wait-list control group for young adult and adolescent cancer survivors. Findings were mixed, suggesting that cancer survivors find psychological telehealth interventions helpful depending on the point in their survivorship journey.

Studies involving chronic illness were also found. Muscara et al. (2020) studied the effects of acceptance and commitment group therapy (ACT) compared to a wait-list control group for parents of children with life threatening illness who experience traumatic stress. Results showed ACT to be more effective in reducing stress for parents regardless of the diagnosis of their child. Douma et al. (2020) also studied the effects of group treatment for parents of children with chronic illness. When compared to the wait-list control group, the intervention (i.e., psychosocial group treatment) was found to significantly decrease depression and anxiety as well as to increase disease-related coping skills. Douma et al. (2021) then studied the effect of online psychosocial groups for adolescents with chronic illness compared to a wait-list control group and found that treatment improved disease-related coping skills and quality of life.

Marshall et al. (2020) studied the effects of support groups for stroke survivors with aphasia delivered via a virtual reality platform. No significant differences were detected on primary outcome measures although evidence for the feasibility of group delivery was supported. Lester et al. (2020) studied adolescents with neurofibromatosis participating in an online mind-body group. Those in the active intervention group experienced significant improvements in several resiliency factors compared to the control group. Lastly, Robinson-Whelen et al. (2020) studied an online self-esteem group intervention for women with spinal cord injuries. The treatment was found to be feasible and to have potential for improving self-esteem. Overall, despite some mixed findings, online group treatment for those with medical conditions appears promising in terms of feasibility and effectiveness.

Neurodevelopmental Concerns

We identified four RCTs on neurodevelopmental concerns. Two examined a virtual mind-body parenting group, the Stress Management and Resiliency Training-Relaxation Response Resiliency Program (SMART-3RP). Among parents of children with autism spectrum disorder (ASD), Kuhlthau et al. (2020) found that parents in SMART-3RP showed greater improvement in resiliency, stress reactivity/stress coping, depression/anxiety, social support, and mindfulness compared to a wait-list control group which was sustained at a three-month follow-up. Among parents of children with learning and attentional disabilities, Park et al. (2020) found that parents in SMART-3RP showed larger improvements in distress, resilience, stress coping, depression, anxiety, social support, mindfulness, and empathy than the wait-list and improvements were again sustained at follow up. Kulbaş and Özabacı (2022) studied another parenting group, the Positive Psychology-Based Online Group Counselling Program (PPBOGCP), among mothers of children with intellectual disabilities. Relative to mothers in the placebo and no intervention groups, mothers in the PPBOGCP group showed significant increases in psychological well-being, hope, and self-compassion; these changes were sustained at a two-month follow-up. The last study (Bioulac et al., 2020) compared virtual cognitive remediation to methylphenidate treatment and individual psychotherapy. Behavioral ratings did not improve after cognitive remediation. Yet, children showed less distractibility and improved attentional performance on an objective measure; results on these variables were equivalent to the methylphenidate group. Further, outcomes for impulsivity were better for the virtual cognitive remediation group than for the methylphenidate group. Based on these results, the authors argue that virtual cognitive remediation may be able to replace methylphenidate treatment in some cases. Collectively, these studies highlight how online group interventions can be effective in the treatment of children with neurodevelopmental concerns and their parents.

Family Relations

We located one RCT related to family relations. Tuntipuchitanon et al. (2022) assessed an eight-week online group positive parenting program (PPP) for parents of healthy children aged three to six. Parents were randomly assigned to the intervention group plus weekly general education via communication application or weekly general education alone. Parents in the PPP group reported a higher sense of competence at 14 weeks, while parents in both groups utilized a more authoritative parenting style and showed significant reductions in children's emotional and behavioral problems.

Internalizing Symptoms, Bereavement, Stress, and Other Outcomes

Several studies investigated the effect of online group treatment on anxiety, depression, bereavement, stress, weight loss, and mindfulness outcomes. Anxiety and depression in particular were variables of interest during the COVID-19 pandemic due to worry about illness and social isolation leading to depressive symptoms. These studies are organized below by outcome (see Table 2.1).

Anxiety

Five studies examined anxiety as a primary outcome with mixed results—some studies indicated decreased anxiety and others showed no difference between the intervention and control groups. Abedishargh et al. (2021) studied virtual group cognitive behavioral therapy (CBT) for weight loss and found no difference in anxiety between intervention, treatment-as-usual (TAU), and wait-list control groups. On the other hand, Naeim et al. (2021) studied virtual group CBT for COVID-19 ICU unit nurses, and they found a significant decrease in anxiety for the intervention. Similarly, Otared et al. (2021) found significant effects for an online group ACT intervention for healthcare workers during the COVID-19 pandemic. They reported a moderate effect size for decreased anxiety symptoms relative to the no-treatment control group. Mirabito and Verhaeghen (2022) studied an online Koru mindfulness intervention for a sample of college students and found lower anxiety in the intervention group. Ritvo et al. (2021) organized a mindfulness virtual community to help with college student depression, anxiety, and stress. They found no significant difference in anxiety between the intervention and control group, although it should be noted that the group intervention was short, just 20 minutes per week.

Depression and Bereavement

Seven studies examined depression and related symptoms, with mixed results similar to those found for anxiety. Schuster et al. (2022) studied a group CBT approach for mildly depressed clients. They found a large decrease in depressive symptoms in the intervention relative to the wait-list control condition. Conversely, Shapira et al. (2021) measured the impact of a group intervention for elderly people on depression, loneliness, and social support. They found no difference between the intervention and control conditions on measures of depression and loneliness. Another study found that an online group CBT intervention for suicide bereavement helped with depression and suicidality symptom improvement, but no more than the wait-list control condition (Wagner et al., 2022). Three studies also found no difference between intervention and wait-list conditions in improvement of depressive symptoms (Abedishargh et al., 2021; Mirabito & Verhaeghen, 2022; Ritvo et al., 2021). Otared et al. (2021) found that an online ACT group intervention significantly improved depressive symptoms compared to the no-treatment control group. In all, studies with individuals who had higher levels of depression found that online group treatments led to symptom improvement. Subclinical and less depressed samples seemed to have less improvement in depressive symptoms.

Stress

Given the widespread burden of the pandemic, stress was also an outcome of interest for researchers. Four studies examined stress as a primary outcome, and most studies indicated that group online treatments decreased stress. Online group CBT and mindfulness approaches decreased stress relative to control groups in three studies (Naeim et al., 2021; Mirabito & Verhaeghen, 2022; Ritvo et al., 2021). Another study found that online group CBT for weight loss did not decrease stress more than the control group (Abedishargh et al., 2021).

Weight Loss and Mindfulness Outcomes

One study examined the effect of online group CBT on weight loss and found that the intervention led to significant decreases in body mass index

Table 2.1 Randomized Controlled Trials of Online Group Therapy

Study	Intervention (n)	Comparison (n)	Population	Outcomes (between group effect size)
Abedishargh et al. (2021)	Internet-based CBT for weight loss (30)	TAU (30) Wait-list control (30)	Women with BMI ≥25	Weight loss* ($\eta_p^2 = 0.3$) Depression ($\eta_p^2 = 0.002$) Anxiety ($\eta_p^2 = 0.01$) Stress ($\eta_p^2 = 0.01$)
Bioulac et al. (2020)	Virtual cognitive remediation (16)	Methylpheni-date (16) Individual therapy (19)	Children with ADHD	Distractibility Attentional performance Impulsivity*
Douma et al. (2020)	Op Koers Online (34)	Wait-list control (33)	Parents with a child with a chronic illness	Anxiety/ depression* ($p < .05$) Disease-related coping skills* ($p < .05$)
Douma et al. (2021)	Op Koers Online (35)	Wait-list control (24)	Adolescents with chronic illness	Internalizing/ externalizing problems ($p = 0.140$; $p = 0.129$; $p = 0.928$; $p = 0.815$) Disease-related coping* ($p < .05$) Health-related quality of life* ($p < .05$)
Kuhlthau et al. (2020)	SMART-3RP (25)	Wait-list (26)	Parents of children with ASD	Distress ($d = 0.38$) Resiliency* ($d = 0.69$) Stress coping* ($d = 1.12$) Worry ($d = 0.31$) Social support* ($d = 0.65$) Positive affect ($d = 0.60$) Empathy ($d = 0.52$) Mindfulness* ($d = 0.77$) Depression/ anxiety* ($d = 0.64$)

Study	Intervention (n)	Comparison (n)	Population	Outcomes (between group effect size)
Kulbaş & Özabacı (2022)	PPBOGCP (12)	Placebo group (11) No intervention (12)	Mothers of children with intellectual disabilities	Psychological wellbeing* $(\eta_p^2 = 0.43)$ Hope* $(\eta_p^2 = 0.38)$ Self-compassion* $(\eta_p^2 = 0.39)$
Lester et al. (2020)	Resilient Youth with Neurofi-bromatosis (RY-NF) (27)	Health Education for Youth with Neurofi-bromatosis (HE-NF) (24)	Adolescents with neurofi-bromatosis	Mindfulness* $(p < .001)$ Resiliency $(p = .150)$ Perceived coping $(p = .408)$ Gratitude* $(p = 0.27)$ Optimism $(p = .514)$ Social support $(p = .101)$
Lleras de Frutos et al. (2020)	Online group positive psychother-apy for cancer survivorship (OPPC) (16)	Face-to-face group positive psychother-apy for cancer survivorship (PPC) (28)	Women with cancer	Emotional dis-tress* $(b = -2.24)$ Post-traumatic stress* $(b = -3.25)$ Post-traumatic growth* $(b = 3.08)$
Marshall et al. (2020)	Social support group (16)	Wait-list (18)	People with aphasia	Mental well-being $(\eta_p^2 = .002)$ Communication activities of daily living $(\eta_p^2 = 0.018)$ Social connectedness $(\eta_p^2 = 0.003)$ Language ability $(\eta_p^2 = 0.12)$ Speaking ability $(\eta_p^2 = 0.004)$

Study	Intervention (n)	Comparison (n)	Population	Outcomes (between group effect size)
Milbury et al. (2021)	Psychosocial group (mindfulness emphasis) (27) Psychosocial group (psychoeducation emphasis) (27)	None	Women with lung cancer	Evidence for feasibility was found
Mirabito & Verhaeghen (2022)	Online group-based Koru mindfulness (58)	Wait-list (53)	College students	Mindfulness* ($d = 0.64$) Depression ($d = 0.33$) Anxiety* ($d = 0.37$) Stress* ($d = 0.65$)
Muscara et al. (2020)	ACT-based group therapy (Take a Breath) (152)	TAU (162)	Parents of children with life threatening illness	Post-traumatic stress* ($d = 1.10$) Depression ($d = 0.51$) Anxiety ($d = 0.60$) Stress ($d = 0.44$) Guilt/worry ($d = 0.74$) Emotional resources* ($d = 0.95$) Unresolved sorrow/anger ($d = 0.82$) Uncertainty* ($d = 1.34$) Negative appraisal* ($d = 0.98$) Family factors ($d = 0.60$)
Naeim et al. (2021)	Virtual CBT (20)	No treatment (20)	COVID-19 ICU nurses	Anxiety* ($\eta^2 = 0.43$) Stress* ($\eta^2 = 0.41$) Fatigue* ($\eta^2 = 0.40$)

Study	Intervention (n)	Comparison (n)	Population	Outcomes (between group effect size)
Otared et al. (2021)	Group-based ACT (20)	No therapy (20)	Healthcare workers with anxiety and depressive symptoms during COVID-19	Depression* ($\eta_p^2 = 0.52$) Anxiety* ($\eta_p^2 = 0.81$) Quality of life* ($\eta_p^2 = 0.42$) Acceptance and act* ($\eta_p^2 = 0.55$)
Park et al. (2020)	SMART-3RP (31)	Wait-list (22)	Parents of children with learning and attentional disabilities	Distress* ($d = 0.83$) Resilience* ($d = 0.83$) Stress coping* ($d = 1.39$) Worry ($d = 0.57$) Social support* ($d = 0.71$) Positive affect ($d = 0.55$) Mindfulness* ($d = 0.86$) Empathy* ($d = 0.77$) Depression/ anxiety* ($d = 0.71$)
Penedo et al. (2021)	Cognitive behavioral stress management (CBSM) (95)	Health Promotion Control Group (97)	Men with advanced prostate cancer	Inflammatory markers Il-10 ($p = 0.894$) Il-8 ($p = 0.592$) Il-6 ($p = 0.053$) CRP ($p = 0.270$) TNF-α ($p = 0.492$) Diurnal cortisol ($p = 0.106$) Overall cortisol output AUC ($p = 0.965$)
Ritvo et al. (2021)	Mindfulness Virtual Community (76)	Wait-list (78)	College students	Depression ($d = 0.04$) Mindfulness ($d = 0.02$) Anxiety ($d = 0.20$) Stress* ($d = 0.24$)

Study	Intervention (n)	Comparison (n)	Population	Outcomes (between group effect size)
Robinson-Whelen et al. (2020)	Self-esteem in Second Life Intervention for Women with Disabilities (SEE-SCI) (12)	Control group (11)	Women with spinal cord injury	Health promoting behaviors* ($p = .049$; $p = .017$) Social support ($p = .27$) Self-efficacy ($p = .81$) Self-esteem ($p = .34$) Depression* ($p = .04$; $p = .035$)
Sansom-Daly et al. (2021)	Recapture Life Intervention (19)	Online Peer-Support Group Control (10) Wait-list (11)	Adolescent and young adult cancer survivors	Positive/negative impact on cancer (all $p \geq 0.46$; $p > 0.14$) Depression and anxiety (p's > 0.3) Identity changes (p-values > 0.35; all p-values > 0.55) Coping strategies ($p = 0.24$) CBT skills* ($p = .027$) Family functioning (p-values > 0.11)
Schuster et al. (2022)	Tele-group CBT for depression (33)	Wait-list (28)	Mildly to moderately depressed participants	Depression* ($d = 0.99$) Depressive behavior* ($d = 0.88$) Cognitive/ behavioral skills* ($d = 0.97$)
Shapira et al. (2021)	Web-based platform for CBT and mindfulness skills (64)	No treatment (18)	Older adults during COVID-19	Depression ($\eta^2 = 0.05$) Loneliness* ($\eta^2 = 0.07$) Social support

Study	Intervention (n)	Comparison (n)	Population	Outcomes (between group effect size)
Tuntipuchi-tanon et al. (2022)	PPP plus weekly general education (52)	Weekly general education alone (51)	Parents of healthy children	Sense of competence* Authoritative parenting style Child emotional/ behavioral problems
Wagner et al. (2022)	Online CBT after suicide bereavement (84)	Wait-list (56)	Adults who have lost a close person through suicide	Depression ($d = 0.19$) Grief ($d = 0.15$) Intrusion ($d = 0.31$) Avoidance* ($d = 0.43$) Hyperarousal ($d = 0.21$)

Note: * Denotes significant difference from comparison group(s).

(BMI) relative to control (Abedishargh et al., 2021). Regarding mindfulness, Mirabito and Verhaeghen (2022) found significant improvements in mindfulness skills in the intervention conditions relative to control. However, Ritvo et al. (2021) found no difference between intervention and control on mindfulness skills after taking part in a mindfulness virtual community.

Online Group Interventions Versus In-Person Interventions

Our search identified nine additional studies comparing online group interventions to in-person interventions. In many instances, outcomes were comparable across formats. For example, outcomes have been comparable for dialectical behavior therapy (DBT)-based intensive outpatient programs (IOP) (Bean et al., 2022), psychoeducation (Karagiozi et al., 2021), mindfulness training (Lim et al., 2021), positive psychotherapy (Lleras de Frutos et al., 2020), CBT (Milosevic et al., 2022), perinatal groups (Paul et al., 2021), and mind-body skills groups (Ranjbar et al., 2021) (see Table 2.2). In a few studies, some outcomes were superior for face-to-face interventions. For example, Milosevic et al. (2022) found a small benefit for face-to-face CBT on symptom outcomes when analyzing the whole sample; notably, when testing subgroups, outcomes only differed for the generalized anxiety disorder group and not for the panic disorder/agoraphobia, social anxiety disorder, or obsessive-compulsive disorder groups. Further, Lopez et al. (2020) found that online DBT group members did not feel as connected to one another as in-person

Table 2.2 Studies with Comparable Outcomes for Online and In-Person Intervention Formats

Study	Intervention	Population	Comparable outcomes
Bean et al. (2022)	DBT-based IOP	Comorbid substance misuse and mental health diagnoses	Depression Anxiety Stress
Karagiozi et al. (2021)	Psychoeducation	Caregivers of patients with dementia	Anxiety Depression Sense of burden
Lim et al. (2021)	Mindfulness training	General community	Stress Attendance
Lleras de Frutos et al. (2020)	Positive psychotherapy	Cancer survivors	Post-traumatic growth Emotional distress Post-traumatic stress
Milosevic et al. (2022)	CBT	Anxiety	Functional improvement Treatment dropout
Paul et al. (2021)	Perinatal groups	Pregnant and postpartum women	Depressive symptoms
Ranjbar et al. (2021)	Mind-body skills group	Psychiatric residents	Attendance Intervention satisfaction

DBT group members. Lastly, Rice and Schroeder (2021) found that clients in in-person mindfulness-based stress reduction (MBSR) experienced greater trust in the instructor, classmates, and self as well as greater class satisfaction compared to clients who attended MBSR via Second Life, a virtual world. Meanwhile, online groups may have their own advantages. For instance, Lopez et al. (2020) found that online DBT had significantly better attendance. In all, this research provides preliminary evidence that outcomes are largely comparable for online and in-person formats, though each format may be associated with unique benefits.

Conclusion

In conclusion, the research on online group therapy conducted between January 2020 and June 2022 is promising, with positive outcomes for clients with varying concerns and largely comparable outcomes to in-person therapy. These results provide initial evidence for the efficacy of online group therapy, indicating that it is likely an effective form of treatment. However, the need for further research is clear, including larger-scale RCTs extending to other presenting concerns (e.g., eating disorders).

Further, there is a lack of research about online process-oriented groups, and long-term ones in particular; this could perhaps be because it takes more time for such research to be conducted. There is also research needed to better understand how group therapeutic factors (e.g., group climate, cohesion, alliance, empathy) compare between online and in-person groups. With additional research, the efficacy of online group therapy will become increasingly clear.

References

Abedishargh, N., Farani, A. R., Gharraee, B., & Farahani, H. (2021). Effectiveness of internet-based cognitive behavioral therapy in weight loss, stress, anxiety, and depression via virtual group therapy. *Iranian Journal of Psychiatry and Behavioral Sciences*, 15(3). http://dx.doi.org/10.5812/ijpbs.113096.

American Psychological Association (APA). (2020, June 5). *Psychologists embrace telehealth to prevent the spread of COVID-19*. Retrieved from https://www.apa services.org/practice/legal/technology/psychologists-embrace-telehealth

Andersson, G. (2016). Internet-delivered psychological treatments. *Annual Review of Clinical Psychology*, 12, 157–179. https://doi.org/10.1146/annurev-clinp sy-021815-093006.

Banbury, A., Nancarrow, S., Dart, J., Gray, L., & Parkinson, L. (2018). Telehealth interventions delivering home-based support group videoconferencing: Systematic review. *Journal of Medical Internet Research*, 20(2), e25. http://dx.doi.org/10.2196/jmir.8090.

Barak, A., Hen, L., Boniel-Nissim, M., & Shapira, N. (2008). A comprehensive review and a meta-Analysis of the effectiveness of Internet-based psychotherapeutic interventions. *Journal of Technology in Human Services*, 26(2–4), 109–160. https://doi.org/10.1080/15228830802094429.

Barker, G. G., & Barker, E. E. (2022). Online therapy: Lessons learned from the COVID-19 health crisis. *British Journal of Guidance & Counselling*, 50(1), 66–81. https://doi.org/10.1080/03069885.2021.1889462.

Bean, C. A. L., Aurora, P., Maddox, C. J., Mekota, R., & Updegraff, A. (2022). A comparison of telehealth versus in-person group therapy: Results from a DBT-based dual diagnosis IOP. *Journal of Clinical Psychology*. https://doi.org/10.1002/jclp.23374.

Berryhill, M. B., Culmer, N., Williams, N., Halli-Tierney, A., Betancourt, A., Roberts, H., & King, M. (2019). Videoconferencing psychotherapy and depression: A systematic review. *Telemedicine and e-Health*, 25(6), 435–446. https://doi.org/10.1089/tmj.2018.0058.

Bioulac, S., Micolaud-Franchi, J. Al., Maire, J., Bouvard, M. P., Rizzo, A. A., Sagaspe, P., & Philip, P. (2020). Virtual remediation versus methylphenidate to improve distractibility in children with ADHD: A controlled randomized clinical trial study. *Journal of Attention Disorders*, 24(2), 326–335. https://doi.org/10.1177/1087054718759751.

Carlbring, P., Andersson, G., Cuijpers, P., Riper, H., & Hedman-Lagerlöf, E. (2018). Internet-based vs. face-to-face cognitive behavior therapy for psychiatric and somatic disorders: An updated systematic review and meta-analysis. *Cognitive Behaviour Therapy*, 47(1). https://doi.org/10.1080/16506073.2017.1401115.

Douma, M., Maurice-Stam, H., Gorter, B., Krol, Y., Verkleij, M., Wiltink, L., Scholten, L., & Grootenhuis, M. A. (2020). Online psychosocial group intervention for parents: Positive effects on anxiety and depression. *Journal of Pediatric Psychology*, 46(2), 123–134. https://doi.org/10.1093/jpepsy/jsaa102.

Douma, M., Maurice-Stam, H., Gorter, B., Houtzager, B. A., Vreugdenhil, H. J. I., Waaldijk, M., Wiltink, L., Grootenhuis, M. A., & Scholten, L. (2021). Online psychosocial group intervention for adolescents with a chronic illness: A randomized controlled trial. *Internet Interventions*, 26, 100447. https://doi.org/10.1016/j.invent.2021.100447.

Gentry, M. T., Lapid, M. I., Clark, M. M., & Rummans, T. A. (2019). Evidence for telehealth groupbased treatment: A systematic review. *Journal of Telemedicine and Telecare*, 25, 327–342. http://dx.doi.org/10.1177/1357633X18775855.

Hariton, E., & Locascio, J. J. (2018). Randomised controlled trials—the gold standard for effectiveness research. *BJOG*, 125(13), 1716.

Karagiozi, K., Margaritidou, P., Tsatali, M., Marina, M., Dimitriou, T., Apostolidis, H., Tasiatsos, T., & Tsolaki, M. (2021). Comparison of on site versus online psycho education groups and reducing caregiver burden. *Clinical Gerontologist*, 1–11. https://doi.org/10.1080/07317115.2021.1940409.

Kuhlthau, K. A., Luberto, C. M., Traeger, L., Millstein, R. A., Perez, G. K., Lindly, O. J., Chad-Friedman, E., Proszynski, J., & Park, E. R. (2020). A virtual resiliency intervention for parents of children with autism: A randomized pilot trial. *Journal of Autism and Developmental Disorders*, 50, 2513–2526. https://doi.org/10.1007/s10803-019-03976-4.

Kulbaş, E., & Özabacı, N. 2022. The effects of the Positive Psychology-Based Online Group Counselling Program on mothers having children with intellectual disabilities. *Journal of Happiness Studies*, 23, 1817–1845. https://doi.org/10.1007/s10902-021-00472-4.

Lemma, A., & Fonagy, P. (2013). Feasibility study of a psychodynamic online group intervention for depression. *Psychoanalytic Psychology*, 30, 367–380. http://dx.doi.org/10.1037/a0033239.

Lester, E. G., Macklin, E. A., Plotkin, S., & Vranceanu, A.-M. (2020). Improvement in resiliency factors among adolescents with neurofibromatosis who participate in a virtual mind-body group program. *Journal of Neuro-Oncology*, 147 (2), 451–457. https://doi.org/10.1007/s11060-020-03441-8.

Lim, J., Leow, Z., Ong, J., Pang, L., & Lim, E. (2021). Effects of web-based group mindfulness training on stress and sleep quality in Singapore during the COVID-19 pandemic: Retrospective equivalence analysis. *JMIR Mental Health*, 8(3). https://doi.org/10.2196/21757.

Lleras de Frutos, M. L., Medina, J. C., Vives, J., Casellas-Grau, A., Marzo, J. L., Borràs, J. M., & Ochoa-Arnedo, C. (2020). Video conference vs face-to-face group psychotherapy for distressed cancer survivors: A randomized controlled trial. *Psycho-Oncology*, 29(12), 1195–2003. https://doi.org/10.1002/pon.5457.

Lopez, A., Rothberg, B., Reaser, E., Schwenk, S., & Griffin, R. (2020). Therapeutic groups via video teleconferencing and the impact on group cohesion. *mHealth*, 6(13), 1–9. http://dx.doi.org/10.21037/mhealth.2019.11.0.

Mariano, T. Y., Wan, L., Edwards, R. R., Lazaridou, A., Ross, E. L., & Jamison, R. N. (2019). Online group pain management for chronic pain: Preliminary results of a novel treatment approach to teletherapy. *Journal of Telemedicine and Telecare*. Advance online publication. http://dx.doi.org/10.1177/1357633X19870369.

Marshall, J., Devane, N., Talbot, R., Caute, A., Cruice, M., Hilari, K., MacKenzie, G., Maguire, K., Patel, A., Roper, A., & Wilson, S. (2020). A randomised trial of Social Support Group intervention for people with aphasia: A novel application of virtual reality. *PLOS ONE*, 15(9). https://doi.org/10.1371/journal.pone.0239715.

Milbury, K., Kroll, J., Chen, A., Antonoff, M. B., Snyder, S., Higgins, H., Yang, C. C., Li, Y., & Bruera, E. (2021). Pilot Randomized Controlled Trial in Women with Non-Small Cell Lung Cancer to Assess the Feasibility of Delivering Group-Based Psychosocial Care via Videoconference. *Integrative Cancer Therapies*, 20, 1–8. https://doi.org/10.1177/15347354211052520.

Milosevic, I., Cameron, D. H., Milanovic, M., McCabe, R. E., & Rowa, K. (2022). Face-to-face versus video teleconference group cognitive behavioural therapy for anxiety and related disorders: A preliminary comparison. *The Canadian Journal of Psychiatry*, 67(5), 391–402. https://doi.org/10.1177/07067437211027319.

Mirabito, G., & Verhaeghen, P. (2022). Remote delivery of a Koru Mindfulness intervention for college students during the COVID-19 pandemic. *Journal of American College Health*, 1–8. https://doi.org/10.1080/07448481.2022.2060708.

Muscara, F., McCarthy, M. C., Rayner, M., Nicholson, J. M., Dimovski, A., McMillan, L., Hearps, S. J. C., Yamada, J., Burke, K., Walser, R., & Anderson, V. A. (2020). Effect of a videoconference-based online group intervention for traumatic stress in parents of children with life-threatening illness: A randomized clinical trial. *JAMA Network Open*, 3(7), 1–14. https://doi.org/10.1001/jamanetworkopen.2020.8507.

Naeim, M., Rezaeisharif, A., & Bagvand, S. G. (2021). The effectiveness of virtual cognitive-behavioral group therapy on anxiety, stress, and fatigue in Coronavirus Intensive Care Unit nurses. *Minerva*, 62(4), 216–222. https://doi.org/10.23736/s2724-6612.21.02141-5.

Otared, N., Moharrampour, N. G., Vojoudi, B., & Najafabadi, A. J. (2021). A group-based online acceptance and commitment therapy treatment for depression, anxiety symptoms and quality of life in healthcare workers during COVID-19 pandemic: A randomized controlled trial. *International Journal of Psychology and Psychological Therapy*, 21(3), 399–411.

Penedo, F. J., Fox, R. S., Walsh, E. A., Yanez, B., Miller, G. E., Oswald, L. B., Estabrook, R., Chatterton, R. T., Mohr, D. C., Begale, M. J., Flury, S. C., Perry, K., Kundu, S. D., & Moreno, P. I. (2021). Effects of web-based cognitive behavioral stress management and health promotion interventions on neuroendocrine and inflammatory markers in men with advanced prostate cancer: A randomized controlled trial. *Brain, Behavior, and Immunity*, 95, 168–177. https://doi.org/10.1016/j.bbi.2021.03.014.

Park, E. R., Perez, G. K., Millstein, R. A., Luberto, C. M., Traeger, L., Proszynski, J., Chad-Friedman, E., & Kuhlthau, K. A. (2020). A virtual resiliency intervention promoting resiliency for parents of children with learning and attentional disabilities: A randomized pilot trial. *Maternal and Child Health Journal*, 24, 39–53. https://doi.org/10.1007/s10995-019-02815-3.

Paul, J. J., Dardar, S., River, L. M., & St. John-Larkin, C. (2021). Telehealth adaptation of perinatal mental health mother-infant group programming for the COVID-19 pandemic. *Infant Mental Health*, 43(1), 85–99. https://doi.org/10.1002/imhj.21960.

Penedo, F. J., Fox, R. S., Walsh, E. A., Yanez, B., Miller, G. E., Oswald, L. B., Estabrook, R., Chatterton, R. T., Mohr, D. C., Begale, M. J., Flury, S. C., Perry, K., Kundu, S. D., & Moreno, P. I. (2021). Effects of web-based cognitive behavioral stress management and health promotion interventions on neuroendocrine and inflammatory markers in men with advanced prostate cancer: A randomized controlled trial. *Brain, Behavior, and Immunity*, 95, 168–177. https://doi.org/10.1016/j.bbi.2021.03.014.

Ranjbar, N., Erb, M., Tomkins, J., Taneja, K., & Villagomez, A. (2021). Implementing a mind-body skills group in psychiatric residency training. *Academic Psychiatry*. https://doi.org/10.1007/s40596-021-01507-x.

Reger, M. A., & Gahm, G. A. (2009). A meta-analysis of the effects of Internet- and computer-based cognitive-behavioral treatments for anxiety. *Journal of Clinical Psychology*, 65(1), 53–75. https://doi.org/10.1002/jclp.20536.

Rice, V. J., & Schroeder, P. J. (2021). In-person and virtual world mindfulness training: Trust, satisfaction, and learning. *Cyberpsychology, Behavior, and Social Networking*, 24(8), 526–535. https://doi.org/10.1089/cyber.2019.0590.

Ritvo, P., Ahmad, F., El Morr, C., Pirbaglou, M., Moineddin, R., & Team, M. V. C. (2021). A mindfulness-based intervention for student depression, anxiety, and stress: Randomized controlled trial. *JMIR Mental Health*, 8(1), e23491. https://mental.jmir.org/2021/1/e23491.

Robinson-Whelen, S., Hughes, R. B., Taylor, H. B., Markley, R., Vega, J. C., Nosek, T. M., & Nosek, M. A. (2020). Promoting psychological health in women with SCI: Development of an online self-esteem intervention. *Disability and Health Journal*, 13(2), 100867. https://doi.org/10.1016/j.dhjo.2019.100867.

Sansom-Daly, U., Wakefield, C., Ellis, S., McGill, B., Donoghoe, M., Butow, P., Bryant, R., Sawyer, S., Patterson, P., Anazodo, A., Plaster, M., Thompson, K., Holland, L., Osborn, M., Maguire, F., O'Dwyer, C., De Abreu Lourenco, R., & Cohn, R. (2021). Online, group-based psychological support for adolescent and Young Adult Cancer Survivors: Results from the recapture life randomized trial. *Cancers*, 13(10), 2460. https://doi.org/10.3390/cancers13102460.

Schuster, R., Fischer, E., Jansen, C., Napravnik, N., Rockinger, S., Steger, N., & Laireiter, A.-R. (2022). Blending Internet-based and tele group treatment: Acceptability, effects, and mechanisms of change of cognitive behavioral treatment for depression. *Internet Interventions*, 100551. https://doi.org/10.1016/j.invent.2022.100551.

Shapira, S., Cohn-Schwartz, E., Yeshua-Katz, D., Aharonson-Daniel, L., Clarfield, A. M., & Sarid, O. (2021). Teaching and practicing cognitive-behavioral and mindfulness skills in a web-based platform among older adults through the COVID-19 pandemic: A pilot randomized controlled trial. *International Journal of Environmental Research and Public Health*, 18(20), 10563. https://www.mdpi.com/journal/ijerph.

Tuntipuchitanon, S., Kangwanthiti, I., Jirakran, K., Trairatvorakul, P., & Chonchaiya, W. (2022). Online positive parenting programme for promoting parenting competencies and skills: randomised controlled trial. *Scientific Report*, 12. https://doi.org/10.1038/s41598-022-10193-0.

Wagner, B., Grafiadeli, R., Schäfer, T., & Hofmann, L. (2022). Efficacy of an online-group intervention after suicide bereavement: A randomized controlled trial. *Internet Interventions*, 28, 100542. https://doi.org/10.1016/j.invent.2022.100542.

Ward, M. M., Ullrich, F., Merchant, K. A. S., Carter, K. D., Bhagianadh, D., Lacks, M., Taylor, E., & Gordon, J. (2022). Describing changes in tele-behavioral health utilization and services delivery in rural school settings in pre- and early stages of the COVID-19 public health emergency. *Journal of School Health*, 92(5), 452–460. https://doi.org/10.1111/josh.13150.

Weinberg, H. (2020). Online group psychotherapy: Challenges and possibilities during COVID-19—A practice review. *Group Dynamics: Theory, Research, and Practice*, 24(3), 201–211. http://dx.doi.org/10.1037/gdn0000140.

Wind, T. R., Rijkeboer, M., Andersson, G., & Riper, H. (2020). The COVID-19 pandemic: The "black swan" for mental health care and a turning point for e-health. *Internet Interventions*, 20, 1–2. https://doi.org/10.1016/j.invent.2020.100317.

Chapter 3

Miles Away

Alliance and Cohesion in Online Group Psychotherapy

Cheri L. Marmarosh, Alexandra Robelo, Alicia Solorio and Feng Xing

Introduction

The therapy relationship is one of the most important aspects of both individual and group psychotherapy and includes the working alliance, the agreement on the tasks and goals of the group, and the bond between the therapist and the client (Norcross & Lambert, 2018; Fluckiger et al., 2018). The same holds true in group therapy. In group psychotherapy, the relationship with the leaders and group members are the most critical aspects of group psychotherapy (Yalom & Leszcz, 2020; Burlingame et al., Yang, 2018). The COVID-19 pandemic has had a powerful impact on us all and has increased our reliance on tele-group therapy (Marmarosh et al., 2020). Instead of meeting only face-to-face, groups are now also meeting online, and our attention has shifted to the differences in the therapy relationship between online and face-to-face treatments. Researchers studying individual therapy have found that clients rate the therapeutic alliance at least equally as strong in online therapy compared to face-to-face treatment, across a variety of diagnoses (Smith et al., 2022).

What about group psychotherapy? This chapter will focus on group treatment and the impact of shifting to the online modality on the relational aspects of group treatment, the alliance and group cohesion. The chapter will examine some of the recent research demonstrating that leaders and members of online therapy groups feel differently about the therapy relationship in online versus face-to-face groups. The chapter will explore factors that likely influence the alliance and group cohesion such as limited eye contact, increased physical distance, and detachment from the body (Weinberg, 2020). The chapter will also review how leaders can facilitate cohesion in online group treatment. Implications for practice and future research will be explored.

Online Groups: Are there Differences?

Conventional wisdom insists that psychotherapy is meant to be delivered face-to-face because of the effectiveness of psychological interventions

DOI: 10.4324/9781003248606-4

contingent on the development of a high-quality therapeutic alliance between therapist and client (Bee et al., 2008). However, there are many external factors preventing patients from engaging in traditional face-to-face mental health services, including the pandemic, financial burdens, difficulties of transportation, mobility-reducing health issues, and scarce availability of clinicians or facilities in the region. The technological innovation of telehealth represents a drastic change in mental health services by empowering patients to exercise greater choice and control (Hollis et al., 2015).

The use of video conferencing or other online platforms possibly hinder the quality of interpersonal interaction due to the diminished auditory and visual information, including eye contact, posture, physical expression, and voice (Wootton et al., 2003). Many are concerned whether the therapist would be compromised in the capacity of communicating warmth, understanding, sensitivity, and empathy through videoconferencing. We turn to the research findings to see how group members are impacted by online group psychotherapy.

Therapeutic Alliance: Online Group Therapy

Although there are variations of the definition of the therapeutic alliance, most agree that (a) the working alliance captures the collaborative element of the client-therapist relationship; (b) the capacity of both clients and therapists to negotiate the breadth and depth of goals and tasks; and (c) the emotional connection between therapist and client (Horvath & Symonds, 1991). The relationship between the quality of the working alliance and the subsequent therapeutic treatment outcome has been extensively studied and was found to be correlated across multiple meta-analyses (Horvath et al., 2011; Horvath & Symonds, 1991).

In group therapy, the alliance is the relationship between the member and the leader/s. Meta-analysis revealed a similar finding that the group therapy alliance is also related to outcome in group psychotherapy (Alldredge et al., 2020). Specifically, studies have found support for online group psychotherapy. A pilot study that delivered group cognitive therapy protocol using online video conferences found that the online group could meet the same professional practice standards and outcomes as face-to-face delivery of the intervention program (Khatri et al., 2014). Morland et al. (2015) found psychotherapy delivered via videoconferencing to be equal to in-person treatment with no significant difference between therapeutic alliance, treatment compliance, and satisfaction.

A recent study by Morel et al. (2021) surveyed 20 group members in online group therapy and asked them about their perceptions of the alliance, satisfaction with treatment, convenience, and cohesion. They found that most of the group members indicated that the alliance and cohesion was either the same or slightly worse in online compared to face-to-face groups. However, they found that most members also found online group therapy to be effective, convenient, and satisfying.

Therapeutic Cohesion: Online Group Therapy

Cohesion, the relationship between group members, is different from the alliance, the relationship between the group member and the leader. Yalom and Leszcz (2020) describe group cohesion as the attractiveness of the group that fosters an emotional experience often described as a sense of "we-ness" or "esprit de corps." Group theorists emphasize the bond between group members (Joyce et al., 2007), the commitment to the group, to the leader, and to the other members (Piper et al., 1983), and the attraction to the group-as-a-whole (Frank, 1957). In addition to the force of attraction to the group, Forsyth (2021) emphasized how cohesion facilitates commitment to the group and a sense of unity. It is not only a necessary condition for meaningful group work, but it is also a prerequisite to change (Yalom & Leszcz, 2020).

Although we know a significant amount about face-to-face group cohesion, we know far less about online group cohesion. One study found a significant difference in patients who reported group cohesion in online and in-person groups. Although there were no differences in the connection to the group leader (group alliance), many in the online group reported less group cohesion and feeling less connected to other group members compared to those in in-person groups (Lopez et al., 2020). They found that in group teletherapy, group cohesion and group member similarity were more important than client-therapist alliance (Heckman et al., 2017). The results reveal that group cohesion is an important force in online groups and may be a bit more challenging to develop in online groups, but the relationship with the leader is less impacted by the online nature of the group modality. This is important information for leaders to be aware of as they begin to lead online groups. They have a significant role in fostering cohesion.

Practical Implications for Online Groups Leaders

Researchers have shown that group members and leaders describe the value of cohesion in online group treatment; therefore, it is even more important to examine what leaders can do to facilitate cohesion in online groups. Burlingame et al. (2001) emphasized six empirically based principles that focus on group leader behaviors that contribute to and foster group cohesion (see Table 3.1.). These principles describe how the leader fosters cohesion via planning, verbal engagement, and facilitation of emotional intimacy in the group. Their work was based on face-to-face groups, and we made additions that reflect the needs of online groups.

Burlingame et al. (2001, 2002) among others emphasize how pre-group preparations that include reviewing client expectations for groups, establishing group procedures that address the online process, and providing information about group boundaries and confidentiality are critical when establishing a therapeutic environment. Online group leaders can prepare patients by conducting individual or group interviews prior to the start of online group and reviewing technology, clinical procedures such as fee payments, time and length of sessions, protocol for the chat and online platform being used, and termination procedures. Leaders can enhance group homogeneity within group members by ensuring an even gender distribution, being sensitive to members' race, culture, and sexual orientation, and including members within the same age range (Yalom & Leszcz, 2020; Ribeiro, 2020). McMillan and Chavis (1986) outline additional factors related to group cohesion, which they describe as a group community. They underscore the importance of positive interactions and a sense of belonging in the group. Frequent contact and stability foster a sense of unity.

In online groups, leaders need to actively try to engage group members to interact and provide the necessary structure to foster a sense of safety in the group. This is especially true in groups that have members from cultures with norms that do not value open disclosure of emotions or prioritization of the self over others (Debiak, 2007; Ribeiro, 2020). One way that leaders can foster safety within the group is by inviting members to share their preferred pronouns during the intake interview, followed by ensuring that other members adhere to the pronouns that have been disclosed. Leaders may inquire about disabilities that may not be seen in an online format in order to assess any mobility constraints that may impact their use of the technology. Online groups have altered the frame of the treatment. Instead of meeting together in a shared space, members may log in from their homes. Leaders may need to help members to address feelings that are triggered when members see other group member's personal living situations, some with more wealth and some with more poverty. Removing the boundary of the therapy room increases exposure to economic differences, religion/faith, culture, and personal values.

It is always difficult to balance group members' disclosure of outside group experiences with ingroup process, and this is magnified when members are sitting at home in the group. For some members, it is harder to step into a different world when they are sitting alone in their room. Group leaders who ensure that the here and now interactions are emphasized, and not avoided, facilitate cohesion because they encourage within group disclosure that facilitates healthy conflict and intimacy (Yalom & Leszcz, 2020; Burlingame et al., 2001, 2002; Tschuschke & Dies, 1994). Group therapists describe how the resolution of conflict facilitates trust, intimacy, and cohesion (Corey et al., 2018; Yalom &

Leszcz, 2020; Tasca et al., 2021), and group researchers have supported the increase of cohesion after periods of conflict (Castonguay et al., 1998; Kivlighan & Lilly, 1997). Two special editions were devoted to rupture and repair in group therapy (Marmarosh, 2021a, 2021b) where experts described the importance of helping members to work through micro-aggressions in the group (Miles et al., 2021), identifying leader micro-aggressions (Rutan, 2021), and monitoring ruptures and repairs after sessions (Svien et al., 2021). We need more research to explore how ruptures are different online and how the repair process may be unique as well.

Modeling corrective feedback by using names when addressing members, maintaining connection despite the loss of eye contact, valuing openness, and encouraging member to member relationships can facilitate closeness within the group (Burlingame et al., 2002). Corey et al. (2018) point out how group leaders can provide a sense of greater connection and belonging between group members by actively encouraging interaction among members and exploring common themes and linking members' experiences. Group leaders are crucial in establishing this trust between group members during the early stages of the group's development.

Not only is the group leader's ability to provide structure, give positive feedback, and encourage risk taking important, the leader must also maintain the emotional climate of the group via the leader's own personal behaviors in the group and their ability to foster that capacity in group members. Johnson et al. (2005) studied the relationship between empathy, group alliance, and cohesion and found that empathy and cohesion were both correlated and loaded onto a common factor described as the positive bonding relationship in groups. In essence, perceived empathy from the leader and members was related to perceived cohesion and contributed to a positive group environment.

An online group leader described an incident in an online group session when a member revealed to the group her desire to kill herself. She walked to the roof of her building and took the group with her on her phone as she described her plan. The group members were terrified, and the leader was able to contain the fear and empathize with the member who was suffering. The leader acknowledged her own fears, empathized with the member and the group, and then group members shared their similar feelings of hopelessness, despair, and desire to help her. They also shared how much they valued her in the group. The member was able to hear the group members' empathy, accept their compassion, and went back to her room and called her individual therapist. She decided not to take her own life, and the group alliance and cohesion had a powerful impact on her that day.

Guidelines for Online Group Therapy

When starting a new online group, the group leader may find benefit in including the group members in the process of creating these guidelines

(Burlingame et al., 2002). By allowing members to have a say in the guidelines, the leader fosters collaboration, communication, and group alliance from the very beginning. When doing online groups, it is helpful to let group members know the guidelines for online group treatment, such as guidelines around cameras being on or off, the use of the chat function, and privacy and confidentiality while using an online format.

Confidentiality and Privacy in Online Group Therapy

Although members may agree to maintain confidentiality during the pre-group preparation, it may be harder to maintain privacy. This freedom of being able to access therapy anywhere also comes with a potential threat to confidentiality. In addition, if other members notice that a member is in a public location or constantly has people walking by in the background during the session, some may be less inclined to participate due to a fear of their private information being heard by non-group members. Group leaders can work to prevent these potential breaches of privacy by encouraging members to log into sessions from a private space. In cases where the member is unable to find a completely secluded area away from others, using headphones during sessions is another option that can also work to prevent others overhearing the group conversation. In addition, members can be directed to sit so their camera is pointed towards a wall. Having cameras on during sessions allows members to maintain some sort of connection with the other members. By sitting with our backs towards a wall instead of a door or windows, we are protecting our fellow members' identities and right to therapeutic privacy.

Challenges and Possibilities: Online Group Therapy

With group sessions being conducted online, leaders have been faced with new challenges and difficulties in building and maintaining alliance among members and cohesion. Listed below are some practices that leaders may find useful to implement in online groups.

Challenge: Loss of Eye Contact

Morel et al. (2021) found that group members in online groups reported more difficulty with having no direct eye contact in online groups compared to face-to-face groups. Using names when addressing someone in an online group is helpful when there is no certainty about eye contact. By using a member's name when speaking specifically to them, we ensure that our message is being delivered to the intended audience. In addition, when names are used and called on, members may feel more inclined to participate since it will not be as easy to blend into the background of the session.

Although there are a variety of valid reasons why a member would choose to keep their camera off during a session, we recommend that leaders request that members keep their cameras on whenever possible to maintain the face-to-face interaction and connection that was an important part of in-person group therapy. Camera usage and preferences should be discussed with members at the formation of the group/whenever there is a new member joining. Leaders may find it helpful to discuss the importance of keeping cameras on. Some members may be uncomfortable with speaking to a "blank" screen because they do not know who is on the other end or if non-group members are present. This can lead to members being less willing to participate or communicate specifically with the members who have their cameras off.

Challenge: Withdrawal and Subgrouping

Many online platforms include a chat function that participants can use to communicate during a meeting. In terms of group alliance, disabling the chat function would most likely be a benefit. If the speaker were to see that group members were "chatting" while they were talking, it could lead to feelings of being ignored or disrespected by the other members. Also, chatting with certain members during a group can lead to the formation of subgroups and people channeling their feelings into a "chat vent" instead of saying something directly in the group.

In addition to chatting while in group, some members may be distracted by emails, phone texts, and other technology. It is important for leaders to discourage this in group preparation, but also to address it when it occurs. Given that many people seek group therapy to address interpersonal difficulties, it should be expected that members might engage in behaviors in online groups that interfere with their relationships. For example, a group member who avoids conflict may find herself looking at her phone during an online session. It may be helpful to examine what motivates this behavior that pulls her away from what is happening in the group. It is also important for the group members to challenge one another as they engage in behaviors that feel hurtful. Processing the ruptures and addressing conflict in the group will foster true group cohesion (Yalom & Leszcz, 2020).

Conclusions and Future Implications

Although online group therapy has limitations and challenges, it is here to stay and provides members with a sense of connection and stability. Researchers are just beginning to explore the group relationships, ruptures, and repairs in online groups, but the research findings so far suggest that online groups do facilitate cohesion. We need additional studies to explore the similarities and differences between online groups and face-to-face groups, especially regarding group process and outcome.

Implications for Future Research

Marmarosh (2019) recommends examining individual difference variables that are likely to influence cohesion and alliance in online group therapy such as member attachment style. Marmarosh et al. (2013) describe how attachment can influence all aspects of group therapy from screening to termination, and one would expect that those members with more attachment avoidance may find the distance of online group therapy more comfortable while those with more attachment anxiety struggle with the increased distance and lack of eye contact. In addition to attachment, culture may influence a member's sense of shame for seeking treatment and online group therapy may feel more acceptable than joining a face-to-face group. A member who is overwhelmed with paranoia or social anxiety may benefit from an online group to begin therapy before eventually transitioning to a face-to-face group when they can tolerate it. Future research is needed to answer these important questions and determine when online groups are more effective (or indeed equally effective) than face-to-face groups and for which patients. It is also important to address group size, co-leadership, and the impact of different technology platforms such as mobile phones, laptops, and tablets.

Implications for Training

As we shift our group work online, we must also help to prepare members and leaders for this specific modality (Weinberg, 2020). Gullo et al. (2022) found that many group leaders had never led a group online before the outbreak of the COVID-19 pandemic. Although there are similarities between face-to-face treatment and online treatment, they are not the same. Leaders do need to revise their informed consent, practice guidelines, and confidentiality agreements. They need to be thoughtful about the new frame and how the different boundaries impact the group. They need to be more thoughtful and intentional about noticing ruptures and addressing them. They need to be more aware of the unexpected intrusions on the group that can occur. There is less control in online groups, and members can be impacted by the things occurring in another's environment. Although there is much for us to learn and to teach the next generation of group therapists, this is an exciting time in the field of group therapy. We can reach more people than ever and have the potential to facilitate long-lasting change.

Table 3.1 Six Empirically Supported Principles for Group Leaders that Facilitate the Group Relationship Amended for Online Groups

Principle I
Conduct online pre-group preparation that sets treatment expectations, defines group rules, and instructs members in appropriate roles and skills needed for effective group participation and group cohesion. Address eye contact, privacy, confidentiality, group policies, and attendance. In online groups, it is important to remind members not to be distracted by texts, cooking, or distractions that are easier to engage in at home.

Principle II
The group leader should establish clarity regarding group processes in early sessions since higher levels of structure probably lead to higher levels of disclosure and cohesion. *When online, model openness to pronouns (have them on the screen), let people know the camera should be on unless it can't be, intervene and provide necessary structure earlier on.*

Principle III
The leader modeling real-time observations, guiding effective interpersonal feedback, and maintaining a moderate level of control and affiliation may positively impact cohesion. *In online groups, the leader may need to remind people to use names when talking to one another since there is a loss of eye contact.*

Principle IV
The timing and delivery of feedback should be pivotal considerations for leaders as they facilitate this relationship-building process. The leader needs to be sensitive to the online nature of interventions. *Tone of voice and expressing self in words is important when providing feedback without having the same eye contact or non-verbal communication.*

Principle V
The group leader's presence not only affects the relationship with individual members, but all group members as they vicariously experience the leader's manner of relating; thus, the therapist's managing of his or her own emotional presence in the service of others is important. *Online groups require more openness to how people are responding with questions like, "I think you looked away just then and I wonder how you are feeling. It is hard online, but it looks as though you were touched by the last interaction." Leaders can model how to be more personal and connected in online groups even when there is a physical distance.*

Principle VI
A primary focus of the group leader should be on facilitating group members' emotional expression, the responsiveness of others to that expression, and the shared meaning derived from such expression. *Online groups are more challenging for emotional expression. It is much easier for a member to pull away and withdraw while looking at their phone. Leaders may need to be more proactive in drawing in members who may disengage during the sessions. In addition, leaders may need to help members who are emotional to feel the presence of others. It may help to invite members to share what they feel. It is helpful to ask members to talk to one another when sharing personal information/feedback even though the screen has multiple faces looking back. It is helpful for the leader to ask how the online platform is impacting them during the sessions.*

Source: Burlingame et al., 2001.

References

Alldredge, C., Burlingame, G., Olsen, J., & Van Epps, J. (2020). Outcome Questionnaire-45 (OQ-45) Progress Alert Rates in Group Versus Individual Treatment: An Archival Replication. *Group Dynamics*, 24(4), 247–260. https://doi.org/10.1037/gdn0000121.

Bee, P. E., Bower, P., Lovell, K., Gilbody, S., Richards, D., Gask, L., & Roach, P. (2008). Psychotherapy mediated by remote communication technologies: A meta-analytic review. *BMC Psychiatry*, 8(1), 60–60. https://doi.org/10.1186/1471-244X-8-60.

Burlingame, G. M., Fuhriman, A., & Johnson, J. E. (2001). Cohesion in group psychotherapy. *Psychotherapy: Theory, Research, Practice, Training*, 38(4), 373–379. https://doi.org/10.1037/0033-3204.38.4.373.

Burlingame, G. M., Fuhriman, A., & Johnson, J. E. (2002). Cohesion in group psychotherapy. *Psychotherapy*, 38, 373–379.

Burlingame, G. M., McClendon, D. T., & Yang, C. (2018). Cohesion in group therapy: A meta-analysis. *Psychotherapy*, 55(4), 384–398. https://doi.org/10.1037/pst0000173.

Castonguay, Louis, Pincus, Aaron, Agras, W. S., & Hines, C. E. (1998). The role of emotion in group cognitive-behavioral therapy for binge eating disorder: When things have to feel worse before they get better. *Psychotherapy Research*, 8. 225–238. doi:10.1080/10503309812331332327.

Corey, M. S., Corey, G., & Corey, G. (2018). *Groups: Process and practice* (10th ed.). Thomson Brooks/Cole Publishing Co.

Debiak, D. (2007). Attending to diversity in group psychotherapy: An ethical imperative. *International Journal of group psychotherapy*, 57, 1–12. doi:10.1521/ijgp.2007.57.1.1.

Flückiger, C., Del Re, A. C., Wampold, B. E., & Horvath, A. O. (2018). The alliance in adult psychotherapy: A meta-analytic synthesis. *Psychotherapy*, 55(4), 316–340. https://doi.org/10.1037/pst0000172.

Forsyth, D. R. (2021). Recent advances in the study of group cohesion. *Group Dynamics*, 25(3), 213–228. https://doi.org/10.1037/gdn0000163.

Frank, J. D. (1957). Some determinants, manifestations, and effects of cohesiveness in therapy groups. *International Journal of Group Psychotherapy*, 7(1), 53–63.

Gullo, S., Lo Coco, G., Leszcz, M., Marmarosh, C. L., Miles, J. R., Shechtman, Z., ... & Tasca, G. A. (2022). Therapists' perceptions of online group therapeutic relationships during the COVID-19 pandemic: A survey-based study. *Group Dynamics: Theory, Research, and Practice*, 26(2), 103–118.

Heckman, T. G., Heckman, B. D., Anderson, T., Bianco, J. A., Sutton, M., & Lovejoy, T. I. (2017). Common factors and depressive symptom relief trajectories in group teletherapy for persons ageing with HIV. *Clinical Psychology and Psychotherapy*, 24(1), 139–148. https://doi.org/10.1002/cpp.1989.

Hollis, C., Morriss, R., Martin, J., Amani, S., Cotton, R., Denis, M., & Lewis, S. (2015). Technological innovations in mental healthcare: Harnessing the digital revolution. *British Journal of Psychiatry*, 206 (4), 263–265. https://doi.org/10.1192/bjp.bp.113.142612.

Horvath, A. O., & Symonds, B. D. (1991). Relation between working alliance and outcome in psychotherapy: A meta-analysis. *Journal of Counseling Psychology*, 38(2), 139–149. https://doi.org/10.1037/0022-0167.38.2.139.

Horvath, A. O., Del Re, A. C., Flückiger, C., & Symonds, D. (2011). Alliance in individual psychotherapy. *Psychotherapy* 48(1), 9–16. https://doi.org/10.1037/a 0022186.

Johnson, J. E., Burlingame, G. M., Olsen, J. A., Davies, D. R., & Gleave, R. L. (2005). Group climate, cohesion, alliance, and empathy in group psychotherapy: Multilevel structural equation models. *Journal of Counseling Psychology*, 52(3), 310–321. https://doi.org/10.1037/0022-0167.52.3.310.

Joyce, A. S., Piper, W. E., & Ogrodniczuk, J. S. (2007). Therapeutic alliance and cohesion variables as predictors of outcome in short-term group psychotherapy. *International Journal of Group Psychotherapy*, 57(3), 269–296.

Khatri, N., Marziali, E., Tchernikov, I., & Shepherd, N. (2014). Comparing telehealth-based and clinic-based group cognitive behavioral therapy for adults with depression and anxiety: A pilot study. *Clinical Interventions in Aging*, 9, 765–770. https://doi.org/10.2147/CIA.S57832.

Kivlighan, D.Jr. (2021). From where is the group? To what is the group?: Contributions of actor–partner interdependence modeling. *Group Dynamics*, 25(3), 229–237. https://doi.org/10.1037/gdn0000164.

Kivlighan, D. M., Jr., & Lilly, R. L. (1997). Developmental changes in group climate as they relate to therapeutic gain. *Group Dynamics: Theory, Research, and Practice*, 1(3), 208–221. https://doi.org/10.1037/1089-2699.1.3.208.

Lopez, A., Rothberg, B., Reaser, E., Schwenk, S., & Griffin, R. (2020). Therapeutic groups via video teleconferencing and the impact on group cohesion. *Health*, 6, 13–13. https://doi.org/10.21037/mhealth.2019.11.04.

Marmarosh, C. L. (2019). Introduction: Attachment in group psychotherapy: Bridging theories, research, and clinical techniques. In *Attachment in Group Psychotherapy* (pp. 1–3). Routledge.

Marmarosh, C. (2021a). Rupture and repair in group psychotherapy: Theory and practice. *International Journal of Group Psychotherapy*.

Marmarosh, C. (2021b). Rupture and repair in group psychotherapy: Theory, assessment, research, and practice. *Group Dynamics: Theory, Research, and Practice*.

Marmarosh, C. L., Forsyth, D. R., Strauss, B., & Burlingame, G. M. (2020). The psychology of the COVID-19 pandemic: A group-level perspective. *Group Dynamics*, 24(3), 122–138. https://doi.org/10.1037/gdn0000142.

Marmarosh, C. L., Markin, R. D., & Spiegel, E. G. (2013). Diversity in group psychotherapy: Attachment, ethnicity, and race. In C. L. Marmarosh, R. D. Markin, & E. B. Spiegel (Eds.), *Attachment in group psychotherapy* (pp. 189–209). American Psychological Association Press. doi:10.1037/14186-005.

Miles, J. R., Anders, C., Kivlighan, D. M., III, & Belcher Platt, A. A. (2021). Cultural ruptures: Addressing microaggressions in group therapy. *Group Dynamics: Theory, Research, and Practice*, 25(1), 74–88. https://doi.org/10. 1037/gdn0000149.

McMillan, D. W., & Chavis, D. M. (1986). Sense of community: A definition and theory. *Journal of Community Psychology*, 14(1), 6–23.

Morel, M., Robelo, A., Solorio, A., Koroma, M.Z., Xing, F., & Marmarosh, C. (2021). *Online group psychotherapy during COVID-19: The group member perspective*. Poster for the Annual American Psychological Association Conference. Online.

Morland, L. A., Mackintosh, M.-A., Rosen, C. S., Willis, E., Resick, P., Chard, K., & Frueh, B. C. (2015). Telemedicine versus in-person delivery of cognitive processing therapy for women with posttraumatic stress disorder: A randomized noninferiority trial. *Depression and Anxiety*, 32(11), 811–820. https://doi.org/10.1002/da.22397.

Norcross, J. C., & Lambert, M. J. (2018). Psychotherapy relationships that work III. *Psychotherapy*, 55(4), 303–315. https://doi.org/10.1037/pst0000193.

Piper, W. E., Marrache, M., Lacroix, R., Richardsen, A. M., & Jones, B. D. (1983). Cohesion as a basic bond in groups. *Human Relations*, 36(2), 93–108.

Ribeiro, M. (2020). *Examining social identities and diversity issues in group therapy: Knocking at the boundaries*. Routledge.

Rutan, J. S. (2021). Rupture and repair: Using leader errors in psychodynamic group psychotherapy. *International Journal of Group Psychotherapy*, 71(2), 310–331. https://doi.org/10.1080/00207284.2020.1808471.

Smith, K., Moller, N., Cooper, M., Gabriel, L., Roddy, J., & Sheehy, R. (2022). Video counselling and psychotherapy: A critical commentary on the evidence base. *Counselling and Psychotherapy Research*, 22(1), 92–97.

Svien, H., Burlingame, G. M., Griner, D., Beecher, M. E., & Alldredge, C. T. (2021). Group therapeutic relationship change: Using routine outcome monitoring to detect the effect of single versus multiple ruptures. *Group Dynamics: Theory, Research, and Practice*, 25(1), 45–52.

Tasca, G. A., Mikail, S. E., & Hewitt, P. L. (2021). *Group psychodynamic-interpersonal psychotherapy*. American Psychological Association.

Tschuschke, V., & Dies, R. R. (1994). Intensive analysis of therapeutic factors and outcome in long-term inpatient groups. *International Journal of Group Psychotherapy*, 44(2), 185–208.

Weinberg, H. (2020). Online group psychotherapy: Challenges and possibilities during COVID-19—A practice review. *Group Dynamics: Theory, Research, and Practice*, 24(3), 201–211. https://doi.org/10.1037/gdn0000140.

Wootton, R., Yellowlees, P., & McLaren, P. (2003). *Telepsychiatry and e-mental health*. Royal Society of Medicine Press.

Yalom, I., & Leszcz, M. (2020). *The theory and practice of group psychotherapy* (6th ed.). Basic Books.

Chapter 4

Online Group Psychotherapy

Is the Body Really Necessary?

Nikolaos Takis

The outbreak of the COVID-19 pandemic in early 2020 brought about significant changes in the practice of individual and group psychotherapy. Remote sessions became the only available option of group work. Group leaders have been forced to move from face-to-face to online environments, without being adequately trained and prepared for this sudden transition. This new reality modified, to a significant extent, the framework of group psychotherapy.

Leaders and members of groups faced multiple unexpected challenges. Primarily, they had to deal with the absence of the physical body (Weinberg, 2020). The spatial reality was also different. Participants did not meet face-to-face in a specific room, but attended sessions remotely, from their private locations. In this chapter, we focus on the repercussions of the physical body's absence on the group process and frame. Our main conjecture is that, despite the significant differences, the body is still vividly present in online sessions albeit in a different way that, if perceived properly, can have significant effects on group members.

The transition to the virtual environment of online platforms questioned some basic principles of psychotherapy's frame. Psychotherapy is deemed to be a process based on physical presence. For example, according to Winnicott (1971), the primary function of therapists is to provide a sense of holding environment for their patients. He describes the holding environment as the illusory space between two people that enables the successful mutual adaptation and healthy development. This sense has clear somatic components, as it originates in the feeling of the infant being in the safety of the mother's arms. Patients should reexperience this feeling in the consultation room, which then becomes for them a motherly environment, and should be allowed to make use of the therapist, according to their needs and deficits.

Seen from the lens of Bowlby's theory (1979), physical presence and, ultimately, proximity is necessary for the sense of having a "secure base." In order to attain this sense, therapists need to develop an ability to draw on attunement and markedness. Attunement pertains to the therapist's

DOI: 10.4324/9781003248606-5

ability to focus the client's thoughts and emotions, so that the latter feels understood (Stern, 1985). Markedness refers to the emotional response to the clients' cues and signals (Fonagy et al., 2002). Once attained, the sense of security and being understood allows for the development of earned secure attachment (Main, 1990), a fundamental component of effective treatment.

Defining the basic principles of the frame of group psychotherapy, Bion (1961) states that groups meet in a specific place, for a predetermined period, one or several days of the week. The spatial dimension is a key component of the framework and boundaries. The physical space becomes the equivalent of "mental skin" (Bick, 1968), or "ego-skin" (Anzieu, 1985), which in the early stages of the infant's life, and indeed the group's, enables the tolerance and processing of internal and external stimulations. The arrangement of the seats in a circle generates the feeling of an environment capable of holding tensions, stress, and unpleasant emotions. The circle of the group, having as a boundary the bodies of the group's members, becomes the group's skin, "incorporating" all the collective and individual functions that take place within the process (Foguel, 1994).

Foulkes (1975) considered looking after and safeguarding the environment and the physical setting of the group, as a major task of the group's leader. It is part of the *dynamic administration*, which enables members to develop a sense of safety, to connect and communicate. Metaphorically, the leader acts in a maternal manner, attending to the members' needs.

The body, being part of the frame, participates in the creation of the group unconscious and the imaginary body of the group. The drives and the internal objects of each member are put at the service of the collective "mental apparatus." Through the group process, it is possible to revisit each member's internal objects and drives, as they are revived in the multiple transferential diffusions within the group (Weinberg, 2014).

The framework enables this revisiting in a safe way. It activates and at the same time sets limits for the regression of group members. Participants, as they engage progressively in the process, experience emotions and desires, and construct erotic or aggressive fantasies towards others. Libidinal and aggressive drives are in a constant mix, fueled by the participants' bodily functions. The rules of the frame (prohibition of bodily contact) ensure that fantasies will not become a reality, thereby preventing impulses from their physical discharge. Their frustration and prohibition, however, is what opens the field to the process of thought and psychic exploration—one of the major aims of psychotherapy. It should be noted that some of these fantasies can also be realized in online settings, without involving the bodily engagement of other group members.

Bion (1961), departing from Freud's view on groups (1921), believes that adults who enter a group resort to mass regression. The feeling that the group exists as a distinct entity is an illusion, indicative of this mass regression. He proposes the term "proto-mental system" to describe the operation of the group at this stage. His three basic assumptions about the group's function, namely dependency, fight-flight, and pairing, derive from phenomena and functions that occur in groups. The manifestations of the proto-mental system always threaten the coherence and evolution of the conscious level of operation of the group, which Bion calls the "work group." However, as he points out, "one of the striking things about a group is that, despite the influence of the basic assumptions, it is the Work Group that triumphs in the long run" (p. 135). Although he does not elaborate further on this issue, it seems that the triumph of the working group is, to a large extent, a result of the smooth functioning of the frame. The group, as another "framing structure" (Green, 1983), gradually achieves the containment of potentially destructive elements of the protomental system, which have bodily origins, such as physical arousal, the feeling of destructiveness or even anxiety, the so-called beta elements (Bion, 1962). It absorbs, metabolizes, and eventually returns these elements to the members as something that can now be endured, even if it causes discomfort. It also transmits to them a mode of operation, a mechanism which is gradually internalized and established as the ability to manage self-destructiveness and bodily stimuli.

All the concepts described thus far constitute pivotal points in the theory and practice of psychodynamic group psychotherapy. They all underscore the significance of the body's participation in the group process. The question that arises is whether, and if so how, they can be applied in an online group. Moreover, how does the polymorphous and multilayered group setting fit into an online environment?

Research on online group psychotherapy remained scarce until recently. In their review of the therapeutic alliance on videoconferencing psychotherapy, Simpson and Reid (2014) reported that many studies reported high levels of alliance for both therapists and clients. Online services were often preferred over the face-to-face services (Mohr et al., 2010; Dunstan & Tooth, 2012). Group cohesion in online settings, although insufficiently studied, is concluded to develop in online groups, but at a slower pace compared to in-person groups (Weinberg, 2021). Video-based groups have been found equally effective to in-person groups for the majority of participants (Gentry et al., 2019). One possible explanation for a client's preference for remote services is that they feel that they can control their level of involvement in the process. They maintain their individuality, set their personal boundaries, and at the same time they are members of a broad network (Weinberg, 2014).

The outbreak of the COVID-19 pandemic sparked an exponential increase in relevant research, as there was a great need for specific guidelines and help on how to move groups online. Furthermore, the pandemic restrictions offered the unique opportunity to study the alterations happening in the case of transition from face-to-face to online settings. A plethora of articles has been published since the outbreak of the pandemic, suggesting how group work can continue online (Stolper & Zigenlaub, 2021), offering practical recommendations for group leaders (Weinberg, 2020), studying the effectiveness of different group interventions (Lleras de Frutos et al., 2020; Fortier et al., 2022; Dark et al., 2022; Nurmagandi et al., 2022), and describing the implementation of alternative group modalities, for example psychodrama (Biancalani et al., 2021) and acceptance and commitment therapy (Otared et al., 2021). The common thread between these studies is the feasibility of the transition to online environments, with some necessary modifications. It is noted that the situation is more complicated when it comes to groups of patients with severe psychopathological disorders. For many of them, the physical presence acts like an anchor to reality. However, as recent experience has shown, even patients in the midst of a first psychotic episode can benefit from online treatment (Wood et al., 2021).

The clinical question that arises is: what is it that makes online groups work, despite the changes that seem to question basic theoretical principles? As systematically confirmed from related studies, the absence of the physical body from the sessions does not impede the delivery of group mental health services nor does it reduce their effectiveness. In fact, according to Lemma (2017), both leaders and members participate in the session with their bodies, in an embodied presence. She explains that the difference is "the experience of our own and the other person's embodiment" (p. 92). She also adds: "When in cyberspace we are still embodied even if we might choose to deny this to ourselves" (p. 19). Therefore, as noted by Weinberg (2020), it is not the body that is missing from the online environment but the body-to-body interaction between the participants. The visual and auditory channels of communication remain intact. Members focus more on the facial expressions, which can be perceived more clearly in the high resolution of the screen. The term face-to-face, often used for in-person communication, could be more suitable for online communication, as the upper part of the head is usually the part of the body that is visible on-screen. This form of physical presence enables the operation of the proto-mental system and the work group that Bion (1961) considered to be major attributes of the group process.

The group's holding environment seems also to have been successfully attained. Fletcher et al. (2014) introduced the term online holding environment as a special form of connectedness that develops in computer mediated relationships. They define it as "a space where supportive relationships can be developed and maintained through the use of technology over time" (p. 91). Regarding the earned secure attachment, a basic prerequisite of the group's cohesion, recent experience confirmed that it can develop in the online groups, so long as the leaders remain attuned to the participants.

The new condition does not seem to impede the emergence of the collective reality of the group either. Weinberg (2014) notes, after many years of experience, that online groups share a common reality as well. He departs from Immanuel Kant's notion that we can never grasp reality itself and that to approach it, we rely on thought which is based on a sense of stability of space and time. The sense of reality is subjective and mediated in each case by other parameters, such as cognition, emotion, and experience.

Expanding on the concept of skin ego that he introduced in 1971, Anzieu suggested the idea of the group skin ego, as an external membrane of the group's body (1999). He claimed that the group, being a discernible entity in its own body, develops an imaginary skin that envelops its internal processes and functioning (Raufman & Weinberg, 2016). The group ego exists within a symbolic skin, deriving from the meeting of the individual skin ego of each participant and the group body. The development of the group skin ego is not impeded by the online environment. On the contrary, given the absence of physical bodies, the setting fosters the use of symbolic functioning and imagination. By not seeing the total body of other members displayed, participants are recreating symbolically the missing parts, within the safety of their private spaces. Therefore, the fantasy of a well-functioning, containing, and enveloping group skin ego is attained successfully in online groups. It is probable that this process happens faster in online groups, due to the enhancement of symbolic functioning as described above. Agazarian (1989) claims similarly that what makes the group important for its members is the internal representation that is created collectively and shared among the participants, the "invisible group" as she names it, that is different to the actual one.

Lastly, one of the major factors for the success of the online groups is the ability of the group leaders to provide the required sense of safety and containment of tensions. They need to perform the dynamic administration, as described by Foulkes (1975), in a virtual setting. They are the first ones to create in their minds the representation of the group-as-a-whole, in order for the common fantasy of the group as a safe place to develop (Weinberg, 2016). Physical absence leads members to invest more in the leaders, being the representatives of the frame. As the spatial dimension is not available, their representation becomes the stable point of reference for the participants. According to Bleger (1967), the foundation of the frame is the therapist's internal structure and stability. This is what allows the patients to reenact and work through the problematic conditions and relations of their past, so as to overcome them. The members need to experience this stability and security provided by the conductors, in order to develop the internal representation of the group as their virtual safe place. The vignette that follows highlights the importance of the group leaders' function for the preservation of the fantasy of the group-as-a-whole in an online environment.

Group Vignette

The following vignette is an excerpt from an online group session, in its second year, led by two group psychotherapists, supervised by the author. It is the second session. The previous year, sessions were held in-person. The group consisted of five members, three males and two females. Some changes have been made in order to ensure confidentiality and to anonymize patient details.

When the therapists announced via telephone calls that the group would continue online, a female member, Rita, stated that she would quit the group. She believed that "group therapy can't be effective if the patients aren't in the same room with the therapists." She said that, for her, it would not work well to see the faces of others on a screen, without being able to "feel" them. She would return only if sessions were held face-to-face. This abrupt termination was not discussed in detail at the session that followed. However, other members commented that her departure was like a sudden death, and that they would have liked for her to continue. An excerpt from the next session follows:

HERA: I come to the session with lots of frustration, I will either burst or cry! I also feel strange because of a quarrel with my friends. The day has not started well, I have a bit of a melancholy after the over-excitement about my new house. Two of my friends gave birth. They reminded me how it is when things are going forward in life. And I always think about what I haven't done, that is, family and children. I am still on my own. The issues of companionship, security also arise. But no, no, I'm happy for my new apartment. It gives me stability and security. I don't need any substitutes to be well.

THERAPIST A: Might the new apartment become a substitute for companionship?

HERA: No, no that's not it.

LEON: I have similar concerns. I'm looking for security and safety too. I feel terribly lonely. It gets worse now, seeing you all from a computer screen!

HERA: For me, the relationship relates to stability and tranquility. As I said, I miss the feeling of having a common or parallel cause with someone. I am afraid that I will not find what I am looking for and this gap will remain.

THERAPIST B: Could you tell us more about this gap?

HERA: It's a big discussion, but I do not want to go "deeper" …

ORESTIS INTERVENES: Ha ha! Why should you ... Are we really in psychotherapy here?

HERA: [laughing] I mean that the socio-economic conditions can be to blame. Or it may be MY CHOICE [she emphasizes the word] that it has not happened [she means being in a relationship]. Sorry, I am monopolizing the group.

THERAPIST A: It is important that this issue is on the table. It concerns all of you. You may be wondering whether we can stay really connected on an online platform.

ORFEUS: I do not feel connected at all! Especially after Rita's dropout!

HERA: This is the reality, and we must accept it. It is like living a test of acceptance of reality. You do not need to know why! [Speaks with a strong tone and then is silent for a few seconds.]

LEON: Wow!

ORESTIS: In all these thoughts of Hera's I can see myself too. These are security issues. If I didn't have my wife for 15 years, I don't know how I would have been now. I try to set some standards. A long-term relationship requires some compromises. Otherwise, you cannot escape loneliness!

THERAPIST B: Like the compromise of meeting online instead of face-to-face?

LEON: In 2008 I met Maria, with whom I was together for five years, and in fact, we lived together for a year. It was my first relationship with a strong element of companionship. From 2013 I was single until 2016, when I met Ioanna. We lived together for two years. Leaving this relationship, I was immediately looking to enter the next one. I was not alone at all, I was always surrounded by people, I thought I was completely weak.

[At this point, therapist A's internet connection was temporarily interrupted and her image on the screen "froze."]

ORFEUS: Oh! Look at her face, I will take a picture of her and send it to you!

THERAPIST B: Orfeus, this is not permitted!

ORFEUS: Okay, I will not do it.

ORESTIS: It's not funny Orfeus! She looks as if she had a stroke!

[After a short break, therapist A reconnects.]

ORESTIS: Oh, you are back! Finally! I thought something bad happened to you!

[Leon yawned many times here.]

ORFEUS: [with several pauses and strokes in his speech] What I understand by listening to you, is that a beautiful puzzle is formed. But at
the same time each one is complementary to the other. I have a hard
time making myself clear, but I will try. I am now in a relationship
with my partner whom I love, for eight years. I mean, it's not easy for
everyone to have a relationship. I will share something with you. For
me and my partner, it is even more difficult because we come from
difficult families. Her mother was alcoholic, and my father was on
antipsychotic medication. I'm trying all my life to shatter the belief
that I'm not crazy too. I tell you all this because I feel that sharing in
the group relieves stress. I also wanted to tell you that my partner and
I made a lot of efforts to have a child, with the help of doctors. I
wanted to say that our families did not teach us how to be in a
functional relationship.

THERAPIST A: It sounds like you are all talking about the issue of loneliness and companionship. I see two different aspects: the ability to be
alone and the ability for relatedness.

THERAPIST B: Although at times it is difficult to follow, today the group
seems to worry about its survival, meeting in an online environment.
On the other hand, many of you shared private information for the
first time. Could that also be an effect of the transition?

LEON: For some reason I felt that today I could focus more on what was
said. In the beginning I was anxious and a bit angry at not addressing
Rita's dropout, but later I felt that the group, although different to
what I knew so far, is still working well.

At the end of the session Hera stated that she felt calmer. Orfeus said
that he felt more connected to her and the group than before. Leon and
Orestis both said they were looking forward to the next session.

This session portrays the major challenges and perspectives of the transition from the in-person to the online environment. The group starts in an
unprecedented tension. The question of connectedness and whether it is
better to be in a relationship or to be alone arises quickly. It relates to the
question of whether it is possible to construct a meaningful relationship
online. Communication is initially fragmented. There is a feeling that there
are parallel monologues, in a common theme. Memories of failed encounters
emerge. Members do not seem to experience the same degree of coherence
and inclusion as when they were all together in the group circle. Orestis asks
as a joke: "Are we really in psychotherapy?" implying that psychotherapy is
not possible through a screen. The attack on the frame is obvious.

Both therapists, experiencing the anxiety of the group, also feel "con-
fused" and become more active and talkative compared to the previous
period. Despite the confusion, they resist the aggression and attempt gradually to restore the indispensable sense of safety and inclusion. The

group's cohesion, although shaken, is restored and strengthened. The framework survives, eventually managing to contain the members' discharges. Even if the physical body is absent, the sense of belonging to the group remains. It is the group's frame, defended by the group leaders, that prevents the disorganization. The interventions of the therapists attempt to make sense of the new experience and symbolically become the articulations that will keep the members together and ensure connection to external reality. The group skin ego holds the parts of the group connected, enabling the survival of the group, despite the casualties. As the session unfolds, participants feel safe enough to share information for the first time in the group. It is probably the safety of the online setting that enables the disclosure. Weinberg (2014) notes that remote participation often makes participants feel less exposed to the sight of others, facilitating the voicing and processing of issues that evoke feelings of guilt and shame.

Orpheus was impressed by the pose of the therapist when her connection was interrupted and wanted to take a picture of her. Orestes worried about her. Their desire to stay connected and mutual concern about the therapist that disappeared are evident. Being deprived of total sight, participants focus more on each other's faces, in order to decode the expression and connect emotionally to each other.

Finally, in response to the question posed in the title of this chapter, physical presence does not seem to be necessary for a therapeutic group process to be delivered. The application of online group psychotherapy during the COVID-19 pandemic, as the only feasible option, established it as an effective method in the field. Even if the group dynamics and interactions differ significantly, in the absence of the physical bodies they can develop in virtual settings as well. However, a revisiting and renewal of our clinical and theoretical tools is required in the light of remote sessions. The results of online practice so far present a successful alternative to the traditional form of group psychotherapy. Group leaders need to be equipped with the necessary skills in order to render this promising modality as effectively as possible.

References

Agazarian, M. Y. (1989) The invisible group: An integrational theory of group-as-a-whole. *Group Analysis*, 22(4), 355–369.

Anzieu, D. (1971). L'illusion groupale. *Nouvelle revue de psychanalyse*, 4(1), 73–93.

Anzieu, D. (1985). *Le moi-peau*. Dunod.

Anzieu, D. (1999). The group skin-ego. *Group Analysis*, 32, 319–329.

Biancalani, G.Franco, C., Guglielmin, M. S., Moretto, L.Orkibi, H., Keisari, S., & Testoni, I. (2021). Tele-psychodrama therapy during the COVID-19 pandemic: Participants' experiences. *Arts in Psychotherapy*, 75, 101836.

Bick, E. (1968). The experience of the skin in early object-relations. *International Journal of Psychoanalysis*, 49, 484–486.

Bion, W. R. (1961). *Experiences in groups and other papers*. Routledge.
Bion, W. R. (1962). *Learning from experience*. Jason Aronson.
Bion, W. R. (1984). *Transformations*. Karnac Books.
Bleger, J. (1967). Psychoanalysis of the psycho-analytic frame. *International Journal of Psychoanalysis*, 48, 511–519.
Bowlby, J. (1979). The Bowlby-Ainsworth attachment theory. *Behavioral and Brain Sciences*, 2(4), 637–638.
Dark, F., Miles, A., Madson, K., & Strochnetter, E. (2022). Adapting evidence-based group therapies following COVID-19 restrictions. *Australasian Psychiatry*, 30(1), 13–17.
Dunstan, D. A., & Tooth, S. M. (2012). Using technology to improve patient assessment and outcome evaluation. *Rural and Remote Health*, 12, 20–48.
Fletcher, K. L., Comer, S. D., & Dunlap, A. (2014). Getting connected: The virtual holding environment. *Psychoanalytic Social Work*, 21(1–2), 90–106.
Foguel, B. S. (1994). The group experienced as mother: Early psychic structures in analytic groups. *Group Analysis*, 27(3), 265–285.
Fonagy, P., Gergely, G., Jurist, E., & Target, M. (2002). *Affect regulation, mentalization and the development of the self*. Other Press.
Fortier, C. B., Currao, A., Kenna, A., Kim, S., Beck, B. M., Katz, D., Hursh, C., & Fonda, J. R. (2022). Online telehealth delivery of group mental health treatment is safe, feasible, and increases enrollment and attendance in post-9/11 U.S. veterans. *Behavior Therapy*, 53(3), 469–480.
Foulkes, S. H. (1975). A short outline of the therapeutic process in group analytic psychotherapy. *Group Analysis*, 34, 59–63.
Freud, S. (1921). Group psychology and the analysis of the ego. In *The Standard Edition of the Complete Psychological Works of Sigmund Freud* (vol. XVIII, pp. 65–144). Hogarth Press.
Gentry, M. T., Lapid, M. I., Clark, M. M., & Rummans, T. A. (2019). Evidence for telehealth group-based treatment: A systematic review. *Journal of Telemedicine and Telecare*, 25, 327–342.
Green, A. (1983). *Narcissisme de vie, narcissisme de mort*. Editions de Minuit.
Lemma A. (2017). *The digital age on the couch*. Routledge.
Lleras de Frutos, M., Medina, J. C., Vives, J., Casellas-Grau, A., Marzo, J. L., Borràs, J. M., & Ochoa-Arnedo, C. (2020). Video conference vs face-to-face group psychotherapy for distressed cancer survivors: A randomized controlled trial. *Psycho-Oncology*, 29(12), 1995–2003.
Main, M. (1990). Parental aversion to infant-initiated contact is correlated with the parent's own rejection during childhood: The effects of experience on signals of security with respect to attachment. In T. B. Brazelton & K. Barnard (Eds.), *Touch* (pp. 461–495). International Universities Press.
Mohr, D. C., Siddique, J., Ho, J., Duffecy, J., Jin, L., & Fokuo, J. (2010). Interest in behavioral and psychological treatments delivered face-to-face, by telephone, and by Internet. *Annals of Behavioral Medicine*, 40, 89–98.
Nurmagandi, B., Hamid, A., Yani, S., & Panjaitan, R. U. (2022). The Influence of Health Education and Group Therapy on Adolescent Online Gamers' Self-Concepts. *European Journal of Mental Health*, 17(1), 37–46.
Otared, N., Moharrampour, N. G., Vojoudi, B., & Najafabadi, A. J. (2021). A group-based online acceptance and commitment therapy treatment for

depression, anxiety symptoms and quality of life in healthcare workers during COVID-19 pandemic: A randomized controlled trial. *International Journal of Psychology & Psychological Therapy*, 21(3), 399–411.

Raufman, R., & Weinberg, H. (2016). To enter one's skin": The concrete and symbolic functions of the skin in the social unconscious, as expressed in fairy tales and group therapy. *International Journal of Group Psychotherapy*, 66(2), 205–224.

Simpson, S., Bell, L., Knox, J., & Mitchell, D. (2005). Therapy via videoconferencing: A route to client empowerment? *Clinical Psychology and Psychotherapy*, 12, 156–165.

Simpson, S. G., & Reid, C. L. (2014). Therapeutic alliance in videoconferencing psychotherapy: A review. *Australian Journal of Rural Health*, 22, 280–299. http://dx.doi.org/10.1111/ajr.12149.

Stern, D. N. (1985). *The interpersonal world of the infant: A view from psychoanalysis and developmental psychology*. Basic Books.

Stolper, E., & Zigenlaub, E. (2021). From the circle to the square: Group psychotherapy in the age of coronavirus. *Journal of the Eastern Group Psychotherapy Society*, 45(1), 11–29.

Weinberg, H. (2014). *The paradox of Internet groups: Alone in the presence of virtual others*. Routledge.

Weinberg, H. (2016). Impossible groups that flourish in leaking containers: Challenging group analytic theory. *Group Analysis*, 49(4), 330–349.

Weinberg, H. (2020). Online group psychotherapy: Challenges and possibilities during COVID-19—A practice review. *Group Dynamics: Theory, Research, and Practice*, 24(3), 201–211.

Weinberg, H. (2021). Obstacles, challenges, and benefits of online group psychotherapy. *American Journal of Psychotherapy*. 74(8), 3–8.

Weinberg, H., & Rolnick, A. (Eds.) (2020). *Theory and practice of online therapy: Internet-delivered interventions for individuals, families, groups, and organizations*. Routledge.

Winnicott, D. W. (1971). *Playing and reality*. Karnac Books.

Wood, H. J., Gannon, J. M., Chengappa, K. N. R., & Sarpal, D. K. (2021). Group teletherapy for first-episode psychosis: Piloting its integration with coordinated specialty care during the COVID-19 pandemic. *Psychology and Psychotherapy: Theory, Research and Practice*, 94(2), 382–389.

Chapter 5

From Shrinkage to Expansion

Online Group Therapy that Enables Acquaintance with "Other" Self-States through Dissociation and Enactment

Enav Karniel Lauer

Introduction

Online group therapy opens an opportunity for patients and therapists to learn more about relationships, through additional experiences. The chapter explores the limits of the online group "container" and its flexibility while analyzing the "online matrix." The matrix offers options for expanding and developing the self via encounters with other self-states that appear on-screen and as a result of the transitions from the circle to the screen, and vice versa. Such transitions enhance coping with changes, separations, and losses.

Online attendance emphasizes the absence of body-to-body interaction and forces patients and therapists to give up and lose the familiar interpersonal intimacy. It is an encounter with the online "other" inside us and the online "other" inside the other, and an acquaintance with the "Zoom self-states," i.e., new self-states that are revealed in the online space.

According to the relational approach, the self is flexible and multiple, constantly changing across times and places. A person's life is an evolving collection of many selves, or in Bromberg's words "self-states" (Bromberg, 1998). Some self-states are kept and become a significant part of the identity and self-definition, while the rest are forgotten, excluded, projected onto others, or experienced as strangers. These self-states that went through dissociation and exist in the dark, engraved in the body, or in the margins of consciousness, can represent aspects of impairment, shame, aggression, and trauma, but can also be aspects of strengths and abilities that were excluded due to negative reactions from the environment. In the face-to-face group and in online group therapy, it is possible to encourage enjoyment, friendship, and recognition of the various self-states, as well as the option to move fluently and flow naturally from one to the other, with a sense of choice rather than automatic response.

Online group therapy encourages familiarity with the self-states, through processes of recognition, mirroring, and resonance, while working in a space of shared trauma and vulnerability in the therapeutic relationship.

DOI: 10.4324/9781003248606-6

Online Group Therapy

Online group therapy became popular during the COVID-19 pandemic. The pandemic, the quarantines and lockdowns that it created, changed the field of psychotherapy overnight from in-person to "virtual" (Tullio et al., 2020). The main benefit of online group therapy is convenience and accessibility. Using online platforms enables accessibility and availability for patients based in various geographic locations, patients who may be unable to leave the house for any reason, or patients who can only afford less expensive care (Andersson, 2018; Weinberg, 2020).

On the other hand, online groups also have significant drawbacks that must be taken into consideration. First, the transition from the circle to online therapy presents a complex challenge for the psychotherapist and the patient due to the change in the work environment and the therapy management skills, both technological and professional. Furthermore, there are patients who cannot join the online groups, either because they lack a safe physical space for the therapy session (such as women experiencing trauma or violence), or because they lack the required technological knowledge to work online (e.g., senior patients). It is important to note that further research on issues such as privacy, confidentiality, safety, and other legal issues is required (Tullio et al., 2020).

Zoom In: Questions about Unique Effects in Online Group Therapy

Online group therapy changes our point of view about relationships, intimacy, and closeness. The "group matrix" (Foulkes, 1990), which is a hypothetical network of verbal and non-verbal communications and of the relations in a given group, occurs through mutual mental permeability and psychosomatic overlapping areas that enable members to "know" each other profoundly. The matrix contains various communication modes: verbal, non-verbal, symbolic, and concrete, implicit, and explicit communication. Subliminal non-verbal communication usually occurs at subliminal velocities and is usually expressed via body language and gestures, while explicit communication of words and sentences is slower.

In this chapter we will look at whether the online space can offer the same opportunities for developing this group matrix, including non-verbal and implicit communication modes that enable creative, playful, passionate, and emotional work. The online space is sometimes experienced as the loss of the familiar and "homely." The Internet is not the "home," but functions as the "other" place—"the Uncanny" (Freud, 1919). It is an important, fascinating, and vital place, but different from the home where we grew up and where our perceptions were shaped.

However, for some people participation in online group therapy in the comfort of their own home might provide a homely feeling.

Patients and therapists who are used to face-to-face therapy sessions may feel like immigrants in the digital world. Sometimes they will be required to learn a new language, and therefore mediate the familiar world into the new world. The group needs to bear the "lack of knowledge," the different and the unfamiliar, and to pause familiar attention and communication skills, while experiencing an attack on attention, focus, and patience. On the other hand, young people are comfortable with the Internet. Many enjoy chatting online, so for them therapy over the computer may feel more comfortable than talking to a therapist face-to-face.

There are questions regarding the quality of the analytical listening that takes place in the "screen relationship" (Isaacs Russell, 2015) as they rely only on the senses of sight and hearing. Is it possible to produce unique analytical and empathic listening to the sounds of the unconscious, which includes the observation of the other, and to produce the same holding environment necessary to create a secure space and to bear the initial regressive processes of the patients (Triest, 2020).

With the removal of face-to-face therapy, there is a need to maintain and foster the therapeutic relationship over the Internet through considering the necessity of cultivating and maintaining a therapeutic presence (Geller 2020). In online therapy where the therapist and the group transform from three-dimensional to two-dimensional figures, certain verbal communication aspects must be emphasized to overcome the absence of the familiar body interactions. It is important to try and make the screen relationship as human and as familiar as possible, thus avoiding alienated and insensitive communication. In a similar way to the circle, intense emotions, crying, anger, and great laughter, also take place in online therapy, as well as regressive effects and acting out.

It is possible to continue listening in online group therapy to the patient's inner world with all the senses: to the fantasies, to the unconscious, to transference and countertransference. Despite the disembodied environment, the therapist can touch the inner world and the patient's experiences, contain, emotionally hold, and clarify behavior patterns, and facilitate change of unhealthy patterns.

Online Group Therapy: A Space for Challenges and Opportunities

It is possible to describe the online group space as a "semi-safe" space, a concept that was introduced by Berman (2018) and describes the group therapy space as one that does not enable absolute safety for the patients:

The "semi-safe space" is an aspect of the group matrix co-related by the conductor and the participants to contain the tension that exists between the poles of safety and unsafety in order to enhance the therapeutic benefits to the group.

(p. 191)

Group members enter the process of group therapy by choice and with the idea that the group space should provide a safe base for the unfolding of meaningful relationships. However, paradoxically, the needed basic safety is created through the risks that group members are ready to take in real time. Thus, the group therapy process is a precarious balance between being "safe, but not too safe" Bromberg (2008). Bromberg warns us that too much safety may be stifling and prevent the birth of new experiencing: "The analytic relationship become a place that supports risk and safety simultaneously—a relationship that allows the painful reliving of early trauma, without the reliving being just a blind repetition of the past" (p. 332).

The online space is subject to disruptions and attacks on the physical boundaries of treatment due to possible exposure to technological failures and due to privacy and confidentiality issues. However, Weinberg (2016) states that even in an online therapeutic environment with the lack of clear boundaries, members of the group can also act in a way that overcomes the limitations of the "leaking container," and indeed they can search for creative ways to bypass the virtual distance. As Weinberg mentions, "The participants can do this by imagining the group as a good-enough holding environment despite its problematic 'real' qualities" (p. 16).

Since the group therapy space is semi-safe, it might invite patients to different, intriguing, and challenging communication experiences. Just as in any place where there is a lack of confidence, there is an opportunity for investigation and learning, as is the case in the online group therapy space. In the "Hall of Mirrors," according to Foulkes and Antony (1957), it affords members an opportunity to get to know themselves through other group participants in new and unfamiliar places. The group and interpersonal experiences are unpredictable and therefore enable personal growth and development.

Considering the challenges of maintaining the boundaries and settings in the online space, special attention is required for issues of enabling a safe physical space, stability, and continuity that will help patients to feel the maximum security and stability during the treatment. The group therapist, who is responsible for the "dynamic administration," the administrative processes required to hold the therapeutic sessions, which has dynamic meaning (Foulkes, 1975), takes on a great responsibility to create a therapeutic space that is attentive to the participants' physical and emotional needs. He/she offers comprehensibility, maintainance, and holding in a safe environment to enable group interaction and participants' confidence in the online platform.

At the same time, as mentioned before, it is not possible to guarantee complete safety without malfunctions. The relationship between the group therapist and the patients is mutual but asymmetrical, as the therapist is responsible for confidence in the treatment. The therapist's responsibility is ethical and moral, together with the mutuality and recognition of the therapist as a subject. In the "shared vulnerability space" between patients and the therapist in online therapy, the therapist can encourage the emotional discourse about loss, change, anxiety and anger and thus help participants to discover new and unfamiliar resources along with new experiences, or in Stern's words (1998) "unbidden experiences". Surprising and spontaneous experiences, which in Stern's opinion are at the center of the therapeutic act, occur when the freedom to experience and a willingness to let go allow the unbidden experience to take place. Furthermore, it is important to process the losses of leaving the familiar and known and the acceptance of the new and different world, where the global reality is changing, as seen in the climate, the COVID-19 pandemic, and resource reduction (Ullman, 2020). The ambivalence that arises in the group discussion can be interpreted for the purpose of understanding, closeness to self and others, and communication. Any psychotherapy is a place where there are doubts or ambivalence, and the group space requires awareness and dialog about it.

A discussion about online difficulties can turn into a conversation about emotional needs in therapy, an opportunity to learn what patients are missing, what their challenges are, concerns, and dilemmas. Sensitivity to the nuances found in patients' internal dialogs with online therapy can open new channels for the self and others.

Multiple Self-states and the Group Analysis

According to the relational approach, self-states are defined as configurations that encompass feelings, experiences, memories, needs, and motivations that can function independently of each other, according to any given context. Our inner world is not one cohesive entity; instead, it comprises multiple self-states that have complex interactions with each other. From within any certain self-state, one's personal experience is of authenticity, experienced as this is "me", while any sign of any other self-state is experienced as "not me" (Bromberg, 1998).

Dissociation is most often used to deal with traumatic situations. It disconnects the mind from its capacity to perceive what is too much for selfhood to bear.

The group space invites movement and connection between the various self-states that are the outcome of use of dissociative mechanisms that are activated to maintain the self-continuity experience, but on the other hand, limit and reduce it. The goal of therapy is to progress from dissociation to conflict while being aware of the patients' various self-states, through recognition and familiarity of the variety of self-states, while moving and choosing. When the different self-states of the patients are recognized and seen, an authentic dialog can take place and enable flexibility between the self-states that are in dissociation.

In the analytic group, the other patients may represent the person's interpersonal worlds. The group is an open and continuous system of interaction between all the participants of the group including the conductor. The "free floating discussion" that, according to Foulkes (1975), characterizes the processes of an analytic group facilitates the creation of a dynamic continuum that invites dissociated self-states. This assembly of self-states acts as a "parallel group" that inhabits our personal world. Thus, an analytic group can be thought of as a crowded space packed with a host of different self-states that struggle to be heard and recognized by each other. Dissociated self-states may be recognized and remembered by other participants. Moreover, dissociated self-states may be expressed by others and processed through group analysis of mirror reactions and resonance (Foulkes and Anthony, 1957). In this way the group may become a "Hall of Self States" (following Foulkes' "Hall of Mirrors") in which different attitudes and points of view co-exist and provide alternative experiences, attitudes, and solutions (Berman, 2014).

The matrix in the online group therapy is a platform for intricate and branched interpersonal and group communication, inviting unexpected and surprising reciprocal games. The unsafe, different, and new online space might create opportunities for new encounters with the self and the group, which leads to unfamiliar and challenging self-states. I suggest that this space might allow the emergence of new self-states that have been in dissociation.

The encounter between the dissociated self-states of the patient and the therapist creates a common dissociative communication, difficult to understand and identify, and as a result the reflective ability of the partners in the process can be destroyed. Sometimes these self-states will appear through an enactment in which there is a collaboration between intolerable parts of the self that appear unconsciously in therapy, sometimes recreating traumatic situations in which the patient and therapist are partners (Howell, 2002). Through the identification of enactment states, accessibility is created between the detached self-states, in which mental turmoil, conflict, and an internal struggle develop. Conflict makes it possible to expose other detached parts and attach to them denied feelings such as suffering, pain, jealousy, and shame. When recognition of these feelings is achieved, a concept of correction to self-esteem emerges and facilitates a connection to the self-states that are in dissociation.

Vignette: An Online Group Meeting

In this section I present an example from an analytical group, consisting of six women, aged 50 to 70, meeting once a week for the past three years. Following the outbreak of the COVID-19 pandemic in March 2020, we moved to online meetings. The technological aspect of the transition was implemented with no special issues. Everyone understood the importance of continuing the group activity, even if this entailed the use of an online format. Shula had a very hard time with the transition to Zoom. She occasionally complained that it is very different from face-to-face meetings. She joined the meetings using her personal smartphone or tablet, (since she did not have a computer) and often complained that she could not see all the other participants (the mobile version of Zoom allows only four participants to be seen on the screen at the same time). Shula came late to some of the meetings, used to wander with her smartphone around her home, and had difficulty finding a quiet place in the house. More than once we saw her husband passing behind her.

Shula, 70 years old, has three children and seven grandchildren. She worked as the principal of a special education school and retired recently. About ten years ago, her eldest daughter died of cancer, three weeks after the birth of the daughter's eldest son. With the transition to the online meetings, the participants often referred to and reflected on Shula's restlessness that was seen on-screen. They expressed sympathy and understanding with the difficulty and asked her to continue to attend the meetings.

On my recommendation and with the encouragement of the other participants, Shula purchased a computer, and her online participation experience improved. She said she did not realize the suffering caused to the other participants by "Zooming" via her smartphone. However, after several meetings she again expressed discomfort from and resentment about the online meetings and said decisively that she would take a break until such time as the group returns to the face-to-face meetings.

SHULA: I'm desperate, drained, not myself, not connected to this medium of on-screen meetings, closeted at home most of the day. I have a very hard time with the loss of control and the absence, I was narrowed down to a small place. I prefer to use the phone, even with Ophir [her son] in New Zealand I usually talk on the phone, and occasionally on Skype, then the granddaughters join the on-screen conversation for a few seconds. But it's more frustrating than enabling because it is not real...

DVORA: You have no choice; you will not communicate with your son and granddaughters ... if you do not make an effort and use Skype

YARDENA: I also have some difficulties in this kind of conversation, I actually feel the opposite, I am afraid to get used to staying at home, and that I would not want to leave it. It is comfortable when you have no commitment outside...

HEDVA: But it is better than nothing ... isn't it?

NOAM: Shula, what is going on with you? It looks like you are really suffering from the entire COVID situation. You are going through a difficult time.

SHULA: Yes, I really suffer, I am not myself at all ... very nervous, not enjoying anything, I am angry, nothing is real...

ME: What is not real for you? ...

SHULA: It is like looking at pictures of Orit [her deceased daughter], I experience something distant and unreal ... it is not the same, it is just pictures.

The other participants refer to "not real" and express empathy, but at the same time acknowledge that at least it is possible to communicate through the screen during these difficult and lonely days of the COVID-19 pandemic.

ME: Shula, it seems like you experience the Zoom conversations as "unreal," you lack the facial expressions, the smell, the touch, and for you, it is like looking at pictures, especially pictures of Orit...

Shula was very excited by my comment and burst into tears.

SHULA: I really did not think about it, that through all this COVID period, I locked myself at home and was not willing to Zoom with people because it is not real, as the connection to Orit through the pictures...

DVORA: And there are people, who are alive, that I cannot meet because they are not in touch anymore.

NOAM: I have no pictures of my brother at all, he did not like us to take pictures of him.

ME (TO SHULA): The Zoom experience becomes unbearable for you because you experience Orit's absence and loss over and over again. Orit's loss becomes too real in light of the emptiness you experience in the pictures or faces on screen.

SHULA: The pictures ... it is not real, the longing is real ... [crying], it is new to me, I never thought I would not like to talk through a screen because it is re-experiencing Orit's absence and loss.

ME: Maybe the restlessness and the anger over Zoom is new to you and is an expression of the loss, longing, and absence of Orit and also of Ofir who is out of the country...

SHULA: I did not notice my complaining, maladaptive, angry, and stubborn side. I always think of myself as the "pleaser type" and a good girl ... I did not realize that I stood out, and disturbed, and that the group suffered...

The members of the group shared how they experienced her in these online meetings; how her restlessness was very noticeable to them, and daring to tell her for the first time that the fact that her husband occasionally appears on the screen bothers them, because it is a violation of the group's security and confidentiality. At the same time, they shared that they now understood the reasons for her behavior, and the meaning of her restlessness.

Discussion

In the above online sessions, a new and unfamiliar self-state of Shula appeared on the screen: stubborn, grumpy, angry, and rebelling against the online work state. Shula does not feel that this part belongs to her and does not recognize it as part of her. These dissociated self-states contain her most personal history of painful experiences (the loss of her daughter). At the same time, it also contains keys to authenticity that was lost (or even squashed) on the way "to fit in." Thus, to retrieve lost feelings, to become "in touch," may be experienced as rather a mixed blessing. From this angle, the authenticity that transpires in the live interactions between Shula and group members can become a threat, as much as it is an opportunity.

The ability to discuss the way we view her on screen, through processes of mirroring and resonance, enabled Shula to connect to strong emotions that were disconnected. The connection and owning of these emotions in which pain, sadness, longing, and missing out allow the behavior to be translated into emotions that connect her to the detached and unfamiliar self-state. In future sessions, Shula may understand from whence these emotions originate, and how they influence her behavior, and she may then agree to accept them as part of her.

At the breaking point where Shula announced her desire to leave, an opportunity for connection became possible. The therapeutic group can move between situations whereby members are able to use the space and occurrences of collapse. The discussion about expressing Shula's desire to leave enables the discourse and observation of the rebellious and angry state of the self that is inaccessible to her, to release difficult and painful emotions within herself, and thus to turn the resisting movement to a connecting movement to herself and others. Following the connection and recognition of this detached self-state that was revealed as a "Zoom self-state," Shula was able to choose to stay in the group. A choice is only possible when self-states that were detached become accessible.

Bromberg (1998) argues that the experience of the interface between the valued and rejected self-state is the source of the patient's greatest anxiety, terror, and shame, but is also his only hope for authentic analytical growth. Out of the inevitable storm, the conflict is precisely the beginning of the reorganization, and enables a discourse. Online group therapy becomes a reference space that allows the revival of the flooding experience "here and now," contained jointly by the therapist and the group and worded, and at the same time, provides good enough confidence to allow it to be processed, and the mental turmoil becomes meaningful.

Staying within the conflict means a pendulum motion between and within the new self-states that have just met. It is a meeting that is not always easy, that takes time and resources from the patient and the group. The entire group was required to contain the restlessness of Shula and the lack of privacy they suffered for a long time until it could be met and processed.

Working with Shula on the self-state that appeared on the screen enabled an open and honest discussion, a closeness was created and felt between the participants.

Working with the group, Shula recognized the idea that the grief and pain over her daughter's death had damaged her relationship with the screen and thus limited the relationship she could have with her family in New Zealand. Through working in a group and after the recognition of and the connection to a detached self-state, Shula could choose to continue working online and stay in the group. She chose a limited relationship, in her opinion, but decided not to leave and experience another loss.

The possibility of discourse on issues related to loss, grief, missing out, and longing, the comparison between the "unreal" experiences on-screen to the memory from the images of the dead, released the hidden and unconscious places that Shula and others projected on the screen and in the online work. The dichotomy between the two truths—that real life occurs only face-to-face and the deadly online experience—could have been interpreted by accepting a dissociated and detached self-state.

Needless to say, this brief vignette provides only a glimpse into complex dynamic processes that can be perceived in many different ways. My purpose here is to use it purely as an illustration of the subtle, unsolicited ways that dissociated self-states present themselves in online group therapy.

Summary

The "online self-states" that stand out via the screen enable us to change the quality of attachment within and between us. The screen offers an intersubjective field of multiple selves and alternating identities between and within the patients, while striving for human, personal, and authentic interaction. The dynamics between the group participants allow each participant to be recognized by the other participants in the group, to recognize other participants in the group, and to identify new self-states that might develop. In other words, a significant therapeutic transformation can occur through the screen and help participants to change their lives in a way that allows them to communicate and behave differently.

References

Andersson, G. (2018). Internet interventions: Past, present, and future. *Internet Interventions*, 12, 181–188. http://dx.doi.org/10.1016/j.invent.2018.03.008.

Berman, A. (2014). Post-traumatic victimhood and group analytic therapy: intersubjectivity, empathic witnessing and otherness. *Group Analysis*, 47(3), 242–256.

Berman, A. (2018). Therapeutic semi-safe space in group analysis. *Group Analysis*, November 24. https://doi.org/10.1177/053331641881502.

Bromberg, P. M. (1998). *Standing in the spaces: Essays on clinical process, trauma and dissociation*. The Analytic Press.

Bromberg, P.M. (2008). Shrinking the tsunami: Affect regulation, dissociation, and the shadow of the flood. *Contemporary Psychoanalysis*, 44, 329–350.

Geller, S. (2020). Cultivating online therapeutic presence: Strengthening therapeutic relationships in teletherapy sessions. *Counselling Psychology Quarterly*, 1–17.

Freud, S. (1919). *The Uncanny*. First published in *Imago*, Bd. V; reprinted in *Sammlung, Fünfte Folge*. [Translated by Alix Strachey]. Hogarth Press.

Foulkes, S. H., &. Anthony, E. J. (1957). *Group psychotherapy: The psychoanalytic approach*. Penguin.

Foulkes, S. H. (1975). *Group analytic psychotherapy: Method and principles*. Karnac Books.

Foulkes, S. H. (1990). *Selected papers: Psychoanalysis and group analysis*. Karnac Books.

Howell, E. F. (2002). Back to the "States": Victim and Abuser States in Borderline Personality Disorder. *Psychoanalytic Dialogues*, 12, 921–957.

Isaacs Russell, G. (2015). *Screen relations: The limits of computer-mediated psychoanalysis and psychotherapy*. Karnac Books.

Stern, D. N. (1998). The process of therapeutic change involving implicit knowledge: Some Implications of developmental observations for adult psychotherapy. *Infant Mental Health Journal*, 19, 300–308.

Tishbi, U. (2020). Thoughts of countertransference in the Corona period. *Sihot in the Days of Corona*.

Triest, Y. (2020). Lists in Corona Time: The Horror Virus. *Sihot in the Days of Corona*.

Tullio, V., Perrone, G., Bilotta, C., Lanzarone, A., & Argo, A. (2020). Psychological support and psychotherapy via digital devices in Covid-19 emergency time: Some critical issues. *Medico-Legal Journal*, 88(2), 73–76. https://doi.org/10.1177/0025817220926942.

Ullman, H. (2020). On three therapeutic difficulties in the days of Corona. *Sihot in the Days of Corona*.

Weinberg, H. (2016). Impossible groups that flourish in leaking containers: Challenging group analytic theory. *Group Analysis*, 49(4), 330–349.

Weinberg, H. (2020). Online group psychotherapy: Challenges and possibilities during COVID-19—A practice review. *Group Dynamics: Theory, Research, and Practice*, 24(3), 201–211. https://doi.org/10.1037/gdn0000140.

Chapter 6

"Can I Join Online?"

Hybrid Group Therapy Integrating Online Participants in Face-to-Face Groups

Efrat Zigenlaub and Ella Stolper

Introduction

This chapter was written in the midst of the fifth wave of the COVID-19 pandemic, during which the need for a hybrid format of group therapy had emerged. "Hybrid" became a popular term in contemporary discussions, and group conductors, as well as universities and organizations, are required to consider how to allow for online participation in face-to-face sessions.

The term "hybrid groups" can refer to two possibilities: (1) some group participants join online while others are physically in the same room; and (2) some group meetings are conducted online while others are conducted in person. This chapter will address the former type of groups and will attempt to explore how participants can use online platforms to participate in predominantly face-to-face groups. We will examine the flexibility required from both conductor and group to combine the various platforms. We will discuss whether the hybrid option is an opportunity or obstacle in the group process, consider the conditions in which hybrid sessions can take place, and reflect on the implications of the hybrid method for group work.

Literature Review

Since the outbreak of the COVID-19 pandemic, a vast literature on online groups has emerged (Stolper & Zigenlaub, 2021; Weinberg, 2020a; Weinberg & Rolnick, 2020). In an earlier paper, we described four central phenomena that characterise the transition to an online format: the visible and the hidden from view; the group conductor as a "host"; the group state during the transition; and the impact of physical distance on the emotional intimacy. Our conclusion was that the transition to an online format created both new possibilities and obstacles, and we proposed to group conductors methods that can turn this two-dimensional experience into a tridimensional one (Stolper & Zigenlaub, 2021).

DOI: 10.4324/9781003248606-7

In contrast to the growing body of research on online group therapy, the lack of research on hybrid group therapy is evident. We therefore expand our scope to relate to studies published on hybrid workplace meetings. A study by Ellis et al. (2022) pointed to some of the advantages and shortcomings of hybrid meetings. Some of the advantages the saving of time wasted on getting to meetings, the ability to invite specialists and guests from faraway places and resilience to personal constraints or quarantines. The shortcomings of the model include online participants' difficulty in following the discussion and recognizing the speaker, which can make them feel isolated, marginal and estranged; distractions that online participants experience in their home space; and communication difficulties due to the loss of nonverbal cues in the interaction. Further studies on hybrid work meetings also suggest similar challenges, mainly communication difficulties due to the lack of nonverbal cues, eye contact and body language, and the difficulty that online participants have in feeling included in the meetings (de Haas, 2021; Saatçi et al., 2019). Some of the studies in the field examined technological tools that can address the challenges involved in conducting hybrid sessions (de Haas, 2021).

The aim of the present chapter is to examine the challenges involved in including online participants in face-to-face groups and to explore the effectiveness of the hybrid format in group therapy.

Method

This study is qualitative, phenomenological, and descriptive, and it outlines and conceptualizes observations that were made during the writers' group sessions, using clinical examples and analyzing and defining them with relevant terms derived from the literature (Mertens, 2014). The study is based on our experiences as conductors of nine psychodynamic groups, including four psychoanalytic groups, and five supervision groups for group conductors in academic settings, when each group was conducted by one of the authors. The phenomena described in these groups took place during 2021–2022, between the third and fifth waves of the COVID-19 pandemic in Israel.

Findings

Opportunities in the Hybrid Space

Online Courage

> Shmuel, a 30-year-old man, had been participating in a therapeutic group for six months, during which he avoided sharing personal information about his life and participated only through cautious

reactions to other participants. He asked to connect to one of the sessions online due to a medical procedure that he had undergone and I allowed it. He was silent for most of the meeting. A week later, he asked whether he could participate online again since he still had not recovered and I agreed once more. In the middle of the meeting, the thought came to my mind that his request was not related to avoidance of contact with the group but expressed his quest for a safer space for self-exposure—something that so far he had not dared to do in face-to-face meetings. I shared this thought with the group and, in reaction, Shmuel began to cry. He said that he did indeed feel burdened with a big secret that he had not dared to share with the group so far, and he felt that he needed to let it go already, and now, when he was physically distant from the group, he felt that he could finally tell his story. He shared his secret with the group with a determination that was uncharacteristic of him, and after the participants had contained him empathically in the physical circle, he said that he felt relieved and that the shame he felt was no longer as threatening as before.

This example shows that sometimes online platforms constitute a safe space that allows self-exposure and confidence to speak that is not possible in face-to-face meetings. This is consistent with the "proximity/distance" theme we discussed in our previous paper on the transition of the whole group to online meetings (Stolper & Zigenlaub, 2021).

Interestingly, we found that the hybrid space can facilitate not only the self-exposure of single participants, but also of a subgroup that joins online, while the rest of the group meets face-to-face. The following example discusses the case of a minority group that connected online while the majority group met face-to-face:

During the terror attacks in Israel in April 2022, Arab students expressed fear of coming to the campus, mainly due to their fear of using public transportation. As a result, the college's management gave them permission to study online, while the Jewish participants did not know of this request and did not receive a similar permission. That week, I facilitated a practicum group that included a majority of Jewish participants sitting together in a circle and a minority of Arab participants who joined online. In that session, the Israeli-Palestinian conflict that had not come up during the six months of the group meeting entered the room for the first time. In that session, the group discussed in a courageous and moving manner the issue of the Arab minority's belonging to Israeli society through personal stories related to belonging and exclusion. A Bedouin student said that she possesses multiple identities, and in fact does not feel belongingness anywhere: "In Mecca, I'm 'damaged goods' because I'm Israeli, among the Palestinians I'm 'damaged goods' because I have a nephew who serves in the IDF [Israel Defense Forces], and I'm scared of taking Israeli buses because I'm a Muslim."

Of course, this moving session was heavily influenced by the external reality that brought the conflict to the group, but the special hybrid setting in which the majority group sat in the physical circle while the minority group joined online contributed significantly to the introduction of a subject that up until then had not been discussed.

This situation was unique, as the subgroup that joined online was already a subgroup before the meeting and had not been established as such due to the mere joint online participation. In therapy groups, we did not encounter situations in which there was more than one participant online and it is interesting to continue exploring the group dynamics in such cases.

Different Self-States Online

Bromberg (1993) argues that the capacity of the individual to live an authentic and self-conscious life depends on the presence of a continuous dialectic between separateness and the unity of his self-states, which allows each self-state to function optimally.

Bromberg argues that in normal development, the individual is only vaguely aware of the presence of individual self-states and their reality, since each self-state functions as a part of a healthy illusion of a cohesive self-identity—a cognitive and experiential state that is experienced as "me." Every self-state is a part of a functional totality that is based on an internal negotiation process with reality, values, influences and others' points of view. Despite collisions and even hostility between aspects of self, it is unusual for each self-state to function entirely outside the sense of "self"—that is, without the participation of other self-states.

According to Bromberg (1993), "mental health is the ability to stand in the spaces between realities without losing any of them—the capacity to feel like oneself while being many" (p. 166). Therapy aims, among other things, to allow the individual to express and move between multiple self-states.

Ronen, a participant in his forties, had been participating in a therapeutic group for two and a half years before the outbreak of the COVID-19 pandemic. Ronen often told the group about his anger outbursts at his wife and children and sadly told that this had led his wife to want a divorce. But in the group, there was no sign of this behavior and the participants were always surprised to hear these stories that seemed inconsistent with his behavior in the group.

During the pandemic, Ronen had to join one of the sessions online as he had contracted the virus. During session, Ronen yelled angrily at two participants, a man and a woman, who were trying to sort out their intimate relationship and who in his view took all the space in the group. Ronen even threatened to leave the group and attacked anyone who tried to protect the couple. The following week, when he returned to the group face-to-face, Ronen apologized for this behavior but to some extent was also pleased that the group had had a chance to witness his aggressive side. This hybrid session allowed Ronen to express an aggressive self-state that he could not express in face-to-face sessions, possibly due to his fear that the group would reject him, just as his wife had.

Levin, in his paper on combined individual and group therapy with the same therapist, argued that in individual and group therapy people express representations of different self-states, and that these move and develop in parallel, consistent with the developmental needs of the patient who then can shift between different modes in therapy (Levin, 2006).

We believe that as in combined therapy, hybrid group therapy, too, allows transition between different self-states. The physical distance from face-to-face sessions and the position behind a screen provides an illusion of safety and sometimes allows brave behaviors that are not always possible when participants are sitting next to each other, as we demonstrated in the previous section. Additionally, participation from the patient's "home" sometimes serves as a "safe space" and allows them to express their more shameful and hidden self-states. Finally, the feelings of "aloneness" and "separateness" in the presence of the group that is meeting face-to-face are realistically increased in the hybrid setting, forcing the individual to cope with issues of lack of belonging, rejection and exclusion in an intensity that is different from that which is experienced in the presence of the group.

Challenges in the Hybrid Space

The Transition to Online Therapy as a "Too Easily Available" Solution

Before the era of online therapy, a large part of the unconscious information was revealed through exploration of moments of "missing out" or "absence." Group reflection and exploration of lateness, absences and missed out experiences deepened the dynamic understanding of the group-analytic symptom of the group. Nowadays, online participation has become so readily available that to a large extent it "fills the spaces" in the group. The access to hidden, complex and unconscious materials of the group is denied. Foulkes (1964) wrote of the role played by the conductor's "location," that is, recognition of the "hot spot" in the group, the area that the group is preoccupied with. Location is usually expressed through implicit information, one of which is participants' absence from certain meetings (for instance, after conflicted or difficult sessions). Location work may suffer from immediate connecting to sessions from anywhere that hides from view precious nonverbal information.

Transition to online therapy is an easy, accessible solution and it is tempting for both participants and conductor to use it in situations in which participants are unable to come to meetings. However, we see that this solution sometimes becomes a "too easily available solution" that constitutes quick and absolute gratification of the patient's wishes, instead of the conductor being a "good enough mother" (Winnicott, 2007) who gradually allows participants to cope with the demands of reality.

The Screen Barrier in Hybrid Therapy

David, a student in a supervision group for group facilitators at the university, joined the group online throughout the whole fall semester due to a medical condition. During the following (spring) semester, he was able to come to face-to-face sessions. In retrospect, the David I had met in the fall semester was completely different from the one revealed to me in the spring semester. During the online sessions, David had a difficult time participating in the group. Even though he was present in all the sessions, joined on time and complied with all the rules of the setting, his presence was absent: he was silent throughout whole sessions and I had to make active efforts to include him in the group discussion. I cleared him time and space and addressed him directly in every session, attention that I did not give to the other group participants. Since I had not met David face-to-face before, I imagined a quiet, introverted and distant participant who needed active help to participate. However, in the face-to-face sessions of the spring semester, I discovered a David who was completely different: happy, vibrant, active and full of life, and—surprisingly—one of the most talkative participants in the group.

The extreme difference between the two appearances of the same participant was striking. The difference may be partly attributed to David's medical condition in the fall semester, which had improved in the spring semester. However, we presume that his special status as the only online participant throughout a whole semester played some part here—given that he had to watch the whole group working face-to-face, while he was disconnected from the discussion from time to time, and at times felt uninvolved and had trouble "overcoming the screen barrier."

In other groups, we have encountered this phenomenon in situations in which one or more participants were forced due to different reasons to connect online throughout a long period of time, while the rest of the group continued meeting face-to-face. In such a continuous situation, we saw that online participants were usually quieter and less involved and needed our active help to take part in the group.

Special Treatment from the Facilitator

Online participation undermines the group rule that "everyone is equal" that is maintained in the circle regarding various aspects, and gives a participant an opportunity to receive special treatment.

The special attention begins even before the meeting, through the technical effort to send a link and check, sometimes through a phone call, whether it has worked, and sometimes involves the facilitator's pre-occupation with their cellphone during the session in an attempt to contact an online participant in the case of disconnection—something that is of course unheard of in regular groups.

In hybrid meetings, we saw that the group had complicated reactions to online participants that included a combination of disregard and jealousy. Often, the difficulty of online participants to overcome the screen barrier led to them being ignored by the group. Still, we often reacted by active mediation that reminded the group to relate to online participants, something that often aroused a feeling of jealousy of online participants among the group. In such incidents, we invited the group to discuss the associated feelings.

Issues Involved in Facilitation of a Hybrid Space

Understanding the Psychodynamic Implications of the Request to Join Online

In a therapy group that I led, there was a high frequency of requests to participate via Zoom. When I brought up the topic for discussion in the group, one of the insights was that due to the recent expansion of the group, participants felt that they did not have enough room and thus unconsciously chose a group solution of "sending one participant to connect online every time" as a way to supposedly decrease the number of group participants.

This example suggests that the transition to online participation was not only a technicality but involved many unconscious considerations on the personal and group level, and that it often constituted an unconscious solution the group found for coping with complicated group dynamics.

We see this act as a "mumbling symptom" (Foulkes and Anthony, 1957) of a group that tries to reveal unconscious aspects of group communication that are not yet ready to be expressed in a direct, overt manner. The mumbling symptom is not only expressed in the mere transition to online participation but also in the attention to what happens in every given moment in the online space and between spaces, beginning with the participants' positions and their changes from session to session, through their body language, preoccupation with other things, people or pets that enter the space, the timing of the decision to speak or remain silent and the timing of disconnections.

The Importance of Technological Holding

Dynamic administration is a term coined by Foulkes (1948) to describe the conductor's routine actions and chores for creating the group setting and boundaries and their dynamic meaning in the group. In normal conditions, these actions include arranging the chairs, making sure that the room temperature is comfortable, taking care of payments, and informing participants of setting-related issues and of changes, absences or lateness or introduction of new group participants. The dynamic implications are revealed before the group when a group discussion of each of these actions develops.

In the transition to online therapy, we discovered the importance of what we call "technological dynamic administration." Technological dynamic administration refers to the technical setting and boundaries of a group that meets online and their dynamic implications on the group. It includes aspects such as participants' location, instructions regarding open camera and microphone, limitations on entering the group in various situations, such as while driving or in the presence of family members in the room, having a stable internet connection, checking that the equipment works and, of course, psychodynamic interpretation of the occurrences.

In facilitation of hybrid groups, the facilitator is responsible for managing and holding two spaces at the same time: the real group room and the room of the "online participants.'" They are also requested to facilitate optimal movement between the two spaces, while considering the psychodynamic aspects of participants' requests to join the group meetings online. In fact, we believe that hybrid work creates a "third space," since the group participants are divided between a virtual space and the real group room and meet on these two levels at the same time.

Management of hybrid group spaces requires advanced skills and technological equipment to overcome the challenging movement between the different dimensions and the facilitator must insist on reflecting on these transitions as dynamic materials in the group life.

In our discussion of previous themes, we emphasized the psychodynamic reflection on the occurrences in the hybrid space, beginning with the request to join online, through every supposedly technical group occurrence, such as disconnection, not seeing, not hearing, etc. In this theme, we want to emphasize the aspect of technological holding, which includes having a stable internet connection and advanced equipment, the decision where to position the camera and rules that determine from which locations participants can connect and how.

The Group State during the Transition to a Hybrid Format

One of the phenomena we observed was the relationship between the group's ability to cope with the hybrid space and its state before the transition. Our impression was that groups that were more mature, that had a more stable, secure and intimate foundation before the transition to a hybrid format, adapted more easily to hybrid work and even found new opportunities in this space. In addition, groups that were more mature were more willing to work through the psychodynamic implications of various aspects of hybrid work, on both the personal and group level. Thus, participants were more willing to explore occurrences and reflect on them, something that in turn helped the group to overcome various enactments. In contrast, in groups that were characterized by tense and conflicted relationships and atmospheres before the transition, the hybrid space led to an increase in the volume of the conflicts. Those findings are similar those described in our earlier paper (Stolper & Zigenlaub, 2021) on the transition of a whole group to an online format.

Discussion

In this chapter, we examined the hybrid model of group therapy, that combines face-to-face groups with online participation of one or several participants. We found two opportunities presented by the hybrid model: online courage and movement between different self-states online, and three challenges: the transition to online participation as a too easily available solution, the screen barrier in hybrid work and special treatment from the facilitator, as well as three issues characteristic of the hybrid space: the dynamic implications of the request to join online, the importance of technological holding and the group state before the transition to a hybrid format.

The Hybrid Model: Threat or Opportunity?

We started this study with the aspiration to examine whether the hybrid model poses a threat or an opportunity, and received a complicated answer to this question, that involves both. We would like to discuss two emerging themes that supposedly contradict. The first theme—"online courage"—sees in this model an opportunity, whereas the theme "online participants' difficulty in overcoming the screen barrier" sees it as a threat.

The theme "online courage" is consistent with the "proximity/distance" theme that emerged in our earlier study, according to which participation in a group from home through online formats could serve as an opportunity for exposure and openness that are not always possible in face-to-face sessions. Previous studies that found a similar phenomenon in online groups explained it through the "screen effect" (Vaimberg & Vaimberg, 2020). This effect results from the idea that when people separate their actions from their real world and identity, they feel less vulnerable and less obligated to endure the consequences of their actions. This effect in fact creates operative dissociation between the individual and his image on the screen. Leszcz, too, argued in his interview with Weinberg that participants express more courage in online groups than in face-to-face groups because of the distance between them (Weinberg & Rolnick, 2020). We found it interesting that the same effect occurred even when a participant saw the rest of the group sitting in the physical circle. We could have expected that the situation of being "one versus many" would be threatening and eliminate this effect.

However, another theme we discovered was the "difficulty of online participants to overcome the screen barrier," which showed that exposure in the hybrid model is more cautious and limited than in face-to-face groups. How can we explain the difference between these themes?

One possible explanation is related to the difference between a one-time or temporary situation of hybrid participation, which we described in the theme "online courage," and a continuous situation of hybrid participation that we described in the theme "the difficulty of online participants to overcome the screen effect." In a one-time situation of hybrid participation, the participants hold in mind the whole group and can "tolerate" this temporary change, and as we have showed, can even see it as an opportunity. However, in a continuous situation in which a participant is "born" into a situation of being "one versus many" or when needing to stay in such a situation for a long time, the difficulty to overcome the screen barrier increases.

Another possible explanation is that the hybrid model suits some groups more than others, for example, groups that are found in more advanced developmental stages, as we have shown in the paper. In addition, perhaps some participants find the hybrid setting as more suitable to their needs than others. In a contemporary review presented by Weinberg (2020b), he argued that some patients (e.g., patients who are in the midst of an acute crisis) find online therapy to be less suitable, while others (e.g., patients with intimacy problems or social anxiety) prefer it over face-to-face group therapy. These variables have not yet been studied in the context of the hybrid model and would be an interesting theme for future research.

One of our main insights in this study is that the "transition to an online format" is not a simple matter, nor is it purely technical. The transition to an online format can tell a whole group story, as we have demonstrated in the example of a group that grew and "sent" one participant to the online space every time to deal with the issue of room. The dynamics of disconnections and connections and the possibility to see and hear is not purely technical and it is important to explore and realize when they occur.

In sum, based on the findings above, we formulated several suggestions for conductors of hybrid groups:

- When a participant asks to join a meeting online, it is important to consider this request through a psychodynamic lens, in addition to the concrete reasons for the request. The conductor should try to understand whether the request expresses a wish to escape the face-to-face group or whether the transition to a different space calls for the emergence of different self-states and allows the participant more courage for self-disclosure.
- In addition to considering the psychodynamic implications of the request, it is important to understand whether the request expresses a group voice that reveals a story that has not yet been told.
- We see in the transition to the hybrid space a "too available solution" that often constitutes a too quick and absolute gratification of the patient's wishes that misses the opportunity to explore moments of "missing" something that would have been available face-to-face. This solution should be used cautiously, holding in mind the aforementioned considerations.
- For hybrid work to be effective, it is important to acquire advanced equipment, including a screen positioned on a chair inside the circle and an external microphone located at the center of the circle. In addition, it is recommended that participants use an external camera, in addition to the laptop camera. Furthermore, it is important to check during the session that the online participant is still connected.
- We recommend using the hybrid model with groups found in more advanced stages and not with groups that are just starting out or that are in the midst of a crisis. In addition, it is recommended to use this model for a session or two and not for extended periods.

Note

1 We thank Dr. Haim Weinberg for his comments and contribution to this chapter.

References

Bromberg, P. M. (1993). Shadow and substance: A relational perspective on clinical process. *Psychoanalytic Psychology*, 10, 147–168.

De Haas, K. (2021). *Improving group dynamics and involvement in hybrid meetings.* TuDelf. http://resolver.tudelft.nl/uuid:0ba37db7-ad11-411d-9097-61e88649f550.

Ellis, R., Goodacre, T., Mortensen, N., Oeppen, R. S., & Brennan, P. A. (2022). Application of human factors at hybrid meetings: Facilitating productivity and inclusivity. *British Journal of Oral and Maxillofacial Surgery*, 60(96), 740–745.

Foulkes, S. H. (1948). *Introduction to group analysis psychotherapy.* Heinemann.

Foulkes, S. H. (1964). Psychodynamic processes in the light of psychoanalysis and group analysis. In S. H. Foulkes (Ed.). *Therapeutic group analysis* (pp. 108–119). Karnac Books.

Foulkes, S. H., & Anthony, E. J. (1957). *Group psychotherapy: The psychoanalytic approach.* Karnac Books.

Levin, U. (2006). The many in the one: Multiple self-states in combined psychotherapy. *Group Analysis*, 50(2), 190–202.

Mertens, D. M. (2014). *Research methods in education and psychology: Integrating diversity with quantitative and qualitative approaches.* SAGE.

Saatçi, B., Rädle, R., Rintel, S., O'Hara, K., & Nylansted Klokmose, N. (2019). *Hybrid meetings in the modern workplace: Stories of success and failure.* In Collaboration Technologies and Social Computing: 25th International Conference, *CRIWG+ CollabTech 2019, Kyoto, Japan, September 4–6, 2019, Proceedings 25* (pp. 45–61). Springer International Publishing.

Stolper, E., & Zigenlaub, E. (2021). From the circle to the square: Group psychotherapy in the age of coronavirus, *Group*, 45(1), 11–29.

Vaimberg, R., & Vaimberg, L. (2020). Transformations through the technological mirror. In H. Weinberg & A. Rolnick (Eds.) *Theory and practice of online therapy* (pp. 188–204). Routledge.

Weinberg, H. (2020a). From the couch to the screen: Online (group) therapy. AGPA Group Circle. https://www.groupanalysis.gr/en/blog-en/203-from-the-couch-to-the-screen-online-group-therapy.html.

Weinberg, H. (2020b). Online group psychotherapy: Challenges and possibilities during COVID-19—A practice review. *Group Dynamics: Theory, Research and Practice*, 24(3), 201–211. http://dx.doi.org/10.1037/gdn0000140.

Weinberg, H., & Rolnick, A. (2020). *Theory and practice of online therapy: Internet-delivered interventions for individuals, groups, families, and organizations.* Routledge.

Winnicott, D. W. (2007). *Play and reality* [in Hebrew]. Am Oved.

Part II

Online Group
Process-Oriented Approaches

Chapter 7

Modern Psychoanalytic Group Therapy Online

Adaptations of Theory and Technique

Aaron E. Black and Ellen L. Wright

Introduction

During an online group, a member said, "I hear you, but I don't feel you." The leader responded, "What would help you feel me?" to which the group member said, "I'm not really sure. Your words seem right but something's missing." Forced online by the COVID-19 pandemic, group leaders confronted novel issues of confidentiality, technology challenges, and foundational changes in group processes with little preparation. As practitioners of modern psychoanalytic group psychotherapy, we migrated groups from in-person to online formats and adapted our approach to this new relational space. In this chapter, we review the core elements of modern psychoanalytic group psychotherapy and reflect upon modifications in theory and technique to better implement this approach online.

Overview: Modern Psychoanalytic Group Therapy

Hyman Spotnitz (1985) originally conceived of the modern psycho-analytic method because he observed that patients functioning at a pre-Oedipal level benefited more from emotional communication than inter-pretations. Spotnitz (1985) recognized that narcissistically regressed patients often misdirect aggression, making it less available to energize personality development. He coined the term *narcissistic defense* to describe how these patients attack their own minds, contributing to developmental arrests. When it was unsafe for the angry child to express that feeling, they turned their aggressive feelings against themselves to protect the parent-child relationship.

Ormont (1992) and others (Levine, 2017; Rosenthal, 1987; Zeisel, 2009) expanded modern psychoanalytic methods for group psychotherapy. Rather than being a source of insight, they viewed the leader as a maturational agent (Levine, 2017; Ormont, 1992) who reduces barriers to emotional connection among group members and invites the verbal expression of all thoughts and feelings (not just aggression). They also

DOI: 10.4324/9781003248606-9

applied Spotnitz's methods to higher functioning clients with "pockets" of pre-Oedipal deficits and conflicts. Modern analytic group leaders demonstrated that resolving group members' difficulties verbalizing their emotional experience vitalized personality growth, differentiated the boundaries between self and other, and reduced the self-absorption characterizing narcissistic mental states. By establishing a clear framework for the group to resist (Brook, 2001), the leader studies and resolves resistances to "progressive emotional communication," namely emotionally rich, non-repetitive disclosures that deepen relationships within the group (Ormont, 1999). The focus is on helping group members to sustain relational engagement through immediacy, the here-and-now of group process. To accomplish this, the leader asks the group to embrace an explicit framework (see below) for group treatment, involving specific goals and guidelines. The group leader simultaneously welcomes, and seeks to resolve, inevitable self-protective resistances to these agreements to promote emotional resilience and maturation (Ormont, 1994).

Modifications to Theory and Technique in the Online Group

Groups that meet online via videoconferencing face special hurdles due to the format itself (Weinberg, 2021). These include: (1) absence of eye contact, physical presence, and limbic resonance; (2) a slower, linear group narrative that can be difficult to interrupt; (3) limited nonverbal communication; (4) elimination of "small talk" before and after the group; (5) distractions on the computer and in the physical space that each member occupies; (6) elevated concerns about privacy and confidentiality; (7) a dissociative mental state created by a combination of these factors; (8) self-consciousness caused by seeing one's own face; and (9) technical and process barriers that can prevent contact with the leader and the group.

These challenges create dilemmas for the modern analytic group leader. Removing natural eye contact impairs the functioning of mirror neurons (Dickerson et al., 2017), slowing the development of group cohesion. Members may over-rely on cognitive "knowing" about their relational interconnections instead of having shared, embodied experiences together. In addition, the online format can create distortions in the process of communicating love, hate, and sexual feelings. Reversing the problem of self-hate, of central concern to modern analytic leaders, involves redirecting aggressive feelings outward to protect the self and engage others. Technology-induced dissociation can drain vitality from expressing aggressive feelings rather than stimulating relational nourishment, potency, and enhanced freedom. The failure to "see" and "feel" physical responses can increase group member anxiety as one's negative feelings may seem cold and distancing as they are expressed into a technological/emotional void. The fear of loss and rejection may be magnified since abandonment is only one click away.

Similarly, the online leader's emotional communications are mediated by technology, requiring creative alterations in technique and the use of self. The video format evokes objectification, rather than intersubjectivity, whereby group members can feel talked at rather than talked with. The leader appears as an equivalent video image, undifferentiated from the members, confusing if not obscuring the power differential between group and leader.

Specific Technical Modifications When Working Online

The Group Agreement

A central aim of modern group analysis is the study of member opposition, compliance and cooperation with the group goals and agreement. The goals include telling the emotionally significant story of one's life (over time) and putting thoughts and feelings about oneself and others into words as one becomes aware of them. Critical elements of the group agreement involve starting, stopping, and paying on time, confidentiality, using words not actions to communicate, no socializing outside of the group, and including the group in the process of ending treatment. Online, additional guidelines may include ensuring privacy, having adequate technology, and leaving one's audio and video on during the meeting. The leader no longer provides the physical meeting space, however, and cannot easily monitor, or contain, the members' behavioral actions. Further, the leader must manage the meeting links and online "room," and ensure that their own technology is an adequate "holding environment" for the group. These elements complicate the group agreement, online.

Still, group leaders must study deviations from group goals and agreements, which illuminate group members' personalities and histories, and examine their countertransference reactions. Doing this online requires both theoretical and technical modifications. In-person groups have greater implicit togetherness than those online. Without physical presence, questions about a late arrival online can be experienced as overly scrutinizing and marginalizing an already disconnected group member. Identifying minor actions as resistance can undermine exploration of more meaningful resistances and can magnify rather than resolve them. Online, we more actively link group members to gently examine diversions from the contract, while reserving direct attention to the treatment of destructive behaviors.

While the elements of the online group agreement vary in importance, inattention to or excessive focus on the group contract can signal countertransference issues in the group leader. With less control over the holding environment, group leaders may seek affirmation of their value by choosing to indulge in rather than explore disruptions to the group process (i.e., lateness, drinking or eating during group, etc.). Increased highlighting and enforcement of the group agreement can exacerbate unexamined issues of systemic racism and bias, particularly as it pertains to privilege in the group leader. Both countertransference driven actions can be understood as compensation for feelings of helplessness, powerlessness, guilt, loss engendered by global health and political issues, and personal challenges experienced by the group leader. Enactment of these countertransference feelings can block the expression of underlying longings, deprivations, and other feelings pressing for discharge. If left unformulated, these actions can create destructive, uncontained power struggles within the group.

Transference and Resistance

Modern analytic theory emphasizes both transference and resistance in group therapy. Of special interest is the narcissistic transference, where another person is experienced as part of, or an extension of, the self. This contrasts with object transference, where the other person (or group as a whole) is experienced as a parent one once had or the child one once was. Developmentally, the narcissistic transference allows access to preverbal experience, while the object transference signals Oedipal-level functioning (and assumes whole object relating). Arrested self-hate at the pre-Oedipal level is a focus in modern group analysis. Relatedly, two forms of resistance are also of interest: transference resistance and resistance to the transference. Transference resistance involves inhibited communication that derives from the transference itself. For example, a member relates superficially to another group member who reminds them of some unwanted aspect of themselves. Resistance to the transference, however, occurs when a member suppresses their transferential feelings to another member or the leader. All forms of transference and resistance induce feelings in the group leader that can be utilized in interventions that remove barriers to sustained emotional contact within the group. From a modern analytic perspective, the ideal circumstance is when the group engages freely, with affect, about their transferential feelings when they become aware of them.

Working online directly influences transference and resistance. The dissociative elements of the online environment produce feelings of neglect, abandonment, and variations of toxic loneliness. Arguably, online groups recreate greater relational neglect than in-person groups, where silent identifications emerge naturally through non-verbal communication. In online groups, object transferences can overwhelm fragile narcissistic transferences (which may be less robust in general due to the limited activation of mirror neurons, see Dickerson et al., 2017). It is easier online to feel like the neglected child of a neglectful parent than to experience aspects of oneself in others. Judicious use of affective self-disclosures signals the leader's presence, emotional availability, and interest in our impact on the group, and the group's impact on us. By offering up "more self" to the group, we can reduce the chronicity of the neglectful parent-child dynamic and stimulate the blooming of narcissistic transference.

Like transference, resistances are filtered through the lens of the online experience. The comment "I didn't feel like coming today" is a more frequent refrain at the start of an online group. While complaining about the online format is common, such objections often carry rich emotional information about transference and resistance. For example, one member who expressed resistance to being online identified a familiar feeling of being forced into a new stepfamily, with relative strangers, and a "flat" unemotional parent (i.e., like the online group leader). Superficial complaining about working online can be deadening, tempting the leader to dismiss or discredit the objection; however, transference, resistance, and enactments remain clinically important phenomena that, when engaged by the leader, help the group to progress.

In online groups members cope with the format's inherent disconnection by remaining in emotionally safe waters, rather than foraying into new and uncharted emotional topics. In this status quo resistance (Rosenthal, 1987), supportive feelings tend to impede progress by sidelining anger. Members who prefer the relational safety of disconnection and non-engagement can also create a status quo resistance, whereby the group clings to comfortable relational distance. For example, in one online group working on something for an extended period, the leader asked who was suppressing a feeling that might disrupt the group's current focus. Sure enough, a silent group member spoke up:

> I have been. I don't want to mess things up. The group's been so loving and supportive to Susan, I feel like my annoyance and boredom have no place. If I voice them, I'm going to end up just like I did in my family, the one who causes all the trouble when everyone else seems perfectly happy.

In this instance, the silent member both supports the status quo resistance and resists her transference, demonstrating how resistances to transference intersect with group-level resistances in disrupting progress in an online group.

The leader explores the underlying meaning of member objections to working online, rather than hopelessly accepting or dismissing them at face value, which can be a reaction to induced feelings of hopelessness or helplessness. We have found it helpful to remember and state that, despite their power, words alone fail to compensate for the missing elements of an in-person group. Accepting the limits of language within this format helps us patiently to field typical complaints online while also listening for the deeper emotional meanings embedded within transference, resistance, and enactment.

Virtual Countertransference

Like our group members who avoid uncomfortable feelings, leaders may not recognize the challenges of online group treatment. The emotionally and physically depriving aspects of being online can also rekindle pre-verbal deprivation in the group leader. If not identified and managed, this Virtual Countertransference (VCT) (Wright, personal communication with Aaron Black) can lead some leaders to over-compensate through increased activity levels and erudition, while others may withdraw into passive observation, protected from or tormented by the toll of emotional disengagement. Similar to analyzing resistance in our group members, leaders can recognize VCT by examining when they adhere to or veer from the customary in-person group leadership approaches.

One of the most compelling expressions of VCT manifests as the intensification of the drive to be the "good enough" group mother and become the "perfect [online] group mother." Leaders may enact this by trying to overcome the countertransferential guilt engendered by the inherent limitations of online group treatment. This "over-functioning" can be seen in increased vigilance and monitoring of group members' feelings, greater reactivity to group members' level of contact or silence and increased projection of the leader's history onto the screen of the group dynamics. These countertransference reactions can be potentially understood as a parallel to the group members' feelings of online deprivation as well as a repetition of the group leaders' early life.

One type of VCT feelings can be recognized as "the bad analyst feelings" (Epstein, 1987) stimulated by the group's transference to us as *both* their neglectful, depriving parent, as well as their experience as a neglected, unvalued child. By examining the emotional and visceral elements of this countertransference, we can gain insight into the deficits of the group members' early lives and form reparative interventions. This type of VCT can become destructive, however, when the group leader interprets these feelings of being the inadequate parent, or unloved child, as a sign of their technical or personal failings. Reacting to the toxicity of these feelings, group leaders can be drawn to compensatory interventions (e.g., increases in attempts at attunement, pressure to provide interpretive insights) or withdrawal into self-attack and dissociation. These reactions further the enactment, rather than the study of, these early traumas in the group process.

Such inadequate compensatory reactions can cause group leaders to experience feelings of depletion, self-hate, and even fantasies of ending a group or leaving the profession. An antidote to these toxic feelings is the development and accessing of the "valuing self" (Wright, 2022). A companion to Epstein's "observing" and "experiencing self," accessing one's "valuing self" enables the group leader's nourishment by internalized sources of professional competency and personal regard. Describing this process, Wright explains,

> These alternate internalized voices help us set aside these toxic projections and inductions long enough to examine what is happening in these challenging group interactions. Without the support of the valuing self, the induced feelings of the online group experience and the negative projections can ring true and overwhelm or disable our competent, therapeutic selves.
>
> (Wright, 2022)

Bridging

Bridging, developed by Lou Ormont, is a critical technique designed to help a modern analytic group to keep progressing. Bridging involves the deliberate linking of different group members to each other, to subgroups, the group-as-a-whole, and to the leader. It can take many forms including bridging over similarities, differences, certain transferences, resistances, defenses, or elements of members' current or past life circumstances. New groups learning how to be a working group require a substantial amount of bridging to help the group form. More advanced groups tend naturally to bridge and have less need for the leader to serve this function. However, online groups, due to the greater built-in disconnection, benefit from continual bridging from the leader. The use of bridging creates an additional safety net for group members whose nascent sense of entitlement or habitual state of isolation can overwhelm them, blocking healing connections. Most online groups—even mature, working groups—can be stymied by the monotonous experience of everyone being separated and alone, staring at a screen. Likewise, silences in-person are often deeply meaningful communications that contain an affective charge which can be accessed to propel the group forward. Silences online can quickly promote or magnify dissociative elements that deplete energy from the group process; therefore, we are more likely to break silences online, often with bridging. Bridging can also be used to invite the group to visualize how their interconnections might be different if they were in-person together. Imagining or retrieving memories of physical closeness can safely connect withdrawn members with their memories of physical closeness without the demand of experiencing it within the riskier format of the group. Bridging through visualization or memory can also be understood as a "join" with a group member's resistance to intimacy, due to fears of engulfment or loss of autonomy stimulated by the group setting.

When bridging in online groups, we pay special attention to non-verbal communications to remind the group of their bodies. An example of this might sound like, "Rachel, why is Sam smiling while you are talking?" Or, "Jonathan, can you tell Miguel what all of your moving about is saying to him?" Or, asking a member where they were noticing the feeling in their body: "Does anyone else feel that kind of pressure in their chest like Kaitlyn is feeling?" Since we have maximized visual coverage of the entire group, visual bridging, i.e., bridging that emphasizes what we are seeing (over what we are hearing), can be very effective. When bridging online, the leader should carefully track their activity level. Too much or too little bridging can yield the same results, namely increased relational disconnection within the group.

Bridging also creates and fosters sibling relationships in the group. Deprived of physical proximity, group members can benefit from references to "group siblings" which serve as an antidote to the relational deprivation of the online format. This added bond is particularly useful when a group member ventures into the fraught arena of criticizing the group leader. Online groups can intensify fears of parental and sibling retaliation, however. The online group leader must keep in mind that speaking in the online group can magnify fears that one is being "too visible" or taking too much group time, risking attack from one's group siblings. The leader can help to narrate these fears and bridge among the members who share them, creating greater safety within a subgroup with similar feelings.

Contact Functioning and the Insulation Barrier

Modern analytic leaders support the contact function, group members' making self-determined, member-centered emotional contact (Margolis, 1983a). In addition to supporting each member's personal agency, and the linking of emotional contact to that agency, attention to contact functioning communicates the acceptance of group members where they are, rather than where others want them to be. Awareness of cultural, racial, and ethnic influences on how and when members choose to speak is essential to help to create safety in the group, supports people working at their own pace, and buoys the ego functioning of vulnerable group members. When the leader initiates contact with a group member, it is sometimes through the use of an object-oriented question (Margolis, 1983b), a question that directs the member's attention to the world outside the self and to which there is no wrong answer. A contact functioning question is a method for making non-intrusive emotional contact with a group member. This might sound like, "John, should I ask you to tell us more about that experience, or have you said enough at the moment?" These object-oriented and contact functioning questions invite engagement that is shaped by the individual member or subgroup rather than the leader.

The inherent over-insulation of members caused by the online group format complicates the leader's attention to contact functioning. Lou Ormont (1994) referred to the "insulation barrier," an aspect of the mind that mediates between our inner and outer experience. An overly porous insulation barrier allows too much stimulation to enter the mind from others, while an overly thick insulation barrier prevents the mind from being affected by emotional communications, making the person less accessible. Technology arrangements create a thicker insulation barrier among group members, as the shared physical space and ways of communicating are dramatically altered. This added emotional insulation online means that traditional attention to the contact function may need to be adjusted. Rather than waiting for group members to initiate contact spontaneously (though that is still desirable), the leader needs to actively seek out individual members who exist on the edges of the group experience. The types of questions outlined above may need to be asked more frequently. In addition, we are more inclined to ask ego-oriented questions—asking a group member about their inner experience to link them more readily to the group. For example, after two group members worked out a conflict successfully, the leader turned to a silent member to ask, "What were you feeling while Karen and Edith were working on their relationship?" This is an example of bridging with an ego-oriented question rather than waiting for the member to make contact. While in-person group members may feel more "put on the spot" by these interventions, online group members can feel helped into the process, reassuring them that they occupy space in the leader's mind.

Each group member's character plays a key role in understanding the issues of contact functioning and emotional insulation. More avoidant people may find added comfort in the online format, as it supports their desired level of intimacy, while online barriers can exacerbate attachment anxiety in others. Because the lack of shared physical presence limits emotional immediacy, information about members' outside lives can take on even greater importance, as members communicate where they are "located" in the world. This sort of "outside the room" material can deaden an in-person group but, if meaningful, these disclosures can help online members to feel more immediately included in each other's lives. The enhanced sense of mutual involvement improves contact functioning, creates feelings of connection, and optimizes the insulation barrier of each individual member. More sharing of current life experiences can be an additional way to help the members of an online group to feel that they matter to one another much as emotional immediacy does in an in-person group. Contact functioning questions, object and ego-oriented questions aimed at emotionally significant current life experiences can, thus, help to build cohesion and intimacy more readily in an online group. The leader needs to help to balance emotionally immediate and "out of group" communications as a way of connecting online group members to each other and to the leader.

Joining, Mirroring, and Emotional Magnification

Modern psychoanalytic theory suggests that treatment resistances are early accommodations to developmental deficits, conflicts, and traumas, that serve a stabilizing function within the personality. Rather than barriers to be eliminated, resistances are addressed with respectful curiosity, so that their function, purpose, and history can be fully articulated and understood. With this in mind, modern analytic leaders use techniques such as joining (siding with), mirroring (emulating or mimicking), and emotional magnification (enlarging the emotion) when addressing resistances (Margolis, 1986). These techniques can reduce defensiveness while highlighting resistance as an object for collective study within the group. Emotional communications are also required to help to resolve the resistance over time. These techniques serve important functions beyond the scope of this chapter; however, a shared primary function is engaging and resolving resistances. When working online, we have found that joining and emotional magnification seem more effective than mirroring, again perhaps due to the lack of physical presence and activation of mirror neurons (Dickerson et al., 2017). The mirroring of aggressive feelings online may be misunderstood as the leader being dangerously angry or defensive, when effective mirroring is meant to communicate that, in this moment, we (the member and leader) are similar. When successful, it is implicitly understood that the leader is sharing in the group member's feeling state, rather than inserting their own separate feeling. Mirroring anger online may inadvertently cause group members to "shut down," given the power differential in the leader-member relationship or to create difficulties in detecting the leader's motivation. The emotional "as if" quality of the intervention can be lost online. Therefore, when leading online groups, we minimize mirroring of aggressive communications in favor of non-defensive inquiry and visible curiosity, and clarify questions to seek deeper understanding. Joining and emotional magnification, in contrast, seem equally effective and less confusing online.

Emotional Communication and Induced Feelings

The modern analytic group leader emphasizes emotional communication to resolve resistances within the group process. Key to successful emotional communication is use of the feelings induced (i.e., projective identification) within the leader's countertransference, or the objective countertransference. Why is this focus important in a modem analytic group? Resistances to the goals of telling the emotionally significant story of one's life and putting thoughts and feelings into words as one becomes aware of them are usually impeded by a desire to avoid uncomfortable psychological states (which emerge within the leader). Using these induced feelings to reconstruct the member's history, the leader seeks to resolve this resistance, thus releasing the split-off feeling within the group in a more regulated form which helps the group to progress. Since virtual countertransference can often meld with the leader's early life (i.e., feelings of deprivation, badness, shame, exclusion), the process of studying one's countertransference has an added urgency when working online. Without this process, the source of the countertransference may be obscured, making the information unavailable for interventional purposes. Recognizing VCT as one source of these feelings can help the leader to detoxify the intensity of some of the disowned feelings that get stimulated in a powerful but more covert manner in the group.

The dance of partial identification (Holmes, 2009) is key in the online format. This is where we identify with group members while holding an outside perspective that supports the wise introduction of needed emotional material. When working online, the leader might restate things that might seem obvious in an in-person group; emotional threads need constant restimulation to counterbalance the inherent disconnection in the online process. In-person, our tone and body language, and the experience or communication expressed in our physical presence, are often enough to communicate the induced feeling back to a group member. In the online environment, where it is harder for the members to implicitly sense the emotional state of the group leader, overt self-disclosure is sometimes needed.

Working with transference, resistance, and countertransference in an online group places new, sometimes greater demands on the group leader for responsiveness, transparency, and relational flexibility. The pressure to be verbally expressive, the likelihood of dissociation, and difficulties feeling with others, are obstacles to the group leader's ability to address pre-Oedipal, pre-verbal deficits. As experienced modern analytic group leaders, we are still learning how to translate these core techniques into an online environment. Despite these challenges, the modern analytic group theory and technique continues to respond, and adapt, to this challenge. It is our hope that this chapter will be the first of many attempts to address and expand the therapeutic power of modern analytic group practice online.

References

Brook, M. (2001). An overview. In L. B. Furgeri (Ed.), *The technique of group treatment: the collected papers of Louis R. Ormont, Ph.D.* (pp. 11–20). Psychosocial Press.

Dickerson, K., Gerhardstein, P., & Moser, A. (2017). The role of the human mirror neuron system in supporting communication in a digital world. *Frontiers in Psychology*, 8, 698. https://doi.org/10.3389/fpsyg.2017.00698.

Epstein, L. (1987). The problem of the analyst's bad feeling. *Modern Psychoanalysis*, 12, 35–45.

Holmes, L. (2009). The technique of partial identification: Waking up to the world. *International Journal of Group Psychotherapy*, 59(2), 253–265.

Levine, R. (2017). A modern psychoanalytic perspective on group therapy. *International Journal of Group Psychotherapy*, 67(Sup 1), S109–S120.

Margolis, B. (1983a). The contact function of the ego: Its role in the narcissistic patient. *Modern Psychoanalysis*, 8, 35–46.

Margolis, B. (1983b). The object-oriented question: A contribution to treatment technique. *Psychoanalytic Review*, 70(1), 69–81.

Margolis, B. (1986). Joining, mirroring, psychoanalytic reflection: Terminology, definitions, theoretical considerations. *Modern Psychoanalysis*, 11(1–2), 19–35.

Ormont, L. (1992). *The group therapy experience: From theory to practice.* Booksurge.

Ormont, L. (1994). Developing emotional insulation. *The International Journal of Group Psychotherapy*, 44(3), 361–375.

Ormont, L. (1999). Progressive emotional communication: Criteria for a well-functioning group. *Group Analysis*, 32(1), 373–384.

Rosenthal, L. (1987). Resistances in group psychotherapy. In *Resolving resistances in group psychotherapy* (pp. 83–103). Jason Aronson.

Spotnitz, H. (1985). *Modern analysis of the schizophrenic patient* (2nd ed.). Hudson Sciences Press.

Weinberg, H. (2021). Obstacles, challenges, and benefits of online group psychotherapy. *The American Journal of Psychotherapy*, 74(2), 83–88.

Wright, E. (2022). *Use of self and care of self: New directions for working with countertransference.* 50th Anniversary Lecture for the Philadelphia School of Psychoanalysis, Philadelphia, April.

Zeisel, E. M. (2009). Affect education and the development of the interpersonal ego in modern group psychoanalysis. *International Journal of Group Psychotherapy*, 59(3), 421–432.

Chapter 8

Group Analytic Therapy and the Online Groups

Some Principles of the Group Analytic Approach to Online Group Therapy

Robi Friedman

Group analysis is "a form of psychotherapy *by* the group, *of* the group, including its conductor" (Foulkes 1975a, p. 3). The individual in therapy is the center of our attention, and the group is the instrument through which their sufferings are cured. The dynamics of the therapeutic group have a strong impact on the individual, usually more of a progressive than a regressive nature. When the group's communicational culture (the group's "matrix") is open and positive, many in the group will be responsive, reflective and will also have a reparative attitude (Schlapobersky, 2016) towards others and themselves, which will be conducive to cure. When the group's aggression is uncontained, scapegoat dynamics of hate and rejection will have a destructive impact on subgroups and the individual. Hence the importance in group analysis of forming a group culture—a matrix—which will facilitate cure and growth through open communicative and relational means. In group analysis this culture is created by the therapist's facilitation of a *shared* reciprocal relational space in which all participants actively take part. This communicational and relational characteristic of group analysis will have to translate from the usual face-to-face group into an online "small windows" format. The creation of such a relational space is necessary for therapy, because change needs to allow a natural re-enacting of past interpersonal patterns. These relation disorders and dysfunction connection patterns are always concerned with feelings ranging from inclusion and rejection. These are the poles of one of the most significant continuums of our social or collective unconscious. It is not surprising to see how distressed and even insulted most participants of group analytic therapy groups feel when they find out how much they are ready to do in order to be included in a relationship, a group or a community. And it is even more distressing when they discover how much everyone is willing to pay in order to not be rejected—an additional painful but helpful group awareness of how great the influence of society's norms and collective preoccupations are on our conscious and unconscious mind and behavior. Group analytic therapy elaborates the impact of society and its norms and exclusion threats on everyday life and western individualistic positions.

DOI: 10.4324/9781003248606-10

The group analytic therapist's challenge is to take up a unique double position in the group. "He is the responsible administrator … Yet he leads the group only exceptionally. Therefore, he has been called the conductor, the guardian and guide, of the group-analytic group" (Foulkes, 1975 p. 3). The main reason for this special kind of "leader who does not lead" (Anthony, 1991) is—as we find out before long—that the real therapist is the group. Thus, the group analyst's position is to try to provide as much space as possible for the development of the communication between all the group's members, including the conductor. Once the group starts (or a new member joins the "slow-open" therapy group, the term used for a continuous group, where newcomers join and veterans leave the group periodically), group conductors have to wean the group from their burgeoning natural dependence on the therapist. In the second stage conductors move to a decentralized position in the group. In the third phase of the development of an analytic group, conductors learn to trust the group and convey this position by their response to the participants in a productive and growth-conducive way. Is all this possible online?

Group analytic concepts, like the few exemplified here, are relational and usually reciprocal, rather than describing the intra-psychic realm. Resonance, for example, an important therapeutic factor in group analysis, means communicating the deepest personal responses to either emotions or persons. Because of the visceral aspects of resonance, its impact online might be somewhat milder than in face-to-face meetings, but will still be influential. Another important therapeutic factor is "mirroring," which describes the process of learning from shared emotions and memories emerging as responses to conscious and unconscious narratives. A group participant will see his own "different" reflection in someone else's behavior. Another participant, by sharing a similar anxiety (mirroring), may be able to demonstrate different refusal or separation responses to such an anxiety, which may contribute a developmental aspect. We have found that mirroring is effectively communicated in online group therapy.

Other group analytic specific concepts such as exchange, which is the ability to give and take in interpersonal situations, need to be transposed (de Maré, 2002) to the online format. Exchange is important as it contributes to the necessary re-enactments of dysfunctional patterns of relating, which are the basis of the therapeutic movement needed. However, the transposition of exchange from the face-to-face setting to the virtual environment can be challenging. Excessive passion, anxiety, neediness and hate, which create destructive relations and arouse exclusion and rejection anxieties, can be better hidden in the online tiles (as many called the Zoom windows). "Rejection and chronic exclusion make you sick. Inclusion cures. Rejection is trauma, inclusion is glory" (Friedman, 2018, p. 5). Rejection and inclusion, these basic influences on our mental health, are sometimes less visible in online settings.

The possibility of re-enactment of dysfunctional patterns, which I have called the Relation Disorders (Friedman, 2007), e.g., the recently discussed authority Relation Disorder (Friedman and Seidler, 2022), which is a requisite of therapy, is challenged in the online space. Group therapy should allow repetitions and enactments of interpersonal patterns, while offering possibilities to change these relational patterns. The main agents of change in group analytic therapy are *insights* (which are intrapersonal new understandings about oneself), and *"outsights"* [emphasis added] (de Maré, 2002), which is a heightened awareness of what happens in external relations. I have found that the transposition of both insights and outsights to the online setting is possible. The next phase of the change of a dysfunctional relation pattern would be what Foulkes (1968) called *"ego-training in action"* [emphasis added] using the learned intra- and interpersonal awareness to try new ways of coping with relational situations. In sum, online settings, in my experience, have some difficulty to fully "put on stage" dysfunctional patterns with the same ease and naturalness as in face-to-face situations.

All the above tries to describe the process of "building a specific group analytic therapeutic matrix" (Foulkes, 1969). The "matrix" is the culture of relations and communication in the group. The reciprocal influence is total. Thus, in order to heal participants and their relations, such a matrix is created by continuously communicating the group analytic principles of dialogue and "free floating discussion" (Foulkes, 1969). By providing maximum space to the group's healing interaction, the therapist's progressive trust in the group is shared by all the participants. The group conductor should not be seduced into becoming the leader or the main therapist of the group. These positions need to be learned by experience and supervision. When participants trust themselves to form healing and otherwise growth promoting relations with others including the conductor, the group analytic matrix can be considered to have been created. This culture will then continuously prevail in the group analytic therapy group for years. Whether such a matrix can be created in an online group is the main issue here. I think that while online relations will have less power, need more maintenance and have a tendency to fade away with time, in my experience significant group analytic work can be done in weekly online therapy groups. Although trust and closeness are strongly bodily related and rooted in a primary mother/child relationship, participants can still experience confidence and basic attachment online. However, my experience is that once- or twice-yearly face-to-face meetings strengthen these relations and make working online easier.

Online Group Therapy: My Personal Experience

Over the past 10 years I have conducted many weekly and twice-monthly online supervision and therapeutic groups. China, Russia, Ukraine and

Italy have provided for diverse cultural backgrounds. I have been conducting an online double session "dreamtelling" group (Friedman, 2008) once a month with colleagues from Padova (Italy), complemented by yearly in-person meetings (with the exception of the COVID-19 pandemic period) when we worked for a whole weekend. In addition, during the two-year-long pandemic I conducted more than 50 group analytic large group meetings (Friedman, 2019). The question of online median and large groups in particular is an issue of considerable interest, and will be discussed later.

Most participants were repeatedly surprised at how well the online setting worked. Despite this overall experience, it seemed that for many participants the encounter through the screen felt uncanny, and it was perceived as unwelcoming and untrustworthy. For many participants a process that lasted for almost a year started with a weird feeling, which changed into more trust only after several months and ended in a satisfactory feeling. Interestingly, for many of the participants this successful process did not produce lasting learning with regards to the experience of the online setting. Every time an encounter ended, participants shared their surprise that they had just gone through an experience of intimacy and authenticity. But after every session, this experience seemed to be forgotten. It was as if for these participants there was no permanent learning that online encounters could have trustworthy qualities. While I could not really get to the root of participants' difficulties in becoming familiar with the meeting media, it evoked the feeling that there is a "natural" obstacle to "loving" video meetings. While these difficulties often did not exhibit the character of anxious defenses or resistances, in "block" settings, where we met over a three- to four-day period for four to five daily video meetings, the adaptation was better than in once-weekly group analytic therapy groups. Did I miss something in the learning process?

The resistances or difficulties with video conferencing remain complex processes waiting for convincing explanation. Sometimes the discomfort with video seemed to be rooted in a *displacement* of the anger and fear aroused by the COVID-19 pandemic. For many group participants, video conferencing unconsciously represented the pandemic and its incomprehensive reality, which was felt as insecure inclusion and even growing concerns of being "ejected." It is possible that ejection (e.g., due to technical glitches) from the video session reminded participants of the main characteristics of the pandemic: lonely illness and isolated death. For many, the dependency on the "online space", which did not feel "inclusion-secure" threatened the relations because of a resistance to the "instrument." Of course, this is a central difference from the face-to-face meetings, in which there is a conscious and unconscious "promise of non-rejection" (Friedman, 2018) which feels therapeutic.

The Difference between Face-to-Face and Online Conception of Leadership

Dependency on leadership can be seen as a main defense of group participants against rejection and exclusion anxieties. During the first wave of the COVID-19 pandemic, I detected two conflicting tendencies in online group participants: many tried and finally succeeded to feel included in online groups, while struggling with the difficulty to gain a sense of security. Others, participants with a stronger need for closeness, could not adapt to this sort of alternative meeting and at the beginning it seemed that their expectation of a strong and *present* leader could not be overcome. In contrast to face-to-face groups, in their unconsciousness, the physical distance in the online group hindered the feeling of being protected by the therapist. This caused a series of affective difficult situations, which generally fell under the concept of the "unreal." Often the *contact* with others in the group was felt by many as *unreal* (rather than unauthentic). Often, group participants would say they had to "relate to others through a veil." Much effort has been invested in understanding the phenomenon which makes it more difficult for some to relate through the screen, and cannot really be approached as a relation dysfunction. Frequently I ask myself the opposite—how strong are the attachment abilities of those who adapt so well to video conferencing?

Another aspect is that although everyone can see all faces, something which cannot be done in small or large groups, one can never really look someone straight in the eye. Although I and others made an effort to feel closer by learning to "play" with an occasional fixing the window (pinning) on the video of another participant, or sharing something in the chat function, which copies something of the nonverbal communication in live meetings, nothing can really substitute the feelings of the face-to-face meetings. When the time came and we returned to face-to-face meetings, the significance of the absence of nonverbal "normal" communication became immediately felt. We were all surprised how much nonverbal information about taste, attraction or avoidance, of cues about anxiety, anger and our bodily messages was lost. As a result of this understanding, I repeatedly encourage online participants to share their bodily sensations in order to improve nonverbal communication.

On the flip side, hearing others becomes much easier in online video group sessions. The larger the group the greater the improvement of hearing. Initially, group conductors of various differently sized groups feared that participants trying to talk simultaneously would make hearing difficult, what happened in reality is that it was easier to communicate and find one's voice. In a large video group with Ukrainian mental health professionals, over the course of a little more than one hour, more than 40 out of the 100-plus participants talked. In group analytic thinking this is the first step of a process in which monologues develop into dialogues (Schlapobersky, 1993) and, as described earlier, it is how a communicative matrix is created. Online large groups have a greater ability to foster verbal communication than large face-to-face groups.

The Body in Online Group Analysis

Small group therapy participants who usually are preoccupied by their physical appearance, may actually feel more comfortable on video. Online therapy in groups, which make the masking or hiding of the body possible, taught me a lesson about treating shame and other corporeal insecurities. It provides a possibility to "use" the setting and this increase of comfort as a transient request for containment. Participants may feel greater inclusion security and slowly work on disarming bodily defenses.

Group therapists must be careful not to reinforce the need to hide and disguise but use the online situation as a way to facilitate the work on avoidance in order to enable real contact. The wish to feel closeness and belonging to the group whatever your body looks like, together with the ability to show your body as a way of communicating is something that is facilitated by online therapy. A later transition to face-to-face meetings may be even more conductive to change.

Online group therapists should be sensitive to the difficulties to communicate. I believe that a group therapist should try to use the greater difficulty for some online participants to depend on the conductor, in order to further decentralize himself/herself in order to encourage the centrality of patient-to-patient communication. The seeming equality of the visual setting of the windows may for some contribute to this growth process which, as mentioned earlier, is the essence of the group analytic thinking on therapy.

Remembering Online Meetings

As noted above, interestingly, *memory* of past online group meetings seemed less vivid as that of face-to-face meetings. This finding was corroborated time and again. The reason can be only guessed at. If I use the principle we found in research, that being in a relationship with a containing person (Friedman, 2002, 2007) enhances both the memory and the sharing of dreams, we may be on the same path we outlined previously. Although online small group therapy meetings are generally a surprisingly good alternative to face-to-face meetings, they are not as efficient in creating close relations as face-to-face groups. The pressure on former face-to-face groups to return to meetings in person may also offer testimony to the need for closer relations and connections than online groups can offer.

I believe that psycho-educational groups or groups which do not need such deep connections and do not work on the unconscious difficulties in relating are less hampered by online communication.

The "It's Not a Group Analytic" Controversy

In a certain group analytic institute, some of the staff refused to participate in the conduction of groups for a whole four-day weekend, reasoning that working online is not "group analytic." They joined after four months, only when it became clear that the COVID-19 pandemic was robbing them of their livelihoods. It seems important to tell this, because I do not actually think that they were opposed to working through video, at a time when online therapy seemed to be the optimal alternative to the prohibited face-to-face meetings. It could not be tested and proved, since the basic conditions for the creation of a group analytic matrix (the possibility to wean the group of its dependence, to create a communicative matrix which provides for therapy by the group's participants, including a decentralized conductor) had been met by video conferencing. I think their avoidance of video conferencing and absence is a solid sign of taking an (non-group analytic) authoritative and restrictive stand on the setting. If the politics of group therapy can be discussed here, I feel that there were many deeper reasons for this first refusal of group therapists. My interpretation of this dynamic is that the unspoken power structures, traditionally dominated by group therapists, were threatened by the emergency changes created by the pandemic. From later inquiries with group conductors it seems that, in addition, the insecurity and inferiority in handling video conferencing software, and envy of the adaptation abilities of the younger generation may also be sources of resistance to online therapy during the early stages of the pandemic. In Germany it was clear that young group analysts were in the frontline of the struggle to allow online group therapy, resisting organized governmental and private rulings about this.

Forming a "Group Culture" on Zoom

As a training group analyst at SGAZ (the Group Analytic Institute Zurich) for the last 10 years I have conducted small and large groups three times each year in "blocks" of four full days. An average candidate, coming from German-speaking countries, participates in this curriculum for five to seven years. Each block includes about 16 sessions of small and large groups. As elsewhere in the world, during the pandemic, we had to switch the setting of some blocks to an online format. We were particularly concerned that the January online blocks, in which usually three participants join the groups replacing the three who have left in

September, would become "leaking containers" (Weinberg, 2016). But experience refuted the anxiety and almost all the new participants seemed to have succeeded in joining the groups.

It is true that in the online experience, all connections, memory and communications seemed to have less impact than what we were used to, but looking at the end result, we felt that the online blocks were definitely adequate. Further, we found that the face-to-face meetings later were a substantial addition and reparation for aspects we could not address or understand in the online block. I think many in the group felt that the face-to-face meetings were actually a kind of "reparation." That is why I recommended that group analytic groups who have to be mostly online should include once- or twice-yearly in-person encounters. I think that in the future many group analytic group settings will have some mix of face-to-face and online meetings, in which inclusion (and rejection) are felt more strongly felt and contribute to the therapeutic work as described above.

The Present "Sandwiches" with Ukrainians

Median and large groups are part and parcel of the group analytic set of instruments which provide information and are also formative and trans-formative (Friedman, 2008). Although not all group analysts agree that the large group has a therapeutic impact (Weinberg and Weishut, 2012), participants of this rather innovative setting regularly report having had significant insights about relating to society and especially to external and personal authority. The group analytic large group (Friedman, 2018) enables encounters with differences, norms and political struggles, which can often only be reflected on and discussed in this setting. By facilitating the meeting with hundreds of participants, the large group provides a unique space where "social psychotherapy" (Foulkes, 1975, p. 250) happens.

Large and median groups have also adopted the online setting, and in the lonely and isolated era of COVID-19 they became enormously popu-lar, changing the meeting of a mass of bodies into one of a mass of faces. It seems only natural to share some experiences about them in this chap-ter. The obvious technical advantages of an online large group comprising at least 100 people are the low cost and ease of use—people can log on from anywhere. All around the world people became familiar with video conferencing platforms, and the large number of online large groups which I conducted in the year and a half prior to writing this chapter are proof of this.

While the feelings engendered by participating in the online groups and face-to-face are quite different, do both allow for a "social psychother-apy"? My response is affirmative. Participating online is never as

Figure 8.1 Illustration of Large Group
Source: Robi Friedman.

Figure 8.2 Illustration of Large Group Online
Source: Vadim Pastuh/stock.adobe.com.

overwhelming emotionally as in a large in-person group, the physical presence of a mass is really sensed as different from meeting on-screen—yet the recurring need for large groups is enormous. It seems that participants' need and wish to come together and to have a dialog about their collective preoccupations is the main issue. Being together with people who share concerns, in a space in which resonance and mirroring to this sharing is possible, may be the explanation why, despite the differences in the settings, for months approximately 100 Ukrainian colleagues living in a war zone were willing to make an enormous twice-weekly effort and meet online for a whole evening.

The Sandwich Model (Friedman, 2016), a mix of small and large groups, facilitates different populations to make better use of the large groups and their contributions to growth and social health. The ease with which video conferencing software is able to divide large groups into small groups is beneficial. Ukrainians living under war conditions, privileged in that they had access to the Internet, used the group analytic large and small groups to prevent primary and secondary PTSD, and to exchange about their own terrible circumstances as well. Experimenting with the online use of an innovative group analytic instrument such as the Sandwich Model showed the world real-time emergency assistance: for the first time, a civil population under fire and living in extremely stressful conditions was helped to cope with the impact of a traumatic situation. The online setting of the Sandwich Model made it possible to contain the containers. The members of the group shared the sound of bombs falling in Kiev and Leviv, and communicated in real time their uncontained hate and mourning processes while experiencing a lethal attack on a center of a small town.

To my surprise, it worked. The Ukrainian large group's request to continue this work is the best evidence that the online small and large groups have a containing influence on the participants.

A Technical Innovation in the Hybrid Small Group Setting: a Final Tip

The problems that arise when a small group meets face-to-face while some members participate online will stay with us. There are many benefits to this format allowing the flexibility of the online format while the majority of the group can enjoy the advantages of a face-to-face meeting. It is the accomplishment of my Padovan dreamtelling group to have solved it technically. Being in another country (Israel), I always attended online, sometimes together with another member. The solution we found was to place on a small table in the middle of the group one laptop for two or three participants. Thus, when the group of eight met, they had four laptops and, on each screen, they saw five windows, four of their colleagues, and one was my window, pinned and large. All but one laptop had to be muted, and the open laptop was connected to an external speaker and microphone. In countries in which I need to work with a translator, who is also often online, the translator can communicate with me via a messaging application such as WhatsApp or WeChat (if the translation option of the video conferencing software is not available). We found that this setup was very effective. Later, in Padova a newer device with two large screens and two 180-degree cameras was used, where two half groups appeared in the windows next to me.

We are on the cusp of a new era of communication offering enormous possibilities for therapeutic meetings which warrant further in-depth investigation.

References

Anthony, E. J. (1991). The dilemma of therapeutic leadership: The leader who does not lead. In S. Tuttman (Ed.), *Psychoanalytic group theory and therapy: Essays in honor of Saul Scheidlinger* (pp. 71–86). International Universities Press.

De Maré, P. (2002). The millennium and the median group. *Group Analysis*, 35(2), 195–208.

Foulkes, S. H. (1968). Group dynamic processes and group analysis. In E. Foulkes (Ed.), *Selected papers* (pp. 175–186). Karnac.

Foulkes, S. H. (1975). *Group analytic psychotherapy: Method and principles.* Gordon and Breach.

Foulkes, S. H. (1975). Problems of the large group from a group-analytical point of view. In L. Kreeger (Ed.), *The large group: Dynamics and therapy* (pp. 33–56). F. E. Peacock.

Foulkes, S. H. (1975). The leader in the group. In E. Foulkes (Ed.), *Selected papers: Psychoanalysis and group analysis* (pp. 285–296). Karnac.

Friedman, R. (2007) Where to look? Supervising group analysis: A Relations Disorder perspective. *Group Analysis*, 40(2), 251–268.

Friedman, R. (2008). Dreamtelling as a request for containment: Three uses of dreams in group therapy. *International Journal of Group Psychotherapy*, 58(3), 327–344.

Friedman, R. (2016) The group sandwich model for international conflict dialog using large groups as a social developmental space. In S. S. Fehr (Ed.), *101 Interventions in group psychotherapy* (pp. 83–85). Routledge.

Friedman, R. (2018) Beyond rejection, glory and the Soldier's Matrix: The heart of my group analysis. *Group Analysis*, 51(4), 1–17.

Friedman, R., & Seidler, C. (2022). Über Beziehungen mit Autoritäten in der Gruppenanalyse. *Gruppenpsychotherapie und Gruppendynamik*, 58, 327–343.

Schlapobersky, J. (1993) The language of the group: Monologue, dialogue and discourse in group analysis. In D. Brown and L. Zinkin *(Eds.), The psyche and the social world: Developments in group analytic theory* (pp. 211–231),Routledge.

Schlapobersky, J. R.(2016). From the couch to the circle. In *The Routledge handbook of group-analytic psychotherapy.* Routledge.

Weinberg, H. (2016). Impossible groups that flourish in "leaking containers": Challenging group analytic theory? *Group Analysis*, 49(4), 330–349.

Weinberg, H., & Weishut, D. J. N. (2012). The large group: Dynamics, social implications and therapeutic value. In J. L. Kleinberg (Ed.) *The Wiley-Blackwell handbook of group psychotherapy* (pp. 457–479). Wiley-Blackwell.

Chapter 9

Interpersonal Group Psychotherapy Conducted Online

Judith Schoenholtz-Read and Ruthellen Josselson

Introduction

Over 50 years ago, Irvin Yalom identified specific therapeutic factors that promote healing in therapy groups. These factors are widely accepted as key characteristics of the mechanisms of change and include instillation of hope, universality, imparting information, altruism, the corrective recapitulation of primary family group, development of socializing techniques, imitative behaviors, interpersonal learning, group cohesiveness, catharsis, and existential factors (Yalom & Leszcz, 2020). This chapter focuses on two central therapeutic factors that we find both essential and challenging in the online environment—interpersonal learning and group cohesion—and highlights how therapists apply the critical therapeutic actions of "working in the here and now," "process illumination," and "activation." Based on our many years of teaching and supervising students and mental health professionals as well as providing therapy in the online environment, we will address the challenges and benefits of interpersonal therapy groups when they take place online.

Interpersonal learning occurs in therapy groups when group members and therapists can explore their emotional-cognitive responses to relationships with others and reflect on these relationships with the goal to better understand members' relational patterns. Group members can provide one another with emotional reactions that lead to new ways of interacting and correct destructive interpersonal responses. For the group to promote healing, it must be cohesive by offering a safe space for members and therapist/s to engage openly, freely, and deeply and in the "here and now" (Yalom & Leszcz, 2005, p. 30).[1]

In online groups, the frame has changed from a physical group space in a room with chairs in a circle to a virtual space with group members appearing on a computer screen in small boxes. It is the phenomenology of the shift in the group frame that intrigues us as it impacts the interpersonal experience and group dynamics of the members and the group therapists. The online group space is not bound by physical space, time

DOI: 10.4324/9781003248606-11

zones, or geography but the relationships that are created in this space are experienced as real and meaningful.

While there is extensive research on online learning and groups, there is limited research on online group therapy (Weinberg, 2020; Gentry et al., 2019). Research on online learning groups finds that the leader's "social presence/copresence" and high levels of interaction with group members increase participants' satisfaction, performance, and feelings of belonging (Isbouts, 2021; McClintock & Stevens-Long, 2020). This is consistent with our clinical experience.

Selecting Group Members

Interpersonal group therapists working online as well as face-to-face seek group members who are interested to learn about themselves and how they are seen by others with the personal goal to change interpersonal patterns that lead to unhappiness. In selecting members for online groups, we hold an individual virtual meeting with prospective members to assess their readiness to join an online group. Importantly, we introduce the interpersonal approach of working in the here and now. Rather than focusing on daily problems, we explain that this group approach uses the group members' reactions to one another and the therapist as a means to learn about members' patterns of engagement in the relational context. In selecting group members, we attempt to include at least some diversity in our membership by inviting people from different geographical regions, gender identities, ages, religions, races, and/or sexual orientations.

The online interview initiates our relationship with each member and provides a sense of their online relatedness. We ask our interviewees about their online experiences and their experience of being with us.

Interviews also focus on the capacity of prospective groups members to participate openly, commit to set meeting times, fee payment schedule, and agreement on group norms. In online groups, due to geographic distances (in most cases), members are encouraged not to contact one another outside the group meetings. If they do make contact, they are asked to inform the group at the next meeting.

The Group Therapist's Attitude and Interpersonal Learning

The therapist's focus is on heightening the interactions among group members and between group members and therapist/s and reflecting on the meaning and dynamics of these interactions. Language, tone of voice, and facial expressions are central to online interactions and present challenges for online therapists. When the group meets in an in-person group space, each person is fully visible to the other members at the same time. But in the online environment, facial expressions are magnified and group members are more likely to notice and comment on others' facial movements. Group members and leader/s can select to see the group as a whole on the screen with each member appearing in a box, or they can select to see the group member who is speaking alone on the screen. We request that group members select to see all members at the same time to ensure that the members experience the online group space as a group container. Group members and therapists can manipulate their screens. For example, some therapists or group members may choose not to see themselves. The online group has the advantage of all members viewing themselves and others simultaneously, but the choices members make about this are also available for reflection.

Group therapists attend to group members' screen presentation. Group members can be seated anywhere in their home or even in their car. They may have the screen close to their face or further away.

> For many weeks, Simone sat in a gloomy room with a stark picture on the wall. As she engaged more openly with the group, she disclosed recent losses. Her feelings of connection to the group were apparent when she suddenly appeared in a brightly lit room. Group members reflected that they felt more welcome in her space. She appreciated their care and attention to her feelings of loss and isolation. Her spirits had lifted as she felt the group connection, and she was ready to appear "in the light."

Members' physical backgrounds are often a form of self-disclosure. Some members appear in front of artworks that they have created or are meaningful to them. Sometimes pets take part. One particularly gruff and angry man would sometimes pet his cat lovingly, giving the group access to his more tender side which people noticed and commented on.

> In one session, a man who had been very giving toward others but asked for nothing for himself was talking about how he couldn't make his needs known in his life either. At that moment, his rather large dog who had been sleeping in his room, woke up and barked. The therapist commented that it seemed that his challenge was to learn to bark more, using the dog's behavior as a kind of interpretation. This metaphor continued through many weeks of the group as he struggled with what and how he could make requests of the group.

Just as in face-to-face groups, all behavior and aspects of the self that are apparent to others constitute material for reflection and understanding. As online interpersonal group therapists seek to develop an interactive and engaging group culture, they are required to be more active observer-participants. They do whatever they can to *feel* and *be* fully present with the group. Silent nodding and reassuring looks by the therapist may not be seen and soft words may not be heard. Therapists have to gauge the impact they are having on the group by considering if and how the members feel their presence and are free to inquire about it. When we call on a member, perhaps one who had been silent, we later ask how they felt about our calling on them. It is essential that therapists are interactive and provide a high level of engagement often by linking members to each other. They may be curious and ask the group how they felt when a member said that they were feeling down. Or they may wonder how a specific member was feeling toward another group member by using their names: "John, what was your reaction to Peter when he said he was afraid to tell Ashley how he felt about her?" Linking members to each other provides support for interpersonal interactions particularly early in the group process when members may be reluctant to respond in the moment to each other's emotional states.

The online setting allows members to watch particular members in detail without their "staring" being noticed as it would be if the group were meeting in-person.

"I was looking at you as Tom was speaking," Linda said to Jane, "and you had an odd smile that would sometimes become a grimace. I wondered what you were feeling." Jane was surprised that her reaction was so closely monitored by Linda and this became a site of investigation. Linda reflected that she feels emotionally out of touch with Jane and was trying to find her at a deeper level. Jane acknowledged that what Tom was sharing was touching old memories that she wasn't sure she wanted to share with the group. In the next session, she did just this and opened painful parts of her history that she had kept away from the group. The therapist, who was trying to look at all the members equally and whose attention was mainly focused on Tom in the previous session, felt grateful that the online setting allowed for the subtleties of member reactions to be noticed.

While in the face-to-face group these slight, often unconscious reactions may be communicated in body language, in the online group the face is highlighted and members learn to "read" each other's facial movements. While direct eye contact is impossible, members are aware of each other's eyes.

The therapist was surprised when Betty told Marvin that he doesn't look at them when he speaks, his gaze is usually directed away from his camera when he talks. Marvin was aware of this and his fear of how others might be reacting to him. Therefore, he looked away, talking to no one. This was perhaps the online equivalent of looking at the floor instead of the group in a face-to-face group and it could be noticed in the online setting.

The therapist can also inquire of a speaking member who they were looking at as they spoke. These are among the adaptations to the therapists' attending attitude that is needed to highlight the interpersonal experience online.

Enhancing Group Cohesion

Group cohesion relates to the importance of the group to its members, and regular attendance is a crucial part of this. Frequent absence and lateness are anathema to group cohesion. One of the benefits of the online group is that there are far fewer absences than in face-to-face groups. Because people can log on from anywhere, people can join even if they are on vacation or on business trips or are mildly ill. In an open-ended group that one of us conducted over a period of three years with eight members, there were very few absences. Group members came to group with the expectation of seeing all the others each time and were very reluctant to have to miss the group for fear of missing something important. The group time became a meaningful and reliable therapeutic space.

Regular attendance is required because the online space may feel somewhat fragile. A member of a long-term online therapy group went into a kind of panic when he, unaware of the change to daylight time, logged on to find no one there. This led to discussion of what would happen if the therapist were to die—their space, he felt, would be obliterated and he would lose all the relationships. This led to reflection and meaning-making about both the solidity and the tenuousness of all relationships. Similarly, technological problems can interfere with the consistency of the online space and this, too, can be processed.

Interpersonal group therapists encourage here and now responses, particularly self-disclosure statements, and they work to shift the power to the group to observe itself (process illumination). In the early group, the interpersonal therapist focuses on the group members' anxieties about joining and their efforts to figure out how to engage with one another. Although the online group's efforts in early group formation have similarities to face-to-face groups, we have noticed that there are challenges for therapists and group members.

In the first group meeting the online therapist begins by asking a group-level question: "let us know your hopes for this group and how you feel being here." Mark jumps in with his wish for the group to be a caring and warm place. He speaks with some urgency. His wish is echoed by others. Roxanne, William, and Robin speak to their loneliness and need for a safe group space. The therapist reflects on their desire to find a way to feel connected and safe with one another. Joan lets the group know she feels pulled away with thoughts about events outside the group. Aron echoes Joan. The issue of how to stay present in the moment is articulated. Powerful images flood the group. William presents an image of walking down a lonely trail anticipating a bear attack. Encouraged to respond to the image, others associate with images of good bears huddled in a cave around a fire. The issue of good and bad bears and how to find safety emerges. The therapist associates the cave with the computer and the vulnerability of being online suspended in space. How can there be security when we cannot touch each other? When the computer can be shut off? Other metaphors of safety and vulnerability emerge. Roger imagines a beach where he builds a castle and the tide washes it away—fears of impermanence emerge. Group members begin to respond directly to each other and join with feelings of isolation and need for connection in their lives. Perhaps the most powerful image comes at the end of the first meeting with the song "Wichita Lineman."

I am a lineman for the county
And I drive the main road
Searchin' in the sun for another overload ...
[Chorus] And I need you more than want you
And I want you for all time
And the Wichita lineman
Is still on the line.

The therapist observes that the song reflects the group's ambivalence about loving and being loved and cared for. The "line" is fragile as is the virtual world on the computer screen. The tenuous nature of the virtual group space has been made explicit. The therapist lets the group know that we are off to a good start. We viewed the Wichita lineman as a metaphor for the group beginning to work together towards online group cohesion.

The interpersonal group differs from real-life social situations by encouraging interpersonal feedback from group members about social behaviors. A group member may ask another: "how did I just come across to you?" Or they might state directly, "I felt that you did not hear me the last time I spoke to you." "You look away every time you are angry with Joan."

In the early meetings of an online process training therapy group, the therapist asks the group to imagine that the group is face-to-face sitting in a circle and to talk about where they would sit and who they would sit next to. Group members quickly engage with the circle image and began to use the image during the course of the group. Jack did not sit in the group but found a place outside so he could observe. Alan wanted to sit near Susan but was fearful that she would see him as coming on to her. Group members' associations with the circle image continued to be important as the group developed and revealed repeating themes of whether the member felt inside or outside the group as well as fears of sexuality. Little mention of the therapists was notable. At the same time group members begin to navigate how to take up group "space" when many felt they lacked space growing up. Amanda noticed that she wanted others to invite her in. With the anxieties around participation made explicit, some group members began to make reference to growing up in their families of origin where they hid emotions to survive. A subgroup of members who felt neglected and guilty about taking group time emerged. As members' stories of neglect and abandonment continued, their tears and deep sadness were brought into the group. The group therapist asked, "how do we express compassion in this medium?" Members began to use their imagination: "I would like to touch your hand."

As the disclosures increased connection between members, capacity for confrontation also increased.

Sally tells Charlene that she tends to talk in generalities and finds it hard to connect and know what she is really feeling. Charlene says that her friends say the same thing. She begins to tear up as she reveals her history of despair and fear that her deep feelings would send her into "outer space." She continues to disclose that her mother was fragile and unpredictable and that she learned to override her emotions with laughter and intellectual distractions. In social groups, she withdrew and feared taking up space. This story resonated with three other group members who reached toward Charlene. The theme of maternal neglect continued with a devastating image described by Roy. He felt that his mother imprisoned him in a medieval torture chamber—an iron maiden, where he could not breathe or move. He felt emasculated.

The need for safety in face of parental, particularly maternal, abuse was palpable. As therapists, we were attuned to the issue of safety as expressed in the maternal iron maiden metaphor that women were dangerous. Given that we were two female therapists, we recognized their implicit fear that we would not protect them. We gave voice to members' anxiety and acknowledged that we heard them. We were aware that the online group process was similar to face-to-face groups in the depth of emotional expression and transference relationships between group members and therapists. Meaningful emotional work that includes all the members enhances group cohesion.

Working with Therapist Transference and Transparency

The interpersonal approach encourages careful use of therapist transparency. By pointing out the research on therapist openness, Yalom and Leszcz (2005 highlight that higher levels of group openness enhance the autonomy and power of the group members.

> From the beginning of a co-led process group, the therapists' first and last names appeared on the screen. As requested, the group members' first names only appeared. In about the 10th meeting, some group members noticed that the cotherapists posted their full names and confronted us. Some members felt that this demonstrated our power/authority position and Steve was particularly resentful about this. The following week, Steve said he felt ignored by the group therapists when he raised the issue and the therapists once again posted their full names. One of the therapists told him she appreciated his sharing his feelings about this and that issues of power and authority were very much open for discussion. She further acknowledged that posting her full name did mark her different role in the group. The other therapist remarked that Steve's sharing his feeling of "being put down" by the therapist and his ability to confront her was a significant therapeutic step for him. Steve's disclosure and the therapists' welcoming of the criticism opened the door for other group members' feelings toward the therapists. Rachel disclosed that a few weeks earlier she posted her full name in her screen box but no one in the group noticed. This highlighted Rachel's feeling of not being seen. Some members wondered if they didn't want to notice Rachel "joining" the therapists and a discussion ensued about who wanted what kind of special response from the therapists. Steve then talked about his lifelong feelings of not "measuring up" and his sensitivity to slights. This then led the group to discussing feelings of inadequacy and shame. Rachel then said that she thinks that posting her full name was a rebellion against the therapists' rules about posting only first names. The therapist then spoke directly to Rachel about how she feels closer to her when she comes out of the shadows. She told Rachel that she had felt her silent rebellion and was glad it had come into the open.

Working in the Here and Now: Applying Process Illumination

In addition to focusing on individual members' interactions with each other in the here and now, therapists focus on the group's progress by observing and reflecting on the process that underlies the meaning of members' interactions with each other and the therapist. Yalom considers the process of "illumination" to be critical for building group cohesion and healing Iom & Leszcz, 2005. We understood the following session to highlight process illumination as group members struggled about how they were "seen" by others in a way that was particularly relevant to the online setting—how do I see myself and how do group members and therapists see me? The visual imagery of "being seen" takes special meaning in online groups due to the limited visual presence.

> After mentioning an attraction to Ellie, one of the female members, in the next meeting Ryan told the group about his fantasy that he "saw" group members naked and that Ellie offered him a coat. Ryan felt ashamed of his attraction and his erotic desires. The fears associated with sexual desire were echoed in other group members. In particular, Oscar shared his self-hatred toward being a cis-man. He associated his manhood with violence, particularly violence toward women, and had long disowned his assigned gender. When asked how others in the group "saw" him, he was seen as quite traditionally "manly" by group members.

Through the illumination process, he began to sort out the cultural dimensions of masculinity and accept his own aggressive impulses. How he was "seen" by others gave him a safe space to begin to change his self-image and find some comfort in the exploration of his assigned gender.

As group cohesion deepens, the need to be seen by others increases. Tellingly, in one group that was moving into a different stage of work, the group spoke of a need to know how tall each member was—height is one dimension that is hidden online. The group then worked on how knowing each other's height changed their experience of one another. This was particularly true for the men.

One group took advantage of the online environment which is connected to their computers when one member chose to express how she saw each of us by making a power point of animals that she felt each person represented. By sharing her screen, she showed each member in an animal pose which led first to laughter and playfulness and then serious consideration of how each person had behaved in the group. Who was the lion, holding the aggression, and who the koala bear, asking to be cuddled?

The online environment has subtle but profound effects on group members' longing for contact.

> In an online group that had been meeting for 18 months, the topic arose about having an in-person meeting which the therapist agreed to. As people were coming from long distances, it was set several months ahead. As the meeting dates were firmed up, fantasies about what it would be like to meet in person were available and a source of rich material. The question "will we hug one another?" led to fantasies about who were the "huggers" in the group. It was not clear why the group unanimously named Carl as the "hugger" although he agreed that he was indeed a hugger. Jill was somewhat insulted because she sees herself as a "major hugger" but no one seemed to sense this about her. Nancy avowed that she hates hugging because it is so wooden and false in both her family and her in-law family, but, she realized, she would like to hug the members of the group because she feels known by them—with the exception of Margie, the newest member who she doesn't feel she knows well enough to hug. All of this, of course, becomes grist for the mill as members can explore their fantasies about one another and their position with each one. This exploration also led to feelings about touching and being touched which was particularly meaningful as many of the members had histories of abuse. For these members, the online environment offered a layer of protection—no one could physically harm them. For other members, the online environment connoted the sterility and absence of physical affection they had felt in their families.

In our experience, the biggest hurdle in the online setting is the loss of eye contact. A meeting of the eyes conveys so much about emotion and the status of the relationship between people. Who is looking at who and whose eyes are smiling at who? Who is avoiding eye contact with particular others? There are no "knowing glances" of affective sharing.

> In the 30th week on an open-ended therapy group, one member expressed anger that in the previous session everyone had been saying bad things about him. He was particularly angry at the therapist for not intervening. The therapist said she hadn't noticed that people were saying bad things about him and the member exploded and logged out of the session. In the next session, the therapist looked at him for signs of whether he had cooled down, but while she could have had a reading of this in a face-to-face group, the lack of eye contact meant that she had to seek him out with words. She could not communicate her concern and care with her eyes alone or get a sense of where he might be emotionally until one or the other of them spoke.

Similarly, when members make comments about how they are feeling, we cannot see who they are looking at and have to ask. Communicating empathy and compassion is similarly more challenging, especially when people share painful experiences. Silence in response can have an empathic texture when people are physically present but can feel simply unresponsive unless put into words in the online space.

Absent the usual social cues that mark connection in person, the group will find its own rhythm and vocabulary to create it online. The therapist must remain attentive to these efforts as part of process illumination.

Conclusion: Tips for Enhancing Online Interpersonal Group Therapy

Online interpersonal group therapists, in common with other group therapists who work online, find the demands of listening and observing very challenging compared to face-to-face groups. Group therapists will need to attend to their feelings of fatigue related to intense listening and visual demands while looking at a screen, feelings of disconnection, and technological frustrations related to working online. They may miss the in-person context and find themselves longing for more physical contact. There is a "sense" of a person we take in when we are together in person that we have to rely on other senses to fill in when we are online—and this may never be as robust as when we are physically together. But we can know enough of each other online to be therapeutically useful. We hear from our online group patients how much they have changed from their experiences in the group, particularly about their growing courage to express themselves, a lessening of their fears of conflict and growth in empathy for others which affects their real-life relationships. Meaningful bonds form, and one of our long-term groups is getting to be very long term with a fairly stable membership.

Working in the here and now online requires interventions that stimulate group interactions and feedback among group members. Therapists need to be more creative and active to build relationships with individual members and between members and be highly sensitive to the visual limits of the online environment.

Therapists are encouraged to inquire about group members' experiences of being together online. Specifically, we find that group members' fantasies and metaphors related to being online vs being face-to-face need to be attended to and explored. We found that group members find ways to imagine being physically together in the metaphors that emerge during the group process.

In general, we find more similarities than differences in working online and value the opportunity to serve a broad range of clients who otherwise would not be able to access group therapy.

Note

1   Although there is a later edition of this text, the quotations in this chapter refer to the fifth edition.

References

Gentry, M. T., Lapid, M. I., Clark, M. M., & Rummans, T. A. (2019). Evidence for telehealth group based treatment: A systematic review. *Journal of Telemedicine and Telecare*, 25, 327–342. http://dx.doi.org/10.1177/1357633X18775855.

Isbouts, J. P. (2021). Student perspectives on online learning experiences. In K. E. Rudestam, J. Schoenholtz-Read, & M. L. Snowden (Eds.), *Handbook of online learning in higher education* (pp. 330–360). Fielding University Press.

McClintock, C., & Stevens-Long, J. (2020). The theory and practice of learner-centered online graduate education. In K. E. Rudestam, J. Schoenholtz-Read, & M. L. Snowden (Eds.). *Handbook of online learning in higher education* (pp. 135–155).

Yalom, I. D., & Leszcz, M. (2005). *The theory and practice of group psychotherapy* (5th ed.). Basic Books.

Yalom, I. D., & Leszcz, M. (2020). *The theory and practice of group psychotherapy* (6th ed.). Basic Books.

Weinberg, H. (2020). Online group psychotherapy: Challenges and possibilities during COVID-19—A practice review. *Group Dynamics: Theory, Research, and Practice*, 24(3), 201–211. http://dx.doi.org/10.1037/gdn0000.

Chapter 10

Systems-Centered Therapy and Training[1] Groups Online

Adapting to the Driving and Restraining Forces in an Online Context

Susan P. Gantt[2]

In March 2020, I quickly discovered that an office that had felt comfortably big enough for my psychotherapy groups for 30-plus years was suddenly too small. As was the case for many of us following the outbreak of the COVID-19 pandemic, my groups which had always met in-person were disrupted. It no longer felt safe to me or group members to meet face-to-face with the pandemic in full force. So as quickly as possible, I signed up for a secure video platform that met confidentiality and security requirements and online meetings became the context for all my psychotherapy and training groups. To this day I continue to meet online with many of my groups.

Overview of Systems-Centered Therapy and Training (SCT) Groups

All the groups I lead are from an SCT orientation. SCT was developed by Yvonne Agazarian (Agazarian & Peters, 1981) in the 1980s and 1990s as she put her theory of living human systems (TLHS) into practice by operationally defining each theoretical construct as a method to guide practice (Agazarian, 1997; Agazarian et al., 2021). As SCT guides my group leadership (Gantt & Agazarian, 2017), I relied on its theory to consider how I and my groups would adapt to online work, thinking theoretically as we experimented with our practical adaptations.

Briefly, looking at a therapy group through the lens of TLHS and its SCT application starts by seeing the group as a living human system in a quasi-stationary equilibrium that can be defined by driving forces oriented to development and restraining forces oriented to survival. SCT (Agazarian, 1997) has defined a set of protocols that modify the predictable restraining forces in each phase of group development in order to free the driving forces toward development. Weakening restraining forces also changes the equilibrium in the group system (and its members) toward more development. Each of SCT's protocols and interventions put theory into practice by implementing one of the four basic methods of *contextualizing, boundarying, vectoring* and *functional subgrouping*.

DOI: 10.4324/9781003248606-12

Contextualizing

Contextualizing interventions orient to seeing oneself in context and as a voice for the group or a subgroup of the group rather than personalizing one's experience, e.g., as we began meeting online, reminding group members that everyone gets anxious in the unknown, and that our meeting online was new and unknown for all of us and remembering to be curious in this unknown would likely make it easier. It was also very useful to normalize for the group (and myself) our anxiety about COVID-19 as a predictable response to being in the unknown.

Boundarying

Boundarying interventions relate to structure and influence the permeability of system boundaries in time, space and reality. For example, weakening ambiguity by asking for specificity opens the boundary for reality-testing, e.g., when a group member talks vaguely about not being sure they will make it if they have to stay home all the time. By asking them to be specific, the member's (and the group's) boundaries open to exploring in the here-and-now to identify in reality how they are "making it" and how they are not, and what helps them make it (driving forces) and what gets in the way (restraining forces).

Vectoring

Vectoring interventions introduce the idea of a "fork-in-the-road." Group members are asked to choose which fork to explore: the fork of their restraining force or their driving force. For many SCT groups during the early phases of the COVID-19 pandemic, a common fork-in-the-road was between "hating being online" versus "discovering" how to work online together effectively. Recognizing this fork enabled the group to explore each fork separately, one at a time by using functional subgrouping.

Functional Subgrouping

All SCT groups use functional subgrouping (Agazarian, 1997; Gantt, 2011; Gantt & Agazarian, 2010, 2011) which establishes the norm of separating differences into two different subgroups: in the above example, those curious about their "hate" explored together in one subgroup, and those with energy for "discovering" how to work online worked in another subgroup. First one subgroup worked, then the other. After both subgroups explored, the group integrated its differences by recognizing with delight the paradox of discovering how to work effectively online to explore their hatred of working online! The group was pleased with its first mastery of adapting functional subgrouping online. Functional sub-grouping is the heart of SCT and enables differences to be explored and integrated rather than stereotyped or scapegoated. All living human systems have both the goal of surviving (staying with the known) by closing to differences as well as the goal of developing by integrating differences as the essential resource for group development.

The remainder of this chapter describes and illustrates how I and my SCT groups discovered how to work with the modifications that online work required for us. I used SCT theory to guide our adaptations and my leadership in this new online context as we learned to apply each of the four SCT methods (contextualizing, boundarying, vectoring and functional subgrouping). Together, we discovered both the driving forces of meeting online and the restraining forces. And as we continued, I discovered more and more about how to weaken the restraining forces of working online by finding new ways of implementing SCT theory in practice which freed us all to explore and use the driving forces that online groups enabled.

Working with Boundaries and Structure Online

Right away, shifting from in-person to online required rethinking how to work with the group boundaries. In SCT, boundaries are structure, essential for containing group energy. As SCT leaders, we do our human best to start and stop on time. The rapid shift to online groups introduced new structures and also meant the loss of familiar ones.

First, my groups no longer gathered in my waiting room prior to group starting. The groups missed this informal time initially. It was also apparent that several members discovered a new freedom from repeating their interpersonal past in the online group context. They described feeling freer of their old protective survivor roles and more able to participate as here-and-now members. It may be that seeing themselves online enabled observing rather than enacting survivor roles. Another hypothesis is that with the online context, without the waiting room social interactions prior to the group, it lowered the implicit past roles that were triggered before group started, making it easier to work with each other in the here-and-now work of the group.

Managing the online challenges in our new structure started as soon as the group started: we all spontaneously helped each other to adjust to online work, with simple reminders to each other to turn on our cameras and unmute when we noticed a mouth moving without hearing sound or to adjust our lighting so our faces were easier to see. There was and still is a camaraderie in the groups mastering the online context together.

It was also helpful to establish norms that supported the context of a psychotherapy group online while still maintaining norms of practice. For example, in my therapy groups, each person was asked to change their name to first name only to maintain confidentiality.[3] I also asked group members to unmute unless there was background noise. Though this was counter to what many participants knew from work meetings, this norm supported greater spontaneity in the group without the delay of turning on a mic. This has worked well in our SCT psychotherapy groups and even in our large SCT training groups of 80–90 members. Both are examples of setting structure to support function—a key theoretical principle in SCT. Similarly, letting the group know that ensuring the privacy boundary was a responsibility for each of us, to support the group's confidentiality and secure boundary for working. The group explored together how they were ensuring the group boundary online. This proved useful as members recognized their responsibility for maintaining the group boundary in the here-and-now. This was a shift from cooperation with the boundaries I had set in my office to the group's recognizing realization that aspects of the boundary online can only be maintained by the group members. My leadership here vectored the group to taking up the role that each of us had to ensure the group boundary and reminding the group of the importance of the boundary for safety, freedom to explore and to maintain each other's confidentiality. Introducing how maintaining the boundary was different online for the group was relatively easily integrated by my groups, quite possibly because they were very familiar with time boundaries and space boundaries being clearly established in our in-person work. In fact, rather quickly in our first online meetings, the groups began subgrouping together to explore and tell each other what each was doing to protect the boundary. For example, one member reported that her partner walked across the room once while we were meeting but could not see the screen nor hear as she was wearing earphones. Another member told us about his wife being home and having tested to make sure she could not hear the group. Someone else chimed in, "I am home alone so there won't be any interruption." The group also helped each other to learn settings to reduce background noise. Members taught each other how to turn off self-view for those who wanted to (most did) as it felt more normal not to see one's self.

SCT leaders do their human best to start and stop on time as both time and space boundaries contain the group energy for work. To this end, the leader begins the group by saying, "We are crossing our time boundary." SCT groups then start with *centering* with its goal of connecting to one's inner-person energy and then crossing the boundary into one's inter-person role as a group member with other group members in the here-and-now. In the centering process, the leader often paces the group: orienting members to connect to their bodies, their energy, their breathing, the support of the earth, the universal energy, and then bringing their energy into group membership.

By centering we can calm the chattering that goes on in our brain and free ourselves from distracting thoughts. We become mindful. When we are centered, we can sit at the edge of the unknown with curiosity, explore our experience, comprehend as well as apprehend our context, turn on our researcher and observe and be aware of ourselves, our roles, and our history in context.

(Agazarian, 2011, p. 6)

It turned out that centering itself was easily done online. What was more of a challenge was to adapt what in-person SCT groups do at the end of the centering process when members transition from connecting to themselves to connecting to others. At the end of centering with in-person groups, SCT leaders say,

From our connection with our energy and our own center where we know without words, open our eyes, take in the whole of the group each of us is part of, and then look around in roving eye contact[4] coming into contact member to member in this here-and-now moment.

Online, we quickly realized that "real" eye contact as we had known it, where I see your eyes and you see mine and I see you seeing me and you see me seeing you, is not actually possible in reality in online groups. Acknowledging this reality helped us to grieve for what we no longer had and enabled us over time to find ways to compensate for this loss.

Similarly, I found myself feeling resistant to an occasional request from a member to look at the camera, as members explained to me that they wanted to "feel" I was in eye contact with them. This seemed a violation of our reality and a flight from our online reality. Later I realized that the "want to feel" that I was in eye contact with them was the essential experience to explore. Rather than reacting to the implicit demand, I asked them to see who else felt similarly and explore the feeling of this "wanting" in a subgroup with others. This was vitally important for all my groups and especially so for those working in the intimacy phase of group development. This was an especially important learning for me as I recognized how easily in the new online context I could respond or react to logistical challenges and miss the underlying dynamic that the request for me to look at the camera contained as a group voice.

Over time, we began to explore different ways that the lack of real eye contact could be managed. For a while, at the end of centering, I asked members to connect with their own energy with an intention to bring this in as they looked around the group and took in the faces of other members. Some time later, we experimented with another strategy that emerged as we worked with the SCT method for crossing boundaries into the group, called "undoing distractions."

Undoing Distractions to Cross the Time and Space Boundaries[5] into the Here-and-Now

SCT groups explore experience in the here-and-now, hypothesizing that change happens in the present when we open our boundaries to discover what we do not know, and learn to live in the unknown rather than reciting the past which keeps us out of the present. After centering, SCT leaders say, "Let the group know if you are here, let me know if you have a distraction keeping your energy out of the group, or let us all know if you have news to bring in." The leader works with anyone who is distracted by asking the member to state the bare bones facts of their distraction, and the feeling about each fact (Agazarian, 1997):

MEMBER: My fact is my mother is getting worse.
LEADER: Can you be specific about what getting worse means?

[Using *boundarying* to lower ambiguity]

MEMBER: She can no longer be left alone because she does not remember where she is and she gets frightened.
LEADER: Is there a specific that happened recently that is distracting you from being here?
MEMBER: Yesterday, she wandered outside. My father couldn't find her for an hour.
LEADER: So first your mother wandered outside. In this moment, how do you feel about that fact?
MEMBER: Sad.
LEADER: Your second fact, your father could not find her. How do you feel right now about that fact?
MEMBER: More sad.
LEADER: Any other facts about yesterday?
MEMBER: No.
LEADER: Connect to your sadness, look around making eye contact with each of us with your sadness so you can be here with it and we can hold sadness with you.[6]

Crossing the boundary into the present and making eye contact with others moves us toward resonant experience with ourselves and others. Once again, I (and we) were faced with the problem of how to accomplish online what we did in-person with resonant eye contact. It took me some months to see how best to work with the challenge that there is no real eye contact as we know it when we are online (Armington et al., 2020), very different from being in-person. Experimenting, I asked the member to name her feeling as she called each of us by name. When she came to me, I nodded, saying, "I'm getting your sadness" or "holding it with you." Members experimented too, nodding or saying "yes" or attuned paraphrasing her word "sadness." I changed my leadership vector to say: "Name and bring your feeling into relationship with each of us, call us by name so we can hold it with you and you can be fully here with it." The groups quickly integrated this and liked the increased sense of contact it enabled.

Solving this problem in the online context enabled us to see how to modify our online centering process too, from the in-person version of looking around and making roving eye contact with the group to one of calling each person's name as one came into contact with them. Spontaneously the group began also to nod or give a short verbal response that reflected seeing the other. This enabled each to have some experience of the other with them in that moment. Finding how to use words to translate what was previously communicated nonverbally has been useful. It has also raised questions for me about what we do lose when we do not have the same access to the wordless contact that touches us all at deeper levels: whether this wordless contact is through our eyes or the sense of being with and sensing other bodies who also sense our bodies. Online work does limit our sense experience and our sensorial knowing of others and of ourselves in our sensory resonance with others, a significant restraining force. At the same time, the online adaptations do work and enable work to happen—an important driving force. One member's voice about this captures hers and others' experience of the driving forces:

> I enjoy our SCT group online. Connection is different than in-person, yet still as meaningful. I have felt close to those who bring their fears, joys and tears to our group and sometimes wonder if the connection is deeper because each of us is home, where we feel comfortable and at ease. I like seeing the homes of group members in the background.
>
> Although most of what I see on screen are faces of group members, I can see their expressions easily enough; and enough of their body or posture to sense their presence and feelings. I hear the tones of their voices and know if someone is angry, enthusiastic, excited or quiet. I do not find that the online format diminishes the connection or the experience of our meeting.

This leads to how we have adapted functional subgrouping to online work and the challenges in doing so, the losses and the gains.

Functional Subgrouping

Functional subgrouping, the core SCT method, operationally defines how living human systems survive, develop and transform (Agazarian, 1997) by discriminating and integrating differences. In practice, when anyone finishes speaking, they invite others to join by saying, "Anyone else?" The next person to speak reflects the previous speaker and then adds something similar from themselves. This continues until someone says, "I have a difference" and asks if the group is ready for a difference (Agazarian et al., 2021; Gantt & Agazarian, 2017). As functional subgrouping is the heart of every SCT group, both therapy and training groups, adaptations for online work were crucial. My previous experience of teaching SCT online helped yet I was still stepping into the unknown. The excerpt below describes how at the start of the COVID-19 pandemic we used functional subgrouping online in a training context:

> After an in-person conference was cancelled, a large systems-centered group of 75 people who had been planning to be together in the conference worked together via video conferencing software. In our first meeting, the group worked to lower anxiety with each person first naming their anxiety-provoking thoughts and, in turn, the next person speaking, reflecting what the previous speaking person had said and then adding their own anxiety-provoking thought. This process of reflecting [the first step in functional subgrouping] built a here-and-now connection and activated ventral vagal relating (Gantt & Badenoch, 2020). Midway through, several members predicted that they were going to feel worse after the group instead of better. Yet as the work continued and each member's anxiety was reflected, the anxiety eased as the reflections provided the co-regulation so vital for all of us as humans, helping to lower the anxiety for the whole group. By the end, the whole group felt better able to live in the multiple unknowns that had been named, and had compassion for the human pull to the negative predictions that activated the sympathetic arousal.
>
> A month later, this same large group met again and very quickly began exploring the frustration and irritation with working online, initially focusing on the lack of connection in this platform and their frustration about this. As this frustrated subgroup worked together, reflecting each other and building, they were co-regulating the sympathetic activation brought on by their frustration and experiencing connection with each other. This led to recognizing a fork between exploring frustration about what was not possible or exploring how to have more of what one could in the online context. The latter subgroup then began working and movingly explored reaching out with their hands toward each other to feel more of the connection [much of the screen was filled with hands for some moments rather than faces]. There was tenderness and warmth in these gestures, and the whole subgroup exploring this was quite touched.
>
> (Armington et al., 2020, p. 13)

Though online work using functional subgrouping was highly effective, absence of eye contact did impact subgrouping, e.g., members felt less connected without it, especially in intimacy phase work. Still, as a colleague noted, group members and leaders got better at listening to the voice tone and energy to get a sense of connection.

For in-person groups when one subgroup holds a difference while another subgroup works, the "holding" subgroup stays in roving eye contact with each other to contain their difference together, which is much easier than holding it alone. We experimented with how to work with this challenge online. At times, we asked those holding a difference to raise their mechanical hand (a feature available on some online platforms that moves these faces to the top of the screen). All those holding the difference were then next to each other on the screen and more easily felt a sense of being together holding their difference. For the working subgroup, we also tried "pinning" members that were in the working subgroup. Pinning enlarges the images of those who are pinned and these enlarged images increase the nonverbal information available. Pinning seemed to increase a sense of connection with members reporting feeling more connected when talking with others who were pinned. It did take some time initially for group members to learn to use these functions, though mostly these functions were easily mastered. Now members spontaneously say, "I'm pinning you to see you better." This use of online capabilities has been more difficult in those therapy groups where members are using their phones. Several members voiced how using a computer helped in seeing and feeling more in contact. On the nontechnical side, group members were helped by reminders to scan faces during the group to replicate the roving eye contact that in-person SCT groups use, making it less likely to talk over each other.

Going Forward

In asking SCT group members and colleagues about their experiences working online in SCT, their feedback was varied:

> "Virtual group is much more valuable than I had negatively predicted when we got started."
>
> "It was a great relief to be able to meet and there were frustrations in the online experience."
>
> "Online has been especially challenging for patients that have trouble being 'behind their eyes' and where learning to make eye contact is vital."
>
> "Online has allowed severely ill members to continue to attend group, including a member who was close to death and wanted to be with his group."

"It is harder for some group members to stay engaged online, they are more distracted by texting and pulled more into themselves."

"Volatile couples have been more contained online than in-person as each worked on their own computer."

"Liking the one-minute commute to group."

In conclusion, working in online groups has been invaluable in this time of COVID-19 and has been sustaining for many of us to maintain connection and contact. Group members who have relocated have still been able to attend group. Learning that we can work effectively in SCT training groups online has opened new doors for us, e.g., people from all over the world have joined online SCT training groups, most of whom would not have access to SCT training otherwise.

Having learned that SCT groups can work online, we are now facing other questions, e.g., when is online preferable (certainly it lowers climate cost compared to in-person groups) and when is the loss of the in-person contact too costly to members or the goal of the group? These, of course, are ongoing discussions not only for us in SCT but for all of us as we continue to explore the driving and restraining forces for working online or in-person or in hybrid options in various formats in relationship to our goals and context, and continue to experiment with how to weaken the restraining forces in each of these contexts.

Notes

1 SCT® and Systems-Centered® are registered trademarks of the Systems-Centered Training and Research Institute, Inc., a non-profit organization.
2 Much appreciation to my colleagues Claudia Byram, Nina Klebanoff and Katherine Straznickas and my group members for their inputs and as always to Kathy Lum for her editing, support and inputs.
3 One of my group members shared with the group that he regularly signed out of his Zoom account that he used for work so that his full name and work context were not visible to the group, preserving the confidentiality boundary of the therapy group.
4 Roving eye contact is usually very settling to our human nervous systems. Roving eye contact is defined as catching someone's eyes for a moment or two, different than gazing into another's eyes which can be a driving force in intimacy or a flight into pairing rather than subgrouping.
5 "Goal: Crossing boundaries in time and space into the systems-centered member role. Survival, development and transformation of oneself as a system depend upon the flow of energy-information between oneself, others and the social context" (Agazarian, 2011, p. 11).
6 The final step is the research question, "Are you more here, less here or the same?"

References

Agazarian, Y. M. (1997). *Systems-centered therapy for groups*. Guilford. (Reprinted in paperback by Karnac Books 2004.)

Agazarian, Y. M. (2011). *Systems-centered core skills*. Good Enough Press.

Agazarian, Y. M., Gantt, S. P., & Carter, F. (Eds.) (2021). *Systems-centered training: An illustrated guide for applying a theory of living human systems*. Routledge.

Agazarian, Y. M., & Peters, R. (1981). *The visible and invisible group*. Routledge & Kegan Paul. (Reprinted in paperback by Karnac Books 1995.)

Armington, R., Badenoch, B., & Gantt, S. P. (2020). Zooming along in the pandemic and beyond. *Systems-Centered News*, 28(2), 12–16.

Gantt, S. P. (2011). Functional subgrouping and the systems-centered approach to group therapy. In J. Kleinberg (Ed.), *The Wiley-Blackwell handbook of group psychotherapy* (pp. 113–138). Wiley.

Gantt, S. P., & Agazarian, Y. M. (2010). Developing the group mind through functional subgrouping: Linking systems-centered training (SCT) and interpersonal neurobiology. *International Journal of Group Psychotherapy*, 60(4), 515–544. doi:10.1521/ijgp.2010.60.4.515.

Gantt, S. P., & Agazarian, Y. M. (2011). The group mind, systems-centred functional subgrouping, and interpersonal neurobiology. In E. Hopper & H. Weinberg (Eds.), *The social unconscious in persons, groups, and societies*. Vol. 1: *Mainly theory* (pp. 99–123). Karnac Books.

Gantt, S. P., & Agazarian, Y. M. (2017). Systems-centered group therapy. *International Journal of Group Psychotherapy*, 67(sup1), S60–S70. doi:10.1080/00207284.2016.1218768.

Gantt, S. P. & Badenoch, B. (2020). Systems-centered group psychotherapy: Developing a group mind that supports right brain function and right-left-right hemispheric integration. In R. Tweedy (Ed.) *The divided therapist: Hemispheric difference and contemporary psychotherapy* (pp. 149–180). Routledge.

Chapter 11

Online Large Groups in Times of Social Turmoil

Helping Individuals and Communities to Work Through Pandemics and Wars

Gila Ofer, Uri Levin and Stavros Charalambides

Introduction

Many theories about large group (LG) dynamics emphasize the chaotic-aggressive, near-psychotic character of the LG, as well as the differences between the seemingly "benign" small group and the "destructive" LG (Freud, 1921; Hopper, 2003; Kreeger, 1975). LGs tend to be regressive, defensive, unexpected, chaotic, and overwhelming. Primitive mechanisms, such as projection, projective identification, and splitting, serve as primary defenses against intense anxieties. Sub-grouping, glorification, and devaluation frequently lead to paranoia, conflicts, or even "wars" over resources (e.g., the demand to translate the communication to other languages in addition to a conference's official language). The primary purpose of such LGs, as Schneider and Weinberg (2003) noted, is to "utilize the large group experience as a laboratory in which to study large group processes, both conscious and unconscious, as a way of understanding their impact and influence upon social, organizational and systemic thinking, feelings and actions" (p. 17).

In a "typical" LG, the atmosphere might be overwhelming and confusing, and finding one's voice becomes difficult, even impossible, for many. Weinberg and Weishut (2012) write that:

> The individual might be lost in the crowd, drawing no response at all, which can become a narcissistic blow for the person who dares to speak ... it is challenging to think clearly in this setting, and not easy to make sense of the experience ... [the] unstable participation in the group sessions enhances regression and evokes fragmentation anxieties.
>
> (p. 458)

They go on relating to the difficulties that individuals, especially during their first LG experiences, encounter:

DOI: 10.4324/9781003248606-13

The large group is not a small group ... sometimes a member brings in a personal problem believing that she will get feedback or a personal response ... [and] she may be very disappointed when the large group fails to act like a small group ... the focus of the leader is not on the individual but on the group-as-a-whole ... it lacks the setting, the boundaries and the rules that usually characterize therapy.

(p. 461)

It is hard to imagine that such an experience might provide therapeutic value for its participants. However, group therapists relate also to the LG's therapeutic side, underlying its creative-constructive potential. This perspective focuses on promoting this potential and on the importance of communication and dialogue among participants and between participants and the conductor(s). The analytic attitude and intervention technique changes from the traditionally strict neutrality, anonymity, and abstinence, as well as from the emphasis on whole-group interpretations, to encouragement of dialogue and of using the conductor's subjectivity to promote the analytic process.

De Maré (1975) stated that "only in the larger group ... [can] cultural dimensions ... be comprehensively explored" (p. 79). Schneider and Weinberg (2003) suggested that "the large group helps in role differentiation and integration in the development of both an individual as well as group identity" (p. 18). Jarrar (2003) stated that "the large group provides members with opportunities to explore and learn about the difficulties we all have ... in recognizing other subjects ... and enhancing mutual recognition" (p. 31). Yalom and Leszcz (2005) mentioned that some of Yalom's most known therapeutic factors are relevant in LGs but did not expand on that.

Weinberg and Weishut (2012) differentiate between Yalom's therapeutic factors that are seldom available in LGs (e.g., group cohesiveness and the corrective recapitulation of the primary family group); therapeutic factors partially available in LGs (e.g., interpersonal learning and altruism); and therapeutic factors fully available in LGs (e.g., catharsis and existential factors). In addition to this differentiation, they offer two complementary therapeutic factors unique to LGs. One is the "representation of society," which is related to developing complex social abilities (e.g., social responsibility). The second is the "struggle for power" as a therapeutic factor (associated with a relatively well-contained LG), which "provides a good playground to experience individual freedom and exercise one's power" (p. 469). In recent years, several models have been developed to enhance the therapeutic possibility of LGs. Robi Friedman's Sandwich Model (2019) and Mojović's Reflective Citizens Discipline (2020) are just two of these attempts. Relevant relational psychoanalytic aspects and the "group turn in relational psychoanalysis" (Charalambides, 2022) have influenced all three authors.

Online Work in Groups

We are in the midst of a technological revolution. In the early days of the new millennium, Shields (2000) predicted the use of extensive online groups as a significant learning experience:

> In the future, a new type of group relations conference might be planned, and a new study event might be designed to address the experience of life in the virtual universe. In this unique event, participants would communicate using electronic communication within the conference itself … new questions and understanding might emerge from such a practical learning experience.
>
> (pp. 45–46)

A decade ago, Weinberg (2014) outlined the "paradox of internet groups," and new concepts have breached our communication. Just six years later, it was as if Weinberg and Rolnick's (2020) book *The Theory and Practice of Online Therapy* had almost predicted the outbreak of the COVID-19 pandemic and its revolutionary effect on psychotherapy. Since February 2020, we have all had to adjust to working online. The world constantly Zooms, and therapists have had to work in settings and with media that many never imagined they would use. Weinberg (quoted in Weinberg & Rolnick, 2020) proposed that the therapist's knowledge of the media and readiness to embrace the challenges of the virtual format are important for such a modality to become therapeutically effective. He suggested that further theorizing is needed to epistemologically articulate aspects of the social unconscious, which he termed the "technological unconscious."

Online institutional LGs have become integral to training programs, such as the Institute for Relational and Group Psychotherapy of Athens, Greece. The candidates and faculty members even voted recently to prolong LGs' online settings (Charalambides, 2022). We know that this is the situation in many countries and institutes.

Specific Dilemmas and Challenges for Online Large Groups vis-à-vis Face-to-Face Large Groups

Our ideas are written with much hesitancy and trepidation, as our reflections on the consequences of the COVID-19 pandemic and the Russia-Ukraine war are much more "under construction" than solid rock. We write this chapter based on our experience gained since April 2020 as organizers and conductors of three online LGs, starting from the outbreak of the pandemic and the Russian invasion of Ukraine. What kind of dialogues can be co-created in online LGs, and why/how do they become meaningful? Can we talk of the "holding function" of an LG?

Can online LGs enhance communities' resilience vis-à-vis atrocities? While we have no new language to offer, what we can do is share with the reader some experiences we co-created with our LGs, filtered through the lens of our sensibilities.

As group analysts with extensive experience conducting large face-to-face groups, we have struggled with a few dilemmas and challenges specific to the online LG setting. There are many particular aspects worth exploring, and in the current chapter, we would like to focus on six of them:

- the virtual setting
- connectivity, globalization and new opportunities
- continuity and containment
- democratic leadership style
- parallel communication via chats
- the inability to smell and touch

Some of these aspects overlap to a certain degree. However, we feel that each of them deserves acknowledgment, attention, and reflection. We will discuss these aspects by referring to three LGs:

1. LG on the early phase of the COVID-19 pandemic (April–May 2020) conducted by Gila Ofer and Uri Levin (for nine meetings[1]).
2. LG in support of Ukraine (April–May 2022) conducted by Gila Ofer and Stavros Charalambides (for two meetings[2]).
3. LG in times of war (March–April 2022) conducted by Uri Levin (for nine meetings[1]).

The Virtual Setting

Moving from the big rooms and the giant halls, where LGs are usually held, to the virtual space, requires not only a technical shift but also a rather conceptual one. Weinberg (quoted in Weinberg & Rolnick, 2020) writes that "moving from the circle to the screen … involves no less a dramatic change in the setting … Shouldn't such a change require a change in theory, then?" (p. 174).

Preparing the room is one of the essential holding elements of Dynamic Administration (Foulkes, 1964). We are used to preparing the room for an LG, by organizing an appropriate number of chairs, according to the expected number of participants. However, how many will attend a virtual LG?

On the days of the first COVID-19 lockdowns and the shocking news about the number of deceased in Italy and Spain, two of us (Gila

Ofer and Uri Levin) felt a great need for communication and "togetherness" in the EFPP[3] community. We had sent an invitation, asking professionals from all over Europe to join an online LG. We had no idea how many would join and—more critical to the discussion—we had no awareness of the 100 participants limit of our video conferencing software package. Surprisingly, we had 100 attendees on our screen within a few minutes, and we began receiving emails from people all over Europe who could not log in to the meeting. We were identified with the leaders of Italy and Spain, who could not supply enough oxygen concentrators to their citizens. We were sad, embarrassed, and guilty; we didn't take good enough care of the people who needed us. We learned our lesson, paid for a 500 participants allowance package, and from then on we had enough "chairs" for everyone who wished to join. However, the experience of not being able to let people in the room due to our insufficient understanding of the technological characteristics of a media—new to us at that time—was alarming to both participants and conductors.

What happened to us in that LG (Ofer, 2022) is one expression of how conductors might lose control of the setting in online LGs. What one can do is take responsibility, learn, and improve in effectively responding to technical difficulties and problems. In his practical guidelines for online group therapists, Weinberg (2020) writes: "Remember that your technical expertise can become a holding environment for the group members, so learn well the application you use for the group meetings" (p. 206).

Losing control of the room's composition, the participants' location, or the background they chose, are still a few other aspects of the need to change our understanding and implication of the idea of dynamic administration in online groups in general and LGs in particular. Weinberg (2020) writes:

> Group members are shown on the screen in boxes ... with no specific order. Actually, we do not even have the same order on all the screens, as each computer is generating a different group composition ... group members decide from where they connect to the meeting ... (and) "decorate" the meeting room in any way they choose.
>
> (p. 178)

In face-to-face LGs, the physical dimensions serve as a channel for holding the group. In the virtual setting, the "physical" is replaced by the "technological," at least to some degree. From the experience gained, we can state that, with good-enough technical support, the holding functions of the online LG can sufficiently be achieved and maintained, allowing the participants and conductors to "do their work."

Connectivity, Globalization, and New Opportunities

As expected and planned, most attendees of the three LGs were European. The EFPP is a European federation, and the war in Ukraine is taking place on European soil. However, it was pleasantly surprising to have a considerable number of participants from the US, Canada, Australia, South America, Asia, and Africa at each meeting.

In many face-to-face LGs, one can notice (and sometimes enjoy) the multinational and multicultural nature of the group. In international professional conferences, it is common to have attendees from many countries, sometimes from more than one or even two continents. However, the online LG opens new possibilities for connecting with the "unconnected" and fragmented parts of the globe. The presence of many nationalities on the screens enhanced the feeling of being connected. Indeed, the healing power of identifying similar elements in groups, has been researched and conceptualized as universality (Yalom, 1996). "No Man is an Island" is at the heart of group analysis, but we might also say, "No Island is an Island." [4]

"Oneness" (Turquet, 1974) or "massification" (Hopper, 2009) are basic assumptions, illusionary unifying defensive group myths against diversity and disintegration anxieties. However, to some extent, the idea that we are "one world," and "one living human tissue," is not merely an illusion. We are increasingly globalized by economics and technology, and the possibility to "erase" time and space differences through the use of technology warrants further exploration and maybe amendment of current theories. Nevertheless, it does not mean that we are "all in one boat," as social structures that preserve injustice and inequality work harder in times of disaster. Not all of us suffered equally from the pandemic or the war, and it is not just a matter of arbitrary fate.

Our prompt response to these stressful events was a critical success factor for the LGs we initiated. The time interval between coming up with the idea of an online LG to having a few hundred anticipatory and thankful participants on our screens was no longer than two to three weeks after the outbreak of the COVID-19 pandemic in Europe, and only a few days after the Russian invasion of Ukraine. Technology not only builds bridges between people all over the planet; it is also the most economical means of doing so in terms of resources. In no time and at almost no cost, we were able to help thousands all over the globe—something we could never have done without the technological privilege of large online meetings.

Continuity and Containment

LGs in professional conferences and training programs usually have no more than three successive sessions. The online setting enabled us to explore LGs' processes and dynamics in two nine-session LGs (the EFPP groups in 2020 and 2022). What was evident in all of the three LGs was the urgency of the LG to "do something" to save the Italians/Spanish/Ukrainians/Russians, etc. This urgency was expressed by a splitting process, typical of the early stages of LGs, as demonstrated in this vignette from the EFPP 2022 LG:

> The LG had split over the idea of "What are we doing here, and why should we come." For many participants, the most crucial and urgent purpose was to organize concrete help for our fellow Ukrainians—making the LG a kind of aid "hub." For many others, what was most important was to let the Ukrainian participants have a space to share their emotions, making the LG a "witnessing space" or a passive container. A third party urged the LG to enable a Russian-Ukrainian dialogue, making the LG a "peace-making mechanism," or at least a space where some normality could be found. Some participants tried to resonate with personal experiences, representing an attempt to use the LG in a more matrix-like group-analytic way.

As all three LGs developed, a space for exploration and reflection had been opened; resonance, dialogue, and discourse replaced speeches and monologues. Many participants continuously participated, which created a sense of familiarity. It made the group less frightening and more intimate. Conflicts had become more open and communicated; dreams, metaphors, and reveries had found their way in; mourning replaced splitting; the LGs had to "get used" to the pandemic, to the war, and to the realistic understanding that the LG can do almost nothing to change situations. We believe that weaning from the "salvation fantasy" is inevitable in conducting LGs in times of human-made or nature-made atrocities. We cannot stop the war; we cannot prevent death; we cannot reverse time. We can stick to our humanity, relate to others and ourselves, give support, and be supported. Maybe it's not much, yet we felt it was meaningful.

Democratic Leadership Style

We are familiar with the phrase "Inter arma silent Musae" (When the guns roar, the muses are silent). What could a large group offer its participants vis-à-vis the concrete and urgent basic needs of the people who cannot easily breathe due to infection with COVID-19 or the Ukrainians who were running for their lives? Which leadership style will help the participants to experience the virtual space as safe, beneficial, and explorative? The primary task of all three LGs was to "explore our current situation," but we did not just have exploration in mind. We wished to open a holding and containing space, which would use our knowledge and experience as group conductors to benefit individuals and communities. Online technology enabled us to open a "relational bubble" in a fearful world. This paragraph outlines a few characteristics of our "leadership style" (although each of us, of course, conducts in his way and out of his exclusive countertransference).

In general, we agreed on democratic leadership with egalitarian manifestations, which restricted the power of the conductor(s) to a minimum. It means, for example, that we refrained, as much as possible, from using the "mute all" function, which symbolizes the redundant power of the conductors over participants. We preferred to ask the participants to mute themselves or to urge them to turn on their cameras rather than controlling and taking over by using the technological advantages of the hosts. As will be described later, we also allowed chat communication, although sometimes this parallel communication felt like an attack on the group's and the conductors' ability to think. We did not intervene more than three to four times a session and generally preferred "nonintrusive and companioning" interventions (Grossmark, 2016) over "know all" interpretation. However, as much as we tried, we had to exert our authority in some moments. The following vignette is from the 2022 EFPP group (Ukraine):

> The anxiety at the first two meetings was enormous (it was the first month of the war). The participants' efforts searching for "the right way to do it" reflected an attempt to control that anxiety by producing certainty and clarity in a deconstructing crazy world. Long speeches—mainly by Ukrainians trying to enlist the large group (world) on their side—started to "conquer" the communication without interference. How do you stop a Ukrainian speaker from lecturing with all his heart over the history of Russian aggressiveness toward Ukraine? The idea of intervening at that point made the conductor feel cruel and aggressive ("Russian"). At the same time, the conductor thought he had to indicate that the large group became "occupied" by long speeches, in resonance with the occupation of Ukraine (a projective identification level of communication). "To say (something) or say anything"—the conductor was trapped in a kind of a Hamletian dilemma. In the end, he decided to reflect on the situation. He remembers trying, as much as possible, to be gentle and empathic in his intervention. It was heartbreaking to stop this man in the middle of his speech.

All three of us carry our social and collective traumas. Therefore, we are more "wounded healers" than "without a scratch conductors." We are not sure whether our relatively democratic, soft, unobtrusive style was due to the technological shift to the virtual space or was it more a reflection of the circumstances (the war and the pandemic). We believe all these factors contributed to our working style in the LGs. In a shaking world, the group needed good-enough leaders—not abandoning or dictating ones. We hope we were able to succeed.

Parallel Communication via Chats

The technological possibility of chatting during an online group session and its influence on online group dynamics has not yet been fully explored. Naturally, there are pros and cons to allowing the participant a "competing" communication channel, and we will briefly describe our impression.

In all three LGs, a back-stage chat-based communication had developed. There were a few sessions in which chat communication was massive, powerful, and stressful. Some participants asked the conductors (the hosts) to block the "chat option." In some highly chaotic moments, it was alluring to (ab)use our power and block this parallel underground communication. However, we felt that although the chat option has a destructive potential (e.g., overloading information on the "system"), we should not enforce our power and control over the LG.

Furthermore, we believe the chat's benefits are more significant than its disadvantages, especially as a "tension regulator." In parallel to spoken communication, the possibility to express oneself in writing enables more participants to feel included—especially those who find it challenging to speak in a LG. As the LG continued and developed, we learned how to work with chats as a form of parallel communication. We believe that there is a need to continue exploring this aspect of online LGs.

The Inability to Smell and Touch

In using video conference technologies, such as Zoom, the use of the senses of sight and hearing is different from face-to-face settings. Intriguingly, face-to-face LGs share specific characteristics with the online setting. In an face-to-face LG, one cannot see everybody nor enjoy the gaze of the conductor(s) and many participants. Hearing is also not always accessible in face-to-face LGs, as in the online setting, where audial disturbances are most common. However, in an online LG, one gets to see better or hear better than in a face-to-face LG, e.g., one can shift screens and see all the participants of the LG. Although much has already been written about these technological effects (Weinberg & Rolnick, 2020), theorizing the impact of the "disembodied group" is more "under construction" than finalized and awaits further research.

Now, what about smelling, touching, and tasting? Many participants mourned over the loss of human hugs and the lack of body warmth; others longed for the scent of perfume or the odor of sweat. In the LG held in the early days of the pandemic, when lockdowns restricted us to our homes and offices, much of the communication related to the loss of ability to use our senses of smell, touch, and taste. It became apparent how important these senses are to our human experience in an "autistic-contiguous" manner (Ogden, 1989).

However, our LGs were composed not only of mourners and grievers. For example, since the fourth or fifth session, the COVID-19 group has had creative attempts to overcome losing smell and touch. Some women shared with the group that they deliberately applied perfume before the LG meetings. Stories told in the LG turned more sensual and libidinal, as in these two examples:

> In the seventh meeting, one participant told the group about his 90-year-old mother. The latter said to him that she does not understand why he disappears every Sunday evening (the scheduled time of the LG) and whether he is going to Paris to meet a lover. The story's content and the way it was told brought liveliness and vitality to the group. We now had Eros in the group.
>
> The last (ninth) meeting dealt with the ending of the LG. Sadness, fear, hope, and gratitude were all mixed and pressed into the session. It was touching to see many of the participants bringing flowers with them and showing them in their Zoom windows, as appreciation to the conductors and the LG work, and maybe also symbolizing the fantasy of being able to smell together and repairing by this act the loss imposed by the virus.

In addition to the creative attempts to restore smell, the online LGs we conducted were more touching, by all means, than the face-to-face LGs we have conducted. This is one example of the contiguous quality of communication in the LG "in support of Ukraine":

> In the second session, we had a moving dialogue between a female Ukrainian child therapist and a female Russian psychotherapist. The Russian colleague volunteered to translate for the Ukrainian participants. The Ukrainian colleague showed us paintings of children in shelters. Her voice was trembling from the tiredness, fear of death, and emotional exhaustion. The group embraced her with respect and sorrow. The Russian colleague expressed guilty feelings because of their government's aggression toward the Ukrainians and apologized numerous times. Their painfully touching dialogue moved the group.

Conclusion

LGs, we believe, are about creating a safe place for controversial as well as complex exchanges. Online LGs are needed when it is difficult to have such exchanges in a physical shared space. During pandemics and times of war, when borders are closed, technology enables "gates" in the closed borders, which are crucial to our well-being. COVID-19 and the Russia-Ukraine war required an international virtual space for dialogue and a witnessing network. While virtual and face-to-face large groups share almost the same structural elements mainly related to the number of participants, they share differences as well. Among others, the main differentiation experienced was that self-alienation, as well as the singleton phenomenon, were less prominent in virtual settings. The virtual dimension of the LG enabled a meeting of minds that otherwise could not quickly occur.

We felt that the three online LGs were very important for those who participated. They offered a space for sharing emotions, containing anxieties, imagining love, smell, and touch in a social distancing world, and dreaming about peace. At the same time, air raids and alarms impinge on one's existence.

"We've got to be as clear-headed about human beings as possible," says the writer James Baldwin (1971), "because we are still each other's only hope." We must keep each other alive and sustain our aliveness. This is why online groups at this time are so important, especially during a global pandemic and war. At a time of social distancing, online groups offer a common purpose and remind us that the human heart is unbeaten.

Notes

1 This group was organized via as an European Federation for Psychoanalytic Psychotherapy (EFPP) initiative. The primary aim of the EFPP is to contribute significantly to the well-being and mental health of people living in Europe and to facilitate communication between psychoanalytic psychotherapists in different parts of Europe. The EFPP is concerned with extending the availability of psychoanalytic psychotherapy and its applications in member organizations in European countries. The EFPP promotes a European community network of psychoanalytic psychotherapists through activities such as the EFPP Conferences and the support of training programs and research. For more information about the EFPP, see https://www.efpp.org/.
2 This group was organized by the Tel Aviv Institute of Contemporary Psychoanalysis, the Greek Institute for Relational and Group Psychotherapy, in collaboration with the Kyiv International School of Relational Psychoanalysis and Psychotherapy (who decided to withdraw after the first one protesting against letting in Russian participants).
3 See https://www.efpp.org.
4 "No Man is an Island" by John Donne.

References

Charalambides, S. (2022). *The executioner of envy* (in Greek). Disigma Publications.

De Maré, P. (1975). *The politics of large groups*. In L. Kreeger (Ed.), *The large group: Dynamics and therapy*. F. E. Peacock.

Foulkes, S. H. (1964). *Therapeutic group* analysis. Karnac. (Reprinted in 1984).

Freud. S. (1921). *Group psychology and the analysis of the ego*. In *The Standard Edition of the Complete Psychological Works of Sigmund Freud* (vol. XVIII). Hogarth Press.

Friedman, R. (2019). *Dreamtelling, relations, and large groups: New developments in group analysis*. Routledge.

Grossmark, R. (2016). Psychoanalytic companioning. *Psychoanalytic Dialogues*, 26, 698–712.

Hopper, E. (2003). *The social unconscious: Selected papers*. Jessica Kingsley Publishers.

Hopper, E. (2009). The theory of the basic assumption of incohesion: Aggregation/massification or (BA) I:A/M. *British Journal of Psychotherapy*, 25(2), 214–229.

Jarrar, L. (2003). A consultant's journey into the large group unconscious. In S. Schneider & H. Weinberg (Eds.), *The large group re-visited*. Jessica Kingsley Publishers.

Kreeger, L. (1975). *The large group: Dynamics and therapy*. Routledge.

Mead, M., & Baldwin, J. (1971). *A rap on race*. J. B. Lippincott Company.

Mojović, M. (2020). The Balkan on the reflective-citizens couch unraveling social-psychic-retreats. In A. Zajenkowska & U. Levin (Eds.), *A psychoanalytic and social-cultural exploration of a continent*. Routledge.

Ofer, G. (2022). *Distance, fear and intimacy in COVID time. Contexts*, 95.

Ogden, T. H. (1989). *The primitive edge of experience*. Jason Aronson.

Schneider, S., & Weinberg, H. (2003). *The large group revisited: The herd, primal horde, crowds and masses*. Jessica Kingsley Publishers.

Shields, W. (2000). The virtual universe, the open large group, and maturational processes in the future. *Group*, 24(1), 33–48.

Turquet, P. M. (1974). Leadership: The individual and the group. In G. S. Gibbard *et al.* (Eds.), *The large group: Therapy and dynamics*. Jossey-Bass.

Weinberg, H. (2014). *The paradox of internet groups: Alone in the presence of virtual others*. Karnac.

Weinberg, H., & Rolnick, A. (2020). *Theory and practice of online therapy: Internet-delivered interventions for individuals, groups, families, and organizations*. Routledge.

Weinberg, H., & Weishut, D. (2012). The large group: Dynamics, social implications and therapeutic value. In Jeffrey L. Kleinberg (Ed.), *The Wiley-Blackwell handbook of group psychotherapy* (1st ed.). John Wiley & Sons.

Yalom, I. D. (1996). *The Yalom reader: Selections from the work of a master therapist and storyteller*. Basic Books.

Yalom, I. D., & Leszcz, M. (2005) *The theory and practice of group psychotherapy*. Basic Books.

Part III

Online Psychodrama, Art Therapy and Adventure-based Methods

Chapter 12

Sociatry and Sociodrama

A New Possibility in Psychodrama Online Reality: Healing Social Trauma

Deniz Altınay

Entering the New Age of Psychotherapy: Online Reality

As the year 2019 drew to a close, an insidious threat was slowly entering everyone's life. No one was aware that we were on the cusp of a new but very difficult period. The COVID-19 pandemic, which quickly reached all countries of the world, became our daily reality. Society became alienated and lonely, insecurity gradually increased, and fear of the future began to show itself more than ever. This was one of the most severe social traumatic events in recent years.

Major social traumas make the affected communities sick, causing intolerable stress and confusion (Altınay, 2021a). They may create countless individual symptoms, societal prejudices and unhealthy sociocultural problems. If these traumas are not treated, the trauma patterns of the traumatized societies continue by being transferred from one generation to the next, consciously and unconsciously. Schützenberger examines transgenerational analysis and psychodrama and how Jacob Levy Moreno's concepts of the co-unconscious and the social atom are applied to transgenerational links. "Family patterns and problems, even traumas, can be transmitted through generations as part of an invisible, unconscious but very present family inheritance" (Schützenberger, 2007, p. 155).

Social traumas can be healed by sociodramatic in-person methods. The question is, can the online realities of the digital world offer a solution to these problems? As online realities enter our lives, to what extent are meetings in virtual environments, online trainings and psychological help sufficient? All around the world, people confined to their homes encountered the online reality and started to reach out to each other in large numbers via apps and web programs. In this extraordinary time, virtual reality has given sociodrama the opportunity to play a much wider role and potentially to be of much greater significance in the international arena (Adderley, 2021, pp. 281, 294).

DOI: 10.4324/9781003248606-15

Consequences of Social Traumas

The important problems seen in communities exposed to social trauma can be summarized as follows (Altınay, 2021a, p. 246):

- conflicts in the family system, increase in crime in society
- social isolation and social anxiety
- increase in social prejudices, increase in ethnic conflicts
- unhealthy changes in the identity of the whole society and groups
- the formation of hostile societies and paranoid societies
- permanent damage to the community's perception of reality, mass psychoses/sociosis
- loveless societies
- lonely societies and depressed societies
- fragmented, segregated societies
- deep feelings of alienation in society

Healing Social Traumas

Major social traumatic events exceed individual pain and enter the universal and collective realm (Kellermann, 2007, p. 9). If this social pain that Kellermann mentions is not treated, it will definitely make society sick and it is likely that it will pass from generation to generation.

From a cultural point of view, Ken Sprague (2005), a sociodramatist from the United Kingdom said that, "Our aim is to save our humanity, which is essential at this stage of evolution if all our other efforts are to succeed" (p. 252). A closer look at sociodrama, "which is a group-based social learning activity" (Wiener, 1997), shows that it cannot only be considered as a therapeutic approach, but also as a sociopolitical approach.

Collective trauma follows a distinct course. In the history of a specific traumatic event, we can usually discern six phases of trauma responses: (1) the onset of the actual event (the shock phase); (2) the time immediately after the event (the reactive phase); (3) a few weeks, or months, after the event (the coping phase); (4) many months, or years, after the event (the long-term effect); (5) generations after the event (the transgenerational transmission of trauma); and (6) centuries after the event (the universal influence of trauma on the history of humankind) (Kellermann, 2007, p. 44).

In the first couple of months of the COVID-19 pandemic as it started to spread widely around the world, almost everyone was in a state of shock and many reactions emerged quickly (reactive phase), precautions were taken, reasons were sought and culprits were looked for. This was followed by the coping phase, when people gradually got used to the situation and started to struggle with the difficulties that arose. People were dissatisfied with the solutions and reacted. The epidemic was only in its second year at the time of writing of this chapter, and although we cannot fully predict its long-term effects, it is possible to say that people have become (and will be) more cautious, insecure and fearful. Education has been interrupted, some of the basic freedoms have been lost, the crisis has revealed the inner face of some more clearly and anxiety has increased in societies. For all these reasons, it has become very important to treat this trauma, and it is inevitable that this should be done online. There is a need and even an obligation to reach large masses quickly, urgently and easily.

Sociatric and Sociodramatic Group Methods

Sociatry and sociodrama are effective group methods in dealing with the current problems of communities and society as a whole. The individual cannot be healthy without a healthy society. Moreno (1953) regards society as an organism explaining, "At this point social role analysis comes to the fore as a field that I am particularly interested in" (p. 75). For traumatized societies the social methods include socio-analysis, clinical sociology, psychodrama and group psychotherapy, and especially sociodrama (Haskell, 1962, p. 105). Mass challenges such as COVID-19 opened the door to the realization of Moreno's dream of reaching the whole society and the revival of sociatry in its broadest sense including sociodrama, ethnodrama and axiodrama (Altınay, 2021, p. 145).

Sociodrama is a method of action of social themes and group relations. It can be used as a form of intervention in relation to collective traumas, political problems that cause crises, social disintegration, prejudice, problems caused by social fragmentation, interpersonal tensions that create intergroup conflicts and subsequent reconciliation efforts.

Axiodrama focuses on ethics and general values. It is a synthesis of sociodrama and axiological meanings, and it tries to put into action and dramatize eternal truths, justice, beauty, grace, piety, perfection, eternity and peace (Moreno, 1948, pp. 435–438).

Ethnodrama is the sociodrama of ethnic groups, the exploration and discovery of different communities and cultures in action, the exploration of ways in which ethnic subgroups within large groups can be understood and coexist.

Sociatry is the healing of society. The term has its roots in Latin and Greek: *socius*, which means the "other fellow," and *iatreia*, "healing." Sociatry treats the pathological syndromes of normal society, of interrelated individuals and of inter-related groups. It is based upon two hypotheses: (1) "The whole of human society develops in accord with definite laws" and (2) "A truly therapeutic procedure cannot have less an objective than the whole of mankind. But no adequate therapy can be prescribed as long as mankind is not a unity in some fashion and as long as its organization remains unknown" (Moreno, 1957, pp. 70–81).

Sociatry focuses on the normality and pathology of large masses of individuals, of entire communities and nations, and, perhaps, someday in the future, of all mankind. Psychiatric concepts such as neurosis and psychosis are not applicable to group and mass processes. A group of individuals may become "normotic" or "sociotic" and the syndromes producing this condition have been called "normosis" or "sociosis" (Moreno, 1964, p. 153).

It should be understood that normasis does not mean normal. Normasis is a compulsion to be normal and it emphasizes the unhealthy process, just like the term sociosis, which describes the alienation of sick societies from reality. Moreno (1946) explains this issue as follows:

> Scientific foundations of group psychotherapy require as a prerequisite a basic science of human relations, widely known as sociometry. It is from "sociatry," a pathological counterpart of such a science that knowledge can be derived as to abnormal organization of groups, the diagnosis and prognosis, prophylaxis and control of deviate group behavior.
>
> (pp. 251–252)

When discussing social trauma interventions, either online or in person, we should describe a few important concepts, namely co-conscious, co-unconscious, collective consciousness and "social unconscious." Kellermann mentioned the concept of "collective consciousness" while examining social pathologies. Kellermann (2007) explained, "individuals in society are burdened with excessive stress, causing social pathology. The shadow of the tragic past history settles in the unconscious as collectively suppressed" (p. 44). Moreno's concept of co-conscious and co-unconscious appear as factors affecting the dynamics of intergroup relations (Moreno, 1961, pp. 235–241). Co-unconscious states, defined by Moreno as the social unconscious, also encompass limitations and ways of remaining unknown to oneself, which are relationally constituted as an implicit modus operandi arising from an infant's contact with its care-giver (Fleury & Knobel, 2011).

What connects a group of people together? What are these invisible ties that make members of a group feel that they belong to the same group? Why do human beings construct and become attached to nations and similar imagined communities? Psychology has moved from a one-person to a two-person psychology (Aron, 1996). Whenever two or more individuals are together there is a shared unconscious field to which they belong and of which by definition they are not aware. We can talk about a "relational unconscious" process co-created by both participants (Weinberg, 2007, p. 308).

The term "social unconscious" was first mentioned by Foulkes. He said that "the group analytic situation, while dealing with the unconscious in the Freudian sense, brings into operation and perspective a totally different area of which the individual is equally unaware ... One might speak of a social or interpersonal unconscious" (Foulkes, 1964, p. 52).

The unconscious dynamics described above affect our social roles. Moreno (2020) mentioned that "As soon as the individuals are treated as collective representatives of community roles and role relations and not as to their private roles and role relations, the psychodrama turns into a 'socio-psychodrama' or short sociodrama" (p. 452). This can be defined as sociotherapy in a broad sense. When Moreno stated that sociodrama (socio-psychodrama) is a deep action method, which deals with inter-group relations and with collective ideologies (Moreno, 1953), he set the foundations for the first social treatment methods.

Sociodrama: An Online Method for Big Groups

Online Psychodrama Group Therapy should be seen as a new form of practice and is not the same as in-person group work. It includes obstacles and difficulties due to lack of physical contact, limited view on the screen, the therapist's relative loss of control over the environment and the group, and the possibility of privacy violations. The founder of TeleDrama (a new online methodology), talks about similar difficulties. "TeleDrama was created a long time before this current pandemic. The method faced strong resistance at first; action methods have been traditionally perceived as in-person applications" (Simmons, 2022. p. 120).

The following are major obstacles in online sociodrama. In terms of group members they include inadequate physical contact; technological inadequacies; disconnections in the internet; danger of being recorded; danger of being hacked; closing of videos; and disruptive effects of the home environment (e.g., household, children, hearing voices, people entering the room, light, etc.). In terms of group leaders they include difficulties in hearing and seeing members; loss of control; time delay in communication; inadequacies in maintaining confidentiality; lack of action; and technological difficulties of virtually setting psychodramatic scenes.

Online applications began to show themselves much earlier. Moreno wrote about the first remote realities in psychotherapy nearly 100 years ago. He described treatments for individuals and groups such as telephone therapy, television psychodrama and therapeutic motion pictures (Moreno, 1963, pp. 124–128). They are described below:

Telephone therapy: The telephone, an intensive part of our technological culture, had already become a therapeutic instrument. If we replace the "audio telephone" with a "video telephone" the patients and therapists can not only hear but also see each other in action.

Television psychodrama: Psychodramatic treatment of alcoholic groups has been effectively supplemented by mass media of communication, such as television.

Therapeutic motion pictures: Motion pictures are used as adjuncts to group psychotherapy and psychodrama sessions and they are effective in stimulating the warming up of the patients. A number of motion pictures have been produced which feature psychodramatic techniques such as the doubling technique or role reversal.(Moreno, 1963, pp. 124–128)

As in all psychotherapy practices and in sociodrama, the relationship stands in the center and individuals connect with each other via "tele," just as they do in real life, and then communicate with each other. By definition, "Tele is defined as a feeling process projected into space and time in which one, two, or more persons may participate (Moreno, 1937, p. 16). "Tele" is a process that is effective from physical contact to more advanced communication, as a form of relationship that works on feelings. The question is, to what extent can this connection be established in online processes? Surprisingly, our experience is that the tele-relationship did not deteriorate in online processes.

Digital media in the world of group psychotherapy, which started to accelerate with the new era, comes with its advantages like reaching larger communities easily as well as disadvantages like putting a distance between individuals. Real contact in the psychodrama scene is incomplete during the online experiences. The director/therapist therefore may have difficulty "feeling" the group and the group members may have trouble "feeling together." The ability to feel the other is important in human communication and may impede the process of sociodrama group work.

Techniques of Psychodrama

In group psychodrama, the protagonist whose subject is studied psychodramatically on stage is always supported by a double—this is called the doubling technique. The protagonist chooses someone from the group to play his or her role on stage.

Another basic technique, namely role reversal, can be defined as going into the roles of others (antagonists) and speaking from that role. The other can be another person, thus demonstrating interpersonal conflict. Alternatively the reversed role can be of the individual's different self-states or intrapersonal roles.

Online Applications of Sociatry and Sociodrama

Over a period of eight months, more than 500 people from within Tür-kiye and abroad met in the virtual environment, and a wide range of sociodramatic work was done in both small and large groups. Three groups of 100 psychodrama students each studied the effects of the pan-demic through online sociodrama in three-hour-long group sessions, and about 120 healthcare professionals focused on the problems they experienced in different groups.

We found that when the number of participants in the group exceeded the 130–160 range, it became more difficult to observe, feel and control the entire group. We tried to overcome these difficulties with the reflection part of the sessions. We think that the importance of the subject and lea-dership attitudes (sincere, genuine) contributed to very few dropouts in group work.

Moreno, 100 years ago, asked the question in his eponymous book "who shall survive?" His clear answer to this question is understood as "those who are creative and spontaneous in action will remain in the future" (Moreno, 1953).

Intervention Aimed at Collective Trauma with Online Sociodrama

Sociodramatic works are classified as theme-centered works, group-centered works, research studies in groups, creative works for solutions, and building cohesion.

In general, the sociodrama session has three main purposes:

- to provide a better understanding of the social situation,
- to develop the knowledge of the roles in which group members take in relation to this situation,
- to provide emotional purification or catharsis by expressing the feelings of individuals (in action) about the subject.(Wiener, 1997)

Online Steps of Sociodramatic Social Trauma Works

There are steps that need to be carefully followed in online trauma work. Skipping or neglecting any of these steps can hinder the healthy progress of the work and there is also a risk of retraumatizing individuals.

- Bringing the agitated (mentally disorganized) group to a workable warming level. Online psychodrama sharing groups can be effective in this regard. The trauma pushes the entire community and the indivi-duals within it out of balance to the point that they lose their spontaneity, including agitation, irritation and freezing.

- Creation of a safe working environment. Online encounter exercises develop cohesion and trust and bring individuals in the group to a point where they can cope with uncertainty and anxiety.
- Looking at the whole reality and balancing the chaotic system of thought and emotion with the help of the online role reversal and double techniques in the group.
- Discovery of the impact of trauma through online action methods. This way, the group reaches maturity and calmness and can see itself from the outside.
- Revealing the factor(s) that create the trauma, finding and determining the triggers or causes. This step is important for the group and society to protect itself from future traumas and to be able to deal more effectively with the present crisis.
- Identification of the actual factors causing the trauma to which anger is directed. Cognitive control and deepening the understanding. Here we identify the trigger for anger, that is, which factors discovered in the previous stage should be confronted. Expression of emotions is possible with the empty chair technique on stage.
- Expressing individual and group anger towards those who are perceived responsible for the trauma. (Expression and purification through online action catharsis, for example by painting together on a virtual whiteboard.) All traumas create anger towards authority (failed dependency), and the emotions can be expressed by online action by using pillows in the group members' rooms, creating catharsis.
- Reconnection, creation of meaning and activation of the new reality (transcendent role and surplus reality). Surplus reality is characterized by re-establishing connections, correcting the meaning of life and feeling the new reality (Altinay, 2021). Being able to portray any situation in online scenes is a huge advantage. It can be easily provided through photographs, music, illustrations and pictures drawn together on the whiteboard.

Online Sociodramatic Social Trauma: A Case Study

Encounters, Learnings, Exchanges and Challenges

As of March 2020, the Istanbul Psychodrama Institute started to experience a very difficult but important process following the outbreak of the COVID-19 pandemic. Social and natural traumas, such as social conflicts, earthquakes, fires and floods were already in the background. At first, everyone tried to deny this situation and perceived it as a temporary condition. Indeed, denial is one of our first defensive responses to loss. This was also the reason for the initial resistance and denial to online studies.

Gradually, the world has turned into a small town where people communicate, learn, share and engage in artistic activities over the internet. The world has begun to live online. Initially I had to prepare and train our trainers for the new situation, calm them down, support them, and help them to move on during this difficult time.

The vast majority of my students and instructors were unaware of the possibility of online psychodrama group psychotherapy education. Initially, psychodrama instructors and trainees thought that online studies were useless. Each had to be persuaded and freed from their prejudices.

Seeing and hearing replaced touch. Action on the real stage changed to action in their own venues at home and even to action on the screen in online applications. In this online reality, it was necessary to warm up everyone to the new situation. Our first step was to have "two-hour psychodramatic sharing groups." Their aim was to gather leaders and group members in the online environment in order to share all the anxieties and fears they experience, their feelings about the future, and nurturing the group cohesion by coming together again.

Students who were used to doing in-person work now had to deal with the online reality and technological challenges. Almost at the same time, we implemented a new psychological help project for health personnel with a group of 110 volunteering psychodramatists. These groups started with online sharing activities, and the first role reversal online was made with a chair image projected on the stage online. Aid groups were formed in groups of between 4–5 people and 30–45 people. Volunteer therapists were recruited weekly for online supervision. Role reversal, doublings and mirroring were used in the online sociodrama. Thus, while we gained experience in online help, volunteer therapists began to warm up to the online psychodrama. We also created the following "online working principles":

- Group sessions should take place via the application preferred by the therapists (WebEx, Zoom, etc.) and the account they share. Members should not use a different personal network (Facebook, Instagram, etc.) to reach the therapist outside the designated time frame.
- Both audio and video connections should be used during the group session. Members should not turn off the video during the session, except during breaks, and should be ready to turn on or off their audio connections.
- During the group session, members should not make phone calls, write e-mails or send messages. They should not engage in any other activities on the screen.
- Unless necessary, it is better to connect from a computer or tablet. The small size of phone screens can reduce the impact of meeting and working contacts.

- Both the therapist and group members should adjust their display on the screen optimally. It is preferable to have two empty chairs in the room where the member can sit when necessary and to use a wireless headset if possible.
- It is recommended that members should be ready with the device and connect five minutes before the group session to overcome initial connection problems.
- In case of a technological failure that makes communication difficult (line disconnecting, etc.), group members must warn the leader. It should be ensured that everything is heard by every member.
- During online group sessions, members should not be traveling or in motion, should not participate in social situations or events, should be in a fixed place and alone, in an empty room free from background noises and pets, children and other electronic devices.
- Online group sessions are confidential. Recording the sessions is forbidden. No other person should be in the room during the work.
- Working times of group sessions are determined by the leader. Members should adjust their schedules according to these times.

The next step was the online large sociodramatic group of 100 people each for our 300 psychodrama trainees. All these studies showed us that highly effective and successful work with large groups can be done online.

We started the first large (100 people) sociodrama group work by sharing a short video. In the video, the planet Earth was calling out to people, "what are you waiting for?" After this online warm-up, pictures of "planet Earth" and "COVID-19" were displayed, and the group members were invited to take the roles of these images. The scene created very important speeches and the roles were further deepened with the help of the doubling technique. Later, the students divided into small groups (using breakout rooms) of 10–15 persons and shared what they had experienced.

It was possible to talk to deceased people we love using the empty chair technique and also by drawing and scribbling on the virtual whiteboard. By using the materials in their rooms, members could experience catharsis and following that reconnect, creating new meaning and activating the new reality.

In the large sociodrama workshop with the second group of 100 students, the members were asked to split into small groups online to warm up and share "what they were most affected by COVID-19." They were asked to decide which theme they want to work on in sociodrama. Themes included life and death, fear, relationship with nature, distrust of governments and politicians, learning from the traumatic process, the selfishness of people.

The third group warmed up with a video. Then, they were asked to come up with simple solutions to the problems presented to them. Each small group presented their solution to the group. About 70% of the groups produced solutions to problems for which others are responsible, such as improving the education system, and politicians developing the right strategies. A few groups managed to creatively find solutions which could be implemented by themselves or others, rather than relying on leaders, politicians or organizations. For example, one group suggested that "everyone make a promise to others on social media about a behavior they decide to change in a positive way." One promise was "I would use and pollute water resources less."

In the online environment, it is possible to use objects to set up past scenes, to use photos of the auxiliary egos and sometimes the protagonist themselves, to keep only the necessary people on the stage with the "hide non-video participants" feature, and to quickly form small groups with the help of breakout rooms.

In sum, online studies have made it easier to reach large masses, brought some technological advantages and provided an effective method for dealing with social traumas. On the other hand, the lack of physical contact increased, privacy problems were experienced, and the therapist's control over the group decreased. We are all pioneers in this new age.

References

Adderley, D. (2021). A year (and more) of sociodrama online: The Covid era 2020/2021. *Z Psychodrama Soziom*, 20, 281–294.

Altınay, D. (2021a). *Psikodrama El Kitabı (Handbook of psychodrama)* (6th ed.). Nobel Publishing.

Altınay, D. (2021b). *Psikodrama 450 Isınma Oyunu (450 Warm-Up Games in Psychodrama)* (16th ed.). Nobel Publishing.

Aron, L. (1996). *A meeting of minds*. Analytic Press.

Fiske, A., Henningsen, P., & Buyx, A. (2019). Your robot therapist will see you now: Ethical implications of embodied artificial intelligence in psychiatry, psychology, and psychotherapy. *J Med Internet Res*, 21(5), e13216.

Fleury, H. J., & Knobel, A. M. (2011) *The concept of the co-unconscious in Moreno's psychodrama: The Social Unconscious in Persons, Groups, and Societies* (1st ed.). Routledge.

Foulkes, S. H. (1964). *Therapeutic Group Analysis*. George Allen & Unwin.

Haskell, M. R. (1962). Socioanalysis and psychoanalysis. In *Group psychotherapy* (vol. 15, pp. 105–113). Taylor & Francis.

Kellermann, P. F. (2007). *Sociodrama and collective trauma*. Jessica Kingsley Publishers.

Moreno, J. L. (1937). Inter-personal therapy and the psychopathology of inter-personal relations. *Sociometry*, 1, 9–76.

Moreno, J. L. (1941). *The words of the father*. Beacon House.

Moreno, J. L. (1945). *Group psychotherapy*. Beacon House.

Moreno, J. L. (1946). Psychodrama and group psychotherapy. *Sociometry*, 9(2/3), 249–253.

Moreno, J. L. (1948). Glossary of terms. *Sociatry*, 2, 435–438.

Moreno, J. L. (1951). *Sociometry, experimental method and the science of society.* Beacon House.

Moreno, J. L. (1953). *Who Shall Survive?: A new approach to the problem of human interrelations* (rev. ed.). Beacon House.

Moreno, J. L. (1955). First note on the sociometric system. *Sociometry*, 18, 88–89.

Moreno, J. L. (1957). Psychodrama of Adolf Hitler. *International Journal of Sociometry and Sociatry*, 1, 70–81.

Moreno, J. L. (1961). Interpersonal therapy and co-unconscious states, a progress report in psychodramatic theory. *Group Psychotherapy*, 14, 235–241.

Moreno, J. L. (1963). The actual trends in group psychotherapy. In *Group psychotherapy* (vol. 16, pp. 117–131).

Moreno, J. L. (1964). The third psychiatric revolution and the scope of psychodrama. *International Journal of Group Psychotherapy*, 17, 149–171.

Moreno, J. L. (2009). Psychodrama and Sociodrama: *Trial Lawyers College Handbook*. New York.

Moreno, J. L. (2020). *Psychodrama* (vol. 1, 6th ed.). Psychodrama Press.

Simmons, D., & Wilches, A. (2022). Tele'drama: International sociometry in the virtual space. *Z Psychodrama Soziom*, 21, 119–129.

Schützenberger, A. A. (2007). Transgenerational analysis and psychodrama: Applying and extending Moreno's concepts of the co-unconscious and the social atom to transgenerational links. In C. Baim, J. Burmeister, & M. Maciel (Eds.), *Psychodrama: Advances in theory and practice* (pp. 155–174). Routledge.

Sprague, K. (2005). Permission to interact: A who, how and why of sociodrama. In M. Karp, P. Holmes, & K. Bradshaw (Eds.), *The handbook of psychodrama* (p. 252). Routledge.

Schreiber, E. (2021). *Social justice tradition: Article for the American Board of Examiners in Psychodrama, Sociometry and Group Psychotherapy.* ASPGG Publishing.

Wiener, R. (1997). *Creative training: Sociodrama and team building* (1st ed.) Jessica Kingsley Publishers.

Weinberg, H. (2007). What is this social unconscious anyway? *Group Analysis*, 40 (3), 307–322.

Chapter 13

Psychodrama on Zoom

The Story of the Soul

Shelley Firestone

Introduction

While traditional psychotherapy relies largely on verbal communication, the genre of expressive therapy conveys experience that is difficult or impossible to fully communicate through words alone. Psychodrama, an expressive therapy technique, helps the participant convey their experience through *action* and *encounter*.

Instead of listening to the participant talk about what has happened outside the therapy session, the therapist guides them to create conversations, events, and challenges *in* the therapy session, as if they are happening *in the here and now*, to allow the participant to access their experience and explore their psychological world.

This chapter demonstrates that psychodrama can be effectively practiced on telehealth platforms. We present several popular techniques, including *role play, role reversal, doubling*, along with the *empty chair*, the *mirror position*, and *concretization*, and the roles of *protagonist* and *antagonist*. Vignettes describe using these psychodrama techniques on telehealth in individual and group psychotherapy sessions and in classical psychodrama, demonstrating their transformational power.

Psyche suggests psycho and *drama* may invoke inauthenticity, and the name may create resistance, but psychodrama literally means "story of the soul." In my experience, psychodrama can be the most effective modality from our therapeutic repertoire. This chapter aims to instruct and inspire.

Modifications for Telehealth Psychodrama

As the global COVID-19 pandemic of 2020 escalated the use of telemedicine, many psychodrama practitioners modified their methodology to work online. The audio has a slight delay, and important interpersonal information, including body temperature, touch, and smell, is lacking on virtual platforms. To see the whole body, participants stand and shift their camera angle.

DOI: 10.4324/9781003248606-16

Our online participants are asked to use virtual imagery to substitute for reality, and to relate to images of people rather than to real people. Nery (2021, p. 107) calls our experience "the imaginary together"; we only imagine the materiality of our bodies on virtual platforms. Without bodies, interpersonal touch is impossible (Firestone & Taylor, in press). Longing for the connection that touch can convey, a participant complained about her online experience: "The therapist who takes her hand, [and] puts her hand on your shoulder ... in moments that touch you deeply, it is a severe lack, [and] you feel ... lonely, even though you are in the group ... you still feel alone" (Biancalani et al., 2021, p. 5).

Interpersonal connections are more challenging to establish online (Biancalani, et al., 2021, p. 5; Firestone & Taylor, in press). When the psychodrama facilitator guides the participant to create their interpersonal experiences in the therapy session, in video conferencing, they do well to provide direction and encouragement more explicitly and assertively than face-to-face (Firestone & Taylor, in press; Nery, 2021, p. 114). In a group session, the warm-up requires careful guidance to create and maintain interpersonal connections, group cohesion, and the experience of safety and belonging for the participants. In a complete psychodrama, clear narration is required to maintain continuity from scene to scene, and breaks are suggested to avoid fatigue.

Psychodrama participants are generally instructed to signal their need for help if they become emotionally overwhelmed; many psychodramatists are concerned that the lack of physical connection makes emotional upset a greater issue online. Some designate an emotional support person to be available, perhaps in a breakout room. Others recognize that because facial expressions and gestures are predominant in the camera online, facilitators can easily identify and attend to distress (Firestone & Taylor, in press).

While admitting the challenges, many psychodrama practitioners have cited advantages to online psychodrama. Some have reported creative ways to work with the technology: using breakout rooms for warm-up exercises, sharing the whiteboard for a group project, and supplementing the session with music, art, or a special background to enhance the experience (Biancalani, et al., 2021, p. 3; Giacommucci, 2021, p. 223). Because psychodrama works by conveying our experiences through action and interaction, the online camera becomes a powerful ally; much of what is lost can be gained visually. Using gestures, like thumbs up and thumbs down, participants efficiently answer questions posed by the facilitator. For example, one participant turned her head sideways and held her nose to remark on the pandemic. Stuffed animals can be hugged to convey affection. A club (perhaps rolled up magazines covered with duct tape) can be pounded on a tabletop to express anger or discharge rage.

Psychodrama uses role play and role reversal extensively to enact conversations, and hats, scarves, and masks, particularly eye-catching in the camera, can be used to track the roles online. A baseball hat may designate a boyfriend, a scarf over the shoulders an elegant mother, and a participant with a white scarf over their head may play the spirit of a deceased grandfather. Props can be used creatively, *concretizing* meaning. A participant showed a toy shovel to symbolize her depression, saying she had dug herself into a hole; the participant playing her role showed a pair of scissors instead, and everyone understood (Firestone & Taylor, in press).

Particularly in a small group, telehealth practice has the advantage over in-person sessions of the facilitator being able to see all the faces simultaneously, allowing them to monitor the engagement of each of the participants (Firestone & Taylor, in press). For example, the proximity of the participant to the camera may signal the degree of engagement, providing critical information for the facilitator. In my experience, on a single screen showing 18 or fewer participants, facial expressions can be read easily and accurately, like a movie star with their face in a close-up. In a psychodrama session, spontaneity and creativity enrich the work (Blatner, 2000, pp. 144–145), bringing levity to the experience and facilitating bonding. Some participants are more spontaneous and creative online than face-to-face, even making faces for the camera. Attitudes can be exaggerated; one participant played an unforgettable grumpy Aunt Martha online, her mouth in a squinch and her forehead furled.

Individual Psychodrama

The vignette that follows illustrates the use of psychodrama action techniques in individual psychotherapy with a new patient to demonstrate how we use these techniques on telehealth.

> J Zoomed in on his phone from his truck wearing a leather jacket and those mirror glasses. He asked, "Doc, whatcha' got for me?" I had a question: "Why did you come for therapy today?" He said he didn't know, his wife had sent him.

To minimize conversation in a psychotherapy session with someone who might be concrete and non-analytical, I selected a psychodrama action technique known as *the empty chair*.

> I suggested that J do an exercise with me, and he consented. I showed a tiny chair (a 3" Christmas ornament) close to the camera so it filled the screen, and suggested he *imagine his wife in the empty chair*. As in a face-to-face session, I prompted him to describe what she was

wearing. J imagined *his wife* in our session online, sitting in the empty chair.

I proposed J *role reverse* with *his wife*, a technique in which the main player, called the *protagonist*, takes on the persona, the spirit, and the role of *the other*. Couple therapists do well to use this technique for husbands and wives to see each other's viewpoints, and group therapists may propose role reversal for two group members who are in conflict.

I suggested J remove his glasses, wiggle over to the other side of his screen, and sprinkle fairy dust to magically become *his wife*. J complied, enjoying his make-believe experience. I asked *her* (J playing the role of his wife) to share a couple of things about *herself* to warm him up to the role, and *she* responded. J was embodying the role of his wife. I asked *her* why J had come today to see a therapist. *She* answered immediately, "J drinks too much."

Next, I *role reversed* J out of the role of his wife and back into the role of himself. As himself, moving to the other side of his screen and replacing his glasses, he admitted, "Yah, Doc, she's right. What do you think?"

I held up the chair to the camera again, and suggested he now imagine *the therapist* in the empty chair. I invited him to talk to the therapist. He said to the therapist he envisioned, "Doc, this drinking!"

Doubling is a psychodrama action technique in which someone else speaks as a voice of the protagonist, to help the protagonist to more fully explore their truth.

I *doubled*, coaching him with, "Drinking upsets my wife." Taking my cue, he elaborated, "I never have money" and "I fight with her and say horrible things" and "Last week—I didn't mean to—I hit her." He concluded, pleading, "Doc, help me! What should I do?"

Concerned he would resist whatever I might advise, I suggested J take the role of *the therapist*.

I directed J to role reverse—take off his glasses, move to the other side of the screen, and become *the therapist*—and talk to J. As the therapist, he answered emphatically, "Go to Alcoholics Anonymous. There's a meeting tonight at 6:00. No excuses!"

In the role of the therapist, J had the clarity, energy, and determination that had previously eluded him.

Group Psychodrama

As demonstrated above, psychodrama moves forward largely through inter-actions the protagonist creates within the session. In setting up a conversa-tion, the therapist may suggest the participant use a pillow, or any object of the participant's choosing, or an empty chair (as with J) to locate an ima-gined person or element not present in the session. In a group session, the therapist can suggest that the protagonist choose a *peer* to play the role, making them an *auxiliary*. This generally enlivens the conversation, and when they reverse roles, the protagonist experiences how they come across, hearing the auxiliary repeat the lines. Meanwhile, playing a role in another person's drama expands the auxiliary's role repertoire (Blatner, 2000).

The challenge for the group therapist is to engage all the group members in the psychodrama; when the drama is working, everyone is contributing. Group members are instructed to listen and resonate with the drama from their own experiences (a warm-up exercise can help to engage them), and offer to double when they feel moved to do so. Psychodrama is commonly practiced in groups, and the other participants generally add invaluable encouragement, empathy and new perspectives, significantly enriching the experience.

As my group settled in, T fumed: "I'm so angry with my boss!" Introducing a warm-up exercise for the group, I presented my tiny chair close to the camera so that it appeared large in the camera view. I directed the group members to each reflect on one time *they* were angry, and to imagine *in the empty chair* one person who upset them. I said, "I would like each of you to take a turn role-reversing with your imagined person." Giving explicit direction, all-important when working online, I instructed, and they followed: "Choose a prop to symbolize the role. Stand up, twirl, and stretch and leave the role of yourself to become the role of the other. Sit down with your prop in the camera view, and show us the posture, attitude, and facial expression of the person you imagine. From *the perspective of this person*, tell us why you have been invited here today."

I suggested M take a turn, role reversing him to *the role of his wife,* as he attached a pandemic mask to designate her role. As in face-to-face work, I directed *her* (*M in the role of his wife*) to say two things about herself to help him to make the transition into the role. Then I asked *her* to tell us why M is angry with her. *She* said she didn't know but went into a rant, saying, "He's selfish! Arrogant! And cheap!" (delighting the group). The group members each took a turn, so that when T became ready to enact her drama, each of the group mem-bers was warmed up to their own anger, and able to personally resonate with T and support her in her work.

As demonstrated with J, the protagonist in the drama is encouraged to *experience being in a conversation* rather than *talking about* a conversation. As noted above, psychodrama encourages us to create a realm of imagination, called *surplus reality*, to manifest our psychological world, allowing us to bring *others* into the interaction through our imagination, and we can imagine an *antagonist*, someone in conflict with the protagonist, in the here and now of the session. Guided by the facilitator, the protagonist can recreate an exchange to experience how they felt in the moment and explore their relationship.

> T chose another group member to play her supervisor, and they enacted their conversation three times. The first time, T portrayed what she had experienced earlier: T was polite and constrained. Role reversing to play her supervisor, she gave her auxiliary, playing her role, harsh—perhaps exaggerated—criticisms of her work. The second time, she added experiences that never happened but were psychologically honest, vehemently pounding a rolled-up newspaper on her desk and using heavy profanity. Group members effectively doubled for her as herself ("I'm so angry I could wring your neck!") ("you are like my b... mother!"), and again, when she role-reversed into being her supervisor ("I like you, I just have trouble letting you know"). The third time, after releasing her anger and accessing a fuller picture, she spoke to her supervisor effectively: "About those typos in the newsletter ... people submitted their articles late! Could we establish a firm deadline seven days before printing, so I can edit them?"

Psychodrama Workshops

Jacob Levy Moreno (1953, p. 3), the father of psychodrama, wrote, "A truly therapeutic procedure cannot have less an objective than the whole of mankind." He envisioned using electronic transmission to create mass audiences, and employed radio, film, and television to teach psychodrama (Hudgins, 2017, p. 139). He held demonstrations in New York City and encouraged the public to participate impromptu. During the pandemic, we invited participants to an online demonstration; 24 people participated, including myself as a participant, in the psychodrama workshop described here.

Warm Up

A classical psychodrama opens with a *warm-up phase* to create a sense of safety and belonging, taking time and greater care online because of the greater challenge of establishing and sustaining interpersonal connections.

As the participants appeared onscreen for our session, the facilitator warmed us up to the realm of our imagination, presenting a bag and inviting us to imagine a mouse inside, and to show thumbs up when we "saw" it. When almost everyone had a "thumbs up," he encouraged us to see a moose. When almost everyone could imagine a moose in the bag, he invited us to see a herd of elephants. "Pink, yellow, or any color you want," he coached. "Or spotted!" People began to giggle, signaling our beginning sense of safety and interpersonal connection, while the many thumbs up attested to our expanding facility with our imagination and creativity. The one holdout without a thumbs up became engaged as we moved on to other exercises.

The facilitator went over guidelines for the workshop, including our pledge of confidentiality. He said we could leave our camera view, but suggested we keep our camera on, indicating our intention to return. He cautioned that psychodrama can be intense, and asked us to each monitor ourselves and let him know if we were to become emotionally overloaded at any time; he said he would stop the process and decide how to proceed.

The facilitator next introduced a Zoom game. We were invited to reflect for a moment on our attributes, and to signal thumbs up when we had one in mind. When everyone signaled thumbs up, the facilitator instructed one person to call on someone, say why they are choosing them, and say "I bring to this workshop ..." naming one of their own attributes. The person chosen was to then call on someone unchosen, say "I am choosing you because ..." being specific about why they are choosing them, *repeat all the attributes that have been named*, and add an attribute of their own. With this exercise, each member was chosen for one attribute, which was surprisingly effective for facilitating a sense of safety and belonging (Firestone & Taylor, in press). When the person whose turn it was became stuck, the other group members prompted them to remember. We increased our awareness of our own attributes, plus other attributes useful in our work. The spirit of the exercise was playful and fun, and humility emerged because almost no one could say the whole list of previously stated qualities, signaling permission to make mistakes.

The warm-up phase builds trust and cohesion, readies the participants for action, and helps them to identify issues that are useful to explore. The facilitator suggested that everyone reflect on someone who has ever upset us, and show thumbs up when we knew who that was. He showed an empty chair in the camera view, and asked us to each reflect on the question: "Who is in this chair for you?" He gave us the option to address the person in the chair, or to role reverse to *become* the person, and, as the imagined person, tell the group why we were here. The exercise further deepened the cohesion and trust throughout the group as we revealed personal difficulties and shared heartfelt communications derived from our most meaningful relationships.

Action

For psychodramatists, the *action phase* offers the opportunity to more thoroughly explore an issue, traditionally using psychodrama, or perhaps another expressive modality, such as sociodrama, drama therapy, or dance therapy (Giacomucci, 2021, p. 193). In a psychodrama enactment, the whole group focuses on the dilemma of the protagonist.

As in a face-to-face session, to select our protagonist, the facilitator asked us to reflect on a personal concern we could work on during the psychodrama. He invited us to share our issue with the group, and to say if we were warmed up to be the protagonist. The group then voted for one of the issues of those who were warmed up, and, thus, our protagonist was chosen. The facilitator asked us to each say to our protagonist: "I relate to your issue because ..." so we would know how we personally related to the work, and the protagonist would know how the work would be useful for others.

As in a face-to-face psychodrama, our protagonist was asked what he wanted from the psychodrama, and he answered "serenity." In a classical psychodrama, whether online or face-to-face, we often explore the issue in a situation from everyday life. The protagonist is encouraged to set up a scene, and ask other participants to play auxiliary roles to support the work. This protagonist took us to his law school, imagining his large classroom with windows looking onto trees and the sidewalk beyond. He was giving a demonstration at the front of the room. At the facilitator's direction, he chose an auxiliary to play the role of his professor and another to play his girlfriend, also in the class. The facilitator then assigned everyone not in another role to serve as a student sitting in the classroom; we all straightened our backs and sat up to listen. He started his presentation and, as happened the week before, he stumbled, and experienced panic.

He was directed to choose someone to play his panic. He chose G and demonstrated the role for him, picking up a monster puppet to signify the role. He hunched his shoulders over and transformed his fingers into claws, and stated he was "Dracula," complaining of his stupidity, hypocrisy, sloppiness, and more, wanting blood.

When the facilitator inquired the origin of the Dracula role, he identified his mother's voice telling him "you messed up!" and he chose another auxiliary to play his mother. When he role reversed to demonstrate her role, *she* said, "I'm sorry, I don't know what you are talking about." She had nothing to say to help him with his torment.

In *doubling* in psychodrama, as noted above, the facilitator or other participant voices something that could prompt the protagonist. Someone from the group doubled, "Dad is more helpful!" and the protagonist countered, "No! My dad was worse!" Invited to explain, he said, "My dad killed himself when I was nine!"

The protagonist was asked if he wanted to show us how he imagined the suicide scene. He nodded, and chose an auxiliary, S, to play his father. Because we never know who will be attending an open session and we are concerned about members experiencing vicarious traumatization when we are conducting trauma work in a group setting we always take special care to establish and sustain safety. Whether in face-to-face sessions or online, we monitor the cohesion of the group throughout the session, and pause the action of the drama to introduce interventions should anyone seem under-involved or over-involved, either bored or overwhelmed. Because of this care, we find we can safely work with a range of experiences, including trauma (Dayton, 2000, pp. 319–321). The facilitator reminded us again to let him know anytime anyone felt upset or disassociated during our work.

The protagonist donned a baseball cap and played out the scene he imagined, demonstrating for the auxiliary: climbing the ladder to the attic with a coil of rope (portrayed by a scarf), looking around the attic and setting up a chair to stand on (embodied by a stack of heavy books on the floor), and stepping up onto the chair (tilting the camera up to catch the action for the group). He stood on the chair, made a noose, threw it over the rafter (suggested by a low-hanging lamp), put the noose over his head and around his neck, and symbolically tightened it; finally, he kicked out the chair (the books) and went limp. The group was still: everyone was engaged.

S took the role and replayed the scene while the protagonist watched (from what's called the *mirror position*), and the facilitator suggested the protagonist talk to his father. He expressed anger, and then, with tears, deep sadness. I looked at the faces in the group; everyone was rapt. Guided by the facilitator, the protagonist role reversed to play his father and, in that role, he expressed great love, apologized for being secretive, selfish, and distant, and, finally, for leaving him. The protagonist role reversed back to himself, and expressed deep, long-buried yearning. They hugged themselves as if they were embracing each other while being embraced by the other, and held their embrace while the protagonist sobbed, until the sobbing abated.

Directed by the facilitator, as the sobbing ebbed, the protagonist returned to the classroom. He told the auxiliary playing his torment to exit, as he wasn't needed anymore. He pushed the monster puppet out of his imaginary classroom, while the auxiliary shook off the negative energy of Dracula and became another student. The protagonist turned to the group member playing his girlfriend and said he wanted to "join the world" she inhabited. He asked her to stay with him forever, role reversed, and, as the girlfriend, answered, "I love you—I will never leave you!"

The experience of the story, the emotions, and the precious, meaningful interaction between father and son, a potential held within the protagonist's soul, might never have emerged without the psychodrama. Previously burdened by the Dracula persona that contained the trauma, the protagonist became liberated by his catharsis and was able to "join the world" more fully.

Sharing

In psychodrama, after the enactment, the participants are asked to share how they resonate with the work. In telehealth, as in a face-to-face workshop, during the *sharing phase*, the protagonist leaves their focus on their personal story and psychologically rejoins the group. They discover they are not alone as others share their experiences. Everyone further integrates the work by hearing multiple perspectives. Access to all the facial expressions simultaneously is again an asset, showing how everyone is impacted by each other's shares. The auxiliaries de-role, and everyone leaves the experience of the drama to return to the reality of their own lives.

After this psychodrama, we were invited to share our experiences, abstaining from offering judgements, criticisms, or advice. The key auxiliaries were invited to de-role, the auxiliary playing his torment saying, "I am not Dracula, I am G," and the auxiliary playing the father saying, "I am not your father, I am S." We each shared how we resonated with some piece of the work. We spoke of our fear and torment from trauma; our anger, pain, and sadness about a father, mother, and sibling; and also our compassion, love, and deep gratitude for a family member or close friend, and, for one person awakened by the experience, God. Another person, identifying with the mother, vowed to be more empathic with her child.

Organic in its process and bonding for the participants, psychodrama brings us catharsis and transformation, a new experience of ourselves and the people in our lives. In this single session, these techniques brought healing to the protagonist and others, facilitating a shift into an experience of deepened emotional connection with self and others, heightened spontaneity and freedom, and an enhanced realization of life and love.

Discussion

As illustrated, psychodrama works by the participant expressing thoughts, attitudes, and events through action, and visuals on telehealth enhance the experience. Facial expressions, gestures, and props facilitate the work online, while enriching the process. The proximity to the camera often signals the degree of engagement of the participants, providing critical information for psychotherapists. Online warm-ups efficiently create cohesion and trust, even among would-be strangers.

Creating experiences within the therapy sessions allows the participants to experience their situations as if they are happening in the *here and now*, offering an opportunity to more fully explore their psychological reality. Popular techniques give the work focus: *surplus reality, the empty chair, role play* and *role reversal, doubling, mirroring*, and *concretization*. An addict might *concretize* his experience by making a sculpture symbolizing the addiction, contorting their body (or the bodies of peers) to portray tragic destructiveness and enormous power. In *role reversal*, perhaps the most transformative technique in our therapeutic repertoire, the participant leaves the role of themselves to play the role of *the other*, and in so doing develops new perspectives.

Psychodrama explores problems in spontaneous, dynamic, and creative ways, bringing to life a situation within the safe setting of psychotherapy and facilitating the expression of thoughts and emotions as they emerge organically. Using the *mirror position*, the protagonist steps outside their own role to observe their situation, facilitating alternative perspectives, perhaps with more compassion for the other, or perhaps for themselves. The work may lead the protagonist to a conversation with a perpetrator, an enabler, or themselves as a child, perhaps assisted by an advocate, played by an auxiliary. Using surplus reality, the protagonist may experience the longed-for nurturing of an ideal parent, also played by an auxiliary.

These techniques provide guidance to the recovery process, creating a model of treatment for depression, anxiety, addictions, and an array of impulsive, compulsive, and other psychological disorders. Because the experiential focus gives access to emotion while replaying events, psychodrama is particularly powerful for recovery from trauma, whether from emotional, physical, or sexual abuse of a child; neglect and abandonment; domestic violence; or death, as illustrated above.

As in any therapeutic modality, the therapist must monitor the participants throughout the process, and only uncover feelings that can be metabolized; otherwise, the participants may become re-traumatized (Korshak et al., 2014, p. 106). Because psychodrama evokes intense emotions, the therapist must be sensitive to the vulnerability of each of the participants, and be prepared to help each of them to manage the emotions evoked.

With increasing appreciation of the value of these techniques in education, business, litigation, theater, and other endeavors, expressive therapy is a growing field today. The experience of connection, freedom, and creativity, the general goal of psychotherapy, is achieved through these techniques. With careful facilitation, telehealth can be as powerful and effective as face-to-face psychodrama in resolving our psychological issues, and, as in face-to-face psychodrama, generate healing, growth, and transformation.

Practical Considerations and Tips

1   Because interpersonal connections are more difficult to establish and maintain online, offer guidance and encouragement more explicitly and assertively than in face-to-face psychodrama.
2   Use Zoom games and other warm-up exercises to build cohesion and trust in the group, while warming up the participants to the methodology and to the issues that concern them.
3   Suggest psychodrama action techniques to create conversations, relationships, and experiences in the therapy session, as if they are happening in the here and now.
4   Encourage the use of props, gestures, and facial expressions to effectively differentiate roles and enhance self-expression.
5   Pay close attention to facial expressions and the proximity of the participants to the camera online, as these suggest the psychological state of the participants. When any participant(s) becomes overwhelmed, offer specific guidance to help.

References

Biancalani, G., Franco, C., Guglielmin, M. S., Moretto, L., Orkibi, H., Keisari, S., & Testoni, I. (2021). Tele-psychodrama therapy during the COVID-19 pandemic: Participants' experiences. *The Arts in Psychotherapy, 75*. https://doi.org/10.1016/j.aip.2021.101836.

Blatner, A. (2000). *The foundations of psychodrama: History, theory and practice.* Springer Publishing Company.

Dayton, T. (2000). *Trauma and addiction.* Health Communications.

Firestone, S., & Taylor, G. (in press). Sociometry and psychodrama online: A model for telehealth psychodrama workshops. *Journal of Psychodrama, Sociometry and Group Psychotherapy, 70*.

Giacomucci, S. (2021). *Social work, sociomtery. and psychodrama: Experiential approaches for group therapists, community leaders, and social workers.* Springer Nature.

Hudgins, K. (2017). Action across the distance with telemedicine: The therapeutic spiral model to treat trauma—online. In S. L. Brooks (Ed.), *Combining the creative therapies with technology: Using social media and online counseling to treat clients* (pp. 137–168). Charles C Thomas.

Korshak, S., Nickow, M., & Straus, B. (2014). *A group therapist's guide to process addictions.* American Group Psychotherapy Association.

Moreno, J. L. (1953). *Who shall survive? A new approach to the problem of interrelations.* Nervous and Mental Disease Publishing.

Nery, M. da P. (2021). Online psychodrama and action methods: Theories and practices. *Revisita Brasiliera de Psicodrama*, 29(2), 107–116. https://revbraspsicodrama.org.br/rbp/artice/view/442.

Chapter 14

Online Psychodrama Groups with Children

Hanan El-Mazahy

Introduction

Online psychodrama groups with children (OPGC) present many challenges and opportunities. The outbreak of the COVID-19 pandemic made it possible to explore the techniques and benefits of using psychodrama with children online.

This chapter starts by comparing different methods of psychodrama with children, as well as the difficulties and opportunities encountered by child psychodramatists in terms of psychodrama techniques and the online environment. The development of a new technique known as "psychodrama games," a method that lets children be simultaneous or sequential protagonists while allowing them to engage in a social game, is discussed. We also examine the relationship between psychodrama games, regular play, and video games.

Next, we explore the setup and techniques used in OPGC, with examples of actual scenarios and integrating online tools into psychodramatic play. We also explore the philosophy of trying to shift face-to-face practice online versus creating new methods to suit the online environment.

Lastly, we discuss the clinical uses of OPGC as a tool for support, as an outlet, and as a regular therapy tool. We also present future directions and possible uses.

Psychodrama for Children

Jacob Levy Moreno first practiced psychodrama in the public gardens of Vienna with groups of children (Hare & Hare, 1996). Although psychodrama started with children, it has not been developed for work with children in the same way as it has for adults. Only a very small number of articles and books have been published on the subject, many of which have appeared in the 2000s, and formal training programs are scarce (Blobel, 2016). The main publications include a book about using action

DOI: 10.4324/9781003248606-17

methods with children (Bannister, 2002), and two important books on psychodrama with children (Kende, 2016; Aichinger & Holl, 2017). Although psychodrama with children is also known to be practiced in the USA, Brazil, Egypt, and other countries, most of the publications and training offerings are European.

Following its introduction by Moreno, psychodrama continued to evolve with its spontaneity core and theatrical roots resulting in the formation of a practice that combines both art and science, albeit that the scientific dimension is less developed. Moreno described psychodrama as "a scientific exploration of truth through dramatic method" (Moreno, 1953). Psychodrama sessions are composed of warm-ups and action, and involve a stage, a protagonist, a group, an auxillary ego, a director, sharing, and processing (Karp et al., 1998). Psychodrama techniques include role reversal during which the protagonist switches with another role to see the other point of view, soliloquy during which the protagonist verbalizes feelings and thoughts about a situation to the audience, and double mirroring, whereby the protagonist sees the whole situation from the outside, in the course of which they develop self-understanding (Yalom & Leszcz, 2005), often with doubling statements verbalizing that which was left unsaid. These techniques are used to help the protagonist to dramatize the issue at hand. Warm-ups are used to warm up for the action and to help the emergence of the protagonist, as well as to find a common topic for the group. Finding a topic happens in dramatic games and sociometry (Cruz et al., 2018). According to the Therapeutic Spiral Model, it is important to build up an individual's safety structures and psychological strengths before being able to face and process traumas (Hudgins, 2013).

Both Kende (2016) and Aichinger and Holl (2017) describe a method of practice that builds upon the imagination of the child. They both refer to the different stages of psychodrama with children which are warm-up, action, and sharing, or exiting from the role. Kende also points out the importance of cooling down as this is often more important than warming up (Kende, 2016). Additionally, they emphasize the importance of playing with child-initiated scenarios, Aichinger actually called pre-existing scenarios "canned goods," while Kende stressed that children know what they need.

Another important emphasis while working the children is managing the different levels of energy at the start of the group and engaging the children in the work of the group. The opportunities offered by psychodrama with children's groups surpass those offered by play therapy because of the existence of real-life people taking roles, the ability to use props and to disguise oneself or others, controlling the role of adults (in sharp contrast to reality), and the strong effects of psychodrama techniques such as role reversal, doubling, and mirroring. Furthermore, these experiences present children with an opportunity for interpersonal learning (Yalom & Leszcz, 2005) which, as we shall see, can be successfully maintained during the transition to online work.

Psychodrama Games

Children will often spontaneously make use of psychodrama techniques such as doubling without being prompted to do so (El-Mazahy et al., 2020). However, the classical format of a single protagonist can be boring for children. Furthermore, we have to consider different developmental levels and different psychiatric conditions, such as autism, as well as other factors that make it difficult for children to engage in long, single-protagonist psychodramas. Psychodrama games were developed as a new technique to remedy this problem (El-Mazahy, 2020). In these game scenarios, children play either as quick sequential single protagonists or as simultaneous protagonists.

One popular game is the Mayor's Game. In this game (inspired by an online video game called SimCity®) each child takes turns to become the mayor of the floor space. The only stable element that they use is a piece of fabric to delineate a street. They can then allocate pieces of fabric as plots for whatever they want to build, such as houses, farms, schools, shops, etc. The next stage entails assigning group members and directors roles as adults or children and telling them where to live and what to do. The child playing the role of the mayor may have to deal with the other children if they do not want to do as he/she has requested. This game offers children with an active imagination the opportunity to build a full scene and to play out a full psychodrama, but it also allows children who do not have the ability to create a full scenario to engage and play in their turn and at least feel the potency of being the mayor while role reversing with responsible adults. By playing this game, children develop their social skills because they understand that cooperating with the mayor may help them when they themselves become mayor. Children may also discover that cooperation does not guarantee future cooperation, and that other children may not like their management style or the city that they have "built," requiring them to deal with frustration. In one instance, the other children asked the protagonist for an airport, then they all boarded a plane and decided to emigrate from the city. The protagonist had to negotiate with them while they were in the air, and learned that they had left because as mayor he was not paying enough attention to them and instead was focused on building perfect houses. In real life, the protagonist (a child with autism) focused on their own interests and did not realize how this can affect others; however, this particular child would not have built a scene that involved other people if they had been asked to develop a story on their own.

COVID-19 and Online Psychodrama Children's Groups

The COVID-19 pandemic will most probably be remembered in history as a landmark event during which activities that previously were done face-to-face moved online and also as a time of considerable technological advances. Before COVID-19, there was no published work nor motivation to develop online psychodrama groups for children. Post-COVID-19, online psychodrama with children is described, albeit only with individual children, not groups (Strauch, 2021). More has been published on online psychodrama with adults (Biancalani et al., 2021; Cardoso, 2021; Nery, 2022)

Therapists running face-to-face psychodrama groups with children changed to the online environment out of necessity. The children's original problems that led them to join the groups in the first place were compounded by the successive lockdowns. Some groups continued online, but others met online just to close the group (Katanics, 2021).

The Online Psychodrama Group Setting and Composition

Children's psychodrama groups are usually closed, time-limited groups that run for a year (Aichinger & Holl, 2017). All psychodrama children's groups face the basic challenge of group composition, with many advocating that they should comprise homogenous groups of children of the same gender and chronological age (Aichinger & Holl, 2017). But heterogenous, open groups have the advantage of simulating reality and offering children a range of developmental levels to fit them no matter what their chronological age is (El-Mazahy et al., 2020).

Many psycho-technological factors were noted to be important in the setting of online child psychodrama groups in addition to the regular factors of face-to-face therapy which still applied:

1   The strength and capacity of the internet connection
    Needless to say, a good internet connection is a basic requirement for joining an online psychodrama group. Children and parents were interviewed online to explain functionalities and to test their internet connectivity. Parents were asked to make sure that there was an adequate internet bundle that would not cut out while the child was in the middle of the group action.
2   Whether the child is connecting from a mobile phone, tablet, or laptop
    See Table 14.1 for a comparison of the characteristics of the different types of equipment using common video conferencing software.

Table 14.1 The differences encountered by a group leader according to the device that the child uses to connect to an online meeting

	Laptop	*Mobile phone*	*Tablet*
Number of participants visible on one screen	About 25	Usually 4	Approx. 12
Physical device stability	Stable	Unstable, will often show the ceiling or parts of the child's face in addition to moving around the house with an open camera.	Also unstable and will often collapse after being propped on an impromptu stand such as furniture.
Using the whiteboard	Steps needed for the drawing toolbar to appear, require that the child can read English or may have to get a parent to help, but once enabled has more colors and abilities.	Easy to enable with one click; however, only a few colors are generally available and no shapes or arrows are available.	Easy to enable with one click; however, fewer colors are generally available and no shapes or arrows are available.
Using backgrounds and filters	Available	Unavailable	Available for iPads, but not all tablet models
Interruptions	The child may play something else on the laptop and the video feed does not freeze.	If the child opens another application, their video freezes. Incoming voice calls freeze the video and mute the sound, with some children being instructed to take the mobile phone to their parents if it rings.	Video mainly freezes if the child opens another application.

3   Software version
    Ensuring that all group members are running the latest or the same software version is important, otherwise some children may have functionalities like video filters and others will not.
4   Where in the house will the child be sitting?
    As with other online therapy modalities this is very important, with privacy a major concern discussed with parents and children during the interview. Also, many children tend to lie on a bed during the session or sit on the floor or an uncomfortable place. It is up to the child psychodrama therapist to use those factors and regulate them.
5   Lighting
    Also similar to other online modalities, faces are best seen when facing the light source and not the opposite, however light can also be used psychodramatically.
6   Availability of a parent
    This is an important factor for safety in case a child needs physical support or technical assistance for online and connection issues.
7   Whether the group is a continuation of a face-to-face group or a new online group where participants have not previously met each other or even the therapists in-person
    It was noted that children and therapists found it easy to continue a group after having met face-to-face and experienced face-to-face psychodrama; however, it remains to be studied whether that ease has a therapeutic value.

Technical Challenges and Opportunities

In addition to the technical challenges explained in the setting above, the idea of not being in the same physical presence of each other was a big barrier at first, as was the fact that participants see other group participants in 2D, often only from the shoulder up and sometimes even without the shoulders. Many of the face-to-face techniques and props were greatly missed and mourned by both the children and the therapists. Children were no longer able to hand objects to each other or to the therapists. They missed the toys and physical props and when they brought their own they were unable to point the camera at them.

The challenges continued when the therapists tried to imitate the face-to-face action online. For example, in the mayor's game the protagonist divided the floor into different sections in front of them and assigned areas that the other members could not touch nor often see. It was soon discovered that the online milieu called for different methods and techniques to be used.

Although the online environment posed many challenges, it also offered many opportunities, as shown in Table 14.2.

Table 14.2 The utility of online video apps features or external websites to psychodrama for children group leaders

Feature	Utility
Whiteboard	Can be used for group drawings (the participant who shares their whiteboard has the ability to erase others' drawings). Collaborative whiteboards with no specific owner. Can be used for playing standard pen and paper games, e.g., XO, Dots & Lines. Can be used for playing psychodrama games (see below).
Change background	This can be used to demonstrate a theme by the protagonist. Children like to use this feature to show and sometimes almost wear a persona (e.g., Spiderman, lion, famous football player, historical character) When the video quality is not good, this feature lends the user a scary transparent look. Can be used as a scene background in psychodrama.
Video filters and avatars	These function as psychodrama props, such as crowns of jewelry and flowers, masks, different hats and animal faces.
Share screen	Can be used by the participating children who may want to show something to the group. Games like football and Monopoly Deal can be played using this feature (see below).
Share screen from YouTube	This can be music, songs, video strips, relaxation, or meditation.
Share sound	This can be used to augment roles in psychodrama, e.g., share a train sound when there is a train in the psychodrama (personal communication with Milán Katanics, October 18, 2021).
Share sand tray	See https://onlinesandtray.com/.
Rename function	Can be used by directors to protect children's identities. Can be used by directors or children to assume an identity.
Text chat feature	Can be used by shy children to communicate.
Mute, stop video, waiting room and breakout room features	The mute, stop video, waiting room, and breakout room features can be used by the director to protect the group, for example, if another person appears on screen with one of the children. Children often use the mute and stop video features to express themselves.
Polling	Can be used for psychometric purposes.

Whiteboard

The whiteboard feature can be used in the same way that a board would be used in the regular face-to-face format. Certain video conferencing applications such as Zoom offer additional whiteboard possibilities:

- When shared by the directors, the directors have the ability to erase not only their drawings but also the drawings of any child, while children can only erase their own work. Some applications allow everyone to see the name of the person who is currently drawing. The erasing function is grounds for a warm-up game and the name identification feature helps when a child is trying to ruin a game on the whiteboard that they do not want to play.
- The Mayor's Game has been successfully played using this feature (see "Action Games").

Background Feature

This feature is used by many people to hide their home or untidy background. Children have spontaneously used this feature to express their mood and to identify with cartoon characters and famous heroes. Some children were able to appear as if they were "wearing" the character with their head appearing normally and the body of the character functioning as a costume. They played spontaneously with trying out different characters.

The background feature is also used to set up a scene, for example at school or on the moon. This is often done by the children, not the director, but the director can ask the children to choose a background. To help children to use this feature they need to have various useful images on their laptop, which can then be used as needed.

Video Filters

Video filters and avatars can be used by children as props in psychodramas, for example different hats, masks, animal masks and the filters expressing a character; artistic, romantic, or pirate. Animal faces also can express cuteness or fierceness, according to the situation. They can be used spontaneously, or the director can use them to double the emotions of a child who may then accept the doubling and use that filter.

Share Screen Feature

Besides the regular use of showing an image or text to the group, the share screen feature may be used to play games either for warm-up, social skills, or psychodrama games. Some game providers allow their

Figure 14.1 A group drawing on the whiteboard with the name of the child actively
     drawing covered to protect privacy. Oral consent of the children's
     parents was obtained to publish their drawings
Source: Photograph taken by the author using the print screen feature.

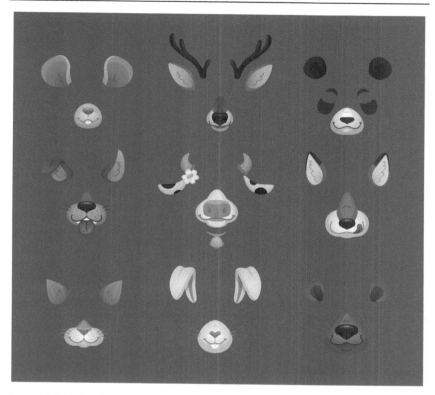

Figure 14.2 Video filters that can be used as psychodrama props
Source: iStock.com/Tetiana Lazunova.

multiplayer games to be played on a platform like Zoom. Two features allow dynamic interaction to take place:

1 Screen sharing on a PowerPoint presentation has been successfully used to imitate the card game Monopoly Deal. Children are dealt their cards on screen, they then place the card they choose to play in the center of the screen and the director moves the card for them. Alternatively, certain video conferencing applications give participants the ability to remotely control the director's screen and thus move their cards independently.

2 Certain video conferencing applications offer annotation tools that can be used whenever a screen is shared. For example, sharing the image of a football field and allowing the children to draw their players and use arrows to demonstrate the pathway of the ball up to the goal where the opponents can move their players to block the ball's path.

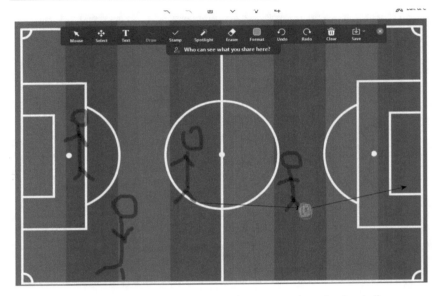

Figure 14.3 The share screen and annotation features used to play football
Source: Photograph taken by the author using the print screen feature.

Share a YouTube Video

This is often used as a warm-up, but it can also be used to increase group cohesiveness by showing a video about a topic to unify the children's experiences and to simulate outings.

Share Sound Feature

This feature is used to complement a scene with sound effects. For example, a child may tell a story that takes place in the forest and the director shares various forest sounds (author's personal communication with Milán Katanics, October 18, 2021).

Virtual Sand Trays

There are a number of websites and applications offering virtual sand trays. One notable example is a free application developed by Dr. K. Fried (Fried, 2022). Virtual sand trays can be used to produce a full psychodrama scene with a group of children.

Rename Function

The rename function is a ready-made role reversal tool. It was accidentally discovered when one child renamed themself by taking the director's name and chatting with the group members who thought they were talking to the director.

Children often divide themselves into teams and rename themselves accordingly, or they may use long and complicated names to express themselves. It is advisable to ask that the children log in using their first names to ensure privacy and to prevent them from finding each other on social media.

Text Chat Feature

The text chat feature can be used as a means of communication for children who have trouble communicating verbally. The hosts (the directors) can choose whether to allow participants to chat exclusively with hosts, with everyone, or with other participants privately. It is advisable not to allow children to chat privately with one another because this may encourage subgrouping and result in privacy problems. As in classical group therapy, measures must be taken to prevent communication outside the group.

Mute, Stop Video, Waiting Room and Breakout Room Features

The director may need to mute a child for safety reasons, either if someone is in the room with one of the children (group setting considerations) or if a child verbally attacks another. The waiting room can be used for time out or in games when a director wants to explain a role to a child without the others hearing. Breakout rooms can be used to split the children into groups and play different games or to take a child out of the main room with a co-therapist.

Polls

Polls can be prepared in advance and launched for children who can read to make anonymous choices and see where they stand in the group as in psychometry exercises where children line up in the physical room. This is especially useful when dealing with sensitive material such as being bullied in the past. This is one example where we can see how universalization as a therapeutic factor (Yalom & Leszcz, 2005) is present in online group psychodrama.

Online Warm-ups

There are different purposes for warm-ups in online children's psycho-drama groups. One purpose is obviously preparing for action; however, warm-ups, especially as children get older, can also be the main event and therefore may need therapeutic elements. In the online environment, warm-ups may also serve the purpose of gradually introducing or moving into the platform that the therapist wants to use for the action phase, for example play XO on the whiteboard prior to the action phase to be carried out on the whiteboard.

Warm-ups to Prepare for Action

- Draw an emotional situation.
- Play charades around a topic, for example school or COVID-19.
- Play hangman (with a plant pot instead of the hanged man).

Warm-ups with Therapeutic Value

- Sandplay warm-ups start by asking a child to choose a single character and then start a story around the chosen character.
- Football game using share screen and annotation functions. (Figure 14.3) This warm-up often brings up memories of problems that happened during playing football in real life, or children who mock the playing style of others. This offers a chance to double, role reverse, and see the mirroring of what they do.
- Warm up around a theme. For example, divide the whiteboard into two sections: the nature section is for drawing trees, flowers, and natural pleasant objects, while the other section is for the dark forces that try to scribble on the drawings in the nature section. The person (s) drawing nature have two tasks, one is to draw and the other is to erase the trespassers' drawings. Children alternate the roles and can share their own whiteboard to have the ability to erase others' drawings. Sometimes the darker forces may win and sometimes nature wins.

Cathartic Games

Participants can play at producing a news program. Children can alternate being the anchor, director, reporter (who can write the news in the chat), script writer (who describes the news to the anchor), or lighting technician who instructs the anchor to move into the light (this role was liked by shy children). During the COVID-19 pandemic, the news was

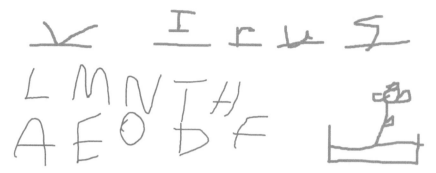

Figure 14.4 Hangman game played using the whiteboard and annotation features with the word "virus"
Source: Photograph taken by the author using the print screen feature.

Figure 14.5 Warm-up is centered around a single character using the sand tray (Fried, 2022) with permission
Source: Photograph taken by the author using the print screen feature.

about COVID-19 and the game was cathartic in that it helped the children to express their fears and to tell the news their way.

Another cathartic game is the School. Children alternate between playing the teacher and the student, and frequently may share their fears, doubts, and annoyance with school. This game can also be repeated with a family or another setup.

Action Games

The mayor's game is an example of psychodrama games played online which offer a full psychodrama experience. Children as sequential protagonists are each given the opportunity of becoming the mayor of the whiteboard area. In the online version it is useful to allow each child as mayor to share their own whiteboard, this way they have the authority to erase what they do not like and deal with any trespassing or vandalism by erasing it.

Another game is the Island Game, during which children play that they are stranded on an island after surviving a shipwreck, and they have to use the few items that they are allowed (seeds, wood, metal) to survive. This is played by the director plotting the land and sea areas with children helping in coloring the sea. The children then draw themselves and can later erase themselves and draw their characters somewhere else on the island. In essence, this is a form of dynamic drawing that resembles a psychodrama production in which children interact with each other.

The Family's Role and Involvement

It is important while setting up OPGC to consider that they take place in the homes of the children. The child's sibling(s) may know that they are "playing," and they are often told not to interrupt them by parents who seem to give the matter more importance than that which siblings might

Figure 14.6 The development of the island game played using Zoom's whiteboard and annotation functions
Source: Photograph taken by the author using the print screen feature.

consider suitable for playtime. Given the added factor that the child is playing with adults, this frequently makes the siblings both jealous and curious, often finding pretexts to enter the room where the child is "playing." We devised a treasure hunt game that we played at the end of a session with all the siblings of each child (or a parent if the child has no siblings). In the treasure hunt game we might ask participants to find five red objects, and the family who assembles the objects more quickly wins. The siblings have a role and are able to take turns which helps the parents to pacify them. This often leads to the group members discussing their family life as well in the next session.

Summary

In this chapter we presented the background to psychodrama and psychodrama with children. We introduced a new technique known as "psychodrama games" and described the setting and composition of OPGC including psycho-technological factors in addition to technical challenges and opportunities. We discussed the development of online techniques to produce warm-ups, catharsis, and action. Lastly, we discussed the families' role and involvement, and presented practical advice on setting up OPGC.

References

Aichinger, A., & Holl, W. (2017). *Group therapy with children: Psychodrama with children*. Springer.

Bannister, A. (2002). Setting the scene: Child development and the use of action methods. In A. Bannister & A. Huntington (Eds.), *Communicating with children and adolescents: Action for change* (p. 240). Jessica Kingsley Publishers.

Biancalani, G., Franco, C., Guglielmin, M. S., Moretto, L., Orkibi, H., Keisari, S., & Testoni, I. (2021). Tele-psychodrama therapy during the COVID-19 pandemic: Participants' experiences. *The Arts in Psychotherapy*, 75, 101836.

Blobel, F. (2016). *The methods for psychodrama with children in Europe*. https://tarashoeva.com/en/the-methods-for-psychodrama-with-children-in-europe.

Cardoso, A. de L., Jr. (2021). Stage, scene and body in online psychodrama. *Revista Brasileira de Psicodrama*, 29(1), 65–70.

Cruz, A., Sales, C. M. D., Alves, P., & Moita, G. (2018). The core techniques of Morenian psychodrama: A systematic review of literature. *Frontiers in Psychology*, 9(July), 1263. https://doi.org/10.3389/FPSYG.2018.01263/BIBTEX.

El-Mazahy, H. (2020). *Psychodrama games for children: A new entity*. 4th International EAGT Conference and 5th IAGP Regional Conference, Cairo, Egypt.

El-Mazahy, H., Gaseau, M., Rakhawy, M., & Sabry, N. (2020). Engaging children in psychodrama: Appropriateness of technique to child development. *Forum: Journal of the International Association for Group Psychotherapy and Group Processes*, 8, 78–86. https://www.iagp.com/docs/forum2020.pdf.

Fried, K. (2022). *Online sand tray by Dr. Karen Fried*. https://Onlinesandtray.Com/.

Hare, A. P., & Hare, J. R. (1996). J L Moreno. In *Key figures in counselling and psychotherapy*. SAGE. https://books.google.com.eg/books?id=71ldMCAyOUkC.

Hudgins, M. K. (2013). Clinical foundations of the therapeutic spiral model: Theoretical orientations and principles of change. In *Psychodrama* (pp. 199–212). Routledge.

Karp, M., Holmes, P., & Tauvon, K. B. (1998). *The handbook of psychodrama*. Psychology Press.

Katanics, M. (2021). *The art of psychodramatist for children and youth: Online groups*. The 2nd International Children and Youth Psychodrama Conference, Zagreb, Croatia.

Kende, H. (2016). *Psychodrama with children: Healing children through their own creativity*. Taylor & Francis.

Moreno, J. L. (1953). *Who shall survive? Foundations of sociometry, group psychotherapy and socio-drama* (2nd ed.). Beacon House. https://psycnet.apa.org/record/1954-04178-000.

Nery, M. da P. (2022). Online psychodrama and action methods: Theories and practices. *Revista Brasileira de Psicodrama*, 29, 107–116.

Strauch, V. (2021). Online psychodrama with children and the psychodramatic sandplay method. *Revista Brasileira de Psicodrama*, 29(2). https://revbraspsicodrama.org.br/rbp/article/view/455.

Yalom, I. D., & Leszcz, M. (2005). *The theory and practice of group psychotherapy*. Basic Books.

Chapter 15

Online Group Art Therapy

Encouraging Creative Healing in the Virtual Space

Iris Lachnit and Meera Rastogi

The shift to online group art therapy during the COVID-19 pandemic has decreased clients and art therapists' reluctance to use the online format (Choudhry & Keane, 2020), and recent literature suggests that art therapy and group art therapy online may be similarly beneficial to in-person (e.g., Hass-Cohen et al., 2021; Lobban & Murphy, 2020). However, the transition to the online format is full of technological challenges while training and research are still limited (Zubala & Hackett, 2020).

This chapter aims to provide an overview and practical guidance for online group art therapy. Based on clinical experience and recent literature, the authors discuss the benefits and limitations of the virtual setting, and provide practical tips for addressing them. Themes covered in the chapter include setting up an online group, making informed choices about art media, designing and presenting art prompts amenable to the online format, facilitating art-making and the processing of artworks, and encouraging group member interaction to build group cohesion. The chapter aims to empower readers to begin to successfully work online with art therapy groups.

Introduction

Many art therapists are challenged with the question of how to replicate the group art therapy session experience in the virtual environment. This transition comes with many concerns and fears; for example, how will clients access art materials? How can art-making be observed? How can assistance be provided with art-making? How can group members see one another's artwork? How can cohesion be created online? Despite research since the 1990s on art therapy and technology, the art therapy community lacks training, practical experience, and evidence-based guidelines to provide virtual art therapy, resulting in low confidence among art therapists (Zubala & Hackett, 2020). This lack of confidence creates a persistent barrier to providing online art therapy. Increasing art therapists' confidence by developing specific skills for virtual group art therapy is

DOI: 10.4324/9781003248606-18

needed more than ever. Based on the most recent literature and the authors' experiences providing online group art therapy with patients with multiple sclerosis, movement disorders, and mental health diagnoses, this chapter aims to give an overview and practical guide for online group art therapists. First, the authors will provide basic information about group art therapy and online group art therapy. The authors will then cover primary considerations when incorporating art-making online, including legal and ethical considerations, technology, art media, art prompts, and building group cohesion. The chapter concludes with some considerations and tips.

Group Art Therapy

As a mental health and human services profession, art therapy combines active art-making, the creative process, and applied psychological theory within a psychotherapeutic relationship (American Art Therapy Association, 2021). Art therapy may reduce anxiety and symptoms of mental health conditions (Abbing et al., 2018; Schouten et al., 2015; Van Lith, 2014), integrate emotional, cognitive, and relational information (King, 2017; King et al., 2019), and activate the reward center in the brain (Kaimal et al., 2017). Art-making may increase behavioral activation, boost self-efficacy (King et al., 2016), and provide beneficial physiological changes (Beerse et al., 2019; Futterman Collier et al., 2016). Besides the effect mechanisms of group therapy (instilling hope, interaction, universality, and altruism; Yalom, 1985), group art therapy engenders relationships through viewing each other's artwork and uncovering connections with others (Rosal, 2016). Creative self-expression gives individuals control over exposure and can reduce anxiety around disclosure in a group (Riley, 2001). Feedback from the group on art images provides additional perspectives and may further illuminate the presenting issue (Waller, 2012).

Benefits and Limitations of Online Group Art Therapy

Although formal online group art therapy research is still lacking, recent literature suggests that the previously described benefits of art therapy and group art therapy are also valid in the virtual setting (e.g., Hass-Cohen et al., 2021; Lobban & Murphy, 2020). One of the most significant benefits of online art therapy is increased accessibility, especially for people with disabilities, mobility problems, or those living in remote locations (Choudhry & Keane, 2020). Holding group therapy online can further reduce practical issues like recruiting enough participants to start a treatment group (Weinberg & Rolnick, 2020). Online group treatment is not only safe for patients with severe illnesses but may have lower dropout rates compared to in-person treatment (Zimmerman et al., 2021). Another benefit of online art therapy is the potential to overcome the barrier of the stigma associated with mental health (Carlier et al., 2020; Spooner et al., 2019). Some clients may benefit from greater privacy as it may be easier to focus on art-making and reduce fear of being judged by appearance (Collie et al., 2017).

Notwithstanding the benefits of online group art therapy, other clients might have less privacy due to family housing conditions (Choudhry & Keane, 2020; Zubala & Hackett, 2020). Other concerns address technological limitations, confidentiality, safety (Zubala et al., 2021), access to art supplies (Choudhry & Keane, 2020), and group members viewing the art product via technology. Another frequently reported concern with online art therapy is the therapist being less involved in the art-making process and missing helpful clinical observations. Nevertheless, the virtual setting may better facilitate the patient-artwork relationship since clients take a more active role in their art-making and treatment process (Levy et al., 2018) which may increase clients' independence but may hinder the transference that can take place in-person.

The authors' main concerns before starting the virtual groups were about replicating the group art therapy experience, especially interpersonal interactions. Some of our considerations were: How can we replicate the sharing of materials and art-making tips with one another? And: How can we enable feedback from members throughout the art-making process? Although these interactions may seem trivial, these small interactions help to build cohesion, confidence, and connection among members, and are the core of group art therapy interventions.

Legal and Ethical Considerations

In addition to typical online group therapy concerns of confidentiality and informed consent (Weinberg, 2020), art therapists are also concerned about the confidentiality of the art product (American Art Therapy Association, 2013; Orr, 2012). The digital informed consent should clearly explain limits to confidentiality and state explicit guidelines for privacy conditions and storing artworks, including that clients do not take screenshots, record, or duplicate any portions of the session (e.g., saving images from other group members).

Technology

The following sections will present technology-related recommendations throughout the steps of setting up an online group, art-making, processing images, and other possibilities with video conferencing applications.

Setting Up an Online Group

The waiting room feature can help to maintain confidentiality as the host must accept participants before they enter the group. The waiting room can also be used to carry out individual technology checks and adjustments such as lighting check or camera height before the session (McBride and Worrall, 2021). Another way to help clients to adjust to technology, reduce technology-related fears, and equalize participants' comfort levels regarding the use of technology, is to offer an orientation session to introduce the platform's functions.

When screening potential participants, art therapists must ensure that participants have access to an appropriate device that possesses a camera (phones or tablets have limited view options and do not allow participants to see all the group members). Availability of caregiver support for technology and art-making should be assured when working with children and participants with disabilities. We recommend pre-meeting with caregivers and parents to discuss how much guidance is needed so that there is no need for them to intervene in the actual artwork and the client works as independently as possible.

Sending a list of supplies needed to group members (McBride & Worrall, 2021) and assessing their preferences and availability of art supplies should be done beforehand (Shaw, 2020). When participants cannot source the required art media, art therapists can mail supplies or have supplies available for pick up, but should weigh the potential loss of confidentiality.

Art-Making Process

Unlike in-person art therapy, whereby both the art-making process and body language (e.g., facial expressions) provide sources of clinical information, currently, online art therapy must manage the trade-off between the camera showing the clients' art-making processes or showing their faces. Also, some clients prefer to move off-camera for art-making. To overcome these limitations, we have two recommendations. To view clients' art-making and their faces, we recommend using external cameras to focus on artworks while integrated cameras focus on clients. This helps art therapists to better assist clients with art-making and can create a sense of cohesion and inspiration among group members. Alternatively, the single camera can be repositioned to view the artwork but clients may be unable to observe other participants. Clients may need encouragement and reassurance that this view of their art-making process will aid the art therapy sessions.

The second recommendation is suited to clients who cannot tolerate these camera positions because they feel exposed or under pressure to perform. If technological and room setup permit, the client can sit at a distance to the camera, allowing for both their faces and art-making to be seen. If clients prefer to show their faces instead of their artworks, art therapists should notice when group members need facilitation.

Group Processing of Images

Presenting artworks online can be problematic as webcams may provide poor image quality. Holding images still for a couple of seconds before speaking allows the camera to focus and enables members to process visual information. The pin/spotlight function allows for highlighting one member's video while the other members' videos, smaller in size, still appear. Since the facial expression of the person sharing is not visible, therapists should carefully listen to the tone of their voice and pause to note how they respond to specific questions or comments. We also recommend using a consistent session structure with enough time to view images when participants first describe them; later, the person sharing can show their face and hold the image up as needed.

Another strategy to deal with blurred images is presenting artworks via screen share (Levy et al., 2018) which provides both an enlarged view of the person's image, and views of their face and any other person speaking. Although screen share is straightforward with digital art, it requires more steps with traditional art, thus may only work for technologically versed and equipped groups.

A third option for sharing artwork online is to post images on an online platform (e.g., Padlet). While this should not be done without participants' consent and informing about potential risks to confidentiality, it is a way to honor artworks individually and as a group and may resemble an art exhibit. Members can either post artworks themselves or send a photograph to the art therapist (e.g., via the chat function). Using screen share and gallery view, therapists can moderate the processing of images by enlarging posted artworks while every person speaking is visible. This method offers the therapist more control over the process and provides different modes to explore group versus individual themes; for example, how long the group views an image, and whether it views one or all images at a time. However, due to confidentiality limitations and the prerequisite that participants must digitalize their images and give therapists access to them, this method may only work for some groups.

A fourth option for sharing artwork is to use a second camera, one focusing on the artwork and another one on the client. As mentioned earlier, this would also allow group members to be more involved in other's art processes and enhance group interaction. Notably, only Zoom currently provides the option of using two cameras. Other platforms (e.g. Teams, Google Meet) allow users to shift between cameras.

To facilitate the processing of images, we recommend incorporating questions on the art-making process, such as: Where did you first start your image? Did you find any part of your creation particularly challenging? Were there any other art materials you wish you could have used? Is there anything that you feel still needs to be added to the image? These questions can address some limitations to the virtual setting by capturing the art-making process and clients' access to art materials.

Other Features of Video Conferencing Applications

Many video conferencing applications provide additional features that may be useful for online art therapy groups. For example, the breakout room provides the possibility for one-on-one assistance if a co-therapist is available. Adjustments of view options (e.g., speaker view) and video options (e.g., hide self-video) may help participants who feel uncomfortable speaking in a group or those with body image concerns (Shaw, 2020). However, hiding self-video prevents the members from working through their difficulties with body image (Weinberg et al., 2023). Another helpful feature is polling, which can be used for anonymous evaluations; for example, to assess treatment efficacy and improve the online format or to check in about timing or pacing during sessions (McBride & Worrall, 2021).

Art Media and Supplies

Art therapy hinges on media use, and considerations around media are crucial for art therapists (Hinz, 2016). Media choices are often based on the idea that media possess different physical properties (e.g., resistive versus fluid) that may affect brain region activity in diverse ways. For example, fluid media such as watercolor is believed to stimulate the limbic system, and thus can promote more affective responses (Graves-Alcorn, 2017; Hinz, 2009). On the other hand, resistive media such as pens may stimulate the cortex, thus promoting more cognitive responses (Hinz, 2009). In the virtual setting, incorporating art materials and different qualitative characteristics and effects of media is challenging for most art therapists (Choudhry & Keane, 2020). The selection of materials depends on fundamental factors rather than media properties, such as availability and access to art supplies or the possibility to use online materials. Using familiar materials or personal belongings from home (Camic et al., 2011) keeps the threshold low. Art therapist Rhonda Johnson had a client use old makeup due to limited access to art supplies during the COVID-19 pandemic (personal communication, October 22, 2020). McBride & Worrall (2021) recommend using felt-tip pens and darker colors to increase artworks' visibility through the webcam.

Another consideration regarding art media and supplies is the use of digital art media, for example, the whiteboard on Zoom. The whiteboard provides several different media (pen, paint, stamps), allows control over thickness and color, and identifies the image's creator. Another option is the use of apps for digital art expression. Digital art applications not only reduce some of the previously discussed limitations of online art therapy but extend and complement the possibilities of traditional media for artistic expression. The programs allow for simply adjusting tools or using tools like cropping to manipulate photographs (McNiff, 2018, p. 101). Finally, the computer's snipping tool, access to the internet, and a Word document are a simple and accessible way to create collages.

To date, the effects of using art apps with art therapy have not been extensively investigated (Malchiodi, 2018, p. 207). Even less is known about digital art-making with online art therapy groups. Regarding in-person settings, the therapeutic value of using tablet technology with pediatric hospital patients has been documented. Garner (2016) provides case reports of integrating digital technology in art therapy, such as videogaming, filmmaking, collage-making, and virtual and immersive environments. Incorporating new media can work as a catalyst in establishing client therapist relationships (Belkofer & Belkofer, 2018, Case Example 3.1) and inspire themes for artistic exploration (Darke, 2016, pp. 141–143).

Clients with limited mobility might benefit from digital art-making technologies (McNiff, 2018, p. 102), as well as people who find the tactile or olfactory process of using traditional media challenging (Darewych et al., 2015), and clients who are comfortable using digital technology (Barber & Garner, 2016, pp. 67–69). In addition, children on the autism spectrum appear to specifically benefit from digital art-making (L'Esperance, 2016, pp. 89–91). Due to the features delete or undo steps, using digital art apps can also help clients who worry about making mistakes (Youhjung, 2019). When incorporating digital media in online groups, similar levels of familiarity with such media among participants may be helpful (Collie et al., 2017). Otherwise, art therapists should accommodate different levels of familiarity (Collie et al., 2006). Malchiodi (2018, p. 208) and Barber and Garner (2016, Appendix 4.1) provide lists of recommended art applications.

Art Prompts

In this chapter, art prompts are defined as a short description that serves as a catalyst for artistic self-expression and relates to treatment goals (for example, "using symbols, lines, shapes, and colors create an image of your mental health emergency kit. Your five senses can help you generate self-soothing ideas using taste, sound, smell, sight, and touch"). Given the previously described limitations with technology and art media, art therapists cannot

simply transfer art prompts from in-person to online groups. Instead, therapists should design art prompts amenable for online groups considering the
following challenges: limited art media, limited facilitation and observation
through the therapist, limited time, increased complexity (if unfamiliar with
the use of technology), potentially increased anxiety around technology and
a new setting (especially when group members have not met before), and
limited interaction among group members. We will address these limitations
with recommendations for time management, reducing performance
pressure, and introducing art directives.

Time Management

McBride and Worrall (2021) recommend planning double the time for
online groups as in-person groups need. Art prompts should be simple
and ample time should be dedicated to processing the images to provide
members possibilities to interact (McBride & Worrall, 2021). With our
groups of between two and eight participants, we usually planned 30
minutes for art-making and 30 to 60 minutes for sharing and processing
images. Check-ins and explaining art prompts took 30 minutes maximum.
One author kept a separate timer to keep track of the time in case the
on-screen time-display was covered up.

Reducing Performance Pressure

Art prompts should be straightforward and adjustable to participants'
needs (McBride & Worrall, 2021). Therapists should emphasize that the
focus is on the experience and content rather than aesthetics or artistic
skills. Allowing participants to use their materials of choice (even when a
specific material is suggested), allowing for modifications to any art
prompt according to their needs or wishes, or sending directives ahead of
time may help to reduce anxiety. However, art therapists should weigh the
pros and cons of knowing the prompts ahead of time. McBride and
Worrall (2021) suggest incorporating independent work between sessions
to reduce performance pressure and providing YouTube video
demonstrations to watch at home to facilitate using new materials.

Introducing Art Prompts

Art prompts that include more than two steps should be presented in
large font on a simple PowerPoint slide or through the chat. Showing
examples of completed works may be helpful for understanding and
inspiration (McBride & Worrall, 2021); however, the examples may interfere with participants' creative and subconscious process. McBride and
Worrall (2021) recommend additional ways to facilitate creative

expression in online groups through presenting concepts, poems, or images to stimulate reflection and conversation about a specific topic. We often used guided meditation to help participants to center, shift their focus to the session, and mentally prepare for the topic before we explained the prompt.

Building Group Cohesion

Social connection and a sense of belonging are central human needs and are among the factors that make group therapy effective (Yalom, 1985). Research in group therapy (Burlingame et al., 2018) repeatedly shows that cohesion is the main factor that positively correlates with outcomes. Building cohesion can be difficult in online groups, especially when group members meet online for the first time. Our two groups had started in-person before the pandemic, thus had already established a sense of cohesion when we moved online. Our challenge was acclimating new members with old members and making sure that everyone felt a sense of cohesion. The small size of the groups certainly helped with the integration of new members as did providing some time for informal conversations at the beginning of sessions. Whenever new members joined the group, we had everyone introduce themselves. When a group member was emotionally upset or had something significant happen in their life, we gave them time to share instead of rushing to art-making. In addition, we strongly encouraged members to turn their videos on and unmute themselves to talk to each other freely and reduce the power differential between facilitators and members (McBride & Worrall, 2021). Co-facilitators should not feel the need to speak right after another or be afraid to offer silence (McBride & Worrall, 2021). During the processing of artworks, we encouraged group members to give feedback and asked if they could relate to the shared experiences. Art therapists should dedicate more time to activities that help members to get to know each other to establish healthy group dynamics (McBride & Worrall, 2021). One way to include new members is using the whiteboard for group projects or as an ice breaker at the beginning of a session (Rosal, 2016). With new groups, McBride and Worrall (2021) recommend setting group guidelines in the first session, referring to individuals' need to connect, feel safe, seen, and nurtured. They also suggest using breakout rooms to work in dyads or small groups to promote extra room for individual sharing and bonding.

Conclusion

This chapter aimed to encourage and equip art therapists to conduct art therapy groups virtually. The authors discussed the benefits and limitations of the virtual setting and provided practical tips to address limitations. Among the themes covered were setting up an online group, making informed choices about art media, designing and presenting art prompts amenable to the online format, facilitating art-making and the processing of artworks, and encouraging group member interaction to build group cohesion. We hope this chapter empowers readers to start working online with art therapy groups.

Practical Considerations and Tips

- Consider pre-meeting group members for technology adjustment, clarifying caregiver support, access to art supplies and private space, and facilitating artwork storage.
- Discuss group preferences for the art-making process (e.g., camera position, microphone setting, silent or conversational).
- Use art media that participants have access to and are familiar with.
- If using new media (e.g., whiteboard), plan enough time to instruct and familiarize participants with it and use several channels for instructing (e.g., YouTube videos, written instructions, demonstrations).
- Take advantage of the new possibilities that videoconferencing features offer for art-making such as camera and view options or the breakout room.
- Keep prompts short and straightforward and allow for individual modifications.
- Use the pin/spotlight function when sharing artworks through the webcam, holding images still for the camera to focus.
- Use screen share in case of digital art or digitalized images.
- Incorporate questions on art processes when sharing and encourage members to ask questions in the processing of images to facilitate group cohesion.
- Consider going beyond visual art-making to facilitate creative expression such as incorporating music, poetry, images.
- Plan enough time and activities to help participants to get to know each other and connect.

References

Abbing, A., Ponstein, A., van Hooren, S., de Sonneville, L., Swaab, H., & Baars, E. (2018). The effectiveness of art therapy for anxiety in adults: A systematic review of randomised and non-randomised controlled trials. *PLOS ONE*, 13 (12), e0208716. https://doi.org/10.1371/journal.pone.0208716.

American Art Therapy Association (2013). *Ethics*. https://arttherapy.org/ethics/.

American Art Therapy Association (2021, February). *About art therapy*. https://arttherapy.org/about-art-therapy/.

Barber, B. S., & Garner, R. (2016). Materials and media: Developmentally appropriate apps. In R. Garner (Ed.), *Digital art therapy*. Jessica Kingsley Publishers. https://ereader.perlego.com/1/book/953516/8.

Beerse, M. E., Van Lith, T., & Stanwood, G. D. (2019). Is there a biofeedback response to art therapy? A technology-assisted approach for reducing anxiety and stress in college students. *SAGE Open*, 9(2). https://doi.org/10.1177/2158244019854646.

Belkofer, K., & Belkofer, C. (2018). Interpersonal downloading: The relational and creative impacts of technology and new media in therapy. In C. Malchiodi (Ed.), *The handbook of art therapy and digital technology*. Jessica Kingsley Publishers. https://ereader.perlego.com/1/book/953387/9.

Burlingame, G. M., McClendon, D. T., & Yang, C. (2018). Cohesion in group therapy: A meta-analysis. *Psychotherapy*, 55(4), 384–398. https://doi.org/10.1037/pst0000173.

Camic, P. M., Brooker, J., & Neal, A. (2011). Found objects in clinical practice: Preliminary evidence. *The Arts in Psychotherapy*, 38(3), 151–159. https://doi.org/10.1016/j.aip.2011.04.002.

Carlier, N. G., Powell, S., El-Halawani, M., Dixon, M., & Weber, A. (2020). COVID-19 transforms art therapy services in the Arabian Gulf. *International Journal of Art Therapy*, 25(4), 202–210. https://doi.org/10.1080/17454832.2020.1845759.

Choudhry, R., & Keane, C. (2020). *Art therapy during a mental health crisis: Coronavirus pandemic impact report*. American Art Therapy Association. https://arttherapy.org/upload/Art-Therapy-Coronavirus-Impact-Report.pdf.

Collie, K., Bottorff, J. L., Long, B. C., & Conati, C. (2006). Distance art groups for women with breast cancer: Guidelines and recommendations. *Supportive Care in Cancer*, 14(8), 849–858. https://doi.org/10.1007/s00520-005-0012-7.

Collie, K., Prins Hankinson, S., Norton, M., Dunlop, C., Mooney, M., Miller, G., & Giese-Davis, J. (2017). Online art therapy groups for young adults with cancer. *Arts & Health*, 9(1), 1–13. https://doi.org/10.1080/17533015.2015.1121882.

Darewych, O. H., Carlton, N. R., & Farrugie, K. W. (2015). Digital technology use in art therapy with adults with developmental disabilities. *Toronto*, 21(2), 95–102.

Darke, K. (2016). IPad apps and traumatic brain injury. In R. Garner (Ed.), *Digital art therapy*. Jessica Kingsley Publishers. https://ereader.perlego.com/1/book/953516/15.

Futterman Collier, A. D., Wayment, H. A., & Birkett, M. (2016). Impact of making textile handcrafts on mood enhancement and inflammatory immune changes. *Art Therapy*, 33(4), 178–185. https://doi.org/10.1080/07421656.2016.1226647.

Garner, R. L. (2016). *Digital art therapy: Material, methods, and applications*. Jessica Kingsley Publishers. https://ereader.perlego.com/1/book/953516/13.

Graves-Alcorn, S. (2017). Media dimension Variables. In S. Graves-Alcorn & C. Kagin (Eds.), *Implementing the expressive therapies continuum* (1st ed., Vol. 1, pp. 8–12). Routledge. https://doi.org/10.4324/9781315624303-2.

Hass-Cohen, N., Bokoch, R., Goodman, K., & Conover, K. J. (2021). Art therapy drawing protocols for chronic pain: Quantitative results from a mixed method pilot study. *The Arts in Psychotherapy*, 73, 101749. https://doi.org/10.1016/j.aip.2020.101749.

Hinz, L. D. (2009). *Expressive therapies continuum: A framework for using art in therapy*. Routledge. https://doi.org/10.4324/9780203893883.

Hinz, L. D. (2016). Media considerations in art therapy: Directions for future research. In D. E. Gussak & M. L. Rosal (Eds.), *The Wiley handbook of art therapy* (Vol. 1, pp. 135–145). John Wiley & Sons. https://doi.org/10.1002/9781118306543.ch13.

Kaimal, G., Ayaz, H., Herres, J., Dieterich-Hartwell, R., Makwana, B., Kaiser, D. H., & Nasser, J. A. (2017). Functional near-infrared spectroscopy assessment of reward perception based on visual self-expression: Coloring, doodling, and free drawing. *The Arts in Psychotherapy*, 55, 85–92. https://doi.org/10.1016/j.aip.2017.05.004.

King, J. L. (2017). Cortical activity changes after art making and rote motor movement as measured by EEG: A preliminary study. *Biomedical Journal of Scientific & Technical Research*, 1(4), 1062–1075. https://doi.org/10.26717/BJSTR.2017.01.000366.

King, J. L., Kaimal, G., Konopka, L., Belkofer, C., & Strang, C. E. (2019). Practical applications of neuroscience-informed art therapy. *Art Therapy*, 36(3), 149–156. https://doi.org/10.1080/07421656.2019.1649549.

King, R., Baker, F., & Nielsen, P. (2016). Introduction. In *Creative arts in counseling and mental health* (pp. 1–7). SAGE.

L'Esperance, N. (2016). Art therapy and technology: Islands of brilliance. In R. Garner (Ed.), *Digital art therapy*. Jessica Kingsley Publishers.

Levy, C. E., Spooner, H., Lee, J. B., Sonke, J., Myers, K., & Snow, E. (2018). Telehealth-based creative arts therapy: Transforming mental health and rehabilitation care for rural veterans. *The Arts in Psychotherapy*, 57, 20–26. https://doi.org/10.1016/j.aip.2017.08.010.

Lobban, J., & Murphy, D. (2020). Military museum collections and art therapy as mental health resources for veterans with PTSD. *International Journal of Art Therapy*, 25(4), 172–182. https://doi.org/10.1080/17454832.2020.1845220.

Malchiodi, C. (2018). There`s an app for that. In C. Malchiodi (Ed.), *The handbook of art therapy and digital technology*. Jessica Kingsley Publishers.

McBride, D. L., & Worrall, A. (2021). Recommendations when shifting gears to running online groups using creative expressive activities. *Canadian Journal of Art Therapy*, 34(1), 18–25. https://doi.org/10.1080/26907240.2021.1943956.

McNiff, S. (2018). New media and their effects in art therapy. In C. Malchiodi (Ed.), *The handbook of art therapy and digital technology*. Jessica Kingsley Publishers.

Orr, P. (2012). Technology use in art therapy practice: 2004 and 2011 comparison. *The Arts in Psychotherapy*, 39(4), 234–238. https://doi.org/10.1016/j.aip.2012.03.010.

Riley, S. (2001). *Group process made visible: Group art therapy*. Taylor & Francis.

Rosal, M. L. (2016). Rethinking and reframing group art therapy: An amalgamation of British and US models. In D. E. Gussak & L. R. Marcia (Eds.), *The Wiley handbook of art therapy* (1st ed., Vol. 1, pp. 231–241). John Wiley & Sons. https://doi.org/10.1002/9781118306543.ch23.

Schouten, K. A., de Niet, G. J., Knipscheer, J. W., Kleber, R. J., & Hutschemaekers, G. J. M. (2015). The effectiveness of art therapy in the treatment of traumatized adults: A systematic review on art therapy and trauma. *Trauma, Violence, & Abuse*, 16(2), 220–228. https://doi.org/10.1177/1524838014555032.

Shaw, L. (2020). "Don't look!" An online art therapy group for adolescents with anorexia nervosa. *International Journal of Art Therapy*, 25(4), 211–217. https://doi.org/10.1080/17454832.2020.1845757.

Spooner, H., Lee, J. B., Langston, D. G., Sonke, J., Myers, K. J., & Levy, C. E. (2019). Using distance technology to deliver the creative arts therapies to veterans: Case studies in art, dance/movement and music therapy. *The Arts in Psychotherapy*, 62, 12–18. https://doi.org/10.1016/j.aip.2018.11.012.

Van Lith, T. (2014). "Painting to find my spirit": Art making as the vehicle to find meaning and connection in the mental health recovery process. *Journal of Spirituality in Mental Health*, 16(1), 19–36. https://doi.org/10.1080/19349637.2013.864542.

Waller, D. (2012). Group art therapy: An interactive approach. In C. Malchiodi (Ed.), *Handbook of art therapy* (Vol. 2, pp. 353–367). Guilford Press. https://go.exlibris.link/jy4tDvsy.

Weinberg, H. (2020). Online group psychotherapy: Challenges and possibilities during COVID-19—A practice review. *Group Dynamics: Theory, Research, and Practice*, 24(3), 201. https://doi.org/10.1037/gdn0000140.

Weinberg, H., & Rolnick, A. (2020). *Theory and practice of online therapy: Internet-delivered interventions for individuals, groups, families, and organizations*. Routledge.

Weinberg, H., Rolnick, A., & Leighton, A. (2023). Epilogue. In H. Weinberg, A. Rolnick, & A. Leighton (Eds.), *Advances in online therapy: Emergence of a new paradigm*. Routledge.

Yalom, I. D. (1985). *The theory and practice of group psychotherapy* (3rd ed.). Basic Books.

Youhjung. (2019, October 16). Digital art therapy exercise using iPad or tablet. *Thirsty for Art*. https://www.thirstyforart.com/blog/digital-art-therapy.

Zimmerman, M., Terrill, D., D'Avanzato, C., & Tirpak, J. W. (2021). Telehealth treatment of patients in an intensive acute care psychiatric setting during the COVID-19 pandemic: Comparative safety and effectiveness to in-person treatment. *The Journal of Clinical Psychiatry*, 82(2). https://doi.org/10.4088/JCP.20m13815.

Zubala, A., & Hackett, S. (2020). Online art therapy practice and client safety: A UK-wide survey in times of COVID-19. *International Journal of Art Therapy*, 25(4), 161–171. https://doi.org/10.1080/17454832.2020.1845221.

Zubala, A., Kennell, N., & Hackett, S. (2021). Art therapy in the digital world: An integrative review of current practice and future directions. *Frontiers in Psychology*, 12, 595536. https://doi.org/10.3389/fpsyg.2021.600070.

Chapter 16

Online Group Art Therapy: The Presence of the Artistic Entity

Experiences with Groups of Senior Citizen Women

Dana Shor

"Can You Hear Me?"

"I can't turn the camera on," "Sit, good dog, sit." Background sounds can be heard from television, the morning news can be heard on the radio, reminder notifications of doctor appointments, a picture of a ceiling fan, far-off voices, black screens, unidentified names and numbers on blurry screens, and metallic sounds blaring from the lack of internet reception. This was the atmosphere during the first session of the online art therapy group for senior citizen women. These women, until recently, had been active individuals who were engaged in various activities, but at this time they found themselves isolated as a result of the COVID-19 pandemic. The aim of the group was to provide a platform for supporting senior citizen women across Israel who had unexpectedly become isolated from society, and showed signs of emotional distress and profound loneliness, in an attempt to protect their physical health.

The initial sessions were characterized by an almost obsessive interest in what could be seen and heard. "I don't see you, but I hear you; can you hear me?" "I can't see anything on the screen," "You're on mute," "What happened to the video conferencing software? It's gone."

The sudden circumstantial changes, together with the adjustment to a new world of digital reality, had led to an overwhelming feeling of complex emotional content including the distress and pain of ageing and retirement, the lack of purpose and human significance, and even the need to be isolated. The need to be socially isolated was not only to prevent the spread of the virus, but also due to the struggles of society to observe old age and the latent desire to isolate this population. All these factors intensified as a result of the COVID-19 pandemic.

I needed to establish a "digital clinic" using Internet programs and applications in the new "digital ecology" environment, while fostering a digital discourse outside of therapy and by using social media (Lieber, 2021). This unfolded within a reality in which an inter-generation distinction exists, between the "digital natives" generation and that of the "digital immigrants" (Prensky, 2001).

DOI: 10.4324/9781003248606-19

The initial sessions held during the first stages of the COVID-19 pandemic dealt with issues of "alignment" and handling basic technological needs. These reflected the women's basic emotional needs to establish their place, to be seen and heard.

Black Windows

Minutes after starting a session, a mosaic spread across the screen, square by square, replacing the more familiar circle of chairs in a therapy room. We saw faces which slowly became familiar; participants noticed new hairdos and bright-colored clothing. The participants' locations on the screen were not determined by them, they did not even know where they were located in relation to other group members. Each participant viewed a different layout on the computer screen. Black squares appeared on the screen, participants came and went, their presence or absence controlled by the fluctuating stability of the Internet connection, or a sudden phone call which interrupted the group at the start of a therapy session.

Online therapy is rife with limitations. During the COVID-19 pandemic, many therapists in a variety of fields described similar difficulties:

1   Risks associated with privacy and unclear boundaries.
2   The partial components of non-verbal connections.
3   Dependence on technological skills and equipment.

The Artistic Entity

Foulkes (1990) described the group matrix as a communication network between group members that is continuously evolving and consists of conscious and unconscious thoughts and feelings. It serves as a common basis, a kind of mother's womb, that gives meaning to the verbal and non-verbal connections between the group members. The processes stem from the dynamic interactions within the group communication matrix. At any given moment, the effectiveness of communication depends on both the morality and type of acceptance of the communication. According to Foulkes, the "I" and the "we" are not separate entities: they exist in a continuous relationship. Group analysis is a meeting place of people beyond the individuals themselves; it is an encounter of mental processes that is enhanced through conversations that flow freely (Foulkes, 2018). I asked myself how I could create a sense of open communication despite the given limitations that would allow for the formation of a group fabric.

McNeilly's (2005) approach and model of "group analytic art therapy" is based on Foulkes' matrix and the view of the group as a whole. McNeilly defines the goal of the analytic group to enable open, personal and collective communication and expression, and claims that this goal becomes easier to implement in groups that are analytic and employ art therapy. An additional dimension of visual symbolic interaction aids the therapist to see the analytical processes of the group more easily, and at times more immediately, and incorporates a sense of concreteness to the process of transforming unconscious content into conscious content.

McNeilly (2005) divided the matrix into three categories: "what is seen," "what is partially seen," and "what is not seen." He distinguished the way these categories are expressed in a group conversation as opposed to expressions in an art group. He observed that in the art group, other dimensions are added to these three categories. For example, what one sees in a conversational group is the number of people in the room and its contents, furniture and the group facilitator, whereas in the art group, there are also the creative materials and the images that are created. McNeilly claims that it is the level of alignment between these three categories that emphasizes the strength of the group matrix.

Lemma's (2017) philosophical insights describe cognitive hybridization, whereby the biological and technical expansion of the individual's emotional and physical abilities becomes possible. The technology becomes an extension of the individual, including his/her physiological and nervous systems, thus affecting the emotional and social being on a macro level. Therefore, the wheel is an extension of our legs, the telephone an extension of our voices, the computer an extension of our minds, and electronic media an extension of our central nervous systems. Similarly, a walking stick for a blind individual is not simply an object, but an extension of the individual's sensory fields which integrates the tool into the body's gestalt.

The presence of the artistic entity in all its permutations serves as an additional platform to expand and extend communication, and thereby compensate for the lack of physical presence. Digital media, by its very visual nature, is complementary to the artistic entity. I will demonstrate how the artistic elements are expressed in an online therapy group and how they are also strengthened in the digital platform. I will then provide a detailed explanation for each artistic element.

Below are the characteristics of the artistic entity:

1   An attentive presence: the creative process contains experiential qualities and an awareness of the present moment.
2   Movement presence: the creative process is an active one, involving the body and physical movement which creates presence and connection.
3   Material presence: the existence of tangible, creative materials involving a heightening of the senses, including emotional or spiritual aspects.
4   Visual presence: the visuality of the product facilitates manifestation, communication and identification. The visual result is accessible and encourages further communication.

5   Atemporal presence: the ability of the visual product to remain present for an unlimited time creates continuity and sequence, fulfilling the need for "witnessing."

These characteristics are "signs of life," bearing witness to the presence of an actual entity whose characteristics provide additional "information" (sensory, experiential, emotional, physical and associative) for group communication, thereby enriching and expanding levels of communication.

All elements are present in a setting that is amplified in a digital environment which by its very nature relies on visual content. In this way, the connection to the artistic medium is a natural connection, which creates a hybrid experience and merges the human and the technological, the foreign and the familiar, and the accessible and the threatening.

I will present these features and their applications in the digital studio/clinic.

Attentive Presence

Working online, participants have heightened attention towards sounds and this increases the level of intimacy. Occasionally, the participants may have wanted to silence the microphone, to turn off the camera, to hide within themselves and not become revealed, aided by the fact that with the simple push of a button, they could disappear. However, the rules of the group prevented this from happening and therefore the sounds and movements continued, sometimes disturbing, frightening and distracting, and occasionally resonating and inspiring. The creative process typically occurs in silence and is accompanied by individual introspection. Research findings (Regev et al., 2016) examining the experience of silence during art therapy showed that silence during art creation enables the creator to turn inwards and develop a significant internal and subjective process, while contributing to the therapeutic relationship. Art plays a central role in evoking moments of silence. During this process of introspection while engaging in art creation, a positive reaction occurs physiologically, similar to processes that occur when practising mindfulness. Zeltser (2017) explains that the act of creation intensifies and awakens a sense of awareness and attention to the present moment and in relation to the activity itself. Here, the ability to be alone, each in her own home but working together through video conferencing software in a joint creative process, reinforced the advantages of online therapy as a means to enable shared listening and attentive presence during which participants not only talk but are present together.

The group participants, who began with many concerns about their ability to integrate into the digital arena, adapted to the group setting in a gentle and soothing way. Gradually, they realized that all they had to do was create inside a cubicle with a camera, microphone and loudspeaker and be present together with the art materials. They could listen to the sounds of creative work and to their own heartbeats. Occasionally, their internal reflections were expressed verbally and openly, indicating a sense of ease and confidence that they began to accumulate.

Attentive Presence in the Digital Clinic

In the first session, I instructed the participants to prepare a small "studio" for themselves inside a box. They were asked to bring tools and materials that they had readily available or that they could take from nature in their immediate surroundings. Given the large gap between our physical and digital spaces, I initially used a variation of Orbach's (2006) method called Open Envelopes, as a mediation technique which is intended for the first stage in art therapy—the stage of embarking on a journey. During this stage of therapy, the patient and therapist embark together on a journey of discovery through a dialogue regarding their expectations and concerns during a first encounter with the art materials. I went beyond the limits of the digital clinical setting and sent each participant a parcel with some basic art supplies. The parcels were minimalistic and contained identical materials. The instructions were to create using only the materials I had sent them inside the parcel without the aid of any other tools. Pictures of the participants' artworks began to appear on the screen. They also added a range of visual and imaginative elements that emerged from their use of similar materials. I uploaded the images to a closed online digital album. The virtual exhibition evoked a great level of excitement among the participants and heightened their sense of universality and shared circumstances. The physical materials served as a transitional object, mediating and alleviating the move from physical to digital.

Movement Presence

Sounds of brushing, painting, plucking, cutting, kneading, engraving, drawing, spreading, slamming and ripping. The group is at the height of the active process which includes physical movements. The creative process is an active one and the movements enable the manipulation of artistic materials, whereby the visual symbol is simultaneously integrated and inherent in the various senses (Markman-Zinemanas, 2011). This strengthens and intensifies the experience and the participants' active participation by hearing sounds such as smearing colors, brushstrokes on the page or hitting clay.

The creation of a symbol involves physical movement, expressing the emotional state of the creator. For example, when the creator of the symbol hits the material as an expression of aggression, the action itself is also aggressive. The presence is expressed through the physical actions of the creator, not merely through verbalization, but also the actual movement as other group members actively participate through watching and hearing the creative act. The results tangibly embody the physical manipulation of the material (Krausz, 2009), expressing the participant's physical presence. From the observation of the physical actions, the participants receive communicative information about the pace of work, the level of mobility of the creator, the way the brushstrokes are created, the amount and density of the paint or material, the development of the symbol itself, and more. Through the brain activity of mirror neurons when observing another's actions, the observer experiences neurological activity in the same areas of the mind required to carry out the action, often experiencing a sense of physical involvement (Markman-Zinemanas, 2012). This neurological activation may indeed increase the sense of embodiment during online group therapy.

The following example illustrates a communication process expressed through Nili's[1] movements. Nili worked vigorously, dampened the paper, covered it with paint in large, heavy movements, then splashed tiny spots of color in small, light movements with the tip of the paintbrush. She then repeatedly turned the paper in different directions, filled it with paint, wetting and splashing, repeating the same actions in a restless and frantic manner. The group members could sense Nili's movements

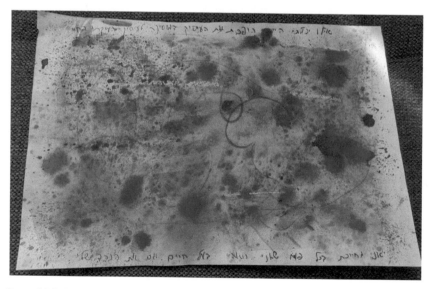

Figure 16.1 Artwork created by Nili
Source: Permission granted by the artist.

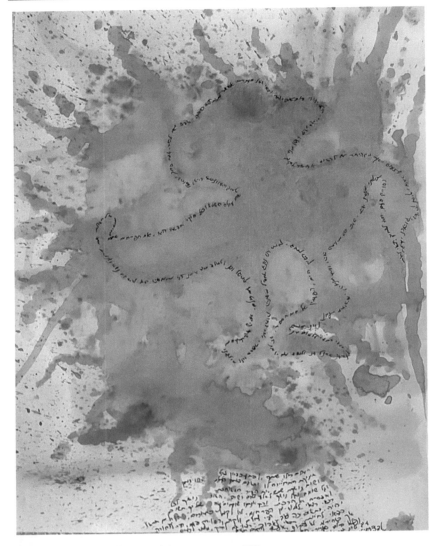

Figure 16.2 Artwork I created in response to Nili
Source: Permission granted by the artist.

and responded at times with movements and verbal reactions. When asked about the meaning of the movements and rhythm that emerged from her video window, Nili replied:

I'm thinking about music. I was involved in music when I was younger, and for some reason I went in other directions. I just think

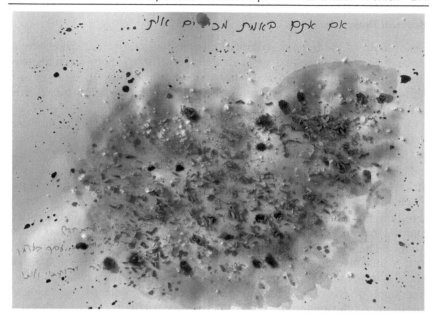

Figure 16.3 Artwork 2 created in response to Nili
Source: Permission granted by the artist.

that I didn't give it enough space and today I use music as a hobby. ... I will no longer become a professional musician. It's no longer as simple today as it was when I was younger. Today there are more limitations if you want to do it [music] seriously. I regret that I didn't try to integrate it into my professional work. I have missed out.

Nili's movements swept the group participants to react creatively and with movement-based responses, which resulted in emotional expressions and further enabled a conversation about their feelings related to old age.

Movement Presence in the Digital Clinic

The video and speakers were activated while everyone was creating in their homes, allowing individuals to move between the screens, and to hear and see each other. This enabled the participants to focus on their senses of hearing and vision which refined and increased the level of intimacy within the group.

Material Presence

The absence of the body is striking; however, the creative materials have a genuine presence expressed through their form, smell, color, weight, texture, and sometimes even their taste. Therefore, in group analytic art therapy, there is a significant supplement of active and creative elements which arouse all the other senses (McNeilly, 2005).

Orbach (2006) addresses the spiritual characteristics of the creative materials and claims that the raw material has significance and a truth of its own. The material refers to the world perceived through the senses, and the tactile aspect in this world is significant and is expressed in a variety of materials, such as oils, liquids, powders, pastes, and lumps, which may all be absorbed through the senses. Every physical material has physical and chemical qualities. The existence of diverse sensory qualities enhances and adds information to the group communication process. The sensory stimulation creates a different dynamic experience, both connective and universal. When participants sense the creative materials together, they feel similar tactile sensations, and this leads to an experience of closeness. Occasionally instructions relate to the physical sensations of the materials, and sometimes participants share with each other and discuss their similar experiences. For example, the clay that dries on their hands and creates cracks, the pulled muscle that holds the pencil, the puddles of liquid paint spots, and so on.

The handling of the material, the dirt, and color produce similar experiences and promote an expansion of communication. The art material adds information in the unknown areas of communication. The creator's choice of material often reflects his/her memories, associations, childhood dreams and even traumas. The actions used with the materials may arouse echoes of past, early physical memories. The material acts as an alternative to the physicality of human contact. Once again there are smells, sights, and tactile elements.

Devorah said:

> I had a difficult feeling, with everything closing in on me, the work with water helped clean it, release it, everything was washed away; I felt a sense of contrast and after dipping the paintbrush in the water and going over everything, the sense of contrast softened. I felt overwhelmed and threw a large amount of paint on the paper. The goal was to wash it, and now it's cleaner. From this experience, something new was born.

Devorah presented her artwork like a sort of X-ray image of a cleaning process and demonstrated how the use of physical material enables her to embark and advance on her processes. Her process was almost contagious, leading others to engage with the materials in the same way, echoing a cleaning desire that each participant desired for herself. For Nitza, "The water really helped me. I felt like I was watering down my emotions, rinsing them, and thanks to the artwork, I am shaping my feelings."

The qualities of the material and the opportunity to feel and interact with them physically facilitated group members to better understand emotions through the feeling of the material, and as such feel empathy and identification. Nitza said:

> I think this pink lump is my heart, it can be squished and extended according to the material. It's made of tissue paper and glue, a material which could harden when it dries and expand when it's wet, just like our own hearts constrict and expand.

For many long, intimate moments there was no longer a need for physical presence, as the intimate contact was so near and so significant.

Visual Presence

The visual medium often serves as the preferred representational medium. Noy (1999) claims that art is communicative and represented by primary, pre-verbal signs that are understood by all. The primary signs are accessible, concrete, and express highly significant information. They are capable of inspiring emotion, conveying experiences in a strong and meaningful way and stimulating the imagination. Markman-Zinemanas (2011) claims that the visual symbol is a concrete entity available for reflective contemplation which can lead to therapeutic change. The artistic product, which is visually marked, serves as an extroverted expression of parts of the Self. Due to its aesthetic characteristics which can be defined in terms of size, color and shape, it enables identification, dialogue and inter-subjective emotional activity. According to McNeilly (2005), the group embraces the imagination and unity of the individuals, providing a concrete form. Through the image, the imagination is more easily seen and shared.

By means of the visual expressions, group members can easily identify the similarities and differences among them. The participants spoke about other's artworks and began to use the plural form when they spoke; the visual image quickly allowed the group to discover that they shared similar concerns and difficulties and had a sense of identification, reflection, hope and even shared advice, which are all primary therapeutic elements for group therapy (Yalom, 2006).

Working with art offers creators a unique visual experience to work with various issues and also has a tendency to accelerate group processes. Furthermore, it provides a special opportunity for development and understanding relationships among group members. Each member is viewed as an individual character with a unique background. The group has a voice, a way of conduct and a way of seeing. Observing forms and shapes together enhances the sense of therapeutic intimacy (McNeilly, 2005).

Visual Presence in the Digital Clinic

In my view as a group facilitator and therapist, ensuring that the art materials were accessible to the participants became a complex task. The preparation of therapy sessions was accompanied by physical activities to prepare and serve the art materials, such as sharpening pencils, cutting plasticine, collecting materials from nature and arranging various work-stations. In order to convey these qualities using digital means, I used slide presentations through which I "presented" materials to the partici-pants and "arranged and organized" tables and workstations. I also col-lected images and inspirational pictures that offered them a visual experience which would allow them to enjoy the richness and diversity and become inspired. During the creative process, I positioned the camera towards my hands so that the participants could observe me creating, and many followed and imitated me. After completing their artworks, they sent photographs of the artworks via the group chat application in order to allow everyone to view the pictures at their leisure and even enlarge the images if necessary.

From the perspective of the participants, another important issue was the convenience and availability of the camera in therapy and the well-known use of chat applications as a tool for sharing images. This affected the ease and speed with which the group members shared their visual artworks and in terms of their availability for reflection and communica-tion after viewing an artwork. To some degree, the opportunity to share within the group became more readily available and accessible and the chat application further enhanced this feature as it was open and available for visual sharing at any time.

Atemporal presence

As a fundamentally visual product, a striking characteristic of the artwork is that it enables consistency and continuity. Moreover, the art product can exist without its owner/creator. Through technological means and expanding the therapy setting to other proportions, the "exhibition" is always available and allows the participants to be "witnesses" for one another in terms of the personal processes which achieve significance from being seen. The presence of witnesses is a significant factor in group art therapy. Moon et al. (2001) assert that witnessing facilitates three central processes: first, it provides the patient with confirmation, validation, acknowledgement and meaning of his/

her presence; second, it may foster empathy; and third, it enables a process of "mirroring" in therapy which allows patients an opportunity to recognize themselves better through the gaze of others.

By using technological tools, we were able to provide a lot of room for the witnessing element of our group. The group maintained its continuity and process between the sessions through the ability of each participant to observe the artworks available using various digital tools. The tools that we used included:

- The group chat application: this was used for messages, updates and links, as well as documenting and sharing the artworks. It is not limited by hour or time of day but exists as a consistent presence that is available for participants to use in any way they choose and does not require active participation. Alongside the advantages of the convenience and availability of the group chat application, the issue of boundaries and safeguarding the group emerged. As the group facilitator, I felt a responsibility to make sure that no one was left without group responses or feedback, and that insensitive or inappropriate content was not conveyed or used as a starting point for a conversation that may be unmanageable during the week.
- Facebook group (separate from the group chat application which was detailed above).
- Padlet board (shared display board): an online collaborative board to which files can be uploaded and viewed together. The Padlet board accompanied us in every session and was accessible for viewing at all times allowing participants to view themselves within the fabric of the group, to address their place or to make changes. The artwork on display adopts a new dimension of meaning due to its uniqueness as well as its placement. In this way, the visual medium and the creative process assisted in developing horizontal thinking, an approach which creates a network of connections among group members (McNeilly, 2005). The participants wait for the moment that they can share their artworks on the mutual display board and are excited to locate their artworks. The presence of the group voice is significant; simply by viewing it and feeling the group as a whole creates a multidimensional process: instead of reducing the unique nature of each object, it increases within the structure of the connections between the objects. Each one expands beyond the limits of its molecular structure into the space between the consciousnesses of the individual group members (McNeilly, 2005).

Conclusion

The "open studio" approach to art therapy, a concept coined by Allen in 1983, recognizes art as the focus of therapeutic work. It is based on the "art as therapy" approach in which the artistic processes and end products are central to therapeutic work and hold restorative qualities.

The studio can also be a state of mind based on the human ability to create metaphors and contexts and believe in their tangibility. What transforms an environment into a studio? A site that was chosen and accepted as a working framework during a defined time with repeated rituals, and a space in which generosity and optimism are present. "The essence of the studio implies allowing ourselves to be present and self-reflective and reflective of others" (Orbach, 2019). Based on these principles, the online environment, insofar as it fulfils these conditions, may serve as a significant therapeutic space.

On a personal level, the therapy sessions with this group during the COVID-19 pandemic were significant and exciting. A central experience of the group members was their feeling of liveliness and vitality, something that was incredibly absent during this period. After reviewing a feedback questionnaire filled out by the participants at the end of the sessions, it was evident that it was a significant experience for them as well. They expressed a sense of belonging to the group, and towards the end of their therapy process, they spoke a common language. The group felt a sense of competence and that they had a space to express their views and individuality. It was a beneficial and positive experience that in my humble opinion was established and experienced quickly, thanks to the artistic entity.

Note

1 Pseudonyms have been used throughout the chapter and all the participants gave their consent to show their artworks.

References

Allen, P. B. (1983). Group art therapy in short-term hospital settings. *American Journal of Art Therapy*, 22(3), 93–95.

Barak, A. (2005). Research and experiences in interventions in online groups: Opportunities and challenges aside difficulties and risks. *Mikbatz*, 10(2), 33–56.

Bar Sadeh, N. (2020). Aloneness and solitude: In the presence and absence of the other—malignant and benign aspects. *Psychoactualia*, 78 (April), 37–45.

Ben-Salmon, A. (2021). Zoom-therapy: Online clinical setting-compromise or an opportunity. *Aca J Cli Psy & Men Heal*, 1(1), 1–3.

Foulkes, S. H. (1990). *Selected papers: Psychoanalysis and group analysis*. Routledge.

Foulkes, S. H. (2018). *Therapeutic group analysis*. Routledge.

Krausz, M. (2009), Creativity and Self-Transformation. In M. Krausz, D. Dutton, & K. Bardsley (Eds.), *The idea of creativity, philosophy and culture* (pp. 191–203, vol. 28). Brill.

Lemma, A. (2017). *The digital age on the couch: Psychoanalytic practice and new media*. Routledge.

Lieber, D. (2020). A ZOOM of her own: A quick jump from studio to technology-mediated therapy. *Art Therapy: Research and De Facto Creation*. Special edition. *Corona* (November), 1007–1016.

Lieber, D. (2021). What's your "story"? Integrating the digital world and therapy with between-the-lines expression and creativity. *Art Therapy: Research and De Facto Creation*. 18, 11–41. Markman-Zinemanas, D. (2011). The additional value of art psychotherapy: Visual symbolization. *Academic Journal of Creative Art Therapies*, 2, 131–139.

Markman-Zinemanas, D. (2012). Intersubjectivity and psychotherapy through art: Diagnostic and therapy repercussions. *In Between the Lines*, 6. http://www.artstherapyjournal.co.il/118153/.

McNeilly, G. (2005). *Group analytic art therapy*. Jessica Kingsley Publishers.

Moon, C. H., & Lachman-Chapin, M. (2001). *Studio art therapy: Cultivating the artist identity in the art therapist*. Jessica Kingsley Publishers.

Noy, P. (1999). *The psychoanalysis of art and creativity*. Modan Publishing.

Orbach, N. (2006). *Extracting the spirit from the material*. Massa.

Orbach, N. (2019). *A good enough studio*. Riesling Publishers.

Orbach, N., & Galkin, L. (2005). *The nature of the material: Art therapy, steps and experiences*. Vol. 1. Sifrei Oranim.

Prensky, M. (2001). Digital natives, digital immigrants. *On the Horizon*, 9(5), 1–6.

Rappaport, l. (Ed.) (2014). *Mindfulness and the arts therapies: Theory and practice* (p. 16). Jessica Kingsley Publishing.

Regev, D., Chasday, H., & Snir, S. (2016). Silence during art therapy: The client's perspective. *The Arts in Psychotherapy*, 48, 69–75.

Schaverien, J. (1999) *the revealing image: Analytical art psychotherapy in theory and practice*. Jessica Kingsley Publishers.

Shufer Engelhardt, E. (2020). Staying within the frame: Meeting through the body in the arena of a computer screen in children's psychotherapy. *Psichologia Ivrit*. https://www.hebpsy.net/articles.asp?id=3994.

Vaknin, O.V., Donski, Y. D., & Soferi, E. S. (2020). HaKol HaReviei: HaWhatsapp HaText HaMelave et HaSha'a HaTipolit (The fourth voice. Whatsapp: The text accompanies the therapy hour between the lines). *Bein HaMilim*, 17, 29–45.

Winnicott, D. W. (1958). The capacity to be alone. *International Journal of Psycho-Analysis*, 39, 416–420.

Winnicott, D. (1971). *Play and reality*. Am Oved.

Yalom, I. (2006). *Group therapy theory and practice*. Kinneret Publishing.

Zeltser, S. (2017). Mindfulness and creation in therapy: A contribution to emotional regulation among children, parents and therapists. *Betipulnet*.

Chapter 17

Adventure-Based Counseling Online

Bringing Novelty, Physical Engagement, and Shared Problem Solving to a Virtual Format

Barney Straus

Introduction

When the world went virtual in 2020, adventure-based therapists were faced with the challenge of how to capture the elements unique to Adventure-Based Counseling (ABC) in a format that limits kinesthetic involvement. Specifically, the attributes of *novelty and play, physical engagement*, and *metaphorical application of meaning* that are central to ABC do not lend themselves easily to transfer of contexts (Ogden and Goldstein, 2020). Gass et al. (2012) have described adventure therapy (AT) as "the prescriptive use of adventure experiences provided by mental health professionals, often conducted in natural settings, that kinesthetically engage clients on cognitive, affective, and behavioral levels." AT is often provided to adolescents at therapeutic schools through long-term camping experiences that foster a sense of self-sufficiency and self-confidence in participants. While long-term camping and exposure to nature cannot be transferred to a virtual environment, ABC, which typically takes place within the context of traditional group therapy framework, can be creatively adapted to virtual settings. This form of AT is well suited to adults and indeed to adolescents and children provided that they can understand the directions to the challenges. Most of the activities used in ABC can be done in a large group room. The challenges given to the group usually involve props and physical movement that are required to complete them.

After explaining how the main precepts of ABC mentioned above complement interpersonal group psychotherapy, this chapter demonstrates through a group vignette how several activities that are often used by adventure-based therapists during live groups can be effectively facilitated in a virtual environment.

DOI: 10.4324/9781003248606-20

ABC as a Complement to Group Psychotherapy

Yalom and Leszcz (2020) have identified 11 therapeutic factors associated with group psychotherapy. They describe the types of structured activities often used in ABC as having an accelerating effect on group development. In particular, the therapeutic factors of altruism, universality, imitative behavior, and group cohesiveness are all amplified through the use of structured exercises. Since ABC invites all group members to work toward a common goal, a sense of universality naturally follows. Group members will often assist each other as they go about solving the puzzles given to them by the group leader; a sense of altruism for those offering the assistance, as well as for those witnessing and receiving such help naturally evolves. An example of this in the physical realm might be one group member offering to help another to balance as they attempt to traverse a suspended wire or a horizontal log. In the virtual world, verbal hints can be offered as group members learn to practice a new skill or attempt a new challenge. As group members witness each other modeling successful approaches to a given skill, they will want to imitate those behaviors that appear to be successful, thus activating the therapeutic factor of imitative behavior. The skilled ABC practitioner will then invite group members to reflect on other behaviors that they would like to emulate in their lives outside the group.

Yalom and Leszcz (2020) posit that group cohesiveness is the most important of all the therapeutic factors. A group that participates in enjoyable activities together is more likely to develop a sense of cohesiveness than a group that does not share a sense of playfulness. Van der Kolk (2014) has written extensively about the therapeutic value of shared play. The sense of novelty inherent in ABC brings out a sense of adventure and a willingness to try something new in group members. Having group members experiment with new behaviors is the very essence of successful group psychotherapy (Narr, 1982).

Novelty and Play

The sense of novelty that is central to ABC is created during in-person ABC sessions through the use of an unfamiliar environment, such as a challenge course, a wooded setting, or unique materials. Adventure therapy theory holds that creating a sense of the unfamiliar has the effect of allowing group members to break free of dysfunctional roles and explore new, more productive behaviors. While the physicality of natural environments can engage all the senses in a way that is impossible to replicate on a screen, the core therapeutic value of allowing participants to become immersed in an unfamiliar environment can be created online through the use of easily accessible props and virtual backgrounds. For example, at a recent conference of the Association for Experiential Education, Itan (2021) and Cain (2021) each suggested ways of incorporating novelty into online groups. Itan suggested using a wide range of activities, including pantomime, improvisation games, and mirroring activities, along with singing and cooking. Cain proposed using the chat feature to meet this purpose through Word Waterfalls (in which each participant writes their response to a prompt and hits "send" simultaneously), and the sharing of six-word stories written by each group member. Word Waterfalls work especially well in large groups, when a prompt such as "write a word or phrase that captures your experience in the group today" can yield a cascade of words and phrases flowing into the chat. Cain also shared several virtual backgrounds that invite group members to work together to solve a series of visual puzzles. Some of these were in the hidden figures tradition (think of the *Where's Waldo?* books) that shows a picture and askes group members to try seeing what was previously hidden from them. This is a metaphor that is easily applied to developing an enhanced self-concept among group members, as it reminds them that there can be more present in the group and within themselves than can be immediately seen.

Being able to speak and act freely and without too much forethought is a tenet that is valued by most interpersonal group therapists and practitioners of ABC alike (Zeisel, 2002; Gass et al., 2012). Spontaneity is invariably compromised in an online environment (Ogden and Goldstein, 2020). For example, impediments to spontaneity are experienced when two people try to speak simultaneously, whereas in live groups, multiple voices are fully audible, allowing speakers to grapple with the interpersonal tension that develops when several people try to speak at once. The unspoken question of which group member will defer to the others presents opportunities for interpersonal learning (Yalom and Leszcz, 2020). In contrast, in an online environment, the technology being used usually broadcasts one voice while muting the others, thus depriving group members of the nuances available during in-person group meetings. Despite this limitation, many activities specifically designed to facilitate both verbal and physical spontaneity among group members can work well in an online environment. Activities such as Group Juggling, improv games, and mirroring activities like Simon Says, all transfer well to the virtual world, with some modifications, as described below.

Physical Engagement

Of the three aspects of group processes under consideration, *physical engagement* is the most difficult to capture in an online format. Limitations of cameras built into computers restrict participants' mobility. Using phone-based cameras can result in unstable images that are difficult for viewers to focus on. The end result is that group members need to be seated during the group. This is anathema to the emphasis ABC places on becoming physically engaged in the group process. The many ABC activities that involve physical contact between group members are likewise unavailable in an online environment. However, the tactile element of ABC can be preserved through the use of easily accessible materials such as writing instruments, pieces of clothing, and sheets of paper measuring 8 ½ x 11 inches. For an example of the latter, see the description of the adapted Tarp Turn later in this chapter. The group leader can also request that the group members direct them to use a sheet of paper and a pair of scissors to create a contiguous frame of paper large enough for them to pass through. During an in-person group, the group members would be given the materials for Paper Doorway (Straus, 2018), and *all* the group members would be challenged to pass through the contiguous circle of paper. The online version of this activity allows group members to grapple with the problem-solving aspect of the activity, but denies them the tactile satisfaction of working with the materials and passing through the paper doorway themselves.

One reason that physical movement is so central to ABC is that movement itself can function as an analogous metaphor for change. Since an overall objective of psychotherapy is personal transformation, the act of moving one's body can represent movement toward such change, as opposed to remaining seated in a chair, which, metaphorically speaking, can be analogous to remaining stuck. One way to create a sense of movement during online groups is through group members repositioning their squares on the screen. This is the online equivalent of changing seats during an in-person group meeting. For many who are new to online learning, it comes as a surprise that they are not "stuck" in one place, but have some agency in being able to position themselves and others according to their preference. Moving squares is easily accomplished on Zoom, for example, by clicking on a square and holding down on the mouse or touchpad while moving the box to a different position on the screen. In this way, group members can create a pattern that all share, as opposed to the pattern that is determined by the program's algorithms. Arranging group members alphabetically by first names is the simplest method, though doing that bypasses a potentially useful discussion about who belongs where in terms of the group dynamics. The leader might want to take a more nuanced approach to forming the sequence of squares. Having a shared pattern on all group members' screens allows for facilitation of activities in which a predetermined order is required, such as One Word Stories, an improv game in which each person adds just one word to an evolving story (Spolin, 1983; Straus, 2018). While the moving of squares on a screen can be fun and can meet some structural needs of a group, it still has everyone remaining seated while they switch the positions of squares on the screen.

Figure 17.1 Group leader passes through the paper doorway that group members
          have co-created by providing verbal directions
Source: Photograph taken by Nancy Straus.

While the online universe has its limitations for adventure-based
therapists, it does provide some opportunities as well (Weinberg and
Rolnick, 2020). For example, virtual breakout rooms allow for subgroups
to work together without being distracted by other subgroups, as commonly happens when large groups splinter off in live settings. Likewise,

group drawing is made possible through use of the annotation feature of Zoom (whiteboard) and other similar platforms. Through the use of this application, all group members are able to draw on the screen simultaneously, and collaborate in a way that would be impossible in a real-world setting. While group drawing allows for the collective artistic expression of the group, the same application can be used to transfer sociometry exercises to the screen. Sociometry is related to both psychodrama and ABC; it involves asking group members to physically position themselves in relation to a specific schema. For example, "If the room were a lifeline, position yourself at the age at which you experienced the greatest stress." Sociometry is an effective way to have group members share about themselves simultaneously.

One example of doing sociometry online can be illustrated by an activity called Take A Stand (commonly known as Spectrogram in psychodrama), during which group members literally take a position in a room according to criteria the group leader defines. For example, the leader might say "If you identify more with a tortoise stand at one the end of the room and if you are more of a hare stand at the other end of the room." This activity allows group members a way to nonverbally share much information about themselves in a relatively brief period of time. An alternative online version of this activity can be done by pre-loading a PowerPoint presentation with slides that indicate the two ends of a continuum, and then group members place their virtual stamps on the page according to how they identify with each criterion. This feature effectively accomplishes the same kind of fast-paced self-reflection and disclosure that takes place during in-person sessions. Some criteria that can be used for this exercise include the following:

Do you believe that nature or nurture is more telling in shaping us?
Are you a head-centered or heart-centered person?
Are you an introvert or an extrovert?
Are you a dog person or a cat person?
Are you trusting or mistrustful?
Are you self-focused or mostly interested in others?
Are you a tortoise or a hare?
Are you judgmental or accepting of others?
Are you self-accepting or critical of yourself?
Depending on the goals and make-up of the group you are working with, you can pause for reflection and discussion following each round. I like to offer an opportunity for group members themselves to suggest other criteria for the group to work with. Doing this supports emergent leadership among group members, attends to their personal interests, and strengthens a sense of collaboration between group leader and participants—the group alliance.

Kinesthetic Metaphor

The third and arguably the most important quality of AT is the concept of *applied metaphor* which involves taking the construct of an activity and applying the dynamics to other areas of participants' lives. Metaphors can be therapeutically applied using language as well as action. Gans (1991) maintains that in order for a metaphor to be meaningful to group members, it must be understood by them. Obtuse verbal metaphors can leave group members feeling ashamed and frustrated. Kinesthetic metaphors, such as those used in ABC, have the advantage of being physically observable, and are therefore easy for group members to apply to their lives outside the group. Gass et al. (2012) define kinesthetic metaphor as intentional actions with isomorphic links to affect, behavior, and cognition that can then be applied to an individual's life and/or treatment goals. For example, in the Group Juggling activity described in the next section, group members remaining focused on the present moment is a key to the group's success. Crane-Okada (2012) has written about the importance of presence in group psychotherapy. A facilitator thinking metaphorically could invite group members to reflect on other aspects of their lives in which remaining focused on the present might be beneficial to them. Framing a question in an open-ended manner allows group members to apply the concept of presence to their personal relationships, professional aspirations, or avocations.

If the mood of the group is noteworthy, the facilitator can likewise ask what the energy in the group reminds them of elsewhere in their lives. If the mood of the group is playful or happy, where else do group members experience these feelings? If the group is feeling frustrated or angry, group members can reflect on how they cope with whatever challenges life has been presenting them with. Though the range of physical engagement is limited in an online environment, the use metaphoric transfer of learning is not, as seen in the examples that follow.

ABC Sequence Adapted to a Virtual Environment

To illustrate how a sequence of ABC activities can be adapted to an online environment, I will now describe how a typical sequence of activities that might be used during an in-person ABC session can be facilitated in the virtual world, while preserving the central therapeutic qualities of spontaneity, physical engagement, collaboration, and effective use of metaphoric transference. As mentioned, physical engagement is the most difficult of these elements to recreate in an online setting, whereas *novelty* and *metaphorical application* transfer fairly seamlessly. In addition, the concept of sequencing that is central to ABC can easily be applied online. Sequencing is related to group development, and essentially entails introducing activities in accordance with the group's developmental stage (Jacobs et al., 2016). This generally results in the group leader introducing less challenging activities before more involved ones, as reflected in the group session described below.

When working with a new group, or with an ongoing group that has gained one or more new group members, many ABC practitioners will start with an activity that helps group members to learn each other's names. One of the most popular of these is known as Group Juggling. During Group Juggling, group members are asked to stand in a circle and pass a beach ball or similar object to each person once without letting it touch any group member twice. Group members are asked to say the name of the person they are throwing the ball to, while tossing the ball. Once the group has successfully completed this initial task, a second and third object can be introduced once the first one is in play. The group is challenged with keeping all three objects in play without any drops for at least one complete cycle, meaning that each person gets each ball at least once.

While the tactile elements of throwing and catching of objects cannot be replicated online, the process of becoming familiar with group members' names while engaging playfully and remaining focused on the present moment can all be captured through the use of pantomime. The facilitator simply introduces an imaginary ball by placing their hands as if they were holding a basketball. The group leader demonstrates making a virtual chest pass with the ball while saying a group member's name aloud.

Figure 17.2 Group member prepares to throw an imaginary ball
Source: Photograph taken by Nancy Straus.

It is best to let the group complete a couple of cycles before introducing a second imaginary ball into the mix. Two virtual balls is probably the maximum number a group can juggle in the cloud at once, since eye contact and visually being able to track objects—two important aids in completing the task in a physical setting—are missing in the virtual world. This added challenge is compensated for by the fact that no one can literally drop an imaginary ball in a virtual environment. However, an invisible ball can still get effectively "dropped" as group members lose track of where the virtual objects are at any given moment. However, if group members become engaged and seem to be enjoying themselves, the group session is off to a good start, and these qualities are more important than whether or not the group completes the task. Attentiveness and having a shared sense of reality are two aspects of this warm-up activity that can be applied to other areas of group members' lives. These two qualities are important components of feeling fully present in a group. In her discussion of centrality of presence in group psychotherapy, Crane-Okada (2012) notes that the process of creating presence for group members begins with the group leader's own sense of being fully engaged and attuned to the group environment and to each of its members.

To further develop a sense of presence in a group, facilitators will frequently choose an activity that requires active listening. As noted by Gans and Counselman (1999), at any given moment most group members are silently listening to others, and becoming a better listener is an opportunity that group therapy is unique in being able to offer. Group therapists often model active listening in their role as group leaders. Yalom and Leszcz (2020) and Crane-Okada (2012) both emphasize the role-modeling aspect of group leadership. Likewise, Gass et al. (2012) have described ABC as an egalitarian method, meaning that group leaders often participate in the activities that they introduce to a group. The act of playing a game with a group in ABC is analogous to the interpersonally oriented group therapist modeling active listening. The task for the adventure-based therapists is to be able to model the behaviors while maintaining a clear role boundary. This is largely accomplished by avoiding doing one's own personal work while processing an activity.

One exercise that develops both active listening and a sense of being fully present is known as Zen Counting. The objective of Zen Counting is for the group to count aloud from 1–15, in sequence, without any number being said twice. Group members are asked to refrain from making a predetermined order in which group members say the numbers. Someone starts by saying "one," and then another group member says "two," and so on and so forth, until 15 is reached. If more than one person says a given number at the same time, the whole group starts over. This activity really encourages slowing down and listening before speaking—sensing when one's participation is likely to be helpful. The old oxymoronic adage "less is more" is relevant here. Through the use of metaphoric transfer, this concept can be applied to situations in which people are preoccupied with trying to change another person, for example. It can likewise apply to group endeavors in which individuals need to be sensitive to the efforts of their peers. Zen Counting transfers fairly seamlessly into an online environment. The audial limitations of Zoom can make it tricky to know whether two people are speaking at once, but being able to see everyone head-on seems to compensate for this limitation, and from my experience group members are fairly good at monitoring themselves.

Once the goals of fostering presence and playful engagement have been established through the use of introductory activities, most adventure-based counselors transition to problem-solving challenges. These challenges almost always engage the body, as kinesthetic learning is a core tenet of ABC (Gass et al., 2012). Examples of some of the best known of such activities include River Crossing, in which group members stand on movable platforms as they try to cross an imaginary river by stepping only on the platforms, and Trust Leans, in which group members physically support each other in a variety of ways. These kinds of activities are designed to foster and under-score the importance of shared problem-solving. In terms of metaphoric transfer of meaning, group members will be invited to reflect on how they enlist and use support to address the issues that brought them to the group. Many of the problem-solving activities used during in-person meetings do not transfer easily to a virtual environment. However, there are ways of get-ting group members out of their chairs and physically involved in shared problem-solving during virtual ABC sessions. Mirroring activities such as Simon Says work well in a virtual space. Itan (2021) reported having had some success using virtual Blind Walking activities, in which one person is blindfolded and then instructed to perform a series of motions by their guide. Use of a cell phone allows for better movement of the camera than does a computer, which, if remaining stationary, will significantly limit the range of motion possible. Please note that caution should be used when leading blind guided activities, as the visual sphere will be limited by use of cameras instead of eyes, and although creating a sense of perceived risk-taking is central to ABC, it is important that actual risk of physical injury be kept to a minimum. Accordingly, sticking to slowed down movements is probably best when using virtual blind guided activities. Other physical activities can be effectively adapted from group to individual challenges that can be attempted in each individual's home environment. One such activity is known as Tarp Flip.

When introducing Tarp Flip during an in-person group meeting, group members are asked to stand on one side of a plastic or canvas tarp and attempt to flip it over, *without stepping off of the tarp*. I have used this activity to capture the essence of the eighth of AA's 12 steps (Straus, 2018): Step 8 reads, *Made a list of all persons we had harmed, and became ready to make amends to them all* (Alcoholics Anonymous, 2001). I accomplish this by asking each group member to write the initials of someone they would like to make amends to on a piece of painter's tape, and then place the strips of tape on the bottom side of the tarp. As the group attempts to flip the tarp back right-side up, they are symbolically indicating that they are becoming ready to make amends to the collective list indicated by the strips of tape. Gass et al. (2012) refer the process of building meaning into an activity before the group commences on attempting as using *structured* metaphor, which the authors distinguish from *spontaneous* and *analogous* metaphors. Itan (2021) refers to this process as front-loading an activity.

Lung et al. (2008) suggest a way of adapting Tarp Flip from a group to an individual challenge. They do this by using standard sheets paper measuring 8 ½ x 11 inches and asking each person to stand on a piece of paper and flip it over *without stepping off of it*. The meaning embedded in my version can easily be accomplished here by simply having each group member write the names of the person(s) they want to make amends to and placing the side of the sheet with the names face-down to start. Because group members do not have each other to physically lean on when working alone at home, you might suggest that your group members use pieces of furniture or other props to help them balance as they attempt this task. For those working with recovering individuals, you might want to follow this exercise with some psychodrama. Psychodrama offers opportunities for group members to practice the act of making amends. (See Chapter 13 in this volume for detailed explanations of how this modality works best in an online environment.)

In addition to the kinds of problem-solving challenges traditionally used in ABC groups, Itan (2021) and Cain (2021) both recommend that the action-oriented group leader explore a variety of alternative methods that more easily transfer to the virtual environment. In addition to Group Drawing, described earlier, they each recommend using Show and Tell as a way for group members to build a sense of cohesion and familiarity with each other. Assuming that each person is logging in from home, items of emotional and/or practical value are likely to be close at hand. Similarly, virtual treasure hunts can be facilitated, although these involve participants leaving their respective computer terminals for brief periods of time.

Since online treatment grew vastly in acceptance during the COVID-19 pandemic, it seems likely that group leaders will continue to have opportunities to engage their group members in active endeavors from afar, and in doing so create a meaningful sense of a shared space that will provide a context in which group members can glean personal insights that can be applied to their lives beyond the screen. I hope that my colleagues who are practicing online group therapy will experiment with some of the activities described in this chapter—I think you and your group members alike will be delighted by the sense of shared play, and then further inspired to work toward their therapeutic goals. As we all know intuitively, anytime *work* starts to feel like play, something positive is taking place.

References

Alcoholics Anonymous (2001). *Alcoholics Anonymous: The story of how many thousands of men and women have recovered from alcoholism* (4th ed.). Alcoholics Anonymous World Service.

Cain, J. (Ed.) (2021). *The learning curve: Navigating the transition from facilitating in the real world to facilitating in a virtual one.* Healthy Living.

Crane-Okada, R. (2012). The concept of presence in group psychotherapy: An operational definition. *Perspectives in Psychiatric Care*, 48(3). doi:10.1111/j.1744-6163.2011.00320.x.

Gans, J. (1991). The leader's use of metaphor on group psychotherapy. *International Journal of Group Psychotherapy*, 41(2), 127–143.

Gans, J., & Counselman, E. (1999). Silence in group psychotherapy: A powerful communication. *International Journal of Group Psychotherapy*, 50(3), 70–83.

Gass, M. A., Gillis, H. L., & Russell, K. C. (2012). *Adventure therapy: Theory, research, and practice.* Routledge.

Itan, C. (2021). *Experiential group work virtually.* Association for Experiential Education International Conference, November 11–14.

Jacobs, E., Schimmel, C., Masson, R., & Harvill, H. (2016). *Group counseling strategies and skills* (8th ed.). Cengage.

Lung, M., Stauffer, G., & Alavarez, A. (2008). *The power of one: Using adventure and experiential activities within one and one counseling sessions.* Wood N' Barnes Publishing.

Narr, R. (1982). *A primer of group psychotherapy.* Human Sciences Press.

Ogden, P., & Goldstein, B. (2020). Sensorimotor psychotherapy from a distance: Engaging the body, creating presence, and building relationship in videoconferencing. In H. Weinberg & A. Rolnick (Eds.), *Theory and practice of online therapy: Internet-delivered interventions for individuals, groups, families, and organizations.* Routledge.

Spolin, V. (1983). *Improvisation for the theatre: A handbook of teaching and directing techniques.* Northwestern University Press.

Spolin, V. (1986). *Theater games for the classroom: A teacher's handbook.* Northwestern University Press.

Straus, B. (2018). *Healing in action: Adventure-based counseling with therapy groups.* Rowman and Littlefield.

Van der Kolk, B. (2014). *The body keeps the score: Brain, mind, and body in the healing of trauma.* The Viking Press.

Weinberg, H., & Rolnick, A. (Eds.) (2020). *Theory and practice of online therapy: Internet-delivered interventions for individuals, groups, families, and organizations.* Routledge.

Yalom, I., & Leszcz, M. (2020). *The theory and practice of group psychotherapy* (6th ed.), Basic Books.

Zeisel, E. (2002). *Working with immediacy.* Conference of the Illinois Group Psychotherapy Society, Schaumburg, Illinois, Fall.

Part IV

Online Person-Centered Mechanisms of Change Approaches: Psychoeducational, CBT, ACT and SE Groups

Chapter 18

Somatic Experiencing Informed Group Psychotherapy Online

Carlos Canales

Introduction

Somatic Experiencing® (SE) is a specialized modality of trauma and resilience treatment. It aims to help people to listen to their bodies, prioritizing the body's natural responses to a variety of situations such as shock, threat, pleasure, distress, and pain. The body has the capacity to capture a felt sense of internal or external stimuli continuously, and simultaneously to organize itself to respond, react, protect, heal, and guide us through every moment. The body keeps a record of our history, most often outside of conscious awareness. According to SE, all trauma and patterns of response reside in our individual nervous systems, not in the events or the stories reported by individuals (Levine, 1997; Riordan et al., 2019; van der Kolk, 2014). Thus, SE is typically practiced in individual therapy rather than in group.

Group psychotherapy is a modality that focuses on the treatment of the individual within a group context (Schlapobersky, 2016; Weinberg & Rolnick, 2020); however, the group is not restricted to the examination of a singular nervous system or intra-psychic process, one mind. Group therapists also track the bodies and minds of shifting subgroupings or of the entire group. Daniel Siegel (2020) defined the mind as an embodied, emergent, self-organizing, and relational process that regulates the flow of energy and information within and between people. When we are part of a group, there are noticeable shared feelings, sensory awareness, and group-as-a-whole experiences, as if members make up a much larger, organic and dynamic unity with regulating or dysregulating qualities.

All virtual therapy starts in a disembodied manner (Weinberg, 2014). Connection is outwardly heady and artificial since it is mediated by technology. By inviting the noticing of our full bodily sensitivities, discernments, and responses, SE initiates a type of centeredness within. It aims at progressively building confidence in locating the self via sensations, facilitating the flow of emotion, and encouraging meaningful whole-body-to-body interactions.

DOI: 10.4324/9781003248606-22

Effective virtual group psychotherapy would readily recognize the interplay of singular and multiple psychologies. Weinberg (2014) points out that "it is all about relationships," underscoring the ebb and flow between a culture of "me-ness," "we-ness," and "in-betweenness." In spite of the physical distance, group members have an idea of who they are, their subjectivity, their sense of belonging, and what is co-created with one another.

A Somatic Experiencing Informed (SE-I) virtual group benefits from the symbolism represented by Leonardo da Vinci's *Vitruvian Man*. In it, da Vinci portrays a naked man in two superimposed positions within both a circle and a square. The circle represents the divine, the infinite, and its revolving repetitions. The square symbolizes the material and mundane, with its sharp edges (Hdez, 2019). Historically, the group circle is viewed as a symbol for interconnectedness and parity (equidistance to the middle) while the square represents order. The artist depicted the body at the center, a microcosm of the universe, intimately interacting with it in perfect proportion. Everything inside connects to everything outside. When working online, our full bodies (nervous systems and minds) are in intimate communication with each other. Each member is in their square, their physical room and their virtual quadrangular; bounded and boundless, inside and outside circles of connections. Our bodies are central to all experience. Group psychotherapy made the transition from examining the psychology of one to the psychology of many (Schalpo-bersky, 2016). When working online, we move from the circle to the square, all registered by our sensate bodies.

The Wisdom of the Body

Freud understood that the psyche has its origins in raw sensory data, experience that is not limited to childhood. He wrote, "The ego [I] is first and foremost a bodily ego" (Freud, 1923). He implied that each person's psychological makeup, their minds, ultimately originate from physical sensation, the skin. However, Freud's most influential proposition was the existence of the unconscious and our propensity to repression, which stimulated a tremendous amount of attention to mental currents and undercurrents, separate from the sensate body. Subsequent therapeutic practices became more focused on understanding our thinking, our mental and interpersonal patterns, rather than attending to the body's wisdom and seeking its guidance (Wong, 2020).

For internal matters, the body is in charge. It seems to intuitively know where to go and how to self-organize. We do not have to think about growing old, circadian rhythms, breathing, salivating, sensing, circulating blood, or fighting illness. The body knows how to feel safe, satisfied, warm or cold. It knows how to provide us with a sense of belonging or

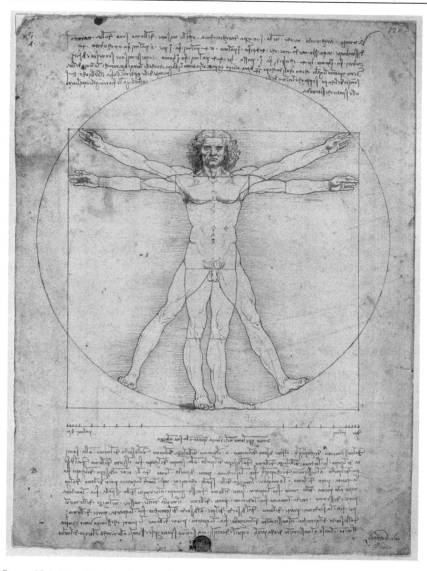

Figure 18.1 Vitruvian Man [pen and ink drawing] by Leonardo da Vinci, ca. 1490
Source: Gallerie Accademia, Venice, Italy.

detect its absence. When we are bruised, injured, or infected, the body immediately mobilizes to restore health and keep us whole. This type of primal wisdom cannot be taught. Hollis (2020) goes one step further and suggests that healing is a mystery of nature, a biological gift. The clinician can maximize the conditions but only nature heals. This notion is often missed in manualized treatments that focus on standardizing interventions. SE is intentional about respecting the body's intelligence and online work requires twice the initiative of looking inside.

The body is always present, forming and informing the foundations of our very existence. Thomas Ogden (1992) referred to this fundamental psychological form of organization as the autistic-contiguous mode of experience. He argued that it is our first way of relating to the world, which never goes away. It is sensory-dominated, pre-verbal, and pre-symbolic. It gives us a notion of where one's experience begins. Ogden (1992) termed it boundedness or "the sense of having (being) a place (more specifically a surface) where one's experience occurs and where a sense of order and containment is generated." In fact, many of us refer to "feeling ourselves" when we are in harmony with our bodies, safe and connected. In psychotherapy, it is paramount to help our clients land into themselves by sensing into their bodies and tracking the body's wisdom.

Principles of Virtual SE-I Groups

The practice of all SE could be summarized as befriending the nervous system of each client while supporting one's own, moment to moment. Doing SE at the individual level is complex enough given that we are tracking and relying on the corporal sensitivity, receptivity, ability to share and make meaning of internal sensory subtleties and movements. In a face-to-face (f2f) group, the therapeutic incorporation of body awareness is facilitated by the collaborative attunement of multiple nervous systems sitting next to each other and their countless ways of interfacing and resonating with one another. Each group member uses their five senses and their emotional intelligence to notice, support, and share. Touch and smell are literal possibilities. By contrast, the interpersonal dynamics of a SE-oriented virtual group relies on audio and visual sensing only. In this manner, the fullness of the engagement is less than in f2f groups. However, the examination of internal processes is the same. In fact, having the possibility of seeing yourself as another group member, another square on the screen, does not add to one's internal curiosity and inner noticing. You have to look inside. Thus, some members prefer to hide their self-view in order to pay attention to their phenomenological innerworkings, while others use their image to examine the congruence of their emotional expression and their image.

Similar to f2f groups, online SE group emphasizes the tracking of subtle and overt body-based behaviors while simultaneously inviting group members to pay attention to their own internal readings: sensations, emotions, and energetic movements. If emotions get too intense, the therapist may focus on regulating the nervous system of the individual member or the activation of various members to more manageable levels. The therapist supports the renegotiating and discharging of pockets of intensified sensation or feeling (sympathetic activation) or partial to global collapses of energy (dissociative or freeze moments) as they show up (Carleton, 2009; Levine, 2010; Payne et al., 2015).

As clients begin to understand that their bodies follow natural biological principles of activation or deactivation, there is less judgment about oneself and others and the group grows in patience and compassion. When clients are unable to know what they feel, they are at a similar loss to know what their peers are experiencing. Empathy and interpersonal resonance increase as members appreciate their own signals and rhythms, and that of their virtual neighbors (Cohen, 2011). Group cohesion is amplified as the group builds solidarity around the task of respecting one's physiological processes and restoring connection (Taylor & Saint-Laurent, 2017).

Virtual groups have many SE advantages. A group member can choose the room from which to participate, increasing familiarity and comfort. There is also the option of distancing or looking away from the screen, responses that are not available during an in-person meeting. To the degree that regulated body awareness is allowed, clients report feeling calmer, more present, curious, compassionate, and creative (Levine, 2010). While in session, group members can use their eyes and scan their homes or offices for objects, paintings, or mementos that represent emotional anchors to them. When connection with these occurs, there can be a noticeable expansion in breath, a change in posture adjusting for increased comfort or relaxation, sometimes even a change in muscular tone or color in the face. When group members feel in their bodies, they settle and orient themselves to the rest of the group with more sturdiness. They also perceive more support from peers.

The life of the group offers ample opportunities for a diversity of activations, disengagements, and energetic renegotiations—patterns that over time become familiar to all present. Individual disclosures are activating; so are absences, latencies, disagreements, and transference and countertransference dynamics. For some, it is too much to receive the group's attention displayed on a two-dimensional screen. In a f2f group, the awareness of the group member is limited to his or her frame of focus, namely that which is immediately in front of them. The experience online is that all members are directly in front, staring. The facilitator could encourage an overly stimulated member to look away from the screen for a few seconds or to observe who in the screen seems more familiar or welcoming and therefore soothing. Then, the invitation is to soak in one's body response, slowly enriching oneself with goodness. Sometimes members complain about not perceiving any eye contact from others and feel frustrated by insufficient or inadequate contact. The facilitator could invite the client to notice the sensations related to seeking connection and invite the tracking of one's self-regulation. There are also internet interruptions, poor connection, frozen images while voices continue talking, and complete disappearances. The mind knows intellectually that it is the internet that failed, but the body often responds with dysregulation.

Clients present a spread of biases about their bodies, emotional competencies, discrepancy in their capacity to notice internal subtleties, and difficulty slowing down and trusting others. Selvam and Parker (2017) list ways to work somatically with developmental issues related to autonomy, need, existence, or performance. By slowing down one's attention to physiological responses, each person recognizes how these active patterns are stored in procedural memory and live in unformulated, not reflective form (Stern, 2003). SE is particularly helpful in addressing this raw data, inviting awareness, allowing the wisdom of the body to guide the work (Riordan et al., 2019). Selvam and Parker (2003) argue that when we do not have access to our bodies, our instinctual energy, we do not feel safe, even when surrounded by people we know and love.

Starting an SE-I Session

When working virtually, there are at least two immediate challenges to beginning every session: the lack of transition to the therapeutic space and what Weinberg and Rolnick (2020) described as the disembodied group or the fact that only the head and shoulders of every member are visible. Thus, it is crucial for the therapist to start grounded and centered, to slow down to our most regulated tempo, and be intentional about using one's body to recognize others. The task is to facilitate the most presence in the therapist and group members.

Most often, a therapist has access to a virtual lobby where group members' names are listed. When the session begins, members are admitted into the virtual session and squares containing faces (circles inside squares) promptly populate the screen. For illustration, there are Peter, Amanda, Mike, Rene, Diego, Nancy, and Jackson. It is clear that everyone is adjusting to the stimulation of suddenly coming in. Mike's eyes are moving back and forth excitedly, as if following a bat's flight. Rene stares rigidly, while one of the squares is void of a person. This group member is identified by the title he used during his previous work meeting. His screen only shows his desk. The group's attention is fragmented and scattered.

Joining an online session is activating! Some members seek the gaze of others, while others avoid being the initiators of interaction. One's ability to be more present is relative to the degree of safety our body offers at any moment. By working on transitioning group members to the session—inviting them to attend to their bodies—the therapist summons the group to become aware of cues for safety and resolve cues for danger.

Typically, there is no transition time for those who work on their computers before they begin therapy; therefore, there is no difference in the physical setting or mental frame from which they relate. Often, their bodies have not adapted or shifted away from their previous engagements.

Most sessions begin with some version of "welcome, take a moment and notice your bodies … notice what your system is doing … look around and look inside and let yourself become aware of what your body is telling you, whatever is relevant in you."

In SE-I work, this intentional pausing and gradual looking around while feeling within allows our systems to begin orienting and settling. Orienting is the natural response of our bodies after scanning the environment for safety and connection. During these few seconds, group members become conscious of their breath, their posture, their energy, their weight on the chair, the hardness of the floor, and their overall wellbeing or lack thereof. Ogden differentiates between overt orienting—when visible physical actions such as turning one's head or seeking with the eyes are present—and covert orienting—where an inner mental shift occurs that is not evident to others (Ogden et al., 2006). Traumatized or overly stimulated clients will likely reveal difficulty orienting because they have trouble sorting out relevant from trivial clues in their environment. Their look is often overly attentive, deer-in-headlights appearance, or numbed out. Arriving at one's inner presence initiates increasing levels of body awareness for the session ahead. It concretely creates a holding and containing process with each participant and the group. In a way, it locates the person of the therapist and the person of the client in time and space (boundedness).

Within seconds, members shift their positions on their chairs, take a literal breath or sigh, nod, and begin describing their awareness. Amanda shares, "I am happy to be in group," to which I reply, "Happy how? How do you know happy in your body?" The interest here is to have Amanda further consider her sensations, how she feels what she says she feels, rather than repeat her pattern of providing conventional niceties. Most often, clients appreciate the invitation to attend to their bodies and they notice more emotions, more sensations, leading to more insight. Gradually, the group builds a culture of acceptance and interest in themselves, which increases self-care and body-to-body communication.

Our nervous system does not tell us who we are or what we are but how we live moment to moment, and this is the information we want to gather to improve cohesion in a group (Dana, 2018). Jackson, beaming, might say, "I am excited to see you all," while Nancy might share that she has not had a break all day, that she has not even had a chance to eat and it is 2 pm. All that matters is present tracking and awareness. The great majority of clients show up to session overwhelmed, disembodied, and distracted. They are often dutifully devoted to their work or the management of relationships. It is a gift to slow them down and hear them report, "It feels good to catch my breath and pay attention to myself."

Session after Session: the Body of the Work

It is commonly said that humans are social animals, that we are born wired to connect, and that we are tribal (Brooks, 2012). However, polyvagal theory (Dana, 2018) would argue that we are born in a helpless and hypervigilant state, constantly reacting to threats and unable to mobilize out of danger. It may be more accurate to say that we are born ready to be seen, held, and supported by others.

From an evolutionary perspective, Stephen Porges (Wong, 2020) found that our autonomic nervous system has three response patterns when it comes to threat. These are the dorsal vagus (immobilization, freeze response), the sympathetic nervous system (mobilization/fight or flight response), and the ventral vagus (social engagement, curiosity/play response). Thus, physiological regulation—feeling safe and secure in our bodies—occurs when our dorsal and sympathetic systems are stable and regulated, allowing our ventral or social system to take the lead. Therefore, physiological regulation is the preamble to bonding, attachment, and learning (Dana, 2018). The more secure we feel in our bodies, the more open we are to being vulnerable and accessible to others. This is an essential ingredient in developing epistemic trust or the ability to believe in the authenticity and relevance of social information (Black, 2019). Virtual SE groups are optimal as they allow members to examine their autonomic responses and their movement toward social engagement.

During our 12th group session, Diego says, "I am fed up with this COVID thing. I want to see you in person, I haven't really met you. I am tired of being in my house all day. I am sick of this working from home!" He appears overwhelmed, his hands are pressing on his cheeks and his eyes squint a bit, as if in pain. Rene adds, "MEEEE too! But it could be worse. At least none of us are sick." Diego quickly turns his head as if aiming a laser beam toward Rene with his eyes. Mike, Nancy, and Peter raise their heads slightly, on alert, but withdraw slightly.

When we operate outside of our window of emotional tolerance, we either move toward sympathetic activation (fight or flight) or para-sympathetic dominion (freeze, collapse) (Ogden et al., 2006). Diego is in fight mode, energized, frustrated, isolated, and angry. In a SE-I group, the therapist's task is to track the present sensations and support the capacity to feel by titration (little bits at the time) and pendulation (renegotiating inherent rhythms of the nervous system, expanding and contracting, back and forth, between sensations that support calmness—resourcing—and distressing stimulation, both at the personal and inter-personal level). When working online, the therapist's expertise in regards to timing the titration, monitoring the rhythm of the pendulation, and tracking the intensity of the experience is crucial. Virtual groups require significantly more attention from the therapist in comparison to f2f groups.

When two or more people slow down and exist together, there is plenty of sensory and mental activity to observe. Peter Levine (2010) suggests that humans make contact through a kind of body resonance. It is the body that subconsciously tunes into what is happening. We are likely to feel sensations similar to others in close proximity, to empathically attune. If someone is anxious or angry next to us, we pick up their signals in our bodies. Ogden and Goldstein (2020) refer to this process as state-sharing, a reciprocal embodied consciousness conveyed and experienced through body-to-body affective communication. However, by virtue of sitting in front of a fixed screen, online group members sustain a more restricted physical stance and point of focus (eyes on the screen) compared to f2f groups. Hence, it is helpful to invite members to notice what is happening in their bodies energetically and how they might want to move.

Attending to the close connection between our bodies and minds, Levine proposes that Sensations can be explored next to Images, Behaviors, Affect, and Meaning (SIBAM). This acronym allows for a complete phenomenological experience (Wong, 2020; Levine, 2010). Therapists can invite clients to notice their sensory awareness and add any or all of these channels to create bigger resonance. When working online, all of these channels are present and the group experience is quite similar to that of f2f groups. This is the essence of bottom-up, sensorimotor processing. Connection with others is always an energetic process and our body is the conductor of this energy.

THERAPIST: Diego, slow … way … down … notice your body. What is it doing? [Scan and locate yourself]
DIEGO: I am pissed! [Affect]
THERAPIST: [Speaks loudly] Sure, you are! What sensations come with being pissed? I can only see your face. What is it like inside? Notice every detail in your entire body.
DIEGO: I don't know. I feel a burning feeling like energy in my neck and arms. I am … don't know. My face is a bit hot. I am annoyed.
THERAPIST: Right! You are angry and your body is with you. You are hot and powerful. Keep on noticing. Stay with you for a moment. You are doing well. Notice your jaw, any sensations there? We are with you.
DIEGO: It is tight and I feel a pressure on my chest.

Diego is allowing the group to pay attention to him and the group is observing and tracking their own responses. Rene, Mike, Nancy, and Peter continue to be alert, but also have a chance to digest their own activation, possibly a fight or flight response. The group slows down a bit. By inviting members to share their whole-body awareness, a virtual group expands the container of what is felt. We become more than heads on the screen and emotion has more room.

Focusing awareness on sensation stimulates nerve cells to fire, which facilitates the flow of feelings. The body is always the place to turn to for deep emotional knowing. Emotions allow for the subjectivity of each member to be recognized, appreciated, and related to. As a SE-I therapist, it is helpful to have a reservoir of invitations for clients to notice themselves. Diego shared the location in his body where he feels the most activation (head, arms, and chest). A therapist could follow this with, "How big is the sensation?" "What color is it?" "Is it painful?" "Enjoyable?" "What tells you inside that you have anger?" "Does it want to do anything?" The interest is to expand Diego's sensitivity and curiosity about himself so as to also increase his capacity to self-regulate. Simultaneously, this process expands the group's resonance and each group member's inquisitiveness about their bodies.

THERAPIST: Diego, what happens to the sensations when you pay attention to them?

DIEGO: It is uncomfortable. It gets worse, but I guess it lessens a bit as I talk about it.

THERAPIST: Notice every detail ... give yourself ample time to know. How does it lessen? What is your breathing doing? [Resourcing or scanning for useful markers of regulation]

DIEGO: It is better, slowing down, I guess.

THERAPIST: Keep tracking. Do you notice anything that your body wants to do?

DIEGO: Hm ... my hands feel ... a little tingly.

THERAPIST: Is that tolerable?

DIEGO: It is OK. It's kind of energizing actually.

THERAPIST: You are alive! Stay with your body. Let the tingly happen ... Notice if the energy has any movement. Keep noticing. [After a few moments] When ready, look around. And group, notice what your bodies are doing.

[Diego looks around with a sheepish smile. His sympathetic (fight) and dorsal (put on the brakes) systems are more regulated. His ventral system is more online. He has wider range for connection.]

NANCY: I feel the same as Diego. I also miss people.

PETER: You are not alone, Diego. This sucks!

[Diego allows himself to further soften, his cheeks relax some and he shows a wider grin. His breathing is deeper.]

THERAPIST: Diego, notice your face. What is your face doing?

DIEGO: I am OK. I am smiling at Nancy and Peter.

THERAPIST: Yes. You are connecting with them. Stay with your feelings.

At this point, there are many options. The therapist could invite others to share what they witnessed and registered somatically. Mike, Nancy, and Peter could elaborate on their initial flight response and see where they are now. Rene could have a second go at linking with Diego. Or, we could all take a moment and observe where the group wants to go next.

THERAPIST: [After about five seconds.] Diego, would you be willing to go back to Rene? When she said that "it could be worse," it looked like you felt something strongly. [Pendulating]

DIEGO: It made me angry. [Face changes expression but it is much softer than the laser beam eyes.] She was discounting what I was saying.

THERAPIST: And what did your body do in response? Could you share that with Rene? [Back to monitoring internal states]

Much of psychotherapy involves practicing new behavioral patterns, which in turn create new synopsis in the brain, new rhythms of interaction. SE-I groups benefit from prioritizing our inner experience, composing an ongoing SIBAM life, especially whenever difficult moments occur.

Summary

The loss of our regulatory capacity changes everything, from feeling safe to thinking, feeling, and bonding. Returning to our bodies provides a fundamental trust inside, which is key to reestablishing connection with others. Therapy that does not include the body lacks the validation that our sensate capacities provide. It is da Vinci's *Vitruvian Man* without the naked body at the center. Therapy that only focuses on the body excludes the highest achievement of evolution, the ventral vagus track, the boundless field of interpersonal possibilities. It would be the drawing without the synergistic square and circle. SE and group therapy go hand in hand, f2f and online.

The driving force in humans is the desire to be connected to others while being fully ourselves. SE-I groups accentuate just this type of living. Its practice introduces rituals of body-centered sentience that enhance presence and deepen connection. Particularly in virtual groups, the more SIBAM we can attain, the deeper we go in our personal and interpersonal interactions.

References

Black, A. (2019). Treating insecure attachment in group therapy: Attachment theory meets modern analytical technique. *International Journal of Group Psychotherapy*, 69, 259–286.

Brooks, D. (2012). *The social animal: The hidden sources of love, character, and achievement*. Random House.

Carleton, J. A. (2009). Somatic treatment of attachment issues: Applying neuro-scientific and experimental research to the clinical situation. *Canadian Society for Psychotherapy Research*. http://www.jacquelineacarletonphd.com/text/pdfs/somatictreatmentofattachmentissues.pdf.

Cohen, S. L. (2011). Coming to our senses: The application of somatic psychology to group psychotherapy. *International Journal of Group Psychotherapy*, 61, 397–413.

Dana, D. (2018). *The polyvagal theory in therapy: Engaging the rhythm of regulation*. W. W. Norton and Company.

Freud, S. (1923). *The ego and the id*. In *The Standard Edition of the Complete Psychological Works of Sigmund Freud* (vol. XIX). W. W. Norton & Company.

Hdez, G. (2019, March 18). *Leonardo da Vinci's Vitruvian Man Explained*. https://owlcation.com/humanities/Leonardo-Da-Vincis-Vitruvian-Man-Explained.

Hollis, J. (2020). What is healing? In *Living between worlds: Finding personal resilience in changing times* (pp. 83–94). Sounds True.

Levine, P. A. (1997). *Waking the tiger: Healing trauma*. North Atlantic Books.

Levine, P. A. (2010). *In an unspoken voice: How the body releases trauma and restores goodness*. North Atlantic Books.

Ogden. P., & Goldstein, B. (2020). Sensorimotor psychotherapy from a distance: Engaging the body, creating presence, and building relationship in video-conferencing. In H. Weinberg & A. Rolnick (Eds.), *Theory and practice of online therapy: Internet-delivered interventions for individuals, groups, families, and organizations*. Routledge.

Ogden, P., Minton, K., & Pain, C. (2006). *Trauma and the body: A sensory motor approach to psychotherapy*. W. W. Norton and Company.

Ogden, T. (1992). *The primitive edge of experience*. Jason Aronson.

Payne, P., Levine, P., & Crane-Godreau, M. (2015). Somatic experiencing: Using interoception and proprioception as core elements of trauma treatment. *Frontiers in Psychology*, 6, 1–18.

Riordan, J. P., Blakeslee, A., & Levine, P. (2019). Attachment focused-somatic experiencing, secure phylogenetic attachment, dyadic trauma, and completion across the life cycle. *International Journal of Neuropsychotherapy*, 7(3), 57–90.

Schlapobersky, J. R. (2016). *From the couch to the circle: Group-analytic psychotherapy in practice*. Taylor & Francis Group.

Selvam, R., & Parker, L. (2003). *Somatic Experiencing: A note on working with anger in the context of an SE session*. http://seaustralia.com.au/downloads/Working_With_Anger_In_SE_Sessions.pdf.

Selvam, R., & Parker, L. (2017, October 22). *Working around developmental defenses in SE sessions*. https://www.bodynamic.com/blog/working-around-developmental-defenses/.

Siegel, D. (2020). *The developing mind: How relationships and the brain interact to share who we are* (3rd ed.). Guildford Press.

Stern, D. (2003). *Unformulated Experience: From dissociation to imagination in psychoanalysis*. Taylor and Francis Group.

Taylor, P. J., & Saint-Laurent, R. (2017). Group psychotherapy informed by the principles of somatic experiencing: Moving beyond trauma to embodied relationships. *International Journal of Group Psychotherapy, 67*, 171–181.

Van der Kolk, B. (2014). *The body keeps the score: Brain, mind, and body in the healing of trauma*. Penguin Books.

Weinberg, H. (2014). *The paradox of internet groups: Alone in the presence of virtual others*. Karnac Books.

Weinberg, H., & Rolnick, A. (2020). *Theory and practice of online therapy: Internet-delivered interventions for individuals, groups, families, and organizations*. Routledge.

Wong, A. (2020, May 7). Why you can't think your way out of trauma. *Psychology Today*. https://www.psychologytoday.com/us/blog/the-body-knows-the-way-home/202005/why-you-cant-think-your-way-out-trauma.

Chapter 19

Fostering Intimacy and Participant Engagement on the Zoom Platform

A Practical Beginner's Manual

Kimberly B. Harrison and Katherine S. Chapman

Introduction

Conducting group therapy on a virtual platform can be either fraught with pitfalls or surprisingly successful. Virtual participants in mental health services have reported a number of benefits of online participation when compared to face-to-face modalities (Di Carlo et al., 2021), including convenience, increased attendance, and feeling more comfortable within the virtual room. While there are many benefits, drawbacks also must be considered. Weinberg (2021) suggests four primary challenges for online groups: managing the frame of the treatment; the disembodied environment; the question of presence; and the transparent background. For some types of groups, many associated issues can be mitigated by using tools available in the online environment. In particular, the Zoom platform provides robust features which can help to create intimate, interactive, and effective group therapy sessions within virtual settings. Tools which allow leaders and participants to share screens, present audio and video, use whiteboards, move members into breakout rooms, and personalize backgrounds and screen appearances can help to improve the disembodied environment identified by Weinberg (2021) and the experience of presence. These tools assist leaders with developing techniques for successful groups across many therapeutic modalities and with a variety of ages and presenting issues. However, these tools are not appropriate for all types of groups.

Many of the interactive tools described in this chapter are well suited for cognitive behavioral, psychoeducational, and active-directive styles of group therapy, as they help to structure types of group engagement which allow for increased expressiveness by group members. Greater opportunities for expressiveness in group therapy have been found to reduce symptoms of depression for many participants (Oei & Browne, 2006). In psychodynamic groups, on the other hand, some of the major factors for group success may be disrupted by use of these platform tools. For

DOI: 10.4324/9781003248606-23

example, psychodynamic groups rely upon group-as-a-whole reactions, the interactions which occur in the interpersonal field of a group, and exploration of transference (Bakali et al., 2010; Rutan et al., 2014). Thus, incorporating tools and techniques which detract from the important group-as-a-whole (Yalom & Leszcz, 2020) dynamic can disrupt and deflect the work of psychodynamic groups.

The foundational keys to success for group therapy remain the same regardless of delivery mode: instillation of hope; universality; imparting information; altruism; the corrective recapitulation of the primary family group; development of socializing techniques; imitative behaviors; interpersonal learning; and group cohesiveness (Bakali et al., 2010; Yalom, 2005). Engagement and intimacy are likewise still essential in online group therapy sessions. Lower engagement has historically been associated with lower symptom reduction and less intimacy with higher dropout rates (Bonsaksen et al., 2013; Yalom, 1966). With skilled leaders and careful use of ancillary tools, online groups can be successful.

Intimacy Development in Individual and Group Psychotherapy

Relationships are an integral part of psychotherapy and are one of the key components of group therapy. Indeed, difficulties with relationships are often primary reasons individuals seek counseling (Kanter et al., 2020). The Interpersonal Process Model of Intimacy (Reis & Shaver, 1988) suggests that intimacy is first formed when two individuals begin a relationship. This type of relational bond happens throughout life and can be healthy or unhealthy. One of the reasons why individual psychotherapy can be helpful is that the therapist-client relationship creates its own intimacy bond which can be used to recreate and rebuild responses to unhealthy bonds from the past. Once intimacy is formed, many factors then contribute to increasing its depth and breadth. Kanter et al. (2020) identified a pattern of intimacy growth in which vulnerable self-disclosure elicits a validating, safe, or giving response and then results in an expression of acceptance and closeness. The depth of this reciprocal disclosure and response has been correlated with the overall degree of intimacy achieved (Kanter et al., 2020).

When seen in terms of group therapy, intimacy and connectedness within the group is integral to positive therapeutic outcomes and higher levels of group cohesion, risk taking and empathetic listening (Yalom & Leszcz, 2020). Group therapy adds another dimension to the formation of intimacy when compared to individual therapy. The power of the group therapy setting is that it provides more connections to build and rebuild a healthy sense of relational engagement (Yalom & Leszcz, 2020). The addition of verbal and nonverbal feedback from multiple individuals in the same room and becoming someone who both asks and gives in a group setting can foster the growth and development of strong relational skills (Kanter et al., 2020). Thus, we see that intimacy creates more intimacy (Cordova & Scott, 2001). Events in group therapy which are conducive to creating deeper connections set the stage for responses which can either strengthen or weaken the development of intimacy (Cordova & Scott, 2001).

With many group therapy settings moving to online platforms, ensuring development of intimacy in the virtual environment is a critical issue. Not every type of group goes about creation of intimacy in the same way. Some will benefit from the tools identified herein as they can enhance the ability to connect. Other groups will rely on more traditional methods which only occasionally use ancillary virtual platform tools. What is most important, however, is to design online group therapy in ways that ensure intimacy development through interpersonal interaction in the here-and-now, as this is one of the most critical mechanisms of therapeutic change (Yalom & Leszcz, 2020).

Administrative Considerations

Rules

Participant engagement starts with the group rules. The group agreement and rules add to the feeling of safety and create the group holding environment (Corey et al., 2014). In addition to standard rules, it is important to have some specific to the virtual platform (Yalom & Leszcz, 2020). First, participants must agree to locate in a place that allows for privacy without interference or the possibility of being overheard by others. Next, require cameras to be turned on unless there is an allowable exception. It would be unacceptable for a person to join an in-person group and not show their face. The literature demonstrates that clients are more likely to disclose information with their cameras turned on, and face-to-face interactions reduce distractions in the client's immediate environment (Baccon et al., 2019; Scholl et al., 2020).

However, drawbacks to being on camera should likewise be considered. Zoom fatigue, or mental prostration related to Zoom use, may result from constant self-monitoring and social interaction anxiety (Ngien & Hogan, 2022; Payne et al., 2020). Zoom fatigue at times has been connected to negative mental and physical health consequences, such as memory problems, stress, depression, tiredness, and headaches. Further, focusing on oneself may exacerbate underlying mental health conditions.

Besides turning off one's camera during a session, one way to help mitigate Zoom fatigue is by hiding the self-view. Doing so reduces the level of self-monitoring and increases focus on interacting with others

(Yalom & Leszcz, 2020). Leaders are encouraged to consider what would be most supportive to the purpose of the group when making rules governing this fatigue.

Other common requirements designated by group leaders can include the participants having a well-lit area, audio turned on or off as needed, and even specifying general distance from the screen. As noted, the full face on screen is usually appropriate for adults, although it may contribute to Zoom fatigue. In some cases, it is also preferable to have participants sit back slightly so more of the body can be seen since body language typically is an important part of group communication (Yalom & Leszcz, 2020). This also helps to prevent multi-tasking on other programs or screens, which disrupts participation and engagement. Remember, the computer may also be a playground, office, or creative space for attendees, and leaders want them to be engaged with the group, not multi-tasking.

Children and teens often participate more if their hands can be seen on camera. Also consider rules surrounding when to use certain features of Zoom, such as emojis, virtual backgrounds, and screen sharing. Guidelines for when it is appropriate to speak or not also may be helpful. For instance, depending upon the size and type of group, interruptions may be reduced if participants use the "raise hand" feature and then wait to be called on by the group facilitator. In other cases, this approach may discourage individuals from speaking or take away from the desired group dynamic.

Overview of Zoom Tools

When planning a virtual group, first think about common ways members interact in an in-person version, then try to find online tools to replicate. For educational and/or activity-based groups, the Zoom whiteboard, chat window, or breakout rooms can replicate many of the features used in person. Many Zoom tools are added and/or updated regularly, thus a comprehensive list is outdated as soon as it is written. While clearly they are not appropriate for all types of group therapy and should only be incorporated if they are helpful to the overall goal of the group, these technology-based enhancements often can help participants to pay attention better.

Views

Choose from either Speaker View or Gallery View. All group members will be seen at the same time on the Gallery View. Conversely, the Speaker View shows the person speaking on most of the screen with the other members in smaller boxes below. Leaders also can use the Spotlight feature on Zoom to create a layout of larger or smaller frames for each participant. Only leaders can control who is highlighted on the screen when using Spotlight. However, sometimes it works best to ask participants to pin their own specific screen layout. The pin feature on Zoom is individually managed. Group leaders can opt to provide instructions throughout the session to switch views as needed.

Screen Sharing

Online groups have the benefit of easily sharing content from one or more computers. Screen sharing is recommended when external content germane to the session is warranted. Sometimes the leader has educational or inspirational webpages, a slide show, or videos which support the topic at hand. Other times participants can share ancillary items to provide more information to the group about themselves or an interest. Leaders can decide if they would like members to be able to share their screens, or if multiple screens are allowed to be shared simultaneously. Other options to consider are whether to allow annotation of shared screens and ways to save content.

Whiteboard

The whiteboard on Zoom serves many of the same purposes as a traditional dry erase board in a group therapy session. Leaders can highlight educational information, provide outlines, or give scheduling information. Virtual groups have the added benefit of all participants being able to write on the whiteboard simultaneously. This feature works well for ice breakers, group discussion, and idea generation. While the host automatically has privileges to write on the board, participants must be granted access.

Chat Window

The Chat feature on Zoom can serve many purposes. Leaders and members can share handouts and other documents, attendance can be logged, and, of course, the Chat window can be used for conversation threads. However, the Chat feature can also create parallel channels of communication which, in many groups—especially psychodynamic—might highlight individual motivation and deflect from group-as-the-whole (Agazarian & Peters, 2018). As with all Zoom features, knowing the purpose and theoretical orientation of the group is critical when considering whether to incorporate Chat and other features. Nevertheless, many group participants thrive in a multi-tasking environment and enjoy using the Chat feature to comment or ask questions while others are speaking.

Reactions and Emojis

Group members can communicate without interrupting through a variety of nonverbal interfaces. Icons for responses such as yes, no, slow down, speed up, raising hand, and coffee cup are found in the Reactions menu on the main Zoom toolbar. Emojis are a more temporary variation of these icons and allow meeting participants to share their feelings without interrupting (e.g., clap, heart, laugh). For some types of groups, incorporating reactions and emojis can be helpful, but for others they can be distracting and deflect from focusing on facial responses. For example, many children and teens have used reactions and emojis when participating in virtual classrooms and have been trained and encouraged to use them to react while minimizing interruption to the lesson. In an online group setting, it can be a way for participants to show a response to a speaker in much the same way they would by changing facial expression or using body language in person. On the other hand, in groups in which focusing on facial expressions is important to the communication and cohesion of the group, reactions and emojis can interfere.

Breakout Rooms

Dividing the larger group into smaller ones is often an effective technique for fostering intimacy, discussion, and extended sharing on a topic in many types of psycho-educational, cognitive-behavioral, or large groups. In psychodynamic groups, however, dividing the group is typically not appropriate as it confounds the group perspective which is accomplished in group-as-a-whole (Agazarian & Peters, 2018). Further, breakout rooms might promote the formation of secret liaisons which could substitute personal gratification for the personal change which the group is designed to foster. Such "acting out" might temporarily relieve frustration about sharing feelings within the larger group by providing a space to avoid dealing with them in a subgroup comprised of those who share a common bond (Yalom & Leszcz, 2020). However, dividing a larger group into smaller ones can be helpful in psycho-educational and cognitive-behavioral groups.

Music and Videos

Whether a meditation track or a funny clip from a movie, groups are often enhanced by music and videos. Zoom makes it easy to share audio and video content, but group leaders are still encouraged to have songs or videos queued up prior to the meeting. Then, when it's time, simply go to Share Screen and click on the prepared content.

Video Filters, Studio Effects, and Virtual Backgrounds

With Video Filters, group members can select hats, glasses, tiaras, or other objects which they then appear to be wearing. Studio Effects are another version of these enhancements and include facial hair and lip color. These filters often provide humor, an outlet for individuality, or information about current moods. Virtual backgrounds provide ways to imaginatively transport to another place or give a neutral background instead of the natural environment. The group leader is encouraged to discuss the pros and cons of using a virtual background in the group rules.

Several issues might arise when using video filters, studio effects, and virtual backgrounds. For example, if seeing the location of participants or verifying what is in the natural environment is important, then virtual backgrounds should not be used. Virtual backgrounds also might mask confidentiality issues because they create a virtual screen whereby group members are unable to see if others are in the environment. Also, filters and effects can be distracting. Nevertheless, children and teens especially enjoy these features, and adults often respond positively to them too.

One reason to use a virtual background includes neutralizing the visual distractions of the natural background. Another reason would be to indicate a change in mood. For example, the native background of a participant's living room could be changed to a beach scene to show the effects of relaxation, or a change to an outer space background might give insight into a person feeling detached. Similarly, using a filter of dark sunglasses might indicate a person's desire to be anonymous, or a tiara could suggest desire to be noticed. Caution should be taken, however, in using the virtual background and other tools to express mood because one of the foundational elements of traditional group therapy requires members to articulate feelings. With that caution in mind, it will be interesting to follow the literature on outcomes of virtual group therapy and use of these platform-based tools as research in the area grows. It is possible that some of these artificial expressions of mood are positive replacements for the nonverbal cues typically available in group. Yalom and Leszcz (2020) suggest that therapists who lead online groups need to be more active and that co-therapists will need to learn new methods to foster connectivity to replace subtle nonverbal cues.

Using Virtual Tools in Session

Introductions and Ice Breakers

If check-ins or introductions are a planned part of the group, decide the mood you want to set. Zoom enhancements and settings can establish a variety of tones for sessions for all ages. For a more lighthearted, inter-active tone, try incorporating music, videos, whiteboards, video filters, virtual backgrounds, or studio effects at the beginning of your session. For example, group members can select a hat or glasses, which tell something about their mood. Since children and teens often like to over-use these tools, having a time at the beginning of the session to incorpo-rate them allows for enjoyment but can then give way to rules about "putting the enhancements away" for the next segment. Another way to incorporate special online features is for group leaders to have an opening song that signifies the beginning of work or a short meditation video to direct focus.

If a more serious introduction time is desired, consider asking group members to switch to the Speaker View and allow each member to check in. This view creates more attention on the speaker and allows for fewer distractions. Sometimes introductions, ice breakers, or check-ins are best facilitated in dyads or triads to allow for more intimacy. Provide a specific question, prompt, or activity, identify a specific amount of time for the conversations, and invite participants to breakout rooms. One of the drawbacks of using a speaker view is that we cannot see how others are responding. On the other hand, Yalom and Leszcz (2020) posit that fatigue is more likely when having to scan multiple faces in a gallery view and thus, occasionally focusing on only one speaker might foster more participation.

Whiteboards also provide an effective way to start sessions. Activities such as "the continuous line" or "continuous story" (detailed below), can foster cohesiveness. Leaders also might write the session topic on the whiteboard and then have participants write or draw their preliminary reactions to the topic. Whiteboard interaction options are endless and can be easily adapted from favorite in-person group activities.

The Heart of the Session

After the introduction, group therapy sessions focus more intently on the purpose of the meeting. Depending on the type of group, any of the Zoom tools noted in this chapter can be used to foster intimacy, connec-tion, and group conversation. For some types of groups, break-out rooms and variations on views (speaker versus gallery) are important tools to incorporate because they allow focus on one person at a time. Process groups, on the other hand, generally would not use these tools, as they could deflect from the group-as-a-whole dynamic and potentially create dysfunctional subgroups (Rutan et al., 2014). Psycho-educational groups may want to integrate slideshow presentations or instructional videos. Social skills groups often benefit from all the above. Adults tend to do well with more talking and listening activities, whereas children and teens usually need more variety to stay engaged.

Closing Activities

This is a time to check in with group members on how they are feeling, what they have learned, insights experienced, and more. It can also be a time to relax and transition. The online environment provides many ways to facilitate closure that are personal and unique.

Examples of Specific Activities

Group therapy activities are limited only by the skill and imagination of the leader, whether in person or online. Often activities used for in-person groups can be modified for online use, so if you have favorites, think through ways to update them for Zoom. Other activities, however, can take advantage of members being in more personalized environments or utilize the tools available online. Here are a few examples of activities which are versions of more traditional ones used for in-person groups that work well in a virtual group environment.

The Continuous Line

Appropriate for children, adolescents, and adults, the continuous line can be an effective ice breaker, closing activity, or both, and assists with fostering group cohesion. Share the screen to the whiteboard and ask one member to start a line. One by one, have each of the other group members add to the line. It can help to decide in advance who will go next, perhaps by assigning a number to each group member and asking them to go in numerical order. Encourage this to be done without talking. After each person has participated, ask the members what shapes they see, what stands out, what feelings are evoked, etc.

The Continuous Story

Appropriate for children, adolescents, and adults, and similar to the continuous line activity, the continuous story allows one group member to build upon the work of another. Leaders can choose to implement the continuous story in a variety of ways, including in the Chat window, on the whiteboard, or through talking. The leader starts the story with a generic prompt such as, "There was a small town...," or "The drive was taking longer than expected..." After the initial prompt, group members take turns adding to the story until the leader ends the process. After the story is complete, discussion takes place about the feelings the story evokes, how characters navigated twists and turns, emotional content, and whatever the leader wants to highlight.

Online Scavenger Hunt

Appropriate for children, adolescents, and adults, this activity takes advantage of the individual group member's environment. It can be used as an ice breaker or for the heart of the session. Ask each participant to find something in their environment which helps them when they feel a specific feeling. For example, you could say, "Find something that comforts you when you feel sad." Then give a time limit and have everyone return and discuss their item. For a lengthier activity, several consecutive rounds can take place, each with a different feeling highlighted, or a list of multiple types of items to find can be given.

Meme Sharing

Appropriate for children, adolescents, and adults, meme sharing is a great way to incorporate lighthearted engagement. Memes are humorous images, videos, or text that capture specific feelings. Having participants share favorite memes at the beginning or end of the session can help with group cohesion. Since some memes might have inappropriate content, however, group leaders need to be clear about content rules.

Color Feelings

One of the downsides of online therapy is diminished perspective of body language. Therefore, incorporating other ways to monitor nonverbal content is important. Art therapists regularly use color to assist with identifying feelings (Buchalter, 2009; Liebmann, 2004). Color and color changes are usually obvious to all group members, and they provide ways for group members to have clues about the emotional content for each other. By simply changing the virtual background color, participants can indicate current mood, reactionary feelings, or shifts in mood.

Progressive Muscle Relaxation and Meditation

Appropriate for children, adolescents, and adults, leaders have a wide array of online sources for incorporating audio and/or video recordings of relaxation and meditation activities. Preview your material and have it queued up so that sharing screen and audio is done quickly.

Mindfulness with Photo

Appropriate for children, adolescents, and adults, this activity involves sharing your screen to reveal an image upon which participants can focus. Images that work well are landscapes, animals, florals, and fruit, but many options can work depending on the focus of the group. Have group members focus on one part of the photo at a time and check in on the feelings evoked, endeavoring to be fully present in the moment with the image and feelings.

Rule Checklist

When setting up a new group, leaders are encouraged to consider rules which allow or disallow some of the Zoom tools and features. Answering these basic questions can assist with defining these rules. Below are some important questions to ask when creating virtual group therapy rules:

1   Would a passcode be appropriate when entering the Zoom meeting?
2   Should participants be placed in a waiting room before being allowed entry?
3   Where should participants be physically located (e.g., private, quiet, well-lit space with secure internet connection)?
4   Should participants' cameras be on or off?

   a   Are there any exceptions?

5   How should cameras be positioned? (i.e., is it appropriate to see just a person's face, or more of their body?)
6   When is muting appropriate?
7   Should participants raise their hand and wait to be called on to speak, or chime in freely?
8   Which Zoom tools might enhance the therapeutic experience?

   a   Which Zoom tools would detract?

9   Are there virtual-specific activities that may improve group engagement and cohesiveness?
10   Which of your favorite traditional group therapy activities might translate best to a virtual setting?

Summary

Video conferencing platforms have allowed traditional group therapy to be modified for online participation, and some tools only available within a virtual environment have become part of the group therapy catalogue. While this chapter focuses on tools available through Zoom, most platforms have an array of enhancements, and these tools are continually evolving. Group leaders are advised to regularly review new materials by attending webinars hosted by developers, watching for information online, and reading the literature. Group participants can also provide a wealth of information about new tools and enhancements. Group rules about when and how virtual tools can be used are important and help to ensure that enhancements contribute to the overall purpose of the group rather than distract. When setting up a virtual group, leaders may find the guiding questions above helpful. As a field, we are still learning about the benefits of online group therapy. What once was considered impossible is now commonplace, and skilled leaders are finding that they can develop intimacy and strong participation in part through use of virtual tools.

References

Agazarian, Y. & Peters, R. (2018). *The visible and invisible group.* Routledge.

Baccon, L. A., Chiarovano, E., & MacDougall, H. G. (2019). Virtual reality for teletherapy: Avatars may combine the benefits of face-to-face communication with the anonymity of online text-based communication. *Cyberpsychology, Behavior, and Social Networking,* 22(2), 158–165. https://doi.org/10.1089/cyber. 2018.0247.

Bailenson, J. N. (2021). Nonverbal overload: A theoretical case for the causes of Zoom Fatigue. *Technology, Mind, and Behavior,* 2(1).

Bakali, J. V., Wilberg, T., Hagtvet, K. A., & Lorentzen, S. (2010). Sources accounting for alliance and cohesion at three stages in group psychotherapy: Variance component analyses. *Group Dynamics: Theory, Research, and Practice,* 14(4), 368–383. https://doi.org/10.1037/a0019170.

Bonsaksen, T., Borge, F.-M., & Hoffart, A. (2013). Group climate as predictor of short- and long-term outcome in group therapy for social phobia. *International Journal of Group Psychotherapy,* 63(3), 395–417. https://doi-org.fgul.idm.oclc. org/10.1521/ijgp.2013.63.3.394.

Buchalter, S. (2009). *Art therapy techniques and applications.* Jessica Kingsley Publishers.

Di Carlo, F. D., Sociali, A., Picutti, E., Pettorruso, M., Vellante, F., Verrastro, V., Martinotti, G., & Giannantonio, M. di. (2021). Telepsychiatry and other cutting-edge technologies in COVID-19 pandemic: Bridging the distance in mental health assistance. *International Journal of Clinical Practice,* 75(1). https://doi. org/10.1111/ijcp.13716.

Cordova, J. V., Scott, R. L. (2001) Intimacy: A behavioral interpretation. *The Behavior Analyst,* 24 (75–86). https://doi.org/10.1007/BF03392020.

Corey, M. S., Corey, G., & Corey, C. (2014). *Groups process and practice* (9th ed.). Brooks/Cole Cengage Learning.

Kanter, J. W., Kuczynski, A. M., Manbeck, K. E., Corey, M. D. Corey, & Wallace, E. C. (2020). An integrative contextual behavioral model of intimate relations. *Journal of Contextual Behavioral Science,* 18, 75–91.

Liebmann, M. (2004). *Art therapy for groups* (2nd ed.). Routledge.

Ngien, A., & Hogan, B. (2022). The relationship between Zoom use with the camera on and Zoom fatigue: Considering self-monitoring and social interaction anxiety. *Information, Communication & Society,* 1–19. https://doi.org/10. 1080/1369118X.2022.2065214.

Oei, T. P. S., & Browne, A. (2006). Components of group processes: Have they contributed to the outcome of mood and anxiety disorder patients in a group cognitive-behaviour therapy program? *American Journal of Psychotherapy*, 60 (1), 53–70. https://doi.org/10.1176/appi.psychotherapy.2006.60.1.53.

Payne, L., Flannery, H., Kambakara Gedara, C., Daniilidi, X., Hitchcock, M., Lambert, D., Taylor, C., & Christie, D. (2020). Business as usual? Psychological support at a distance. *Clinical Child Psychology and Psychiatry*, 25(3), 672–686. https://doi.org/10.1177/1359104520937378.

Reis, H. T., & Shaver, P. (1988). Intimacy as an interpersonal process. In *Handbook of personal relationships* (pp. 367–389). Wiley & Sons.

Rutan, J. S., Stone, W. N., & Shay, J. J. (2014). Psychodynamic group psychotherapy (5th ed.). Guilford Press.

Scholl, A., Sassenberg, K., Zapf, B., & Pummerer, L. (2020). Out of sight, out of mind: Power-holders feel responsible when anticipating face-to-face, but not digital contact with others. *Computers in Human Behavior*, 112, 106472. https://doi.org/10.1016/j.chb.2020.106472.

Weinberg, H. (2021). Obstacles, challenges and benefits of online group psychotherapy. *American Journal of Psychotherapy*. https://doi.org/10.1176/appi.psychotherapy.20200034.

Yalom, I. D. (1966). A study of group therapy dropouts. *Archives of General Psychiatry*, 14(4), 393–414. https://doi.org/10.1001/archpsyc.1966.01730100057008.

Yalom, I. D. (2005). *Theory and practice of group psychotherapy* (5th ed.). Station Hill Press.

Yalom, I. D., & Leszcz, M. (2020). *The theory and practice of group psychotherapy* (6th ed.). Station Hill Press.

Chapter 20

Online Psychoeducational Groups

Nina W. Brown

Introduction

Group therapy made significant changes because of the COVID-19 pandemic. While groups had been conducted virtually and this was continuing to increase, the need for delivering group therapy in an online format expanded tremendously during the pandemic. It is anticipated that the use of online groups will remain constant and even increase.

There have been numerous studies on the effectiveness of online therapy and psychoeducational groups for various issues, conditions and problems and more will emerge rapidly because of the need to go virtual owing to the outbreak of the COVID-19 pandemic. Researchers have recorded favorable outcomes for online treatment for panic disorder (Lauckner & Whitten, 2016; Lustgarten, 2017), anxiety, depression (Lauckner & Whitten 2016; Lustgarten, 2017), PTSD (Lauckner & Whitten, 2016; Lustgarten, 2017), military-related combat PTSD (Acierno et al., 2016; Wierwille et al., 2016; Yuen et al., 2015), substance abuse (Lustgarten, 2017), chronic pain (Lustgarten, 2017), obsessive-compulsive disorder (Stubbings et al., 2015), anger management (Braeuer et al., 2022), depression (Pang et al., 2021), alcohol misuse (Frohlich et al., 2021) and bipolar disorder (Rentala, 2021). Studies of different populations have also found favorable results such as juvenile offenders (Batastini, 2016), parent training (Comer et al., 2017), refugees with PTSD (Ghumann et al., 2016), at risk of suicide (Gilmore & Ward-Ciesielski, 2017), adolescent depression (Kobak et al., 2015), military with depression (Luxton et al., 2016), community support groups (Eysenback et al., 2004), and caregivers (Hepburn et al., 2021; Karagiozi et al., 2021; Meyer et al., 2022; Teles et al., 2022).

This chapter presents the definition and description of psychoeducational groups with a focus on adults, the benefits and challenges for online groups, planning and organizing online sessions, technology and equipment concerns, the ethics and professional issues related to online groups, and suggestions for managing group factors and interactions.

DOI: 10.4324/9781003248606-24

Definition and Description of Psychoeducational Groups

Group therapy was started as psychoeducational group in 1907 when Dr. Joseph Pratt used the process to help with tuberculosis patients. Brown (1998, 2003, 2005, 2006, 2009, 2018, 2019) defines psychoeducational groups as a balanced blend of cognitive and affective components, whereby the cognitive component consists of information to be disseminated, the planning that is needed, the method(s) for dissemination, the use of learning theories and styles of learning, and other educational and learning activities. The affective component includes promotion of feeling expressions and providing the means for that expression, a focus on the here and now experiencing of group members, the importance of the therapeutic alliance and how that is established and maintained, empathic responding, group process, the emergence of group therapeutic factors and managing group members' intense feelings, among many other affective processes and procedures.

A literature search on Google Scholar and PubMed for the past 10 years listed a total of 5,317 articles about psychoeducational groups.

Some distinguishing features of psychoeducational groups include planned dissemination of information whereby the group leader intentionally plans in advance what and how to present information related to the issue or problem or concern that is the basis for the group, an intentional balance of cognitive and affective components whereby each is of importance. In addition, sessions have planned structures and direction and while some elements may emerge during the process, the leader always has a plan for the session. Sessions can be used to teach socializing skills and techniques as well as communication skills, foster the development of relationship attributes, demonstrate conflict resolution, and other such helpful relating skills. Other distinguishing features include how group process is used and the value of group process commentary, a variety of means for delivering content and guiding members in self-exploration such as the use of activities and various forms of media.

Tips for all psychoeducational groups:

- Maintain a balance of cognitive and affective factors for the duration of the group and for most group sessions.
- Stay mindful of time constraints such as the number of sessions that may not be productive or appropriate to engage in deep exploration.
- Be mindful of the leader's need to "go deeper" as time may not permit, or members may not benefit, or that this was not their purpose for attending the group.
- Regard each session as self-contained instead of expecting to build on them as consistent attendance for some groups or members may not be feasible.

- Use guidance for increasing members' knowledge and self-awareness as modest goals.
- Develop attainable goals for the group and for members.
- Focus on the group-as-a-whole as well as on individual group members as this is valuable information for what group members want and need, although they may express this in different ways.
- Continually identify and emphasize similarities as this helps to promote group cohesion even in shorter-term psychoeducational groups.
- Stay aware of the impact and influences of members' culture and diversity characteristics and how these will play a role in their participation.
- Attend to group process and use process illumination.
- Remain emotionally present to promote here and now interactions among group members.

It is also important to attend to some of the usual group therapy factors and facilitation skills as these also contribute to the success of psychoeducational groups. Factors such as fostering the emergence of group therapeutic factors, illuminating process and making process commentary can also be used. Facilitation skills can include discerning the group's session themes as valid information about group members' needs, acting as a container for the members' intense feelings, and using the resources of the group as aids to assist individual group members.

The Virtual Environment for Psychoeducational Groups: Advantages and Disadvantages

Batastini et al. (2020) and Weinberg (2020, 2021) describe the advantages and disadvantages of online groups that also apply to online psychoeducational groups. Benefits for members include increased access to services, the possibility of feeling less anxious or threatened, decreased emotional contagion, increased ability to be emotionally present in sessions, fewer missed sessions and/or tardiness, and increased ability to attend sessions. Increased access to services includes costs to the member such as transportation and childcare, member availability at designated times is easier, and members in rural and other such areas can receive treatment that might not be available in their communities. Group members can have less anxiety about their inclusion in or exclusion from the group, how they will be perceived by group members, a reduction in emotional contagion due to the distance and separation of group members, and members' ability to be and stay emotionally present in sessions could be increased.

Disadvantages include lacking the necessary reliable technology, members' space for attending the group may be harder to ensure owing to disruptions and intrusions, and technical difficulties that cause frustration during sessions. In addition, some members may experience a lessening of their verbal spontaneity for input and responses, have uncertainty about when to speak, and may find it more difficult to develop a therapeutic alliance.

Benefits for group leaders include greater assurance of members' attendance, the ability to provide treatment and care for remote group members and thus increase their access to care, and it may be easier to structure and direct psychoeducational group sessions (Lopez et al., 2020; Barak et al., 2008), and sites such as prisons, residential facilities, nursing homes and other venues can receive therapeutic group services. Adjusting to a virtual group environment presents many challenges for group leaders in terms of technology requirements, ethical considerations, establishing a therapeutic relationship, constraints of some group factors, and the inability to use some group facilitation strategies and techniques.

Planning the Dissemination of Information

One of the most important tasks for psychoeducational groups is the dissemination of information and it is essential that the group leader plans this task in advance. Although basic considerations for disseminating information also apply for other types of groups such as cognitive behavioral group therapy (CBGT), the information and intent differ. For example, for CBGT the primary foci for information to be disseminated are to explain cognitive restructuring and its application to the therapy and principles while other types of psychoeducational groups can have many different forms of information to disseminate. In addition, major additional concerns of online psychoeducational groups are the technology considerations and variables which are addressed in the next section. This section will present examples of how information will be disseminated, some major objectives, and suggestions for group leaders for presentations.

Some examples of strategies for the dissemination of information in the virtual environment are lectures, media, activities, readings and other print materials, web-based presentations and guest speakers. Lectures are effective ways to present a considerable amount of material but group leaders will want to limit the amount of material to be sufficient for the audience, the usefulness of the information, and a realization that the usual time for attending to a lecture is 20 minutes and may be less for some audiences whose members may have difficulty attending for long amounts of time.

Media such as DVDs, videos, and YouTube presentations may also be helpful in the dissemination of information. These should be selected with the audience's characteristics in mind, be limited in time, and provide opportunities for group members to discuss the material to ensure understanding.

Activities can also be helpful in that they allow all group members to participate at the same time, provide for members' personal associations, and can be helpful stimuli for awareness and insight. Sample activities are writing, drawing, imagery, and collage (Brown, 2013).

Readings and other print materials can help to extend group members' knowledge and be additions to the information presented in sessions. It can be important that group leaders incorporate discussions for outside readings in group sessions and to also show how that material can be used by group members.

Web-based presentations and/or guest presenters are invited to group sessions as these may feature experts in the topics or subject matter for the particular group. Timing and time available may be important things to consider when using these to highlight important information.

Two major issues to consider in planning are ethical and professional considerations and the culture and diversity of group members. Most of the ethical and professional issues that apply in other settings also apply in online settings; however, the most important ethical concern is that not all members' virtual environments can ensure confidentiality and group members should be aware of this when the group begins.

Following are some tips for planning the dissemination of information:

- Limit the amount of information presented to the minimum necessary.
- Do not overwhelm members with too much information at any one time.
- Plan to sequence the presentation of information and be prepared for members' absences which may impact building on the previous session, and/or make accommodations for them to receive the materials.
- Attend to the format for presenting and remain mindful that the group is not a class and members can learn in other ways.
- When lecturing or leading discussions, use language appropriate for the members' educational levels, SES, and other cultural and diversity factors.

Technology Considerations for Planning and Organizing Online Psychoeducational Group Sessions

Crowe (2021) describes the technology requirements and security for online sessions as a computer, camera, microphone, internet connection, and appropriate videoconferencing software. Lustgarten (2017), Luxton et al. (2016), and Swenson et al. (2016) explain that the sessions must be in accord with HIPAA requirements and propose that there should be an algorithmic encryption of the video signal to ensure confidentiality. There should be a backup plan for any technological failures with the details of the plan as a part of the written consent, and that it is helpful to have someone with technical expertise on hand to help to manage problems.

Following are some tips and options that may be especially helpful for online psychoeducational groups:

- Breakout rooms can be used to form small groups for discussion or activities.
- Screen sharing can be done by either the group leader and/or group members to share written materials, PowerPoint presentations, handouts for discussions directions for activities, and so on.
- The whiteboard option is used for drawing or writing and through screen sharing can be available to both the leader and the group members.
- The chat icon is very helpful for group members and the group leader can ask them to record their thoughts, feelings and questions for the group and/or for the leader through the chat with the understanding that the leader may not be able to view these during the session. Material put under chat is available for viewing by all group members.

Lopez et al. (2020) recommends that group leaders use practice sessions to become familiar with the technology as they report that group members are more at ease when the group leader is familiar and comfortable with using it. They also recommend that group members be offered a practice session.

Another technology-related task is to decide how speaking will be organized so that members can be guided to speak, decrease interruptions, and allow for interactions and discussions. Group members can signal their desire to speak by raising their hand either physically or electronically.

Tip: both the group leader and members are encouraged to create their space so that it is free from distractions, disruptions, or interruptions to include silencing phones and other devices.

The group leader should ensure that all the necessary materials are readily available before starting the session. It is very disruptive to the process when materials and the like have to be secured from another location, even if that location is just next door.

Orientation Session

Plan to have an orientation session either before the group begins or as an integral part of the first session. The orientation should include group rules and expectations and the technical aspects of online sessions. While members may have had experience with other types of groups, it can reduce some of their anxiety about the ambiguity and uncertainty around this particular psychoeducational group experience to present some information about the rules of the group and expectations of members. This may also help reduce some resistance (Teles et al. 2022).

Tip: suggested basic group rules would include the following:

- Attend all session and arrive on time.
- Notify the group leader when sessions will be missed.
- Attend sessions where there are no distractions, disruptions, and the like to maintain confidentiality for group members.
- Actively participate.

Some group members may not be familiar with technology and can find that their participation is affected because of this lack of information. This is why the orientation session is best held before the group begins. Members can be told what the session will cover and can elect to be absent if they do not need the information. Technical aspects that can be a part of the virtual sessions and that are helpful to cover in the orientation session include muting, how to be recognized, how and when to use the chat function, and screen sharing.

Fostering and Managing Group Facilitation

Some group facilitation factors that will need to be managed and may be more difficult to accomplish in a virtual environment are building the connections so that trust and safety are established for group members, for the leader to be able to tune in to the group's feeling tone as a cue for what the group may be feeling, encouraging members' expression of their thoughts and feelings, and fostering interactions among group members. Possible reasons for the difficulty are the loss of group-as-a-whole nonverbal communications, members not sure of when to speak, lack of eye contact between the speaker and receiver, and other such actions that occur in face-to-face sessions. Although some studies have shown that establishing a relationship with the leader is easier for group members than it is for them to establish meaningful connections with each other, there are several strategies that may be helpful for group leaders (Lopez et al., 2020). Examples of these include encouraging members to talk about what is and is not working for them in the online group, to identify the losses they are experiencing such as not being able to see some nonverbal cues, and to talk to each other by using their names that are visible on the screen.

While it may be more difficult to tune in to the group's feeling tone and to have members express their feelings, group leaders can ask members to identify their feelings either verbally or through the chat icon to get a sense of the general feeling tone of the group. Tip: Leaders can encourage members to use the chat icon during the session to write their thoughts, feelings, and ideas or questions as these emerge during the session as this is another means to encourage participation where members may be reluctant to interrupt either the members who are speaking or the leader.

Encouraging member-to-member interactions may also be a challenge with virtual group sessions as members may be unfamiliar with group interactions in general but especially so using technology. Tip: just as with in-person sessions, the leader can ask members to use each other's names to direct their comments and remarks, to talk to each other instead of just to and through the leader, or even to raise their hands, physically or electronically, to talk to each other.

There are also some group-level concerns that must be attended to and managed in the virtual setting. Among these are *group-level resistance, conflict*, and *difficult member behaviors*. Group-level resistance occurs when the group-as-a-whole is avoiding, ignoring, or suppressing something members find to be threatening or dangerous about or in the group at that time, such as the emergence of conflict with other members and/or the group leader, or there can be fears around intimacy in the group. This can be detected in behaviors such as circular discussions and prolonged silence.

Conflict will emerge in the group and this can range from mild disagreements to very intense exchanges. Members are in separate spaces so there is less likelihood that physical aggression will result. Tolerance of conflict and working through differences—even minor ones—can be a valuable teaching tool for psychoeducational groups to illustrate to members how to work through conflicts, the value of trying to resolve minor differences so that they do not become major ones, and that relationships do not have to be destroyed through conflict.

Online groups will also have some difficult member behaviors that can negatively affect the group and its progress. Members will bring their usual selves and behaviors to the group regardless of the venue; for example, if they monopolize in their everyday lives, they will do the same in the group setting.

Cues for Online Sessions

Although many of the usual cues are not available for online sessions, there are some nonverbal communication cues that will be helpful for group leaders to look for and attend to. Among these are facial expressions, voice tone, and upper body gestures.

Notice facial expressions especially when there are changes and shifts. Cues can be discerned from the eye movements, presence or absence of smiles, and noticing the general impression of the facial expression. Some information can be gleaned from the overall impression the group leader receives when looking at the member's face. Voice tones can be revealing of the person's emotional state. For example, when someone talks fast, choppy, and loud, that can be an indication of some emotional intensity about the topic or disclosure. Notice when group members' voice tones change during the session, are different in a particular session, and what impression or reaction is provoked in the group leader. These can be cues for suppression of feelings, especially intense negative feelings, which can then lead to more effective interventions. Although the entire body is not usually seen on the computer screen, there are some cues to what members may be experiencing at that moment from the positions and/or movement of their heads, shoulders, hand gestures, and/or head positions. This is why it can be helpful for the group leader to attend to how the member is physically presenting themself on the computer screen.

Final Tips

- Keep information sessions short, focused and session contained.
- Integrate creative activities into lectures.
- Balance cognitive and affective components for group and for most sessions.
- Instill hope and universality in the first session.
- Define improvement for the group/members such as reduced minutes of distress, increased minutes of pleasure, fewer disagreements with co-workers.

The use of psychoeducational groups continues to grow, and more evidence of their effectiveness is emerging. Probably the most pressing issue for group leaders will be their adjustment to the virtual group format where they will need to modify their perceptions and facilitation skills to that format. It can be helpful to remember that leaders can continue to use helpful group factors such as group developmental stages, therapeutic group factor, and group-as-a-whole process and process commentary. Finally, leaders must take care to maintain a balance of cognitive and affective aspects for the group and to not overly emphasize either.

References

Acierno, R. D., et al. (2016). Behavioral activation and therapeutic exposure for posttraumatic stress disorder: A noninferiority trial of treatment delivered in person versus home-based telehealth. *Depression and Anxiety*, 33(5), 415–423. doi:10.1002/da.22476.

Barak, A., Boniel-Nissim, M., & Suler, J. (2008). Fostering empowerment in online support groups. *Computers and Human Behavior*, 1867–1883. doi:10.1016/jchb.2008.02.004.

Batastini, A., Paprzychi, P., & Ashley, C., & MacLean, N. (2020). Are video-conferenced mental and behavioral health services just as good as in-person? A meta-analysis of a fast growing practice. *Clinical Psychology Review.* doi:10:1016/j.cpe.2020.101944.

Braeuer, K., Noble, N., & Yi, S. (2022). The efficacy of an online anger management program for justice-involved youth. *Journal of Addictions & Offender Counseling*, 43(1), 26–37. https://doi.org/10.1002/jaoc.12101.

Brown, N. (1998). *Psychoeducational groups: Process and practice.* Accelerated Development.

Brown, N. (2003). *Psychoeducational groups: Process and practice.* (2nd ed.). Brunner-Routledge.

Brown, N. (2005). Psychoeducational groups. In S. Wheelan (Ed.), *The handbook of group research and practice* (pp. 511–530). SAGE.

Brown, N. (2006). *Psychoeducational groups: Process and practice* (3rd ed.). Routledge.

Brown, N. (2009). *Becoming a group leader.* Pearson.

Brown, N. (2013). *Creative techniques for group therapy.* Routledge.

Brown, N. (2018). *Psychoeducational groups: Process and practice* (4th ed.). Routledge.

Brown, N. (2019). *Conducting effective and productive psychoeducational groups.* Routledge.

Colijn S., Hoencamp, E., Snijders, H., Van Der Spek, M., & Duivenvoorden, H. (1991). A comparison of curative factors in different types of group psychotherapy. *International Journal of Group Psychotherapy*, 41, 365–378. doi:10.1080/00207284.1991.11490663.

Comer, J., *et al.* (2017). Remotely delivering real-time parent training to the home: An initial randomized of internet delivered Parent-Child Interaction Therapy (I-PCIT). *Journal of Consulting and Clinical Psychology*, 85(8), 831–834. https://doi.org/10.1037/ccp0000230.

Crowe, T. (2016). Is telemental health services a viable alternative to traditional psychotherapy for deaf individuals? *Community Mental Health Journal*, 5(3), 2. doi:10.1007/s10597-016-0025-3.

Eysenback, G., *et al.* (2004). Health related virtual communities and electronic support groups: Systematic review of the effects of online peer to peer interactions. *BMJ*, 328. doi:10.1136/bmj.328.7449.1166.

Fowers, B., & Davidov, B. (2006). The virtue of multiculturalism: Personal transformation, character, and openness to the other. *American Psychologist*, 61(6), 581–594. doi:10.1037/0003-066X.61.6.581.

Frohlich, J. R., Rapinda, K. K., Schaub, M. P., Wenger, A., Baumgartner, C., Johnson, E. A., O'Connor, R. M., Vincent, N., Blankers, M., Ebert, D. D., Hadjistavropoulos, H. D., Mackenzie, C. S., Wardell, J. D., Augsburger, M., Goldberg, J. O., & Keough, M. T. (2021). Efficacy of a minimally guided internet treatment for alcohol misuse and emotional problems in young adults: Results of a randomized controlled trial. *Addictive Behaviors Reports*, 14, 100390. https://doi.org/10.1016/j.abrep.2021.100390.

Ghumman, U., McCord, C., & Chang, J. (2016). Posttraumatic stress disorder in Syrian refugees: A review. *Canadian Psychology*, 57(4), 246–253.

Gilmore, A., & Ward-Ciesielski, E. (2017). Perceived risks and use of psychotherapy via telemedicine for patients at risk for suicide. *Journal of Telemedicine and Telecare*. doi:10.1177/1357633X17735559.

Hepburn, K., Nocera, J., Higgins, M., Epps, F., Brewster, G. S., Lindauer, A., Morhardt, D., Shah, R., Bonds, K., Nash, R., & Griffiths, P. C. (2021). Results of a randomized trial testing the efficacy of Tele-Savvy, an online synchronous/ asynchronous psychoeducation program for family caregivers of persons living with dementia. *The Gerontologist*, 62(4), 616–628. doi:10.1093/geront/gnab029.

Karagiozi, K., Margaritidou, P., Tsatali, M., Marina, M., Dimitriou, T., Apostolidis, H., Tsiatsos, T., & Tsolaki, M. (2021). Comparison of on site versus online psycho education groups and reducing caregiver burden. *Clinical Gerontologist*, 1–11. https://doi.org/10.1080/07317115.2021.1940409.

Kobak, K., Mundt, J., & Kennard, B. (2015). Integrating technology into cognitive behavior therapy for adolescent depression: A pilot study. *Annals of General Psychiatry*, 14, 37–47. https://doi.org/10.1186/s12991-015-0077-8.

Lauckner, C., & Whitten, P. (2016). The state and sustainability of telepsychiatry programs. *Journal of Behavioral Health Services & Research*, 305–318. doi:10:1007/s11414-015-9461-z.

Lopez, A., Rothberg, B., Reaser, E., Schwenk, S., & Griffin, R. (2020). Therapeutic groups via video teleconferencing and the impact on group cohesion. *MHealth*. doi:10.21037/mhealth.2019.11.04.

Lustgarten, S. (2017). Ethical concern for telemental health therapy amidst governmental surveillance. *American Psychologist*, 72(2), 159–170. https://psycnet.apa.org/doi/10.1037/a0040321.

Luxton, D., *et al.* (2016). Home-based telebehavioral health for U.S. military personnel and veterans with depression: A randomized controlled trial. *Journal of Consulting and Clinical Psychology*, 84(11), 923–934. doi:10.1037/ ccp0000135.

Meyer, K., Glassner, A., Norman, R., James, D., Sculley, R., LealVasquez, L., Hepburn, K., Liu, J., & White, C. (2022). Caregiver self-efficacy improves following complex care training: Results from the Learning Skills Together pilot study. *Geriatric Nursing*, 45, 147–152. https://doi.org/10.1016/j.gerinurse.2022.03.013.

Pang, Y., Zhang, X., Gao, R., Xu, L., Shen, M., Shi, H., Li, Y., & Li, F. (2021). Efficacy of web-based self-management interventions for depressive symptoms: a meta-analysis of randomized controlled trials. *BMC Psychiatry*, 21(1). https://doi.org/10.1186/s12888-021-03396-8.

Rentala, S. (2021). Efficacy of psychoeducation to improve medication adherence among bipolar affective disorder: A systematic review. *Indian Journal of Psychiatric Nursing*, 18(1), 55.

Soching, I. (2014). *Cognitive behavioral group therapy: Challenges and opportunities*. Wiley & Sons.

Stubbings, D., Rees, C., & Roberts, L. (2015). New avenues to facilitate engagement in psychotherapy: The use of videoconferencing and text-chat in a severe case of obsessive-compulsive disorder. *Australian Psychologist*, 50(4), 265–270. https://doi.org/10.1111/ap.12111.

Swenson, J., Smothermon, J., Rosenblad, S., & Chalmers, B. (2016). The future is here: Ethical practices of telemental health. *Journal of Psychology and Christianity*. 35(4), 310–319.

Teles, S., Ferreira, A., & Paúl, C. (2022). Attitudes and preferences of digitally skilled dementia caregivers towards online psychoeducation: A cross-sectional study. *Behaviour & Information Technology*, 42(4), 1–15.

Weinberg, H (2020). Online group psychotherapy: Challenges and possibilities during COVID-19—A practice review. *Group Dynamics: Theory, Research, and Practice*, 24(3), 201–211.

Weinberg, H. (2021). Obstacles, challenges and benefits of online group psychotherapy. *American Journal of Psychotherapy*, 74(2), 83–88.

Wierwille, J., Pukay-Martin, N., Chard, K., & Klump, M. (2016). Effectiveness of PTSD telehealth treatment in a VA clinical sample. *Psychological Services*, 13 (4), 373–379. doi:10.1037/ser0000106.

Yalom, I., & Leszcz. M. (2021). *The theory and practice of group psychotherapy* (6th ed.). Basic Books.

Yuen, E., *et al.* (2015). Randomized controlled trial of home-based telehealth versus in-person prolonged exposure for combat-related PTSD in veterans: Preliminary results. *Journal of Clinical Psychology*, 71(6), 500–512. doi:10.1002/jclp.22168.

Chapter 21

Cognitive Behavioral Group Therapy Virtually

Ingrid Söchting

Transition from In-Person to Virtual CBT Groups

The COVID-19 pandemic profoundly disrupted our personal and professional lives to the point where the question was not so much about when we might return to normal, but more about what the new normal would look like. For mental health practitioners, the new normal would certainly include more online professional activities once it was entirely safe to meet in person. For therapists trained in cognitive behavioral therapy (CBT), the possibility—and reality—of working online with our clients was present long before the pandemic began (Andersson, 2018) and has taken off over the past decade.

CBT typically involves a large didactic component in the form of psychoeducation, followed by a treatment rationale presented to the client. Then various behavioral and cognitive coping skills are presented and tried out with an emphasis on practicing (homework) between sessions. For example, a person with panic disorder will learn that the body sensations they fear (e.g., a racing heart, tightening throat sensations, sense of unreality, etc.) are not harmful in and of themselves. They will engage in a conversation with their therapist about why treatment will involve deliberately bringing on those very feared sensations in order to become desensitized and also to bring themselves into real-life situations, which they associate with believing that a panic attack is more likely to occur. If the rationale makes sense, they will commit to it, including to home practice. It is noteworthy that the CBT groups described in this chapter are different from psychoeducational groups, primarily because they include additional components after the psychoeducational one, and also due to the importance of encouraging group cohesion.

This didactic style of CBT—at times bordering on a lecture or the feeling of a course—lends itself very well to various virtual formats. Slides can be created, psychoeducational models drawn, and instructions for practicing skills provided. In fact, many CBT therapists quickly fell in love with the Zoom "whiteboard" feature—as soon as they transcended their discomfort with the awkward virtual "pen."

DOI: 10.4324/9781003248606-25

CBT clinical researchers and therapists have created, evaluated, and engaged with numerous online therapy programs. Some examples of excellent virtual programs include MoodGym, E-Couch, and This Way Up (all developed in Australia but shared for free or at a modest price with the entire globe; see thiswayup.org.au). In Canada, there are similar e-mental health programs for depression and anxiety e.g., Hadjistavropoulos et al. (2022).

The decade-long tradition of virtual CBT mental health programs, along with the explicit didactic theoretical underpinning, has allowed the CBT group format to experience a somewhat smoother transition to fully online compared to more process-focused groups. CBT groups have an advantage with the explicit didactic approach, namely that there is more focus on what is taught in the group, and less focus on the process, that is, how the group members relate to each other and their leaders. The latter is also understood as *group cohesion*, and is considered the sine qua non for productive work (Yalom & Leszcz, 2005). One can also think of a CBT group as one in which the work is being done *in* the group, as opposed to a process group in which the work is done *by* the group. Given that the virtual environment reduces full-bodied and multidimensional human beings to two-dimensional "talking heads," or the "disembodied group," as Weinberg aptly refers to it (Weinberg, 2020), it is not surprising that process group therapists wondered how on earth (pun intended) anybody could benefit from a group taking place in the Wi-Fi stratosphere. But precisely because CBT groups favor a more therapist-focused lecture style, the virtual CBT group is at risk of becoming overly didactic. This risk is mitigated by group therapists becoming even more aware of how to promote connection and cohesion among the virtual group members. I offer several examples of how to do this throughout the remainder of this chapter.

Despite initial concerns, many kinds of CBT groups have been successfully run and indeed have flourished since the outbreak of the COVID-19 pandemic. Several mental health programs have continued to offer them or some hybrid version. It is exciting to think that people with obsessive-compulsive disorder (OCD) living 2,000 kilometers north of the nearest OCD program in Vancouver, for example, were able to access online group services.

Below, I will outline some general tips and pointers for the virtual CBT group environment, followed by further discussion of the unique demands of group members and group therapists. I will also point to some of the unexpected benefits of the online environment. I will use clinical examples of an OCD group, a depression group, and a trauma group. The groups discussed are all closed groups typically comprising 6–10 members, sessions last for two hours every week for 12 weeks, homogenous with a focus on a shared problem following a careful virtual assessment, and led by two co-facilitators.

Technical Tips including Ethical Considerations before the Group Starts

The Zoom format has proven to be one of the best options for CBT groups, with consistent high levels of group member satisfaction. Various versions of Zoom exist and it is important to reassure clients that the most secure version of Zoom has been purchased and is the one used for the groups. This assuages the understandable concern about gross violations of confidentiality, which occur when meetings are "Zoom bombed." A secure Zoom licence costs about $300 but less expensive accounts, that are HIPAA compliant, are also available. It is thus not out of reach of most programs, including private practices. Still, nothing is entirely certain in life, and it is important to include a line in the consent to clinical services form about how, despite the program using the most secure version of Zoom and the guarantee that the therapists are sitting in a private room, they cannot control the environment at the client's end.

Prior to the outbreak of the COVID-19 pandemic we had implemented a pre-group orientation meeting, and during the pandemic it became clear how valuable such a virtual pre-group orientation is. Only after this first group orientation do group members make a full commitment to the group. Initially, the primary purpose of the orientation was to prevent dropouts by ensuring that prospective members had sufficiently high expectations of their chosen group (expectation has been identified as a critical variable in predicting dropouts; Söchting et al., 2018). However, for virtual groups this orientation is even more critical.

The group leaders lead this orientation meeting. They focus on explaining how the treatment group will work, but also on offering potential members an actual sample experience of what the group will feel like. In the virtual group, this experiential part starts with the facilitators first establishing, reviewing, and trouble-shooting the technological frame—the virtual container—for the group.

It is imperative that facilitators appear competent with their chosen e-platform, such as Zoom, Google Meet, Microsoft Teams, and others. It is equally important to not downplay the technology or make it sound as if there is an assumption that all the group members are knowledgeable about and comfortable with Zoom. Too much technological fumbling on the part of the leaders can undermine critical aspects of the group process.

This is obviously especially an issue for more senior group therapists. If you self-identify as a "new technology immigrant" within your own country, you may want to invest in paying for a session of technical professional development. We have found that this technological caretaking makes a substantial difference in getting groups off to a strong start, including promoting cohesion, trust, and a sense of safety. The latter two are the especial responsibility of the group leaders. Similarly to an in-person group, the leaders influence how members experience the frame. Do they sense the leaders as competent, yet flexible and responsive? Group members wonder if the leaders will keep them safe even if and when they take risks (almost all CBT anxiety groups involve considerable risk-taking during graduated exposure challenges). The term *virtual holding function* (Weinberg, 2020) is apt and important.

The orientation group allows for a discussion of how privacy will be ensured in the individual rooms the members connect from. Securing privacy is not always easy for people who live with several other family members, especially younger clients. The group can discuss ways around this. Can other family members arrange to be out of the home during group time? It is important that the Zoom meeting is password protected (clients are told to not share the password with anyone else), that the Zoom meeting has a waiting-room function and allows for breakout rooms. The breakout rooms are tried and tested during the orientation meeting (leaders have to know how to make themselves *co-hosts*), and can be a good place to have a smaller group discussion about fears and hopes for the group. Whoever is coordinating the group sessions will send out the invitation for the upcoming group the day before, or the morning of, the meeting and it is important to double-check that the Zoom invitation includes the correct day, time, and duration of the meeting. How lateness will be handled is also discussed. Will the virtual door close after 10 minutes or not? Leaders can also check that everyone is using their first name only (no "sticky" name tags and pens are needed as Zoom provides these features) and that this is their preferred name.

The leaders demonstrate their expertise with the app by showing how to do all this. The leaders also express their preference for all the group members to use the *gallery view* option on Zoom as this creates a sense of closeness. When conducting CBT, where there is more focus on the teaching by the leaders, we recommend that it is especially important to not highlight this; thus there is greater emphasis on encouraging members to opt for *speaker view*. This promotes cohesion. Sometime clients connect to the group from a bus or car. For obvious reasons, a private, parked car is OK, but a bus full of people is not. The importance of showing one's full face (and not a picture of one's pet) is discussed. The leaders usually do this by asking a Socratic question that gets to why we feel it is important to show one's face, even though it is tempting to avoid doing so. The leaders normalize the desire that all humans have at times not to show their face, and how Zoom has made this very easy to avoid. Instead, we encourage people to say if they have had a bad day, feel tired, or whatever.

Lastly, the orientation group reminds participants that, despite the high reliability of Zoom, internet connections invariably vary and group members' Zoom video may freeze or be entirely disconnected involuntarily. It is important to have a plan for these not uncommon scenarios. A list of group member contacts, including emergency contact numbers and email addresses, is helpful. A plan for whether a member can dial in and be put on speakerphone is helpful. Group members can also be told they may voluntarily disconnect for various reasons, including anger or other emotional challenges.

The Demands of Facilitating Virtual CBT Groups

Despite the emphasis on teaching, the group process is paramount in CBT (Söchting, 2014). CBT group therapists must manage the content, the teaching, the process, and the way in which the members interact and relate to each other and the leaders. Adding to this, the empirically supported group leader is critical in CBT. Meta-analyses of CBT groups identifies several valuable group leader characteristics, including warmth, humor, the ability to encourage people to try new behaviors and, interestingly, creative and flexible use of treatment protocols (Johnson & Thimm, 2018).

The virtual environment in CBT groups is less psychologically intense than in-person groups, which is both an advantage and a disadvantage. For people with anxiety it can therefore become easier to not apply oneself as fully, to hold off on various exposures. It is hard for the leaders and other group members to get the same sense of how a person is managing a particular challenge when one cannot see or get a sense of the whole person. On the plus side, someone may have been reluctant to leave their home and enter into a "germ-filled" group room, but they were prepared to connect to a virtual group.

As for the delivery of CBT, a major downside is how easily the meeting can evolve into a classroom-type lecture. The virtual environment makes this even more likely, especially if the leaders use *presenter view* for slides to illustrate key treatment points and principles. In fact, our experience suggests that it is best to avoid actual slides and slide shows—tempting as it is to put them up on Zoom. Instead, use the *Zoom whiteboard* option and sketch as you engage the entire group, ideally with examples based on their experiences.

Other ways to promote cohesion and connection is to encourage group members to share their home practice by showing, for example, a decline in subjective anxiety as they faced feared situations. Pictures of worksheets can easily be held up to the computer camera, or, for the more tech-savvy group members, screen sharing is an option. Again, the group leaders' own comfort with the online technology will support expanded ways of promoting the online group processes.

To bring further life to the group and encourage a sense of togetherness, various warm-up exercises can be used. Only the leaders' creativity will limit options. A favorite game for groups that can only be played virtually and not in-person is the Scavenger Hunt: all members are given a list of items to collect over a five-minute period and to then share them when everyone returns to the screen. Items can include a childhood photo, a favourite mug, best book, and "something I use when it is summer." It's not hard to imagine how a simple game like this promotes connection—and cohesion.

Other ways to create that sense of connection (one of the most frustrating aspects of the Zoom room is that one cannot tell who is looking at whom) is to actively encourage the judicious use of the *chat line* and the small set of emojis available on Zoom, including "clapping hands," "thumbs up," and "a party popper." The chat line has proven surprisingly valuable, as members offer a few words of support, empathy, and celebration after difficult exposures during debriefing. We have found that groups use these aids responsibly and sparingly so as not to dilute their impact, nor distract from the main group session.

Virtual Groups for Obsessive-Compulsive Disorder

OCD affects 2% of people and is characterized by recurrent and persistent thoughts, urges, or images that are experienced as intrusive and unwanted and causing marked anxiety, distress, and often fear, guilt, and shame. Compulsions are repetitive behaviors designed to undo the content of the obsession. For example, a person who has distressing obsessions involving an image of pushing a loved one into traffic may attempt to replace the image with one of hugging them, or a mental reassurance ritual: "I am a nice person; I am a good person." They may also need to tap their finger on a surface in a ritualized way in an attempt to undo and neutralize the distressing image. A best practice recommended treatment for OCD involves *specialized CBT* (Sookman, 2016; Sookman et al., 2021) with an emphasis on *exposure and response prevention* (ERP). For example, a youth sitting in a classroom will begin to doubt whether they locked their locker properly (obsession) and will feel a strong urge to leave the room and check the locker. They may repeat the OCD cycle several times, leaving the classroom up to five times, which renders them unable to focus on what is being taught. When they engage in ERP they will learn *not* to take the obsession at face value, trust themselves more, and develop skill helping them to refrain from giving in to their compulsive need to get up and go check the locker. Over time, through the repeated exposures, they will learn to tolerate anxiety and realize that their worst fear (e.g., someone will break into my locker because I forgot to lock it) is highly unlikely to come true, and even if it did they could cope and replace content.

For the virtual OCD group, an incredible upside was the new opportunities for group members to support each other in coping with ERPs in their home environments. The virtual environment continues to surprise group leaders with its possibilities. Group members would literally follow someone with contamination obsessions into the kitchen, see them handle raw meat, wash their hands only once. Or, group members would follow another member out of the home, see them come back in, lock the door just once, no checking, and return to their desk. The person would voice a strong urge to go and check the front door. They were able to track their anxiety, experience a decrease over the remainder of the session, and express appreciation for the support from the group.

Cognitive interventions are also used, and may involve a discussion of the probability of a locked locker vs. an unlocked locker being broken into. Are there any statistics from the person's school? Has it happened to them before or to someone else they know? The Zoom whiteboard is helpful for sketching probability figures and contrasting them with the actual figures vs. the emotional probability estimate (often close to 100%) during an OCD episode. The Zoom chatline can be used to brainstorm the benefits of checking one's locker (e.g., pleasant feeling of temporary certainty, or of not having to bother with replacing any items), compared to the downsides (e.g., missing important learning).

As it is possible to support people in a Zoom group who are directly facing critical triggers (it is hard or impossible, of course, to bring someone's fridge or front door to an in-person group), some group members improved more than they likely would have in an in-person group. Who could have predicted that? But, for some people with OCD, the most distressing triggers are outside of their homes such as public washrooms. In an ideal world, the pre-group assessment would determine whether a virtual or in-person group option would be most helpful.

Finally, the Zoom breakout room obsession is excellent for a larger OCD group. Because the illness of OCD expresses itself in so many different ways, the group leaders can create in-session exposure subgroups based on themes. For example, members with contamination concerns will have more in common in terms of triggers and compulsions than members with sexual concerns. The group time is thus used more efficiently if 40 minutes involves this breakout room option. We also ensure that everyone begins and ends together. The ending includes debriefing in a go-round manner where each member in turn explains what their exposure entailed, how they coped by not giving into their compulsion, and what they learned.

Virtual Groups for Depression

Depression is a major public health concern across the globe with significant personal and societal costs, including disability payments. Major depressive disorder affects about 5%–9% of the population at any time, and persistent depressive disorder (a milder, more chronic form of depression) about 3% (APA, 2013). Both types of depression are characterized by low mood almost every day, and a loss of interest or pleasure in most daily activities and previously enjoyed work and leisure pursuits. Other symptoms include problems with sleep, appetite, energy levels, motivation, inability to focus, helplessness, and hopelessness. In more severe cases, a person may experience thoughts about not wanting to live, and engage in plans for dying by suicide. Depression is a chronic illness with many people experiencing several episodes throughout their lives. After one episode a person is 50% more likely to have a second, and there is a 70% chance of a third (APA, 2013).

Fortunately, psychotherapy for depression is available, with at least three major treatment modalities considered effective (Short-term psychodynamic, interpersonal therapy, and CBT). For people who are especially prone to engaging in self-denigrating talk (e.g., "why even try looking for a part-time job, nobody would want to hire a downer like me"), CBT may be a preferred option. Treatment components in group CBT usually involve psychoeducation with a focus on the *cognitive model of depression*, followed by strategies aimed at increasing behavioural activity. often in the form of goal setting. Thereafter cognitive strategies are used that focus on helping people to identify, catch, and replace overly self-critical thinking with more reality-based, helpful thinking. There are detailed session-by-session group CBT protocols for depressions (Söchting, 2014).

An ongoing challenge for leaders in in-person depression groups is to keep the energy levels up and increase a sense of hope. Managing those twin challenges in the virtual CBT group is not easy. The scenario of dealing with several minutes of silence can make even the most I-am-comfortable-with-silence group leader wonder whether anybody is "with us." And as so often happens in Zoom, two or more people then start talking exactly at the same time. I posit that this is due to the lack of noticing the subtle bodily changes that usually precede a person starting to talk.

One way to mobilize energy is to literally engage in some group movement activities. These can take the form of upper body stretching, or getting off one's chair and standing. It disrupts the usual situation, which is seeing only a face in a square, and invariably elicits some smiles and occasional laughter. Such group activity can then be discussed from the perspective of how people felt before and after, with consensus usually being that it felt easier once we got into it, and once into it, most felt like keeping going. The leaders will then facilitate a discussion of how, in depression, if we wait to feel motivated to start an activity, it is not likely to happen.

As the group engages in setting behavioral goals, it helps to be as concrete and specific as possible. For example, a group member will show the actual drawer in their home that they will plan to spend 20 minutes organizing, or the pile of laundry, the income tax or file folder they have been procrastinating on. In a similar way to the OCD group, allowing group members in for a virtual tour can boost energy levels, and even help each member to feel more committed to being accountable for their chosen goals. This is another unexpected upside of the virtual CBT group for depression, one that is not possible in the in-person group.

Cognitive restructuring is a critical part of a CBT depression group. Again, the Zoom whiteboard lends itself to a beautiful sketching of the cognitive model of depression. The leader could start with how early life experiences may have led to a formation of unhelpful *core beliefs* (e.g., "I am unlovable"), which in turn gives rise to assumptions and rules for living (e.g., "If I don't aim to please others all the time, then I will be rejected"), which then get activated during stressful life events. This activation can in turn lead to ongoing self-critical commentary referred to *negative automatic thoughts* along with the full range of symptoms of depression. After the general group discussion of the cognitive model, members work on completing My Cognitive Model. In the virtual group, these individual member examples can be shared and discussed using the Zoom *share screen option*. Because no copies of other members' personal information are handed out, confidentiality is ensured in ways that would not be possible in in-person groups. Thought Records can also easily be sketched on the whiteboard with group members participating as each member in turns becomes the focus of reviewing the evidence that may or may not support the idea that they, for example, "will never be hired," or "I am a disappointment to others." As always in depression groups, members are encouraged to offer their experience of the person in the "hot seat" and may express the positive impact that the person in question has had on them. A sense of group support and in turn of having a positive impact on others is a critical part of recovery from depression. Again, the seemingly silly Zoom emojis of expressing support and applause can feel welcome to a person who has been isolated and is taking steps to break out of their depression bubble.

Virtual Groups for Trauma

Group treatment for trauma has been around for a couple of decades, be that specific post-traumatic stress disorder (PTSD) (APA, 2013) or more general trauma presentations that may not meet formal diagnostic criteria. A recent article concluded that several types of groups for trauma appear to be equally effective (Greene, 2021).

In our experience, effective trauma groups involve both a talking (verbal processing) part and a body (calming) part, as well as a body calming or self-care skills (see Söchting, 2014 for a full description of this group protocol). Trauma groups can also be heterogenous meaning that people with different kinds of trauma in the same group can be effective (Barrera et al., 2013).

Virtual trauma groups are no exception; however, various ethical issues need attention. It can be difficult for group members and leaders alike to gauge when a person is ready for more intense exposure. Without being able to observe the full body, the virtual therapist must err on under-shooting the therapeutic window, or have full confidence in any individual follow-up plan with a person who may leave the virtual group due to distress, which could include vomiting, dissociation, and fainting (and all of these do happen). It is important to have a clear agreement about what the group leaders will do in the event the person does not reconnect back to the group. In addition to having up-to-date next of kin information, it is also a good idea to schedule brief individual virtual or phone check-ins the day after the trauma group.

Similarly to the virtual depression group, psychoeducation presenting fight, flight, or freeze reactions can be sketched on the Zoom whiteboard, and breakout rooms can be used to group people with similar traumas to create a smaller and more intimate place to begin the recounting of the trauma (the exposure). We always use a gradual approach to trauma exposure and start with a written sketch in the third person (e.g., she arrived at the train station). This written sketch can be written in the chatline and more easily shared with others. Increasingly, accounts become more detailed. Sensory details, such as sounds and smells, are especially important. This eventually involves a verbal account in the first person (e.g., I arrive on the train station, I see ... and I hear ...). Similarly to the in-person group, the virtual trauma group may start with a practice of self-care skills, such as a grounding exercise ("four things I feel, see, hear, smell"). An upside to the virtual trauma group is that group members can create a more secure, grounded atmosphere in their homes, including by wrapping themselves in blankets, playing soft soothing music, and even burning candles or aromatherapy. These individually tailored self-soothing and calming arrangements are just not feasible in in-person group settings. They can all support more effective exposures. But similarly to some OCD presentations, entering back into the real world can be a challenge—and the online trauma group must be mindful of ways to also support this reintegration into a fuller life.

In sum, whether some virtual groups prove to be more effective due to the many upsides will ultimately be an empirical question. Clinical experience thus far suggests that virtual CBT groups are helpful and more accessible. And we also realize the unexpected vast potential in virtual CBT groups for enhancing core treatment principles such as exposure and goal setting.

References

Andersson, G. (2018). Internet interventions: Past, present, and future. *Internet Interventions*, 12, 181–188.

American Psychiatric Association (APA) (2013). *Diagnostic and statistical manual of mental disorders (DSM-5)* (5th ed). APA.

Barrera, T. L., Mott, J. M., Hofstein, R. F., & Teng, E. J. (2013). A meta-analytic review of exposure in group cognitive behavioral therapy for posttraumatic stress disorder. *Clinical Psychology Review*, 33(1), 24–32. http://dx.doi.org.visn1kis.idm.oclc.org/10.1016/j.cpr.2012.09.005.

Greene, L. (2021). The research-practice psychotherapy wars: The case of group psychotherapy in the treatment of PTSD. *International Journal of Group Psychotherapy*, 71, 393–423. https://doi.org/10.1080/00207284.2021.1890088.

Hadjistavropoulos, H. D., Peynenburg, V, Thiessen, D., Nugent, M., Karin, E., Staples, L., Dear, B. F., & Titov, N. (2022). Utilization, patient characteristics, and longitudinal improvement among patients from a provincially funded transdiagnostic internet-delivered cognitive behavioual therapy program: Observational study of trends over 6 years. *The Canadian Journal of Psychiatry*, 67(3), 192–206.

Johnson, J. J., & Thimm, J. C. (2018). A meta-analysis of group cognitive-behavioral therapy as an antidepressive treatment: Are we getting better? *Canadian Psychology*, 59(1), 15–30.

Söchting, I. (2014). *Group cognitive behavioral therapy: Challenges and opportunities*. Wiley-Blackwell.

Söchting, I., Lau, M., & Ogrodniczuk, J. (2018). Predicting compliance in group CBT using the Group Therapy Questionnaire. *International Journal of Group Psychotherapy*, 68(2), 184–194.

Sookman, D. (2016). *Specialized cognitive behavior therapy for obsessive compulsive disorder: An expert clinician guidebook*. Routledge.

Sookman, D., Anholt, G. E., Bream, V., Challacombe, F., Coughtrey, A., Craske, M. G., Foa, E., Gagné, J. P., Huppert, J. D., Jacobi, D., Lovell, K., McLean, C., Neziroglu, F., Pinto, A., Pollard, C. A., Radomsky, A. S., Riemann, B., Shafran, R., Söchting, I., Summerfeldt, L. J., Szymanski, J., Treanor, M., Van Noppen, B., van Oppen, P., Whittal, M., Williams, M., & Yadin, E. (2021). Knowledge and competency standards recommended for specialized cognitive behavior therapy (CBT) for adult obsessive-compulsive disorder (OCD). *Psychiatry Research*, 303. doi:10.1016/j.psychres.2021.113752.

Weinberg, H. (2020). Online group therapy. In H. Weinberg, & A. Rolnick (Eds.), *Theory and practice of online therapy: Internet-delivered interventions for individuals, groups, families, and organizations*. Routledge.

Yalom, I. D., & Leszcz, M. (2005). *The theory and practice of group psychotherapy* (5th ed.). Basic Books.

Chapter 22

ACT as a Group Teletherapy

Darrah Westrup

This chapter explores the potential of Acceptance and Commitment Therapy (ACT) as a teletherapy for groups. While the empirical data on ACT encompasses hundreds of internationally published studies including over 800 randomized control trials (Gloster et al., 2020; Hayes, 2021), there is limited information regarding the efficacy of ACT as a group teletherapy. Studies have shown promising results from ACT delivered as a stand-alone online course, as well as in mixed interventions combining online modules with the use of mobile apps and/or opportunities to interface with a therapist (Bricker et al., 2014; Bricker et al., 2013; Ong et al., 2021; Van der Graaf et al., 2021). There is less data on ACT conducted as a straight teletherapy, though studies are beginning to emerge (Smith et al., 2021; Wood et al., 2021). Overall, there is little published data on ACT as a group teletherapy and much remains to be learned.

In this chapter we will explore the viability of ACT as a group teletherapy, beginning with its theoretical underpinnings and how these naturally translate to an online modality. We will examine ways in which ACT can help to overcome the remote nature of online work, and how it can capitalize on features of videoconferencing for therapeutic gain. We will wrap up with some suggestions as to how experiential exercises—an important feature of ACT—can be modified to increase their effectiveness in teletherapy groups.

What is ACT?

ACT was developed from over three decades of applied research grounded in functional contextualism. This philosophy of science recognizes that an event or act is inseparable from the context in which it occurs. Its inherent "truth," then, cannot be established as contextual influences are always present. This philosophy is reflected in ACT's pragmatic focus on "what works" (Hayes et al., 2012, p. 33) and in the fact that unpleasant thoughts or feelings are not viewed as inherently bad in and of themselves. Contextual approaches such as ACT do not seek to change or eliminate

DOI: 10.4324/9781003248606-26

difficult thoughts or feelings and, in fact, view such change or control efforts as problematic.

A second central feature of ACT is that this decades-long behavior analytic research program resulted in a theory of human language and cognition known as relational frame theory (RFT) (Hayes et al., 2001). This work identified unique abilities that enable humans to acquire language and clarified how "languaging" (referring to all verbal behavior, including cognition) plays a pivotal role in human pathology and suffering. Only humans, for example, can acquire the concept of "failure" and then attach that concept to another acquired concept (e.g., their "identity"). Only humans, via distinct verbal learning processes, have come to know the meaning of "death," or to believe something is wrong with them if they are thinking or feeling a certain way. RFT provides an account of the verbal processes that enable such phenomena and illuminates how quickly and easily our relationship with language becomes problematic.

Importantly, clarity in the verbal processes that lead to suffering pointed to ways this might be alleviated. For example, in understanding how our self-concepts (identities) are constructed, we understand why clients rigidly hold onto their self-concepts even if they are problematic, and, in turn, how they can learn to hold these more lightly. Understanding how humans come to relate to their verbal world in problematic ways guides the ACT clinician to help clients to recognize that they *have* thoughts and feelings as opposed to *being* their thoughts and feelings. This paves the way for a fundamental shift in awareness—clients become aware of themselves as larger than, and distinct from, the internal experiences of the moment. They learn to "notice the Noticer." It is not a stretch from here to recognize the Noticer as being whole and intact despite thoughts and feelings to the contrary. Clients learn to recognize when they are lost in a fruitless battle with their internal experience, engaging in control or avoidant strategies that are keeping them stuck. In learning to relate differently to their internal experience, clients are freed up to engage in their lives, *to be*, in a way that promotes vitality and well-being. This "psychological flexibility" is the overarching aim of ACT and encapsulates six distinct but interrelated processes that are the focus of therapy:

1 *Contacting the present*: Rather than being "stuck in their heads," clients learn to bring their attention to the present moment.
2 *Willingness* (often used interchangeably with *acceptance*): Rather than work to avoid, fix, or change thoughts and feelings, clients learn to relate their internal experience with openness and curiosity—to have what is there to be had without defense.
3 *Cognitive defusion*: Rather than "fuse with" the contents of their mind (i.e., relating to their thoughts as being literally true, being

solely "in" their thoughts), clients learn to step back and observe their thoughts as an ongoing process and as just one aspect of their present experience.

4 *Self as context*: Rather than rigidly identifying with their self-concepts, clients recognize that self-concepts are verbal constructions and that they are "larger than" such constructs. New perspective-taking helps clients to contact the Self that is constant through time, and to experience this Self as whole and intact.

5 *Values*: Clients are guided to identify their personal values, to articulate how they want to "be" (e.g., engaged, kind) in various domains (e.g., friendship, partnership, community).

6 *Committed action*: Clients learn to link their personal values with specific actions that move them forward in a chosen direction. They learn they can make value-driven choices regardless of the thoughts and feelings of the moment.

In short, clients learn to be *open, centered*, and *engaged* as they move through their lives (Hayes et al., 2012).

Why ACT is a Fit for Group Teletherapy

ACT lends itself well to group therapy for reasons that are equally applicable to in-person and online groups. As a starting point, the model provides a way to progress treatment despite the inherent variation and complexity in a group of individuals who each have their own struggles and agendas. An ACT therapist uses all the tools at their disposal—interpersonal learning, psychoeducation, modeling, practice, and use of experiential exercises—to introduce group members to the core ACT processes and help them to learn new ways of relating to their experience. Familiarity with these processes helps the therapist to recognize them in session and work effectively with whatever is occurring in the moment. It is not just that everything is clinical fodder, but that everything can be used in an intentional, consistent manner to move the therapy forward. This unifying tenet of ACT, so helpful with the convolutions of group work, is just as applicable to therapy done remotely as that conducted face-to-face.

It is important to emphasize that content—that which a group member shares in group—is not ignored, but clinical interventions target the process(es) reflected in either what is shared or in the act of sharing itself. The following short excerpt would be applicable to either an online or an in-person group:

GROUP MEMBER ("BILL"): "My boss is such a jerk! He got on my case yesterday for being late and didn't even want to hear why. I was so ticked off!"

THERAPIST: "That sounds frustrating! What else showed up for you when he got on your case? You had thoughts about him being a jerk, the feeling of anger..."

(Rather than aligning with Bill's focus on his boss, what his boss said or even why Bill was late, the therapist targets self as context and defusion by making a distinction between Bill and his experience in the moment he has described. The therapist could also target these processes by having Bill identify what he is currently experiencing as he shares this, or by inquiring what sorts of thoughts and feelings are showing up for others in the group. The therapist could then help group members to practice willingness by inviting them to simply notice and hold what they are experiencing for a few moments.)

The fact that the same clinical goals apply to all members facilitates interpersonal learning. Group members learn from watching others build the same set of skills they themselves are working on, skills that will help all of them to move forward in their lives. This clarity enables group members to support one another in that shared effort rather than align with agendas that are self-defeating (e.g., trying to get others to change, waiting to have different thoughts and feelings before living). Lack of ability with core processes (e.g., avoidance rather than willingness, fusing with thoughts rather than being able to notice them as an ongoing process, rigid attachment to a conceptualized self) also apply to all, so there are ample opportunities to observe at first-hand how such behaviors keep group members stuck.

For readers less familiar with ACT, it may be helpful to learn that this theory-driven approach fosters many elements of group work long considered to be key by experts from other orientations (such as Yalom's (1970) "therapeutic factors") and that have been found to promote change in online groups (Weinberg and Raufman, 2014). Many of these elements arise from the work rather than being specifically pursued. For example, while cohesion per se is not an articulated treatment focus in ACT, it makes sense that a group whose members are participating in an *open, centered*, and *engaged* fashion demonstrates cohesiveness. As we will see throughout the following discussion, cohesion is built as members learn to relate to others and themselves in a way that fosters authentic connection and growth (e.g., learning to be *present, willing* to experience what arises, noticing and *defusing* from unhelpful thoughts and judgements, and choosing *value-driven actions*). Similarly, rather than attempting to "establish hope" (Yalom, 1970), hope as a *feeling* is viewed as an experience that is likely to ebb and flow, and the therapy would instead focus on fostering active engagement and openness to experience as a value-driven stance even when one is not feeling particularly hopeful.

This is not to say that an ACT therapist would not strive to engage group members and provide encouragement—the difference is in the articulated purpose of such interventions (i.e., fostering a feeling vs. ways of being, with both these goals being in the service of promoting meaningful engagement in the group and in life). In ACT, group members are guided to articulate deeply held values and to envision lives wherein more often than not they have made choices in accordance with how they want to be living their lives. It could be said that the goal is to engender hope as an attitude, evidenced by *willingness* and *value-based, committed action.*

"Universality" (Yalom, 1970) is an essential feature of ACT as the model is based on fundamental principles of human behavior that cut across diagnoses, labels and presenting problems. Group members learn that they have similar struggles (e.g., trying to flee or mitigate distressing thoughts and feelings, buying into what their mind is telling them about themselves and their lives), irrespective of their individual histories and presenting problems. A subtle but important distinction between Yalom's conceptualization and the ACT approach is the latter's emphasis on process rather than content. That is, in ACT it is not so much the awareness that "there is no human deed or thought that is fully outside the experience of other people" (Yalom, 1995, p. 6) that is viewed as beneficial, but the recognition that as verbal beings we have similar *ways of relating to our experiences* that lead to suffering, that we are essentially set up as verbal beings to fall into this trap. Put another way, it is not that group members might share the same shameful thought, but that as verbal beings we are set up to produce such thoughts and then to relate to them in a way that causes difficulty.

Yalom (1995) pointed to the therapeutic power of acceptance in group therapy, that it is not just the commonality of experience but the mutual understanding and acceptance of one another's experience that is a mechanism of change. In an ACT group members learn to view themselves as being normal and acceptable for reasons that are equally applicable to their peers. Along with fostering acceptance by highlighting how and why humans struggle similarly, ACT frames these struggles as a normal—though difficult—part of the human condition. It is not uncommon in an ACT group for members to report accessing a deep compassion for all human beings. That being said, acceptance of others and of what might arise in group is targeted in ACT; again, not so much as a feeling, but more as a stance. That is, the *feeling* of acceptance may come and go, but one can choose to *be* accepting in any moment (e.g., attentive and considerate of another's experience, willing to experience what is showing up in the group even if uncomfortable, behaving respectfully regardless of what one might be thinking and feeling). Judgement may arise—in fact it inevitably will—but group members learn to notice and defuse from such thoughts and participate in group in a way that fosters growth for all. (Consider the difference between one group member remarking to another, "Man, you are such an arrogant SOB!" and "Wow, I am having all sorts of negative thoughts and feelings about what you just said!")

There is great relief to be found in the realization that far from being broken or defective in some way, one has simply been behaving as verbal beings do. However, there is a sobering realization in this as well, one that reflects the existential factors about which Yalom (1980, 1995) has written extensively. That is, in ACT groups members are quickly disabused of the notion that they can escape the pain of life, that they can get rid of unwanted thoughts or feelings or find some "fix" that will result in happiness. Additionally, group members come to the tough realization that since thoughts and feelings are not actually in charge, they are fully on the hook for the choices they make in their lives. Though values work in ACT is seen as an answer for "what now?", the ACT therapist makes it clear that living a value-driven life is ultimately up to each group member.

How ACT Helps to Overcome Challenges in Online Groups

The discussion above highlights ways in which ACT fosters therapeutically powerful aspects of group work, and how by their very nature these benefits apply as much to online groups as those done face-to-face. In this section we will explore aspects of the model that helps therapists to work effectively with challenges particular to teletherapy.

A common concern with group teletherapy is the "media barrier" (Weinberg, 2020, p. 183) and to what degree this prevents or lessens the transformative possibilities of group therapy. It is important for therapists to acknowledge the nature of working remotely and to make a concerted effort to establish connection and cohesion while using this modality (Weinberg & Rolnick, 2020). ACT naturally lends itself to this effort as it targets skills that promote vital engagement—in life, in relationships, and in a therapy session. For example, learning to be fully present and noticing what one is thinking, feeling, and experiencing here-and-now is a central skill in ACT and is a focus from the onset of the therapy. Sessions typically start with a brief mindfulness exercise not only to further core processes (i.e., *contacting the present, willingness, defusion, self as context*), but to mark the session as a time set aside for important work (*values, committed action*). The fact that participants are online can be brought into such an exercise:

> Now bring your awareness across the distance to the others in this group … become aware of your peers who are sharing this experience with you right now … who are also thinking … feeling … breathing … Notice they have also set aside this time because like you, they

are about something here ... Notice how they too are in this moment with you.

This way of framing the online experience can overcome perceived distance and, in fact, underscores again the universality of the human condition.

As mentioned above, trying to fix or avoid discomfort during therapy is contraindicated in ACT. Instead, the aim is to help group members to learn that they can remain present and engaged in session despite uncomfortable thoughts and feelings, just as they can learn to hold such experiences as they make value-driven choices in their lives. The model thus takes therapists off the hook for fixing challenging dynamics of online work, while also providing a framework for using such challenges to progress the therapy. For example, rather than striving to repair apparent disengagement or awkwardness in a particular teletherapy session, the ACT therapist might transparently model their experience:

> I am noticing I'm having some worries about our group today. It's hard to tell from my screen what you all are thinking or feeling ... to me the group feels distant, sort of disengaged today ... Is anyone else experiencing this?

This simple intervention models core abilities targeted in ACT; *contacting the present, willingness* to simply notice and hold one's experience, and noticing (*defusing* from) thoughts. Even if not explicitly stated, the language used ("I *am noticing I'm having* some worries," "Is anyone else *having that experience* right now?") supports experiencing *self as context*, and the therapist's choice to share their experience reflects their *values* around the therapy and *committed action* in the service of those values. Rather than fixing, the therapist uses what is happening as a learning and practice opportunity as demonstrated below (watch for *contacting the present, willingness, defusion, values,* and *committed action*):

> Yeah, so it sounds like a few of you are feeling a little tuned out this morning. Me too! And, here is an opportunity for us to choose to engage anyway. We can make the choice to be here right along with those thoughts and feelings, to participate because we are about something in this group. Are you willing to do that with me?

Along with the emphasis on universality in the above example, readers might recognize Yalom's (1995) "altruism." The therapist highlights that despite their physical distance, members are choosing to engage with one another because they are "about something" in this group. It is typical for an ACT therapist to point to such instances of valued action as they occur in group, and to use the type of self-disclosure demonstrated in these examples to model core ACT processes. As ACT is based on fundamental principles of human behavior, the therapist is necessarily "in the same soup" as their clients. This central tenet of ACT is actively utilized throughout the therapy, not to bring unnecessary attention to the content of a therapist's life, but to further core processes in play (e.g., that the therapist is *having an experience*, that they are *noticing and holding* thoughts and feelings). As pointed out by Weinberg (2020, pp. 183–184), when used appropriately therapist transparency can mitigate the remote aspect of teletherapy and show group members how to reach across the distance inherent in online work.

Adapting ACT for Teletherapy Groups

Before moving into suggestions for adapting ACT for a teletherapy group, a point should be made about video cameras. ACT's clinical focus on *willingness* means refraining from supporting avoidance strategies that can occur in session, such as turning off one's video camera, and/or temporarily leaving the session to gather oneself. To be sure, any discomfort or distress is carefully attended to, but such experiences are treated as a doable, understandable human reaction rather than a problem that needs to be fixed or hidden. The therapist sets the stage for this at the outset of the group, establishing this level of engagement as a requirement for participating in the group. Group members agree to leave cameras and microphones on whenever possible (technical difficulties and other logistical issues are sometimes unavoidable), and to remain connected to the group regardless of what they are experiencing.

The main adjustment to ACT for teletherapy concerns the experiential work. An essential feature of an ACT session—when done well—is that it is a felt experience. The therapy is less about transferring knowledge from one individual to another and more about being and doing. This is particularly important in online work, in that sitting and talking at one another through screens and monitors pulls for a reliance on dialogue and thinking and can shortchange other learning mechanisms (Weinberg, 2020). ACT addresses such "mindiness" with well-timed experiential exercises that bring participants out of their heads and into the present, and that provide in-the-moment opportunities to learn and practice the processes at the heart of the therapy.

Fortunately, many of the experiential exercises found in the ACT literature translate well to group teletherapy. When considering an exercise for online work, it is important to be clear on the intended function(s) of the exercise and to consider whether those will transfer to a multi-screen, videoconferencing platform. It is also important to find ways to elicit active participation from all group members.

To provide an example, the well-known "tug-of-war" ACT exercise (Hayes et al., 1999) clearly will not work in the usual way. (This exercise is commonly used as a physical demonstration of the futility and cost of struggling with unwanted thoughts and feelings, and to introduce *willingness*—represented as dropping the rope—as an alternative). When done in person, the therapist uses a rope to enact a tug-of-war with a group member, with the therapist representing what the client has identified as their main issue, such as having anxiety, or the belief that they are not "good enough." The following is an alternative exercise that shares the intended function of this exercise but that would be more effective in an online group. Group members are asked in advance of the session to have a heavy book or similar object nearby. To begin the exercise, the therapist invites members to imagine their books as being "the thing they have been struggling with" (e.g., anxiety, feeling not good enough). Then, to represent their struggle with these unwanted experiences, they are asked to stand and hold their books with their arms straight out in front of them and as far away as possible (the therapist would engage in this activity as well). In this position the books soon become untenably heavy. The therapist would hold this moment, cueing the group to notice the difficulty and cost of the struggle they are in. After a bit, group members would be guided to bring their books back in and to tuck them under their arms (denoting *willingness* and *self as context*). The therapist would guide the group members to notice the difference between the two positions and invite everyone to walk around their space a bit, pointing out how even with their book, they are now free to move.

We can see how this exercise highlights the core processes targeted by the traditional tug-of-war exercise. We can also use unique features of teletherapy to enhance the work. That is, as all participants are standing with books held out, and then tucked in, the therapist could guide the group to regard one another on their screens, to notice their peers as they struggle, and what it looks like as thoughts and feelings are taken in and simply held. The therapist could further this perspective-taking (an important aspect of *self as context)* by asking members to regard their own video camera image as well, cuing them to notice that they are fully able to carry their books, and that they are "larger than" their books, just as others in the group are larger than their unwanted experiences. The therapist can continue to utilize group members' screens in this way throughout the therapy as an effective means to help group members "notice the Noticer."

The Label Parade (Walser & Westrup, 2007) is another exercise that can be modified to optimize the online modality. This *self as context* exercise provides a graphic demonstration of the distinction between a person (context) and their "content" (i.e., thoughts, feelings, sensations). In a typical in-person group, the therapist engages in a dialogue with one or more members of the group to create a physical representation of the sorts of thoughts and feelings they struggle with. That is, as members are cued to share difficult thoughts and feelings, the therapist writes each thought or feeling separately on a piece of paper and asks the members to tape the pieces somewhere on their body. When the group members are essentially covered in paper, they are invited to stand and move to a distance from the group. The therapist then asks all the group members to simply regard one another, and after a few moments invites the group members to share what they see as they regard their fellow group members covered in pieces of paper. It is usually the case that someone in the group will remark something to the effect that they "just see their friends," or that there are "just people here with a bunch of stuff stuck on them." The ensuing discussion underscores this point and the fact that not only are group members able to carry their cards, they are intact and distinct from what they carry.

This exercise can be modified easily for a videoconferencing platform. Group members would need to know in advance to have a marker, tape, and paper on hand during the session. The therapist could then model the process for the group, sharing a worry and the feelings and thoughts that typically arise with the worry, and then taping the paper representations of those experiences on their upper body where it can be seen on camera. The therapist could then work with individual members or cue the group to engage in this process together. And now we see how the therapist can utilize the unique vantage point of a video camera to enhance the perspective-taking needed to experience *self as context*. That is, not only can the therapist cue the group to regard one another, but to spend a few moments regarding their own video images as well. The visual limitations of a screen can be helpful here, making it difficult to see the content on the cards and facilitating the perception that, despite what the taped papers say, what "matters" is the individual who is larger than all the stuff. The group members experientially contact the distinction between themselves and their struggles and can clearly see that this distinction stands for others as well.

There are dozens of experiential exercises detailed in the ACT literature and innumerable ways to creatively implement experiential learning online. The function of these exercises is always to further core ACT processes. Bringing our discussion full circle, we can also see how exercises such as those described above help to build group cohesion, universality, acceptance, and altruism, and optimize the online modality as a learning mechanism.

Summary

This chapter examined the use of ACT as a group teletherapy. Anecdotal and emerging empirical data suggests that ACT holds promise in this context and, in fact, lends itself well to a videoconferencing platform. Consistent with the theoretical framework on which it is based, the model provides a guide for navigating this new terrain, helping therapists to overcome some of the challenges of online work and maximize this medium. We can expect to learn more as the online provision of mental health continues to grow, and, as the literature catches up with real-world practice, to develop increasingly effective ways to harness the therapeutic promise of online groups.

References

Bricker, J. B., Mull, K. E., Kientz, J. A., Vilardaga, R. M., Mercer, L. D., Akioka, K., & Heffner, J. L. (2014). Randomized, controlled pilot trial of a smartphone app for smoking cessation using acceptance and commitment therapy. *Drug Alcohol Depen*, 143, 87–94.

Bricker, J., Wyszynski, C., Comstock, B., & Heffner, J. L. (2013). Pilot randomized controlled trial of web-based acceptance and commitment therapy for smoking cessation. *Nicotine Tob Res*, 10, 1756–1764.

Gloster, A. T., Walder, N., Levin, M. E., Twohig, M. P., & Karekla, M. (2020). The empirical status of acceptance and commitment therapy: A review of meta-analyses . *Journal of Contextual Behavioral Science*, 18, 181–192.

Hayes, S. C. (2021). *State of the ACT evidence*. Association for Contextual Behavioral Science. https://contextualscience.org/state_of_the_act_evidence.

Hayes, S. C., Barnes-Holmes, D., & Roche, B. (2001). *Relational frame theory: A post-Skinnerian account of human language and cognition*. Plenum Press.

Hayes, S. C., Strosahl, K. D., & Wilson, K. G. (1999). *Acceptance and commitment therapy: An experiential approach to behavior change*. Guilford Press.

Hayes, S. C., Strosahl, K. D., & Wilson, K. G. (2012). *Acceptance and commitment therapy: The process and practice of mindful change* (2nd ed.). Guilford Press.

Ong, C. W, Krafft, J., Panoussi, F., Petersen, J. M., Levin, M. E., & Twohig, M. P. (2021). In-person and online-delivered acceptance and commitment therapy for hoarding disorder: A multiple baseline study. *Journal of Contextual Behavioral Science*, 20, 108–117.

Smith, B. P., Coe, E., & Meyer, E. C. (2021). Acceptance and commitment therapy delivered via telehealth for the treatment of co-occurring depression, PTSD, and nicotine use in a male veteran. *Clinical Case Studies*, 20(1), 75–91.

Van der Graaf, D. L., Trompetter, H. R., Smeets, T. & Mols, F. (2021). Online acceptance and commitment therapy (ACT) interventions for chronic pain: A systematic literature review. *Internet Interventions*, 26, 100465. doi:10.1016/j.invent.2021.100465.

Walser, R., & Westrup, D. (2007). *Acceptance & commitment therapy for the treatment of post-traumatic stress disorder & trauma-related problems: A practitioner's guide to using mindfulness & acceptance strategies*. New Harbinger.

Weinberg, H. (2014). *The paradox of internet groups: Alone in the presence of virtual others*. Karnac Books.

Weinberg, H. (2020). Online group therapy: In search of a new therapy? In H. Weinberg & A. Rolnick (Eds.), *Theory and practice of online therapy: Internet-*

delivered interventions for individuals, groups, families, and organizations (pp. 146–187). Routledge.

Weinberg, H., & Raufman, R. (2014). Yalom's therapeutic factors virtually examined. In H. Weinberg, *The paradox of internet groups: Alone in the presence of virtual others* (pp. 149–168). London: Karnac Books.

Weinberg, H., & Rolnick, A. (2020). Introduction. In H. Weinberg & A. Rolnick (Eds.), *Theory and practice of online therapy: Internet-delivered interventions for individuals, groups, families, and organizations*. Routledge.

Westrup, D., & Wright, J. (2017). *Learning ACT in groups: An acceptance and commitment therapy skills training manual for therapists*. New Harbinger.

Wood, H. J., Gannon, J. M., Roy Chengappa, K. N., & Sarpal, D. K. (2021). Group teletherapy for first-episode psychosis: Piloting its integration with coordinated specialty care during the Covid-19 pandemic. *Psychol Psychother,* 94(2), 382–389.

Yalom, I. D. (1970). *The theory and practice of group psychotherapy* (1st ed.). Basic Books.

Yalom, I. D. (1980). *Existential psychotherapy.* Basic Books.

Yalom, I. D. (1995). *The theory and practice of group psychotherapy* (4th ed.). Basic Books.

Chapter 23

"Can We Zoom Out of the Hospital?"

Online Behavioral Stress Management Groups

Reut Ron and Anat Laronne

Introduction

Stress management is a psychological treatment that is found to improve mental health and increase health outcomes. Online group therapy (OGT) is a relatively new modality for behavioral stress management (BSM), and its effectiveness is unknown.

For the past 10 years, Assuta Medical Centers (AMC) have been providing psychological face-to-face support services. The COVID-19 pandemic led to the diversion to online modality of psychotherapy. Alongside this change, a mixed methods study was conducted with patients from the oncology institute, the IVF unit, and the pain clinic. Each group had four sessions at weekly intervals. Study participants were asked to complete an online questionnaire before the first session, and again after the fourth session. Group facilitators were interviewed in two focus groups. In this chapter, we will detail methods and results of the study, conclusions, and practical insights.

Background

Stress management is a psychological treatment that utilizes elements of behavioral interventions and stress management skills. Behavioral stress management (BSM) helps chronic patients to develop skills to increase both physical and mental relaxation, and provides a buffer against the negative effects of their disease (Tang et al., 2020). Several studies and systematic reviews have found that BSM is effective for treating individuals with chronic diseases such as breast and prostate cancer, AIDS, and post-traumatic stress disorder, and indicated that the intervention can improve mental health parameters and increase health outcomes (Kapogiannis et al., 2018).

Three main BSM techniques are some of the most effective means of stress reduction: progressive muscle relaxation, breathing therapies, and guided imagery (Mann & Contrada, 2016). Progressive muscle relaxation (PMR) is a deep relaxation technique that has been effectively used to control stress and anxiety, relieve insomnia, and reduce symptoms of

DOI: 10.4324/9781003248606-27

certain types of chronic pain. PMR (sometimes known as the Jacobson Relaxation Technique) is based on the simple practice of tensing or tightening one muscle group at a time followed by a relaxation phase with release of the tension (McCallie et al., 2006). Guided imagery is a therapeutic approach that uses mental imagery to activate the mind-body connection in order to enhance the individual's sense of well-being, to control stress and to reduce anxiety (Krau, 2020).

Personal or group BSM treatments are usually conducted face-to-face. The meetings last between 30 minutes and two hours, depending on the method being used (progressive muscle relaxation, breathing therapies, or guided imagery). Some BSM methods require several meetings each week, while other methods require less frequent meetings. The method is usually taught by a trained professional who is an instructor in the field. The purpose of the instructor is to help the patient experience the intervention fully without deviating from other, often unwanted, experiences (Foulkes & Pines, 2018).

It was suggested that group BSM interventions might affect patients differently than personal interventions. A growing body of research supports the idea that group psychosocial interventions may improve many aspects of patients' recovery from disease and quality of life (Tang et al., 2020). In this context supportive group discussion is less aimed at sharing illness experience and more oriented toward sharing coping strategies.

The outbreak of the COVID-19 pandemic restrictions ushered in a golden age in the practice of and the research into providing online health services in general and online psychotherapy treatments in particular. OGT, being a relatively new modality for leading psychotherapy groups in general and BSM group therapy in particular, has limited evidence, systematic reviews, and publications. Knowledge on the effectiveness of online BSM group therapy is still scarce and there are no clear guidelines on how to implement it. Recent publications focus on closely related modalities such as online mindfulness-based group cognitive behavioral therapy, showing effectiveness in reducing symptoms of misophonia, depression, anxiety, and stress (Ghorbani et al., 2022). Other publications focused on the fact that group therapists have been forced to move online without sufficient training in leading online groups (Weinberg, 2021) showing that online groups present specific challenges to therapists' work with patients (Gullo et al., 2022) and highlighting that more research is needed, especially on specific elements of online group therapy (Weinberg, 2020).

The Setting: Online BSM Group Therapy at Assuta Medical Centers, Israel

AMC is a private network of medical centers in Israel. For the past 10 years, AMC's Ramat HaHayal Hospital has been providing psychological support services to patients with chronic diseases and to those in long-term treatment. BSM group therapy, which focuses on psychoeducation and practicing relaxation and guided imagery methods, is one of the most active and desired services. BSM groups are open to all cancer, IVF, and pain clinic patients. Each group usually has up to 10 participants.

The social distancing and isolation restrictions brought about by the pandemic in March 2020 led to the diversion of all new BSM group meetings to online video conferences, using an online video conferencing software platform. A validated face-to-face group intervention protocol for cancer patients using relaxation techniques and guided imagery was adapted to the online platform (Cohen & Fried, 2007). Each group was guided and accompanied by at least one facilitator—a medical psychology intern or expert. Patients were informed, via a phone call prior to the first meeting, about group-setting rules including days, time and frequency of the meetings, and the importance of participating in all four meetings. They were also requested to procure the appropriate technical equipment and private space for the meetings.

Alongside the implementation of this change, we conducted a mixed methods study to evaluate the efficiency of the online BSM groups and the satisfaction of patients and facilitators. We also aimed to identify barriers and facilitators to using this modality in order to examine whether online groups should be continued after the end of the COVID-19 pandemic.

The Study: Participants and Methods

The study was conducted between March 2020 and August 2021. The approval of AMC's ethics committee was obtained prior to study recruitment. The study population included individuals who were referred to BSM group treatment by healthcare professionals working at AMC, and individuals who contacted the therapists in response to information pamphlets or a text message sent to their mobile phones. These individuals were then contacted by phone and were provided with more information about the intervention. The individuals who decided not to participate at this point (mostly due to the day and time of the meetings) were not included in the study's dropout rate.

Individuals were included in the study if they were patients at AMC's oncology institute, IVF units, or the pain clinic, if they could read and speak Hebrew fluently, and if they could use the online platform by phone or another device. All participants signed an informed consent prior to enrolling in the study guaranteeing anonymity and privacy regarding patients' responses. Groups were opened consecutively when at least eight verified participants with the same condition (cancer, fertility, or pain) were recruited. Each group had four sessions at weekly intervals.

The groups were led by one or two facilitators (depending on the facilitators' self-assurance level and their acquaintance with the unique challenges of the group population and its health circumstances). The facilitators' teams included six female interns and specialists in medical psychology. Most facilitators had prior experience in leading relaxation and guided imagery therapy for stress reduction in individual and group therapy sessions using a similar protocol at AMC's Oncology Institute. The study protocol was introduced to the facilitators verbally and was written down for standardization.

Study participants were asked to complete an online questionnaire before the first session, and again after the fourth session. The questionnaire consisted of valid measurement tools on stress management and mental health status: Perceived Stress Scale (PSS) (Cohen et al., 1983), Depression Anxiety Stress Scales (DASS) (Lovibond & Lovibond, 1995), and Hospital Anxiety and Depression Scale (HADS) (Zigmond & Snaith, 1983). The questionnaire also included questions on treatment expectations and experiences in the online group therapy.

To collect the facilitators' experience of online groups, all the group facilitators were interviewed in two focus groups. The discourse of the focus groups was recorded and transcribed for qualitative analysis of repeated themes.

Results

During the study period, 128 patients participated in 19 online BMS groups: 78 patients in 13 oncology groups, 38 patients in five IVF groups, and 10 patients in two pain clinic groups. Almost two-thirds of the patients (77. 61%) attended all four BMS online sessions and completed both questionnaires. These included 52 oncology patients, 19 IVF patients, and six pain clinic patients. The remainder (51.39%) were considered study dropouts. The participants' characteristics are summarized in Table 23.1. Participants' median age was 47 years (range, 27–83 years). Most of them (98.7%) were women, 69% lived with a spouse, and 63% worked full-time.

Is the Intervention Effective?

Comparison of the questionnaires completed before the first session and after the fourth (final) session showed improvement in all scores after participation in the BSM group. Patients' average scores on selected questions is shown in Figure 23.2.

Stress: The ultimate goal of the BSM intervention is to reduce patients' stress by providing tools for managing stress and practicing them. Overall, the average PSS score decreased by 0.24 ($p < 0.01$) and the average

Table 23.1 Demographic characteristics of the study population

		All participants	Cancer patients	IVF patients	Pain clinic patients
		N = 77	N = 52	N = 19	N = 6
Age (in years)	Median (minimum, maximum)	47 (27–83)	52 (32–83)	38 (27–47)	43 (28–50)
Gender	Female	99%	98%	100%	100%
Marital and residential status	Living alone	14%	23%	8%	33%
	Living with a spouse and/or children	85%	75%	92%	67%
	Living with parents	1%	2%	0%	0%
Employment Status	Receives pension allowance	6%	10%	0%	0%
	Currently not working	30%	30%	26%	33%
	A full-time or part-time employee	64%	60%	74%	67%
Mobility level	Needs assistance to leave the house	17%	23%	0%	17%
	Mobile using public transport	8%	6%	16%	0%
	Mobile using a private car	75%	71%	84%	83%
Psychological therapy experience	Yes (individual therapy only)	53%	60%	32%	67%
	Yes (group therapy)	3%	2%	5%	0%
	No experience at all	44%	38%	63%	33%
Digital literacy	Frequent user of smart phone, WhatsApp, email, and video calls	91%	90%	95%	83%

DASS stress score decreased by 0.84 (p = 0.170) between the start and end of the intervention, indicating a clinically meaningful improvement in participants' stress levels. In both questionnaires half of the items also showed a statistically significant improvement.

Anxiety: Analyzing all participants, anxiety levels measured by DASS did not show statistically significant differences between the start and end of the intervention. However, the oncology patients showed a clinically

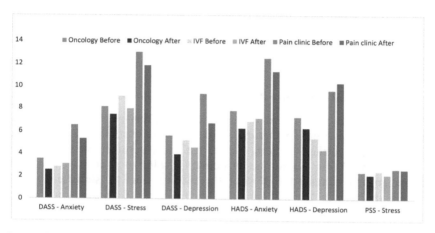

Figure 23.1 Final grades of questions by condition before and after the intervention
Source: Compiled by the authors.

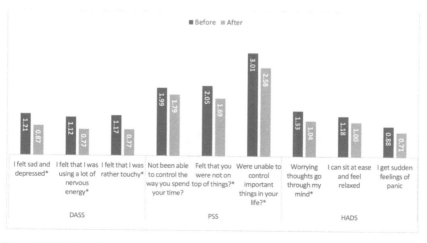

Figure 23.2 Patients' average scores on selected questions
Source: Compiled by the authors.

meaningful decrease in the DASS anxiety score (–0.98, p = 0.077), and in the HADS anxiety score (–1.56, p = 0.03), indicating reduced anxiety following the intervention.

Depression: Although BSM interventions and guided imagery are not intended to address depression, the effect of the intervention on depression was examined as part of the questionnaires used in this study. The analysis showed a clinically significant decreased DASS depression score (–1.48, p = 0.02) and HADS depression score (–0.84, p = 0.21).

Subgroup analysis by patient condition shows differences, especially for pain clinic patients, as shown in Figure 23.1. Among the three subgroups analyzed, the pain clinic patients perceived stress and anxiety at higher levels than the oncology and IVF patients.

Participants' and Facilitators' Perceptions of Online Meetings

The participants were asked to rate four questions regarding their perceptions of online group therapy in general; for example, "I think that online group meetings are better" or "I feel more comfortable with online therapy." In all four questions, participants' willingness to participate in online groups increased following the intervention. A statistically significant increase in the willingness of participants to recommend online group meetings to a close friend was observed between the start and end of the intervention (0.61, p < 0.001).

Participants were also asked to rate 13 questions regarding difficulties, challenges, and benefits of online group therapy meetings; for example, "It is harder for me to concentrate in online meetings" or "Eliminating the need for physical arrival is a significant advantage for me." Patients'

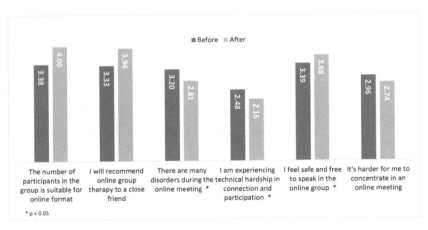

Figure 23.3 Patients' perceptions of online group therapy: selected questions
Source: Compiled by the authors.

perceptions towards online groups improved in all questions, except for the question on the interaction among group members, which showed a decrease in the average score at the end of the intervention. Notably, the perceptions of pain clinic patients towards online groups did not improve following the intervention. We cannot attribute the lack of improvement in perception towards online groups to the online experience itself, as the use of the chosen BSM online intervention may be less effective in the population of chronic pain patients and therefore may interact with their attitudes towards online group participation.

Group Facilitators' Experience

Sense of Alienation, Level of Commitment, and Dropout

The facilitators perceived that the participants had a decreased sense of commitment to online group therapy. They associated it with the absence of physical meetings, increased embarrassment, and reduced number of interconnections among participants before and during meetings. Some facilitators also noted that the participants rarely asked personal questions after online meetings, which they interpreted as indicating less connection.

During the focus groups, the facilitators emphasized their perceptions that the online format lacks the social support component of the group that is experienced in the face-to-face groups. To encourage participants to interact freely, one facilitator requested that participants leave their microphones open during meetings and another made sure to call on each participant to share their experience after every practice. Others used psychoeducational information and training material sent to an online messaging platform between meetings to compensate for the lack of after-meeting contact and to promote interpersonal connection with group facilitators. Yet the weaker interpersonal connections within groups and with the facilitator left the facilitators feeling that participants had lower commitment to the intervention compared to face-to-face meetings.

Technological and Cultural Issues

During both focus groups, all facilitators started by referring to the technological difficulties of leading an online group. First, they referred to the participants' lack of knowledge in the use of the video conferencing software, specifically by older people, and mainly in the first groups and meetings. This challenge was resolved by offering a pre-meeting session to help the participants to use the technology, and to check internet connectivity and the audio connection. Leading the group in a dyad helped to address technological issues during the meetings. Facilitators also noted that the group population's technological literacy increased during the study period.

While the use of mobile computers and smartphones was helpful in enabling participants to access the group from different locations, it was also challenging. Some participants accessed the group when their surroundings were neither quiet nor private. This challenge occurred despite the fact that participants were asked to ensure that they had access to a suitable private setting for group meetings. However, it is noteworthy that working with an ill population or those who are undergoing medical treatment requires facilitators to allow for more flexible settings as patients' schedules are often changed due to health-related issues.

Lack of Physical Presence

Stress reduction through the use of relaxation techniques and guided imagery is a physical practice. The physical aspect is even more pronounced when considering that participants are dealing with illness and health issues. Interestingly, the facilitators perceived that the lack of physical presence was not challenging or even influential. A facilitator of an oncology group said: "The lack of physical presence was not felt. The content raised was as difficult and complex as in face-to-face groups." Another noted: "Much of the conversation was oriented to the body, therefore even if it is not fully shown, the body was very pronounced." The facilitator of the pain clinic group added that "everybody dealt with the body, that was the purpose of the group—they talked about physical pain." In fact, some facilitators felt that participants' facial expressions compensated for the lack of physical presence and enabled intimacy. They noted the ability to see through the camera the slightest changes in participants' facial expressions and relied on them when identifying emotional changes. Facilitators compared this experience with face-to-face groups whereby they found it more difficult to see facial changes in such detail and observed body gestures to understand better participants' emotional experiences.

In addition, being at home while participating in the group had some benefits. Several facilitators mentioned that the fact that the patients could sit comfortably and practice the methods in their natural home environment, encouraged better implementation to everyday life. One facilitator said: "I feel they are more open within their familiar environment, they don't need to bother themselves with what to do with their hands or how to sit on a chair in front of strangers."

Setting Issues: Required Changes in the Content, Training Mode, and Group Size

Relying on the camera to see participants practice was restricting. The specific video conferencing application we used is convenient for seeing faces but less so for observing the chest and abdomen. The facilitators asked the participants to move back from the camera while practicing, but they also had to deal with participants who wanted to practice outside the camera's view in more comfortable locations, such as a bed, which did not allow for proper supervision. They also noted that although they feared that they would not be able to notice distress through the camera, the participants' facial expressions were very indicative and sufficed.

The facilitators noted that teaching progressive muscle relaxation (the Jacobson technique) was the most difficult to teach online compared to face-to-face meetings, because they struggled to present and later see the different body parts as they were contracted and relaxed. During the focus groups, the option was raised to use videos with demonstrations in a meeting instead of demonstrating live.

Another required change was the need to clarify to participants that they should ensure that their setting while participating in the group was private. Due to lockdowns, children often interfered during meetings. Attending meetings while driving was also mentioned.

Facilitators reported that the size of online groups differed from that of face-to-face groups, with the former averaging 5–7 participants and the latter estimated as larger and averaging 8–10 participants. The difference in size was due to dropout rates that caused the online groups to stabilize at a lower number than face-to-face groups. Facilitators perceived that pain clinic patients had greater attention and concentration difficulties and were less inclined to share their feelings and practice. The recruitment process among pain clinic patients was also more difficult, resulting in smaller groups, and, as mentioned earlier, this population benefited the least from the intervention. IVF groups were successfully recruited only for the online modality and showed a high level of interest and participation.

Are There Any Advantages to Online Meetings?

The most obvious advantage of online groups compared to face-to-face ones is the increased accessibility to treatment rather than having to come to the hospital (drive, find a parking space, etc.). Prior efforts to promote face-to-face stress reduction groups among patients treated in pain and IVF clinics failed. This implies that the convenience of attending such groups online encouraged these patients to participate. As previously mentioned, there is a clinical advantage to online practice in a natural setting that enables implementation in real-life situations.

Additional advantages were mentioned by the facilitators. For example, in one of the groups, an oncology patient and her spouse both participated in the group but each of them entered the meeting using a different device so that they each had a "square" in the meeting. According to the facilitator, in this way the spouse felt much more comfortable to freely participate in group discussions. Another noted advantage is that group members were able to be at the same time present and absent from their concrete space at home. One facilitator noted: "I think many patients who come to groups are people who cannot find time for themselves, especially at home due to their spouses, children, and occupations. The participation in the online group forced them to take a quiet hour alone during their daily home routine, and so they learned it is possible."

Conclusions and Applicable Recommendations

Until the outbreak of the COVID-19 pandemic, all BSM groups at AMC's Ramat HaHayal Hospital convened in face-to-face meetings. The population for which the intervention was developed, and who participated in this study, has double vulnerability to stress, namely their medical backgrounds and the pandemic. We therefore saw great importance in providing a group intervention that would allow a sense of togetherness, while providing the tools for stress reduction, which is essential to the wellbeing of this population. Due to social distancing restrictions, self-isolation requirements and lockdowns, it was decided to divert all new groups to an online video conferencing platform. A mixed methods study was conducted in parallel to the implementation of this change, to evaluate the efficiency of the online BSM groups and the satisfaction of both patients and facilitators. Although this is not a classical randomized controlled study comparing the results of groups online and offline (we did not include a control group), its results are still important in evaluating the efficacy of the intervention.

The online BSM group intervention was found to be effective in reducing participants' stress, anxiety, and depression. Participants' positive attitudes toward the online group therapy were high and improved further after joining the group. An exception was the perceptions of the pain clinic participants toward online BSM meetings, which did not improve following the meetings. This patient population also showed the least improvement in stress, anxiety, and depression. One optional explanation is that the BSM group intervention is less effective for this population and there is a need to include more cognitive-oriented or third wave cognitive behavioral interventions to benefit this population.

Participants presented relatively low anxiety levels at the beginning of the study, creating a floor effect, which probably led to the relatively small level of improvement found in the study. It is not clear to us whether these low anxiety levels reflect those who chose to join the groups (volunteer effect) or the general population. Although we expected to find an improvement in stress and anxiety indices, we were surprised to see unexpected effectiveness in reducing depression among participants. This finding may be attributed to the creation of a treatment routine, the provision of coping tools, or the effect of group support. Therefore, even when groups are online, and are less connected, the impact is noticeable. This finding was also described in previous studies (Qan'ir & Song, 2019). These are only cautious hypotheses in light of the absence of a control group; further studies may wish to test this in the near future through the use of a control group.

Analysis of group facilitators' experience showed that the greatest advantage of online groups is the increased accessibility to treatment. Another advantage is the presence of the participants in their natural setting while in the meeting, which enables implementation of the BSM tools to real-life situations. Difficulties and challenges raised by group facilitators included technological and cultural issues, lack of physical presence, setting issues, the need to adapt the content of the meeting, the training aids and group size to the online platform, the sense of alienation among participants, and the participants' dropout rate and their commitment to the group.

Previous studies on online group therapy (Weinberg, 2020, 2021) have already defined the main obstacles of this method, including the quality of the relationship among participants, the absence of physical interactions and eye contact, and too many distractions, but highlighted the need for more research on cohesion in online groups. Our study partially confirmed these findings, as the lack of informal interpersonal interaction, which naturally accrues before and after a face-to-face group meeting, adversely affected the quality of the relationship and therefore impaired group cohesion and engagement with other participants and with the facilitator. Nevertheless, the lack of physical presence and the absence of eye contact were not perceived by the patients or by the facilitators as a difficulty or a disadvantage. Some facilitators felt that the facial expressions compensated for the lack of physical presence and enabled intimacy.

The study results are limited by the relatively high dropout rate, and the different sample size of each patient population may limit the ability to generalize the results, particularly the small number of pain clinic participants. The strength of this study lies in its mixed methodology, which allowed us to compare the perceptions of patients and facilitators.

The findings of this study also indicated the suitability of the questionnaires used for the study population. The PSS and DASS questionnaires showed good statistical significance for all patients in the study, whereas the use of the HADS questionnaire showed significant improvement only for oncology patients. This should be considered in future studies.

The use of a multi-group intervention model makes it possible to test the relative variability among groups; these gaps validate the effectiveness of the group following the intervention and eliminate the possibility of changes attributed to time, events such as going in and out of COVID-19-related quarantine, or adaptation to a new way of life post-pandemic. Comparison of the anxiety, stress, and depression scores obtained for the different patient populations in the study (Figure 23.1) may indicate that this intervention contributes differently to different populations and different health conditions, and may require specific adjustments accordingly.

The results of the study also indicate the importance of adapting the content and structure of the group to online platforms. Facilitators should dedicate time to clarifying the challenges posed by participants' settings and their responsibility for ensuring privacy during meetings. Digital literacy and technological abilities may be improved by adding an extra pre-intervention meeting and adding a co-facilitator. The facilitators suggested demonstrating particular training features, such as diaphragmatic breathing and muscle relaxation, by using videos or animations, rather than a live demonstration. Psychoeducation materials sent to participants between meetings may improve the relationship with the facilitator enabling direct and personal communication and increase trust in the technique. This promotes commitment and helps to reduce dropout rates. Future interventions and follow-up studies will seek to make further adjustments to the content and structure of BSM groups and examine how these aspects can be strengthened remotely. Furthermore, while the therapeutic group processes were beyond the scope of the chapter data certainly shows that the impact of online therapy on the group processes require further research.

Practical Considerations and Tips

- Online BSM group interventions are effective for reducing stress, anxiety, and depression for people suffering from various medical conditions. It contributes differently to different populations, and may require specific adjustments accordingly.
- Participants' positive attitudes toward the online group therapy improve over time. *It takes time and practice!*
- The greatest advantage of online groups is the increased accessibility to treatment and the presence of the participants in their natural setting enabling implementation of the BSM tools to real-life situations. *Do not be afraid of it, take advantage of it!*
- *You need to prepare in advance.* Adapt the content of the meeting, the training aids, and group size to the online platform.
- *Setting and cultural issues are important.* Facilitators should dedicate time to clarifying the challenges posed by participants' settings and their responsibility for ensuring privacy. Culture norms need to be acknowledged.
- Digital literacy and technological abilities may be improved by adding an extra pre-intervention meeting and adding a co-facilitator.

Acknowledgments

The authors would like to acknowledge the contribution of the following to the research and to thank them for thoughtfully conducting the groups: Mayan Tsur Ungar, Elena Gurevich, Ruth Rinat, Sharon Kitron, Sapir Ashkeloni, and Raphaelle Aylon.

References

Cohen, M., & Fried, G. (2007). Comparing relaxation training and cognitive-behavioral group therapy for women with breast cancer. *Research on Social Work Practice*, 17(3), 313–332.

Cohen, S., Kamarck, T., & Mermelstein, R. (1983). A global measure of perceived stress. *Journal of Health and Social Behavior*, 24, 385–396.

Fawzy, F., Fawzy, N., & Hyun, C. (1993). Malignant melanoma: Effects of an early structured psychiatric intervention, coping and affective state on recurrence and survival 6 years later. *Arch Gen Psychiatr*, 50, 681–689.

Foulkes, E., & Pines, M. (2018). Some basic concepts in group psychotherapy. In E. Foulkes (Ed.), *Selected Papers of S. H. Foulkes: Psychoanalysis and group analysis* (pp. 151–158.). Routledge.

Ghorbani, S., Ashouri, A., Gharraee, B., & Farahan, H. (2022). Effectiveness of online group-mindfulness and acceptance-based therapy and cognitive-behavioral therapy on misophonia. *Iranian Journal of Psychiatry and Behavioral Sciences*, 16(2), e120159.

Gullo, S., Lo Coco, G., Leszcz, M., Marmarosh, C., Miles, J., Shechtman, Z., ... Giorgio, A. (2022). Therapists' perceptions of online group therapeutic relationships during the COVID-19 pandemic: A survey-based study. *Group Dynamics: Theory, Research, and Practice*, 26(2), 103.

Kapogiannis, A., Tsoli, S., & Chrousos, G. (2018). Investigating the effects of the progressive muscle relaxation-guided imagery combination on patients with cancer receiving chemotherapy treatment: A systematic review of randomized controlled trials. *Explore*, 14(2), 137–143.

Krau, S. (2020). The multiple uses of guided imagery. *Nursing Clinics of North America*, 55(4), 467–474.

Lovibond, S., & Lovibond, P. (1995). *Manual for the depression anxiety & stress scales* (2nd Ed.). Psychology Foundation.

Mann, S., & Contrada, R. (2016). Cognitive-behavioral approaches to stress management. In C. M. Nezu and A. M. Nezu (Eds.), *The Oxford handbook of cognitive and behavioral therapies* (pp. 264–288). Oxford University Press.

McCallie, M., Blum, C., & Hood, C. (2006). Progressive muscle relaxation. *Journal of human behavior in the social environment*, 13(3), 51–66.

Qan'ir, Y., & Song, L. (2019). Systematic review of technology-based interventions to improve anxiety, depression, and health-related quality of life among patients with prostate cancer. *Psycho-oncology*, 28(8), 1601–1613.

Tang, M., Liu, X., Wu, Q., & Shi, Y. (2020). The effects of cognitive-behavioral stress management for breast cancer patients: A systematic review and meta-analysis of randomized controlled trials. *Cancer Nursing*, 43(3), 222–237.

Weinberg, H. (2020). Online group psychotherapy: Challenges and possibilities during COVID-19—A practice review. *Group Dynamics: Theory, Research, and Practice*, 24(3), 201.

Weinberg, H. (2021). Obstacles, challenges, and benefits of online group psychotherapy. *American Journal of Psychotherapy*, 74(2), 83–88.

Zigmond, A., & Snaith, R. (1983). The hospital anxiety and depression scale. *Acta Psychiatr Scand*, 67, 361–370.

Part V

Training, Teaching and Supervising Groups Online

Chapter 24

Online Group Psychotherapy Training

Haim Weinberg

Introduction

The American Psychological Association (APA) has officially recognized group psychotherapy as a specialized field, which requires a specific sequence of education and training to demonstrate advanced knowledge and skills.[1] Despite established guidelines and standards, many mental health professionals assume the role of a group therapist without specialized training. Such professionals are sometimes asked to lead a group due to the high volume of referrals and limited resources. When the hapless therapist argues that s/he does not know anything about group therapy, the clinical director responds: "you are an experienced and qualified therapist and that is enough."

But is it really enough? Imagine therapists who are trained in individual therapy facing a scapegoating situation in a group they lead. Most of them would focus on the scapegoat's contribution to the problematic situation since they are used to the individual approach. If you learn about group dynamics and especially about the projection mechanism that is involved in scapegoating, you know that the first thing you should do in such an incident is to work with the group members' projections in order to return them to their source. Without proper training in group therapy, colleagues who are used to working with individuals are prone to make serious mistakes in this and in other difficult group-related situations.

The same criteria should hold for online group therapy. Moving from the physical circle to the online squares requires not just a technical adjustment. Foulkes' (1964) idea about *dynamic administration* (explained in detail below) indicates that the administrative function of the group therapist has a dynamic meaning. Although Foulkes represents the group analytic approach, dynamic administration is relevant to all group therapy approaches. Administrative functions provide the group with a sense of safety and continuity and enhance a dynamic flow of communication. Some of the administrative functions (such as arranging the chairs in a

DOI: 10.4324/9781003248606-29

circle) are absent online and the group therapist can compensate for their absence with some technical skills (e.g., registration of the members to the forum, providing instructions on how to use video conferencing software).

Resistances

Following the outbreak of the COVID-19 pandemic in early 2020, therapists had to shift to virtual meetings without any preparation or training, within days. Adjusting to the new situation and understanding that telehealth is a necessary fact was not easy for many of our colleagues. Psychoanalysts claimed, "this is not psychoanalysis." For example, Gillian Russell, in her excellent 2015 book *Screen Relations* wrote: "a bed is not a couch, and a car is not a consulting room." In the group therapy world, group analysts argued vehemently that online groups could not be "true" group analysis (e.g., a discussion on the International Group Analytic Society forum), claiming that it is impossible to create the same group connections, presence, cohesion, and dynamics online as it occurs offline. The only caveat was that they never experienced it.

During the COVID-19 pandemic, therapists who had never considered online therapy were compelled to conduct it regularly. Due to the novelty of this modality, there was a lack of organized training, with only a handful of one-time webinars offered by experienced experts. As a result, therapists had to learn through trial and error.

The Necessity of Training for Online Psychotherapy

Previous research had suggested a need for training in telehealth even before the outbreak of the pandemic (Callan et al., 2017). Research conducted by Glueckauf et al. (2018) found that around 90% of psychologists indicated that "mental health practitioners should undergo training about the clinical, legal, and/or ethical issues related to telehealth." In their study, most participants reported the need for training on technical issues when delivering mental telehealth services. In self-assessments, around 40% of psychologists reported insufficient telehealth training or education and about half reported inadequate skills in managing emergency situations when using online counseling modalities. A recent study found that an important barrier to using telepsychology was therapists' lack of self-efficacy due in part to insufficient opportunities for training (Perry et al., 2020).

Sampaio et al. (2021) measured how many therapists used online therapy before and during the outbreak of the COVID-19 pandemic: 39% of survey respondents used telepsychology before the pandemic compared to 98% during the pandemic. The conclusion reached by the researchers was that a number of therapists still had ethical, training, and personal concerns regarding the use of telepsychology, and that gaps in therapists' knowledge on these topics were evident, indicating a strong need for increased telepsychology training for therapists in the future. In a pilot study (Messina & Loffler-Stastka, 2021), the researchers found that therapists providing online therapy reported significantly fewer clinical skills in comparison to live therapy.

Shifting from conducting offline to online groups needs even more training than moving from individual in-person meetings to online ones since, in addition to the shift from in-person to online, group dynamics and processes might be different in cyberspace. Just as we require group therapists to have specific training when moving from the couch to the circle, moving from the office circle to the screen requires new knowledge and training.

So, what do we need to know about online therapy and online groups, and what are the specific training factors that we need to address?

The Therapeutic Setting in General

The setting is an important concept in psychotherapy in general. It is related to the "technical laws," according to Freud. The setting embodies the characteristics of the framework and system of laws that are established a priori to ensure the environmental conditions necessary for the existence and effective conduct of the treatment. The therapist creates and maintains the setting in order to advance the work of treatment, ensuring and securing it as much as possible from disturbances, "noises," and ruptures, whether conscious or unconscious. In groups, due to the many factors and layers involved, it is more difficult to establish a setting that creates the holding environment.

This concept went through many changes in the history of psychoanalysis, creating different types of settings. Triest (2010) refers to two principal conceptions of the setting. The first includes formal aspects ("the law of the father"): meeting time, duration, frequency, payment, and method of payment. These elements are expected to remain largely unchanged in the online setting. These aspects also include the basic rules of neutrality, anonymity, and abstinence of the therapist. They are relevant to groups as well, sometimes more challenging (like staying neutral in times of a group conflict), and sometimes easier to keep (like abstinence). They were emphasized by Freud's successors and heightened the rigid aspect of the therapeutic setting, dictated by a rigid and forbidding father figure. Abstinence can be kept more easily online, while anonymity is more challenged when the participants and therapist connect from home.

With the formulation of object relations theory through the writings of Melanie Klein and later Winnicott, the concept of the treatment framework became more affected by the stereotype of the mother figure. The holding environment was conceived as a womb—warm, safe, containing, and protected from the outside world. The group circle easily associates with the image of the womb and the safe container. Emphasis on the maternal aspects of the setting means that instead of the patient being required to adapt to reality, reality (at least the interpersonal one) is required to adapt to the patient. This aspect of the holding environment is one that is questionable online. Since the group loses its circular arrangement online, it reduces the association with the womb. Clearly, the online setting is different from the traditional one in our office. Weinberg and Rolnick (2020) and Weinberg (2020) related to the fact that the therapist cannot create the conditions on the patient's side of the screen to guarantee a holding environment. Thus, the therapist should educate the patients on how to create a safe environment. This is an important issue that should be emphasized again and again and should become part of the online training, especially in groups: prepare your patient for the online meeting, and instruct them on how to keep privacy, stay focused, etc.

The Setting in Groups: Dynamic Administration

As mentioned above, in groups the question of the setting is manifested by Foulkes' (1964) term "dynamic administration," which indicates that facilitating the group always acquires a dynamic meaning. The group therapist takes charge of the administration of the group's setting and translates "external material" brought within these boundaries as a matter pertaining to the dynamic flow of communication "here-and-now." Psychodynamic-oriented therapists tend not to pay attention to the impact of their physical actions on their patients, because they usually focus on psychological processes and may see the practical issues as less important. Non-psychodynamic therapists may not pay attention to the dynamic meaning of the setting, as it may not be part of their training or the main focus of their work with the group. Taking care of the environment sends the message that we take care of the patient's needs. It creates a holding environment. Administrative functions provide the group with a sense of safety and continuity. Symbolically, the group therapist is acting like a maternal figure creating a holding environment for the group. In small face-to-face groups, the holding function of the group leader is similar to the work of the blue collar worker. The leader provides the basic conditions for making the environment comfortable. The group members should be free of worries about the physical environment in order to be able to work on their psychological issues.

Moving from physical reality to cyberspace tears this container apart. Therapists cannot directly control the environment anymore, as they cannot shape the environments from which the patients, or group members, connect. They cannot even guarantee whether anyone listens to the group conversation at the member's end. In addition, the online group loses its classical format of people sitting in a circle: the circle is squared. In a face-to-face group, when the group therapist arranges the chairs for the group in a circle, this closed circular form, with its archaic associations of a womb, conveys the unconscious meaning of a perfect maternal container. In video conferencing groups, group members are shown on the screen in boxes, one beside, above, and below the other, in no specific order. Actually, we do not necessarily have the same order on all the screens, as each computer is generating a different group composition, and this arrangement changes every session. In Zoom it is now possible to maintain the order. This can now become the therapist's responsibility. It raises additional questions, as the host is usually the only person who can control the sitting order.

There are some ways in which the group therapist can still achieve this dynamic administration function on the Internet. In the simplest form, holding occurs by being available to quickly respond to technical questions and solve technological difficulties. We need to remember that many older adults participating in virtual communication behave like immigrants who do not know the norms and language and depend on their children's competence and skills to navigate in this scary land. They still feel anxious when they enter this unknown terrain. Of course, younger participants who were born into the Internet era might not need the leader's technical help. This does not mean that the group therapist should be an IT expert, but that s/he should learn the application used for the group meetings and certainly be more experienced in overcoming technical difficulties than the average group member. In a way, the group therapist should compensate for the loss of control over the setting by developing suitable online administrative functions.

As mentioned above, the group therapist should prepare the group members to take care of their environment and to create a private, quiet, holding environment themselves. The responsibility is transferred to the group members. One possible result of shifting the responsibility to the client might be that we encourage more adult coping skills and less regression. It can be an advantage or a disadvantage, depending on the point of view and the specific client. These functions and their consequences should be part of the training program for conducting groups online.

Harris and Tylim (2018) note that the concept of the framework has undergone far-reaching changes as social, cultural, and *technological* forces had a decisive influence on the concept of setting. In the case of online therapy, technology clearly affects the setting. In face-to-face groups, paying attention to materialistic aspects, the quality of light and sound, the location of the chairs, or the decoration, can contribute to the positive effects of the frame. The same guidelines hold for online groups. It is often the work of restabilizing the framework that enables the occurrence of a powerful change. Taking this idea to our online setting, the main conclusion is that discussing the technical changes, obstacles, difficulties, and challenges (including group members' associations and fantasies) should be the correct thing to do in order to re-create a safe and holding environment. The implications for the psychotherapeutic technique are that the setting itself must be related to. These implications are especially true in cyberspace and should be added to a training program.

Internet Unconscious?

How do we adjust to a disembodied environment and how do we stay human when the "Other" becomes two-dimensional (if we connect through video) or even a unidimensional (if we connect through text alone) abstract concept? Moving from using multiple senses to just two (visual and auditory) affects our perception and interpretation of the situation. Theoretically, the only missing sense is smell. The key difference is the "depth" of each sense. Sight is two-dimensional and limited in area. This environment is intermediated by technology.

The *tripartite matrix* (Hopper, 2023), meaning the network of communication and relationships in the background of each group, which so far has included dimensions such as norms, values, gender, communication, and relations, is expanded to include the *technological dimension*. This dimension evokes shared anxieties, associations, and unconscious fantasies, in psychodynamic terms *adding a technological dimension to the social unconscious*. In online groups, technology not only determines the group outcomes (no less than the group cohesion or therapeutic alliance) but is also internalized as another unconscious element that affects human behavior, and the group therapist should pay attention to this influence and learn to notice its impact. For example, in the first year of the pandemic, when there was so much uncertainty, loneliness and isolation, and the fear of death was common, people felt the online groups as connecting them deeply to their shared trauma. Whenever their Internet connection was interrupted (a technical issue), group members felt anxious beyond reason, probably since unconsciously it was associated with the many losses around them (an unconscious dynamic meaning).

A good example of the impact of technology on group cohesion is the fact that the location of the camera determines whether group members would seem to be looking directly at other people or looking aside. Another example is the difficulties in hybrid meetings when some people are online and others are in the same room (see Chapter 6 in this volume). The positive results of such a meeting depend entirely on the technology used, such as the quality and the position of the microphone.

Keyword: Flexibility

> *An online group member seemed quite constrained and quiet for a long time in the group sessions. When the group inquired what is happening to him and why he is so quiet and passive, he revealed that he is having serious problems in his marriage, but since he is connecting from home and the walls in his house are thin, he does not feel that it's safe to talk about his intimate issues and difficulties in his relationship with his wife when she is behind the wall. The group therapist (me) suggested that he go to his parked car and connect from there.*[2]

One of the main factors that impacts online therapy and its outcomes is the question of flexibility. We should stop being obsessed with the question of how much online group therapy is similar to an in-person session (a mistake that many of my colleagues still make) and acknowledge that it is *not* the same as in-person therapy: the setting is not controlled and structured by the therapist; failures of communication are inevitable; and it is difficult to establish conditions of safety and a holding environment. We have to flex the usual rigid boundaries and rules of conservative psychotherapy.

The simple example at the beginning of this section shows that if we want to adjust ourselves to the new conditions of online group therapy we must be flexible, especially regarding the setting and boundaries of the group sessions. This flexibility negates the long tradition of psychodynamic psychotherapy in its conservative form, which assumes that the therapist should establish rigid boundaries in order to guarantee a better holding environment. Please remember that online at least half of the setting is determined by the group members, so we cannot strictly attach to the old notion that the group therapist is the only one controlling the setting. We share responsibility with the group members for creating a safe environment, recruiting their ego functions and strength, and preventing some deeper regression. Collaboration becomes the factor for the group's success. All these factors should be taken into consideration when we move to online groups. Teaching flexibility and training group therapists to be more flexible is not an easy task, and one of the difficulties is deciding how far we go. Bringing case examples for discussion is one way to train group therapists to change their rigid rules.

Presence

Therapeutic presence (Geller & Greenberg, 2012) is a way of *being* with clients that enriches the *doing* or therapeutic approach and techniques that therapists offer in therapy. Therapeutic presence is defined as bringing one's whole self to the engagement with the client and being fully in the moment with and for the client, with few self-centered purposes or goals in mind. When you conduct groups it is like being egoless, focusing on the group members' needs. Therapists' presence is understood as the ultimate state of moment-by-moment receptivity and deep relational contact, becoming deeply rooted in the moment on a physical, emotional, cognitive, relational, and spiritual level. Clients can perceive this presence as creating safety. They feel met and understood (Geller, 2017). For many reasons, it is much more difficult to stay present online. There are too many distractions, and the screen barrier might decrease and dilute the presence of the therapist. However, just as some television presenters can pass the screen and transmit their presence through the ether, group therapists can learn to do so as well. In the section detailing a model for a training program, I describe the concrete implications for training. Research suggests that psychological presence is essential to build and strengthen therapeutic alliances online (Haddouk, 2015). Therapists who feel less competent in providing online therapy and who experience more perceived difficulties tend to experience decreased presence. Considering the significant role of presence in therapeutic relationships, technical training should help to improve therapeutic presence online.

Engaging the Virtual Body

One of the main obstacles in online therapy, including in groups, is the loss of the in-person body, its immediacy, and intimacy. In fact, what is lost in online groups is body-to-body communication. This has been and remains one of the most serious losses when we transit to online groups. The body is a gateway to connect with one's full human experience. An example of this disembodied environment is the absence of the leader's gaze online. In the face-to-face group, the group therapist looks at every group member, sustaining his/her gaze, holding them with the gaze, encouraging the member to speak out, or making them feel appreciated for what they said, just like the mother's mirroring, looking at the infant with glittering eyes, making him or her feel accepted, worthy, and even admired. This important gaze option is clearly lacking in online groups. Even if the group therapist tries deliberately to look at a specific member in video meetings, this member will not be able to perceive that.

There are other ways to compensate for the lack of body-to-body communication online. We can encourage group members to report their body sensations. Group therapists who come from the Somatic Experience (see Chapter 18 in this volume), Sensori-Motor (Ogden and Goldstein, 2020), or Gestalt approach know how to do it well. We can also be more active in asking group members to get closer to or further away from the camera, move around the room, etc. The passive approach is less suitable for engaging the body in online therapy and groups. The group leader should take a more active approach. Creativity is also very important in finding ways to bring the body back to the screen and training programs should include exercises and case studies to practice it.

Online Presence

In a training program for online group therapy, we can teach the following techniques to increase presence online. Additional tips appear in Chapter 3 in this volume.

1   Use yourself more. More self-disclosure is helpful in creating presence. The appropriate kind of self-disclosure and transparency is about the here-and-now, namely our feelings toward the group members and the group-as-a-whole. Of course, using self-disclosure immediately brings to the fore how much it is appropriate for the group therapist to reveal. Yalom and Leszcz (2020) suggested that appropriate self-disclosure is about the feelings of the group therapist (essentially the here-and-now) and not about the therapist's history (the there-and-then).

2   Paying close attention to the facial expressions of *all* the group members (which we see better online since we can zoom into the face) can help us to identify unexpressed frustration and dissatisfaction, especially about the group therapist's interventions. In fact, this is one of the advantages of online groups. However, it requires discipline on the part of the therapist to conspicuously scan all the participants' faces, although the software usually highlights the speaker. In training, we can design exercises on reading the faces of those who are not talking. Below is an example that combines the above recommendations:[3]

One of the group members in an online group requested feedback from the group. The member, Sheila, shared that she is usually satisfied with her life, happy and easygoing. She wondered whether she was denying something. Some group members said that they find it hard to believe that she is always content. Summarizing the responses, the group leader suggested to Sheila that her limited range of emotions is perceived as superficial by the group members. The leader noticed that some group members' facial expressions online seemed shocked or irritated (but not Sheila's). After some reflection, he got back to Sheila and said that he wanted to correct his previous intervention because it might have been understood as if Sheila is superficial, which was not the therapist's intention. He corrected himself by telling Sheila that when she only expresses joy and never any sign of irritation, dissatisfaction or any negative emotions, it makes it difficult for him, the group leader, to get closer to Sheila. She had a strong emotional reaction to this intervention and later on it became clear how much her parents did not allow for any emotional strong reaction, and never acknowledged that they had made mistakes.

3   As seen from the above example, taking responsibility for mistakes and for empathic failures is another way of increasing the presence of the group therapist.

4   Use of imagination: Imagination usually activates the brain as if we experience the situation imagined right now. Using it in online groups increases the experiential component and the sense of presence. Below is an example:

A group member expressed irritation and sadness about the loss of sitting in a circle, not sensing the "real" presence of the participants. She complained about the squares that appear on her screen whose positions change every meeting and sometimes even during the meeting (whenever someone's Internet disconnects). My response as the group leader was: "Please close your eyes and imagine that we are now sitting in a circle in the same room. Whom would you like to sit beside you? Whom would you like to sit across the room far away from you?" Using imagination and discussing her fantasy about possible group seating instigated a deep conversation about intimacy, closeness, disconnection, and distance between group members.

5   Naming sensations, observations and people's names: This is a simple technique that we tend to ignore. A lot of the interaction information in online groups is lost because of the screen barrier. Simply mentioning the therapist's sensations, his/her perception of other members' sensations (*"John, as I look at you, I feel confusion, does this reflect what you are feeling?"*) and sharing subjective observations (*John, I am not sure to whom you refer when you say "you"*) more than in the offline meetings is helpful in strengthening the connections between group members.

6   The therapist should educate group members to address one another by their names since the direction of eye contact is lost online.

7   What to pay attention to: Groups usually flood the therapist with a lot of information, and it is always a difficult decision about what to pay attention to, and what to comment about. Some group therapists just comment on whatever they see or whatever comes to their mind, ignoring the important guideline to comment or interpret only incidents or events that seem to block the group or members' progress (resistances). Online we have more decisions to make regarding what to comment about since there is a lot going on in the background. For example, the fact that group members connect from home brings into the meetings the presence of pets that usually group participants

do not bring to in-person meetings. Should we always comment on the presence of the cat whose tail suddenly waves in front of the camera? In my opinion, we should explore the presence of such pets only if it clearly seems that this presence replaces or interferes with some of the group connections.

8   The issue of what deserves attention also includes the fact that in online group therapy, both group therapists and participants tend to overlook instances of boundary violations that occur in the members' virtual spaces. In an offline group session, if an uninvited person enters the physical room, they are immediately recognized as an intruder, and the therapist or members will object. However, in the online setting, if a family member suddenly appears in the background of a group member's video feed, it often goes unnoticed and unaddressed, even by the therapist. Given that one of the responsibilities of the group therapist is to maintain appropriate boundaries, they should receive training on how to effectively respond to such situations.

A Description of a Training Program for Online Group Therapy

This program is aimed at previously trained group therapists. It can also be integrated in regular group therapy training programs in addition to the basic training.

APA provides education and training guidelines for group therapy[4] detailing knowledge, skills, and competencies in many topics, from the history of group psychotherapy to applications for specific audiences. The specific topics of these guidelines that are relevant to online groups are as follows:

1   The role of group therapeutic factors for group members' healing, growth, and development.
2   Group leaders' skills, tasks, and techniques.
3   Empirically supported group interventions.
4   The impact and roles of culture and diversity for group members, the group, and the leader.
5   Ethical, legal, and professional standards relevant to groups.
6   Selection and use of assessments and measurements appropriate for groups.
7   Group planning, facilitation, outcome assessment and follow-up.
8   Applications for target audiences, settings, and conditions.

All these topics should be covered in a training program for online therapy. Diversity and cultural issues should receive special attention: online groups may bring to the fore more diversity than in-person groups since the pool of candidates for the group is larger. For example, when these groups include therapists from other countries, it can help North American therapists to meet different norms and standards than those common in the United States. Addressing racism, microaggressions, and other issues that are bound to surface in racially/ethnically diverse groups is a very delicate and difficult matter and sometimes conflicts around these issues can split the group. The online modality faces similar challenges but also provides more opportunities to work through them. The presence of therapists/group members from different countries and cultures softens potential conflicts since they bring a different perspective.

Any training program in group psychotherapy includes three elements: theory, practice, and supervision. These are the pillars of a training program for online groups as well.

Theoretical Part

All the above topics that APA suggests and that are relevant to online groups should be included in the theoretical part, in addition to topics such as interpersonal neurobiology and their relation to remote therapy (Badenoch & Gantt, 2019). The latest knowledge on facial expressions and their emotional context should also be included (Cowen et al., 2021) and a review of AI applications for analyzing facial expressions. It will teach the participants about the importance of interpersonal synchronization and the question of how it happens even in remote therapy.

Technology Part

Another significant part will deal with technology and video conferencing software. Important peripheral measures will be reviewed (types of cameras, microphones, screens, sitting distance from the screen, lighting, etc.)

Experiential/Practical Part

Experiential learning is an essential part of any group facilitator's training. Kolb (1984) defined experiential learning as "the process whereby knowledge is created through the transformation of experience" (p. 38). Studies found that experiential growth groups (EGG) are essential in the development of group therapists (McCarthy et al., 2014) and are a valuable experience for them (Hahn et al., 2022). Although these studies focus primarily on in-person training groups, they have relevance for online groups, as we now have a growing body of empirical evidence for the kinds of experiences trainees take away from these groups. Training for online groups should include an online EGG. Weinberg (2023) proposed a model for an online training process group for therapists that includes experiential and didactic parts.

The Deliberate Practice approach (Rousmaniere et al., 2017) is purposeful and systematic. It requires focused attention and is conducted with the specific goal of improving performance, giving immediate feedback to therapists about their performance and impact on their clients. Accordingly, I suggest adding the following practical/experiential part. First, there will be individual practice with feedback for each therapist on the way they perceive the other from a distance. Then they will receive immediate feedback when they lead online groups about their performance.

Of course, the main experience will be on understanding group processes in remote therapy, preferably from the participants' own experience in online groups, also from recorded segments of remote group treatments. For interventions that utilize particular strategies and methods, such as cognitive behavioral therapy (CBT), acceptance and commitment therapy (ACT), and other active techniques (Weinberg & Rolnick, 2020), there is added value in learning how to adapt and effectively employ these techniques in the online environment. Several chapters in our previous book (Weinberg et al., 2023), as well as in this volume, provide useful guidance on adapting particular approaches and techniques to the virtual setting. These resources can be valuable for gaining proficiency in employing these methods online.

As previously discussed in this chapter and in other chapters in the book, the effective engagement of online groups demands an active approach and the utilization of supplementary techniques and strategies. To ensure successful group participation, the training program must incorporate the training and application of these methods, such as virtual icebreakers, along with the underlying rationale and theory. Demonstration groups (e.g., fishbowl—see below) are also an essential experiential part of the training. Participating in an unstructured continuous online group (Weinberg, 2023) is the best way to internalize online group processes and learn from an experienced online group leader in vivo.

Fishbowl/Demonstration Group and its Online Advantages

Demonstration groups (sometimes called fishbowls) are common at group therapy conferences in the United States (e.g., the American Group Psychotherapy Association) and in group therapy training institutes as a way to learn about groups by observing a live group. Kane (1995) suggested fishbowl training for group counselors in 1995. Gans et al. (2002) describe them thus:

A demonstration group is comprised of mental health professionals and/or trainees (usually between six and eight) who volunteer to be members of a group to be conducted by a senior group therapist in front of an observing group of students, peers, and colleagues. The demonstration group usually meets only once, though on occasion it may meet several times throughout the course of a workshop or conference with the added benefit of viewing leadership style and group dynamics in further developmental stages.

(p. 234)

Weinberg (2016) describes the many conditions that hinder such a group's progress, including the following:

The physical group boundaries consist of a circle of chairs with no walls defining the group space and a very permeable membrane exists between the demonstration group and the observers. The audience is observing and listening to everything that the members of the group say or do, so confidentiality is threatened.

(p. 7)

Even Gans et al. (2002) concluded: "Boundary issues in demonstration groups can be so complex and confusing that some wonder if effective teaching is even possible" (p. 240).

Demonstration groups are an important component of any group training and should be part of the training for leading online groups. Since the demonstration replicates the groups for which we train the participants, the trainees can observe the unique processes, obstacles, and solutions of online groups in vivo, and experience them as participants if they volunteer for the demonstration.

The online format creates a huge advantage for these groups. As mentioned above, their main drawback is the loose boundaries between the participants who volunteer for the fishbowl and the observers. Technical options help these boundaries to be clearer and sounder online. The observers are requested to turn off their videos. Online applications (e.g., Zoom) allow each member to select the "hide non-video participants" option, thus removing the images of the observers from the volunteers' screens. The only members that they see on the screen now are their group participants, thus helping them to ignore or even forget the presence of other people who are not part of the demonstration group.

Format

Although most of the sessions of the training program will be conducted remotely, it is very important to hold in-person meetings too, which will allow a comparison of the interpersonal experience in an Internet-based group to a group that meets face-to-face. Indeed, Weinberg's (2023) model includes such an intensive two-day in-person meeting.

Supervision

Upon completion of the training program, participants will undergo a period of remote training, primarily based on recordings of the groups that the intern has facilitated. It is also possible for the training provider to observe the intern's group sessions in real time remotely (see Chapter 26 on online group supervision in this volume).

Conclusion: New Training Process for Group Therapists

As we approach the end of this book it becomes clear that group therapy training must be changed or enhanced. Online groups should be added to any training program in group therapy. Just as conducting groups requires training for individual therapists, so do online groups require training for offline therapists. This training should include the topics mentioned in the chapter and some of those suggested by APA for a group therapy training program: creating the online holding environment and managing the dynamic administration of the online setting; increasing the online presence of group therapists and members; and engaging the virtual body and learning to be flexible and creative in conducting online groups.

When we planned our second book *Advances in Online Therapy: The Emergence of a New Paradigm* (Weinberg et al., 2023) we intended to include only a short section on online group psychotherapy. However, we were blessed to receive a significant number of chapters dealing with moving to online group therapy. On reading these chapters, it became clear to us that we would have to publish a third book focusing on group therapy.

We were impressed by the wide range of chapters describing unique conceptions of group therapy. We noticed that most authors understand that moving online is not just a technical step. We believe that working online will change the way we conduct groups. The flexibility demonstrated by the contributors to this volume shows how moving online allows classical group therapy theories to be more adaptive and flexible. Both CBT and dynamic group therapists agree that online group therapy is here to stay and that we all have to adapt our approaches: some dynamic theories must include more technical and practical aspects while some practical and focused approaches must find a way to incorporate interpersonal concepts such as alliance and cohesion. This chapter addresses the significant changes that must be made to the training process.

Notes

1 https://www.apadivisions.org/division-49/leadership/committees/group-specialty.
2 A version of this example appears in the introduction to Weinberg et al. (2023).
3 A version of this case appears in Weinberg (2020).
4 https://www.apadivisions.org/division-49/leadership/committees/education-train
  ing.pdf.

References

Badenoch, B., & Gantt, S. P. (2019). *The interpersonal neurobiology of group psychotherapy and group process.* Routledge. https://doi.org/10.4324/9780429482120.

Callan, J. E., Maheu, M. M., & Bucky, S. F. (2017). "Crisis in the behavioral health classroom: Enhancing knowledge, skills, and attitudes in telehealth training." In M. Maheu, K. Drude,, & S. Wright (Eds.), *Career paths in telemental health* (pp. 63–80). Springer.

Cowen, A.S., Keltner, D., Schroff, F., Jou, B., Adam, H., & Prasad, G. (2021). Sixteen facial expressions occur in similar contexts worldwide. *Nature*, 589, 251–257. https://doi.org/10.1038/s41586-020-3037-7.

Foulkes, S. H. (1964). *Therapeutic group analysis.* George Allen and Unwin.

Gans, J. S., Rutan, J., & Lape, E. (2002). The demonstration group: A tool for observing group process and leadership style. *International Journal of Group Psychotherapy*, 52(2), 233–252.

Geller, S. M. (2017). *A practical guide to cultivating therapeutic presence.* American Psychological Association.

Geller, S. M., & Greenberg, L. S. (2012). *Therapeutic presence: A mindful approach to effective therapy.* American Psychological Association.

Glueckauf, R. L., Maheu, M. M., Drude, K. P., Wells, B. A., Wang, Y., Gustafson, D. J., & Nelson, E. L. (2018). Survey of psychologists' telebehavioral health practices: Technology use, ethical issues, and training needs. *Prof. Psychol. Res. Pract.*, 49, 205–219. doi:10.1037/pro0000188.

Haddouk, L. (2015). Presence at a distance. *Annual Review of Cybertherapy and Telemedicine*, 13, 208–212.

Hahn, A., Paquin, J. D., Glean, E., McQuillan, K., & Hamilton, D. (2022). Developing into a group therapist: An empirical investigation of expert group therapists' training experiences. *American Psychologist*, 77(5), 691–709. https://doi.org/10.1037/amp0000956.

Harris, A., & Tylim, I. (2018). Introduction: The frame. In A. Harris & I. Tylim (Eds.), *Reconsidering the moveable frame in psychoanalysis: Its function and structure in contemporary psychoanalytic theory* (pp. 1–11). Routledge.

Hopper, E. (2023). The tripartite matrix in Foulkesian group analysis. In E. Hopper (Ed.), *Continuing explorations and clinical implications of the study of the social unconscious in persons, groups and societies* (vol. 4). Routledge.

Kane, C. M. (1995) Fishbowl training in group process. *The Journal for Specialists in Group Work*, 20(3), 183–188. doi:10.1080/01933929508411342.

Kolb, D. A. (1984). *Experiential learning: Experience as the source of learning and development.* Prentice Hall.

McCarthy, C. J., Falco, L. D., & Villalba, J. (2014). Ethical and professional issues in experiential growth groups: Moving forward. *Journal for Specialists in Group Work*, 39(3), 186–193. https://doi.org/10.1080/01933922.2014.924722.

Messina, I., & Loffler-Stastka, H. (2021). Psychotherapists' perception of their clinical skills and in-session feelings in live therapy *versus* online therapy during the COVID-19 pandemic: A pilot study. *Research in Psychotherapy: Psychopathology, Process and Outcome*, 24(1), 514. https://doi.org/10.4081/ripppo.2021.514.

Perry, K., Gold, S., & Shearer, E. M. (2020). Identifying and addressing mental health providers' perceived barriers to clinical video telehealth utilization. *J. Clin. Psychol.*, 76, 1125–1134. doi:10.1002/jclp.22770.

Ogden, P., & Goldstein, B. (2020). Sensorimotor psychotherapy from a distance: Engaging the body, creating presence, and building relationship in video-conferencing. In H. Weinberg & A. Rolnick (Eds.) *Theory and practice of online therapy* (pp. 47–65). Routledge.

Rousmaniere, T., Goodyear, R. K., Miller, S. D., & Wampold, B. E. (2017). *The cycle of excellence: Using deliberate practice to improve supervision and training.* John Wiley & Sons.

Russell, G. I. (2015). *Screen relations.* Karnac Books.

Sampaio, M., Navarro, H. M. V., De Sousa, B., Vieira, M. W., & Hoffman, H. G. (2021). Therapists make the switch to telepsychology to safely continue treating their patients during the COVID-19 pandemic. *Frontiers in Virtual Reality*, 1(36).

Triest, Y. (2010). *Between "law" and "lap."* Lecture at the Israeli Association of Psychoanalytic Psychotherapy, June 24. https://www.hebpsy.net/articles.asp?id=2622 (in Hebrew).

Weinberg, H. (2016). Impossible groups that flourish in leaking containers: Challenging group analytic theory. *Group Analysis*, 49(4), 330–349.

Weinberg, H. (2020). Online group psychotherapy: Challenges and possibilities during COVID-19—A practice review. *Group Dynamics: Theory, Research, and Practice*, 24(3), 201–211.

Weinberg, H. (2023). Online training process groups for therapists: A proposed model. *International Journal of Group Psychotherapy*, 73(2).

Weinberg, H., & Rolnick, A. (Eds.) (2020). *Theory and practice of online therapy: Internet-delivered interventions for individuals, groups, families, and organizations.* Routledge.

Weinberg, H., & Rolnick, A., & Leighton, A. (Eds.) (2023). *Advances in online therapy.* Routledge.

Yalom, I., & Leszcz, M. (2020). *The theory and practice of group psychotherapy* (6th ed.). Basic Books.

Zigenlaub, E., & Stolper, E. (2022). "Can I join online?" Hybrid group therapy that integrates online participants in face-to-face groups. In H. Weinberg, A. Rolnick, & A. Leighton (Eds.) *Practicing online group therapy: Theory, research, and technical considerations.* Routledge.

Chapter 25

Establishing a Group Program in Business School and Shifting to the Virtual World

Darryl L. Pure and Lisa Stefanac

This chapter discusses an innovative course utilizing T-group to teach Interpersonal Dynamics at a top-tier business school. Within a two-week spring break, the course, its lectures, exercises, and the group itself required major adaptations. The solutions reached are discussed in addition to their implications for clinical groups that are technique- or relationship-oriented.

T-group and the Laboratory Training Method (Benne et al., 1964; Clayton and Lucas, 1999) began in 1946 when Kurt Lewin was asked to train group leaders who could help to deal with intergroup difficulties arising out of racial tensions in Connecticut communities. Enlisting Leland Bradford, Kenneth Benne, and Ronald Lippitt, Lewin began the first T-group and Training Lab where group leaders could use experiential groups to learn how to learn. The National Training Lab (NTL) emerged from this experiment. While the T-group served as the learning laboratory for participants to try out new behaviors, the entire Laboratory Training Method included lectures and exercises which were designed to help group members to develop new skills.

NTL trained group psychologists in addition to consultants to the business world, on groups, group dynamics, and the use of groups to facilitate learning. Eventually, the world of organizational consultation and the mental health world started to use this powerful methodology to achieve different goals and divided into separate camps. In 1968, David Bradford brought the Laboratory Method and T-group to Stanford's Graduate School of Business (Batista, 2018). Over the ensuing 45 years, it grew through the efforts of Ken Knight, David Bradford, Jerry Porras, and Mary Ann Huckabay. At Chicago Booth, the class was built in 2019 by Rob Vishny, Darryl Pure, and Lisa Stefanac. The course at both schools is formally called Interpersonal Dynamics (affectionately called "touchy feely" at Stanford and shortened to "ID" at Chicago Booth). MBA students at both schools resoundingly declare that Interpersonal Dynamics is one of the most useful and applicable courses they take during their MBA program.

DOI: 10.4324/9781003248606-30

T-group (Training group) is different from other groups in significant ways. Though T-group functions and appears much like a therapy group, the purpose of the group is to learn about interpersonal feedback versus amelioration of psychological distress, the members of the groups are students versus clients, the facilitators are not necessarily mental health professionals, and the group is for training not group therapy.

An intentional vacuum gets created when there are no leaders (facilitators are members of the group who also have a special organizing role) and no agenda. Students and facilitators alike come with specific learning goals that aid them in the experiential process of T-group. We are in a constant state of learning how to learn (Agyris, 1994) and others offer useful mirrors to help us in learning about ourselves. Students learn to speak from their reality or "their side of the net" (a metaphor used in the course) and use inquiry to find out the other person's reality/experience. They learn that intent does not always equal impact and when that happens, the students have opportunities to practice repairing the relationship.

The class structure toggles between short lectures, exercises to help illustrate the key points of each lecture, and T-group. The vast majority of class time is spent in T-group, and there is an intensive T-group weekend during the quarter. Each T-group consists of 12 students and two facilitators. When in person, specific learning goals composed by each student and facilitator line the walls around the T-group for quick access and reminder of the productive changes each person is aiming to create for themselves and with each other.

The purpose of Interpersonal Dynamics can be summed up in one sentence: to learn how to effectively give and receive feedback in a way that sustains and builds relationships. Through T-group, students learn about intention versus impact. They practice offering appropriate vulnerability and making themselves more known. The students are learning how to not just be good managers capable of developing themselves and their people through giving/receiving feedback; they are learning how to be strong leaders who can create the necessary psychological safety that will bring out the best in their future team/s. The students love this class for the direct applicability it offers through experiential learning in real time. At times they also struggle with the degree of discomfort it creates when they have to take risks and do things well outside their comfort zone. By the end of the quarter, the risk-taking pays off and they have discovered and practiced new behaviors that support them in creating more productive interpersonal dynamics in both their personal and professional lives.

A Sudden Shift and its Challenges

On March 7, 2020 one of the co-authors of this chapter (Darryl Pure) took a workshop on video conference-delivered group therapy with Haim Weinberg.

Little did he realize it was prescient. Returning on March 8, the world seemed well with just a few reported cases of COVID-19 in the United States. This changed after he received an email informing him that he had had numerous primary exposures to the virus and that many of his colleagues were unwell. Similar rise in exposure was happening at Chicago Booth, and March 16 was the last in-person class session until September 2021.

"There is no way a virtual T-group will work!" As mental models go, this was strong and persistent when we were first met with the adaptive challenge of switching an entire class to remote-only at one of the top business schools in the world. Not only had virtual T-group at a business school never been done before, we were also being asked to make the switch from in-person to fully virtual in just over two weeks between quarters. We reached out to our colleagues at Stanford Graduate School of Business to find out how they were approaching the challenge. We were told that "it is just not possible to maintain the quality of T-group in a virtual setting." In other words, a similar mental model to the one we had: "there is no way."

"Or is there?" asked Darryl Pure and Britt Raphling, an adjunct assistant professor for the course. Challenging a mental model can start with offering doubt in the perceived truth of the stated belief. To this end, Ron Heifetz noted, "Adaptive work is required when our deeply held beliefs are challenged, when the values that made us successful become less relevant, and when legitimate yet competing perspectives emerge" (Heifetz and Laurie, 2001). Though skeptical, we discussed how it might work. Britt had successfully run a couple of virtual therapy groups for years and could offer a clear description of how she made it work. In spite of these doubts, we thought the quarter-length T-group experience at Chicago Booth could build off of Britt's experience with ongoing therapy groups. We dove into the adaptive challenge with all our might.

When the pandemic forced everyone to shift to virtual settings, our biggest adaptive challenge became ensuring the same high-quality delivery and outcomes while using video conferencing software including in T-group which benefits from the ability to see full non-verbal body language in addition to what is actually being spoken. We adopted a new mental model, "we can do this," and we set out to make it work.

Fortunately, having taken the workshop on working with groups in virtual settings, we had good grounding in how to proceed. The university, for its part, quickly shipped to faculty large monitors, cameras (which soon became difficult to find), iPads, and industrial-strength versions of video conferencing software. The authors quickly started meeting to revamp the curriculum and to get our co-facilitators up to speed. Given the nature of the course, our challenges were in four areas: calming students and assuring them that though delivered virtually, they would receive a different yet equally valuable experience; modifying the short lectures; revamping the exercises and tools we use to highlight data for the T-groups; and the T-groups themselves together with the intensive T-group weekend that is part of the course. Each will be addressed separately.

The model we are describing sits between what Rolnick (2020) describes as the Techniques Camp and the Relationship Camp of group therapy. Though our T-groups are not psychotherapy groups, they certainly utilize assignments and exercises as do the Techniques Camp. The Relationship Camp is represented by the T-group itself. Given that this is a hybrid model with elements relevant to both "camps," we faced challenges and generated solutions useful to both. As our model utilizes lectures and exercises to intensify the learning, we resolved challenges that will be useful for those who run psychodrama groups, utilize sociometry, and for those who do cognitive behavioral therapy (CBT) groups involving in vivo exercises and practice. The need for T-group to develop meaningful relationships and connections between members created challenges for the virtual environment and our solutions may be helpful to those in the Relationship Camp.

Perhaps with some surprise, we discovered that the Techniques side of the equation seemed particularly challenging as it required massive shifts in delivery. We will start with that issue.

Lectures

The lectures were the easiest to revamp as we already had slide decks which we used when teaching the required skills face-to-face. Each week's lecture presents concepts for the students to consider, experiment with in the T-group, and hopefully master. Simply presenting the lecture along with the slides was easy as we could screen share. More difficult, given the medium, was finding ways to keep the students engaged and interactive. Live, the same lecture allows emphasis to be added by moving around the room while talking, using gesticulations which are often hidden on screen, and using other forms of body language. Being static on the screen required putting the same liveliness into voice tones and qualities, and to notice and name internal feelings which would normally be displayed in body language. It also became important to create engagement by calling on students to comment on the concepts of the lectures or to answer questions.

Also related to the lectures was finding a way to create more of a bond with the facilitators which happens rather easily in the in-person context. One solution we developed was to add two individual virtual coaching sessions for each participant. This individual time with the facilitator seemed to create a stronger bond for both the group member and for the facilitator. This was a more relaxed time (30–60 minutes) to get to know one another and to answer questions, help with stuck areas, etc.

New Norms for the Virtual Environment

For exercises that focused on self-disclosure as well as for the intimate T-group experience, our biggest challenge was ensuring the psychological safety of the group while using video conferencing software. This meant establishing additional norms specific to the virtual setting. Our already established norms for the class were:

- Commitment: Being present physically and emotionally, being on time for the start of class, and coming back on time from breaks.
- Confidentiality: You can only share what you are learning about yourself and your related personal stories; you cannot share others' learning or personal stories. In other words, "what happens in T-group stays in T-group."
- Be curious: Notice your judgments and practice naming and suspending those judgments. Get curious about your reactions. Be curious about others' reactions.

We then added another layer of norms to ensure safety in the virtual setting.

- Confidentiality (second layer): Are you in a physical location where you can speak freely and where others in your location cannot overhear the group?

We found that many students chose to wear headphones and turn their computer screen away from others in their location so they could not accidentally see the screen and who was on it. We also had a number of creative solutions with students dialing in from their parked cars or joining from inside their closet so they could not be overheard.

- Video on: Everyone must have their video on so we can see as much non-verbal communication as possible.

This added norm helped to ensure we could collect as much data as possible during our T-group sessions. This also helped the professors during the lectures so we could notice if someone had a quizzical look on their face or if their hand was up.

- Speak your non-verbals: Notice and verbalize anything going on in your body that relates to what is happening in the room.

This norm became particularly helpful during T-group in the event that someone's leg was bouncing under their chair or someone was picking at their fingers, etc. Unless the person spoke up and declared what they were doing non-verbally outside of the screen display, none of us would have been able to know. This became a surprise benefit of the virtual experience because it taught each student to be more mindful of their body language and how it related to what was going on in the room.

- Use gallery view: This enables you to see everyone at the same time so you can track what is in the room.

Though the gallery view option in video conferencing software inevitably shrinks the image of each person down to an even smaller picture box on the screen, the benefits of using that feature far exceed the cost of the size of the people on the screen. We actually found it delightful to be able to view the full room in an equitable way. When a T-group meets in person, everyone is seated in a circle. There is therefore a bit of a blind spot with those sitting immediately to one's left and right. In gallery view, that blind spot effectively disappears and both facilitators and all the students gain an equal view to everyone at any given time.

- Be 100% present: Absolutely no multi-tasking and limit distractions.

We knew this final added norm was going to be really tough for business students. By nature, business school trains people to engage in effective multitasking. Add the use of a computer and multiple windows that can be open at any given time, and students will be tempted to toggle and shift their attention. However, the nature of T-group requires their undivided attention as a huge learning or key interpersonal exchange can happen at any moment. So, we set the norm of silencing computer notifications, closing down (or at least not toggling to) open windows, and keeping their attention on the task at hand: T-group. Switching computer windows creates a change in the light on someone's face and reading text messages on a phone requires looking down or to the side. We became adept at spotting that activity and given the new norm, we could name it and use that confrontation to bring them back into the group. Talk about raising discomfort!

The final big adaptive change we needed to make was to address the unavoidable number of hours required for the class and therefore to be on a computer screen. We were wary of this for ourselves and our students. The class has in it a capstone weekend intensive experience starting on a Friday evening and ending on Sunday early afternoon. The in-person experience of the weekend stretches across 15 hours of T-group time. We knew that the number of hours on a screen, over two days, would likely make us all go mad or begin to lose our vision!

Our solution was to break up the weekend hours and distribute them across the entire quarter. While each in-person class is three hours, the solution required every other class to extend to four hours. That way, over the course of a nine-week quarter, were able to distribute five hours away from the intensive weekend. This ensured the much-needed T-group time for the quarter and the students' learning while helping to reduce the amount of screen time over the weekend experience.

Exercises

The exercises we used to generate data for the T-groups were quite challenging to modify for a virtual environment. Given that we originally had 10 weeks which suddenly became nine weeks, we used various exercises to highlight aspects of the lecture, helped to speed up the development of the group, and gradually increased the interpersonal risks taken by group members. Each weekly session has 1–3 exercises which can take 10 minutes to a full hour depending on the exercise and the week. Exercises can be divided into the following categories: subgroup exercises (pairs or trios), fishbowl experiences, individual sharing in the group, sociometric explorations, and developing and sharing explicit learning goals for each participant as they navigate the course.

Learning Goals

At the start of the quarter, participants are asked to survey family, friends, and co-workers and based on the feedback received, generate 3–5 learning goals for the quarter. In person, these goals are written on flip chart paper that is posted around the room at each meeting so that any group member can see the goals of each member. As the group progresses, members may elect to modify their goals as they accomplish some and identify others which are important to them.

Modifying these sheets seemed difficult at first until Lisa suggested using a Google Doc with a 3x5 table which allowed each member (and the two facilitators) to claim their cell and write out their learning goals. The beauty of this is that it easily allowed group members to have a copy of everyone's goals on their monitor as the group progressed. Additionally, adding, editing or deleting goals was easy and evident to all.

Subgroup Exercises

Given that the group members often struggle with being emotionally present and open in a group of 14 people, we have a number of exercises which allow them to ease into openness. In person this is accomplished by breaking them into dyads for a number of conversations and having them work with a different person for each. This format helps them to have one-to-one contact with a few people, thus breaking the ice.

In person, these dyads are formed by the individuals selecting someone they wish to know better. In the virtual environment this was accomplished by placing the group members in breakout rooms. This resulted in less milling around and deciding who each member wished to choose for the conversation.

In person, we had an exercise for the members to choose a support group trio to aid each other in sharpening their learning goals and offering support for accomplishing these goals. Typically, this occurred in week five. Shifting to the virtual environment, we decided to randomly assign group members to trios in week one. This was achieved by randomly assigning members to breakout rooms. In week five, once the members better knew each other, we had them actually choose a new support group utilizing a method we will describe later.

Fishbowl Experiences

A few exercises in the in-person environment required half of the group to be in an inner circle engaging in the exercise while the remainder were in the outer circle observing. Eventually, the two subgroups swapped roles. We modified these exercises by having the observing subgroup turn off their cameras while they watched the other subgroup work. Once finished, the roles were reversed. This adaptation seemed to work flawlessly.

Sociometric Exercises

The final group of exercises are those where group members would line up along a continuum related to a dimension we were trying to make explicit. For instance, when dealing with issues of diversity, one pole might represent people of color while the other pole would be white identified members. The middle would represent intersectional members, those who identify along the continuum. In person, this is easy to effect. In the virtual environment we were initially at a loss as to how to operationalize such an exercise. Once again, Lisa suggested a simple and elegant solution; we designed a Google Slide that all members could access and edit. Each group member was given their name in a text box and they could move their marker around in the slide to the place on the continuum which fit their identification. This worked for line-up exercises too, allowing members to show where they would place themselves on various continua (age, socioeconomic status, race, number of languages spoken, etc.).

It also worked in week five where the exercise required selecting a support group trio to replace the assigned one. This is a very tense exercise as it limits the support group to three people and thus requires choice and acceptance/rejection. In this case, students had to move the text box with their name to a landing zone constructed for only three persons. There were opportunities to try out trios before the final round which would last for the rest of the group's life.

In person, these exercises are accomplished by students moving about the room. In addition to choosing support group trios, one exercise requires engaging in a dynamic influence line-up where everyone needs to shuffle into a forced-rank line-up from "more influential" to "less influential." The in-person discomfort created in these activities is where the learning and change occurs. We had to find ways to raise and hold that discomfort in the virtual environment. These exercises tend to be the most productive feedback sessions during T-group, so the students' learning depended on us holding the tension.

What we developed mimicked a live, multiplayer video game. Through Google Slides, we created a slide accessible to and editable by everyone. When it became time to jump into the exercise, we would post the link to the slide in the live chat feature of the video conferencing software. Everyone then toggled over to the slide and synchronously moved their tile with their name on it (their "avatar") to where they wished to position themselves (see sample below). What we found in the translation to the virtual setting was how important it became to create more structure and rules for these exercises. We also learned that it helped for us to play more of a narrator or moderator role during these activities when in the in-person experience we tended to be less vocal and much more observant.

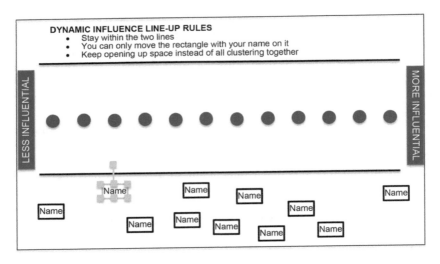

Figure 25.1 Dynamic influence line-up game
Source: Compiled by the authors.

T-group

The exercises, readings, and assignments between classes all generate various feelings and nudge the members into taking risks. In the T-group literature, such a combination is referred to as a Training Laboratory (Benne et al., 1964). Our experience is that it accelerates group formation and revelations about self, resulting in a cohesive group and a positive outcome. What begins as an ambiguous void with few explicit boundaries (confidentiality, time-liness, staying a member of the group, etc., similar to the practice guidelines of the American Group Psychotherapy Association) and much anxiety gra-dually shifts, inviting members to give feedback to each other in the here-and-now. Another dimension which is stressed is there-and-now experiences which can be thought of as transference or ways that the past is coloring the present. Together, trust and cohesiveness emerge.

Having resolved methods to deliver lectures, tools to use for feedback, and exercises, the next challenge was virtual T-group. As noted by Wein-berg and Rolnick (2020) there are at least eight dimensions that experts grapple with in differentiating in-person therapy from video conference-delivered therapy. One challenge we faced, that they do not mention, is the hesitation of group members to enroll in a group that is delivered virtually versus waiting for the opportunity to meet in person at a later time. This does not pose a challenge when the members are dispersed throughout the United States and the world at large. Under any circum-stances, at least one of our groups meets virtually as the members are dispersed or part-time students living outside of the area. Full-time stu-dents, however, value their interconnections and were afraid that they would miss having the full T-group experience. While the virtual experi-ence is not identical to being in the room, we emphasized two points. First, we reminded potential members that the opportunity to be in T-group was a scarce resource given their finite time in business school. Second, as these are students in a top-tier business school, we noted that increasingly the environments in which they work are becoming virtual with work teams spread across the globe.

Implications for Group Psychotherapy in the Virtual World

Given the nature of our endeavor, we have ideas that impact both the Tech-niques Camp and the Relationship Camp of group therapeutic approaches.

Technique Camp

Our groups, just as psychodrama, CBT, and dialectical behavior therapy groups utilize assignments, in vivo exercises, and the practicing of skills in the group. Changing these from the in-person format to the virtual setting was challenging, yet we found workable solutions that may help others. Practicing in fishbowl groups can easily be done by having the observing members turn off their cameras while the others stay on. Dyadic and small subgroups can practice skills by being assigned to breakout rooms. Exercises that require moving group members in the in-person situation can be modeled by using Google Slides with each member represented by a text box bearing their name. These simple work-arounds helped us to achieve the same ends as we did in person.

Relationship Camp

As noted by Agar (2020), whether in person or on video, relationships are everything. Certainly, there are technical difficulties and challenges to boundaries and confidentiality, yet these can be overcome provided that the facilitator and group members pay close attention and name things that disturb them or bring up any other emotion. It is particularly important to have members address each other directly and express their feelings towards one another. When feedback is delivered starting with intent, naming the behavior of the other, and then being clear about the feeling it engendered (how it landed), we find it is often well received and the parties can clarify their interactions.

As members address each other directly and based on their *feelings*, they come to learn about each other. Often one member's curiosity about another leads to sharing there-and-now information which is very helpful in understanding each other. Together, this creates increasing closeness and a strong feeling of cohesion in the group. We have found that this is the same whether delivered in person or by way of video conferencing.

Overall, whether in the Techniques Camp or the Relationship Camp it is possible to deliver high-quality group therapy services in person and via video conferencing.

References

Agar, G. (2020). The Clinic Offers No Advantage Over the Screen, for Relationship is Everything: Video Psychotherapy and its Dynamics. In H. Weinberg, & A. Rolnick (Eds.), *Theory and practice of online therapy: Internet-delivered interventions for individuals, groups, families, and organizations*. Routledge.

Agyris, C. (1994). Good communication that blocks learning. *Harvard Business Review*, July–Aug.

Batista, E. (2018). A brief history of T-groups. *Ed Batista Newsletter*, June 18. https://www.edbatista.com/2018/06/a-brief-history-of-t-groups.html.

Benne, K. D., Bradford, L. P., & Lippitt, R (1964). The Laboratory Method. In L. P. Bradford, J. R. Gibb, & K. D. Benne (Eds.), *T-group theory and laboratory method: Innovation in re-education* John Wiley & Sons.

Clayton, W. B., & Lucas, D. G. (1999). History of NTL: A story worth sharing. In A. L. Cooke, M. Brazzel, A. S. Craig, & B. Greig (Eds.), *Reading book for human relations training* (8th ed). NTL Institute for Applied Behavioral Science.

Heifetz, R. A., & Laurie, D. L. (2001). The work of leadership. *Harvard Business Review*, Dec.

Rolnick, A. (2020). Introduction to the general consideration: Principles of internet-based treatment. In H. Weinberg, & A. Rolnick (Eds.), *Theory and practice of online therapy: internet-delivered interventions for individuals, groups, families, and organizations* (pp. 13–22). Routledge. https://doi.org/10.4324/9781315545530.

Chapter 26

Enhancing Supervision Practices

The Promise and Potential of Online Group Supervision

Arnon Rolnick, Adam Leighton, Haim Weinberg and Cliff Briggie

Introduction

Many of the chapters in this book were influenced by the COVID-19 pandemic, which led to a widespread shift to remote work. The adoption of group supervision via video conferencing, however, predates the pandemic and has been on the rise for some time. The authors of this chapter have been using group supervision for over a decade, as it allows them to bring together a group of therapists who are located in different geographical areas and is time efficient. While the transition to remote group work was initially met with some reservations, it has proved to be effective in the authors' experience.

Although there were academic publications on online group supervision before the outbreak of the COVID-19 pandemic, such as Abbass et al. (2011), Morton (2017), Elliot et al. (2016), and Pennington et al. (2020), there was limited qualitative research on the topic. More recently, Nadan et al. (2020) and Traube et al. (2021) have conducted qualitative surveys indicating the feasibility of online group supervision. Geller et al. (2023) compared the experiences of 250 psychology graduate students in Israel and found no differences between online and in-person group supervision in terms of the students' reports of group processes and professional identity statuses.

In this chapter, we argue that the transition to online group supervision has met a critical need and has enabled the implementation of changes and innovations in supervision practices that may not have been possible in an in-person setting. We will describe an improved therapist group supervision model, focusing specifically on individual therapists receiving supervision in a group setting, rather than group therapists receiving supervision. Although the content may be relevant to the supervision of group therapists, the chapter's scope does not include this unique aspect, as it adds another layer of complexity. It is important to note that this chapter will examine ongoing supervision rather than training supervision, which is covered in Chapter 24 in this volume.

We will first provide a general definition of supervision and discuss the limitations of verbatim-based training. Then, we will introduce the "driving

DOI: 10.4324/9781003248606-31

instruction model" and the possibility for the supervisor to monitor the progress of the supervisee. Next, we will examine various aspects of group supervision and examine how these are impacted by the shift to remote group supervision. Additionally, we will address the challenges embodied in online supervision. Finally, we will delve into the numerous benefits of online supervision, including the ability to learn skills and techniques remotely.

The authors of this chapter would like to acknowledge the late Clifford R. Briggie, who passed away while contributing to this chapter. We have endeavored to honor his memory by including his work and embodying his spirit throughout the content.

Supervision Goals

According to Falender and Shafranske (2014), "Effective supervision is defined as practice that encourages supervisee development and autonomy, facilitates the supervisory relationship, protects the client, and enhances both client and supervisee outcomes." These supervision goals are achieved in various ways, including skill development and maintenance, self-learning and introspection (as the Delphic maxim states, "know thyself"), and support for therapist wellbeing. Klein et al. (2010) propose that supervision can be *formative*, helping therapists to develop and improve their skills and adhere to established frameworks. It can also be *restorative*, promoting self-care and promoting the therapist's overall wellbeing. Additionally, supervision can provide *normative* support, helping therapists to manage their workloads and cases effectively (Inskipp & Proctor, 2009). In terms of patient care, supervision can focus on case review, addressing specific issues or dilemmas, and managing countertransference issues. It can also ensure that the therapist-patient fit is appropriate, taking into account the therapist's competence and qualifications, as well as any potential countertransference issues.

The Limitation of Current Models of Group Supervision

Rousmaniere et al. (2017) and Watkins (2011) both observe that the impact of traditional psychotherapy supervision on client outcomes is uncertain, while Beutler et al. (1994) find that traditional training and supervision methods are not very successful in improving therapist effectiveness. We believe that technology can change this situation.

The traditional method of supervision and training in psychotherapy, verbatim-based supervision, relies on the therapist recalling and relaying their experiences in therapy sessions to the instructor and to the group after the session, rather than allowing for real-time observation and interaction. This is the equivalent to learning to drive, with the driver instructor waiting in his room and providing his instructions based on the young driver's recollection of his driving experiences.

The model that will be described in this chapter suggests using video recordings during online group supervision, offering substantial benefits, and improving the efficacy of supervision and the therapist's effectiveness.

Proctor (2008) describes the concept of "the group as a supervisor" (p. 12). We will adopt this in the following paragraphs, when referring to the supervisor we are including the supervision group.

The Driving Instruction Model

We suggest that supervision of therapists, similarly to learning to pilot an airplane or drive a vehicle, requires a hands-on approach with real-time observation and feedback from an instructor. However, verbatim-based supervision lacks the opportunity for in-depth examination of the therapist's decisions and reactions to patient behaviors and expressions. An alternative approach, whereby the instructor and therapist work together in a treatment session, allows for a more comprehensive understanding of the therapeutic process and enhances the training experience.

Therapy Sessions as "the Garden of Forking Paths"

In verbatim-based supervision, important elements such as voice, intonation, and prosody are rarely considered. Additionally, the timing of different topics and the connection between the therapist's interventions and the progression of the conversation's content, or "forking paths," are lost. Psychotherapy can be thought of as a garden of diverging paths or a tree with many branches, each representing a decision made by the therapist in response to the patient's behavior or non-verbal expressions. In traditional supervision, it is challenging for the supervisor to examine the specific junction points where the therapist made choices, including lingering, asking questions, or interpreting. Additionally, classic supervision does not provide the opportunity for the supervisor to observe the supervisee's treatment techniques or for the supervisee to gain insight into the supervisor's understanding of subtle nuances in the patient's reactions and responses. If the supervisor and supervisee were to work together in treatment sessions, they would have the opportunity to observe and discuss the decision-making process in real time, leading to a more beneficial training experience and improved treatment process.

Exploring the Spectrum of In-Person and Distanced Supervision

Prior to presenting an alternative model, we would like to introduce an additional dimension for characterizing supervision approaches. Various formats of supervision exist, ranging from in situ, where the supervisor is physically present in the therapy room, to ex situ therapist-oriented relational supervision, in which the therapist's *experiences* are the focus of the supervision session and are discussed with the supervisor. This spectrum refers to the conceptual distance from the supervised activity in terms of cognitive, emotional, and somatic aspects, rather than distinguishing between offline and online. Additional formats on this continuum include:

- Supervisor and group members are not remotely present during an online session.
- Review and discussion of recorded sessions.
- Use of roleplay.
- Verbatim case review.

Supervision practices exist along this continuum, each offering its own unique benefits and opportunities for learning and growth. However, to maximize the effectiveness of supervision in meeting both supervisors' and supervisees' goals, we suggest that the supervision format should strive to be as close to in situ supervision as possible. We believe that this approach enhances the formative and normative aspects of supervision, minimizing the conceptual distance between supervision and therapy, as we shall now elaborate.

The Apprenticeship Model

Brattland et al. (2022) describe "An apprenticeship model in the training of psychotherapy students." The authors emphasize that "performing a task together with someone who knows it better is, without a doubt, a basic mechanism for transferring knowledge and human skills."

This approach to learning is based on the idea that hands-on observation and participation in therapy sessions is a more effective way to learn and gain practical skills than simply hearing a verbal report of the sessions. There are several ways that this model can be implemented, including the supervisee observing the work of the supervisor, the supervisor observing the supervisee's therapy sessions, and the supervisor watching video recordings of the supervisee's sessions. We shall describe various methods and applications of the apprenticeship model in group therapy supervision, but first we will briefly discuss remote therapy and supervision.

Remote Therapy's Impact on Supervision

The rise of remote therapy has had a profound effect not just on the therapy itself, but has also ushered in a revolution in therapy training and supervision. Video conferencing software allows therapists and supervisors to easily record sessions, eliminating the need for specialized equipment. This enables them to review and analyze the sessions at a later time, providing a valuable tool for training and supervision.

The use of video conferencing software's abilities is not limited to remote therapy. Even if the therapist and client are in the same room with a computer present, it is now easy to use software such as Zoom or other platforms to record the session. The ability to review recorded sessions offers the opportunity for a close examination of key decision points and the interventions made by the therapist, providing insight into potential intervention points.

An additional opportunity that remote therapy allows is that the supervisor joins a supervisee's session with a patient. In the past, coordinating a therapy session between a therapist and trainee was a complex process, requiring both parties to find a mutually convenient location and time. With remote treatment, this has become much simpler.

Online Group Supervision

Group supervision offers many advantages including interpersonal learning and skill development, as well as self-learning. The methods used for group supervision can differ greatly, depending on the approach of the therapist. The focus of group supervision may include skills-oriented methods like the Portland Supervision Model (Thompson et al., 2015), exploration of parallel processes (explained below), examination of transference and countertransference, and working with projective identifications (Bernard, 1999). Furthermore, group supervision is often a more cost-effective alternative to individual supervision. Our proposal is that online group supervision can be performed effectively, and the apprenticeship model is suitable for online groups and can be adapted to various group supervision methods.

Online group supervision offers additional benefits, including increased accessibility and the ability to review sessions through recordings. These advantages provide strong support for our proposed group supervision model.

The chapters in this book outline various challenges and strategies for dealing with the distinctive features of online group therapy. Rather than rehashing these, our focus will be on the specific qualities of online group supervision and the application of the apprenticeship model.

Online Group Supervision: Feasibility and Key Considerations

In this section, we will explore various elements of group supervision to address the disparities between face-to-face and online sessions. By doing so, we also aim to showcase the feasibility of conducting group supervision online.

This analysis draws on elements described in two distinct sources, each with its own research methodology and approach. The first source is Proctor's (2008) Group Supervision Alliance Model, which outlines the various roles and responsibilities involved in group supervision. The second source is Mastoras and Andrews' (2011) research, which reviews multiple studies on supervisees' experiences of group supervision and identifies several essential elements of group supervision.

Professional Alliances and Contracts

In Chapter 3 in this volume, the authors explore how the group alliance remains largely unaffected by the shift to online format. Meanwhile, Chapter 8 addresses the challenge some participants face in the absence of a strong and present *leader* during online therapy. We believe that these findings are applicable to supervision groups. However, in online supervision groups the alliance with the leader/supervisor can have an additional enhancing factor, namely the supervisor's professional experience and knowledge.

While the transition to online group supervision should not negatively impact the group contract, it should be adjusted to account for the unique aspects of online therapy, especially in terms of engagement. The group contract can help to address distractions like reading emails during supervision sessions, which can be easily concealed from the group.

Participative Maintenance and Repair

As noted by Weinberg et al. (2022, pp. 7–8), the virtual environment is prone to creating instances of ruptures, which may arise from direct factors such as communication challenges, or indirect factors as discussed in this chapter and throughout the book. In light of this, when conducting group supervision online, the supervisor must be especially mindful of the importance and potential benefits of openly addressing issues of rupture and repair. Similar to other methods applied in supervision sessions, utilizing rupture and repair techniques can be advantageous not only for the supervision group itself, but also for modeling the implementation of these techniques.

Creative Methods

Proctor (2008) highlights the significance of creativity in group supervision, as it enables supervision to "reach parts other methods can't reach" (p. 12). Weinberg et al. (2022) similarly stress the value of creativity in online therapeutic work. This is further described specifically in online group work in Chapter 26 in this volume. These views align with Proctor's, emphasizing the importance of creativity in online group supervision.

The Group as a Supervisor

Proctor (2008) emphasizes the role of the group in group supervision, believing that "at its best, a group is a great deal more than the sum of its parts" (p. 12). This requires greater self-management skills, particularly during online group supervision as group members may need to take more responsibility for their participation and engagement in the absence of in-person social cues and prompts. The ease of disengagement as described above may also hinder the development of the group's ability to supervise.

Encouraging Peer Feedback and Managing Supervision Responses

Online group supervision can provide a diverse range of approaches and cultural perspectives, contributing to a more enriched learning experience for all participants. However, there is a need for further research to determine if online supervision groups, as opposed to face-to-face, increase hesitance among participants to share their own cases and difficulties. The importance of addressing participant equality is crucial, and various factors such as the use of similar platforms, the speaker's volume, and presentation size on the screen, can influence it. It is also essential for supervisors to address the limitations of present voice conferencing platforms that do not allow multiple people to be heard in parallel. Therefore, supervisors should ensure that everyone is heard and that all participants are encouraged to give feedback, contributing to a productive and inclusive online group supervision environment.

Balancing the Multiple Roles and Responsibilities of the Supervisor

The group supervisor has multiple roles and responsibilities. Online group supervision requires additional roles that are necessary for a successful and productive learning experience. One of these roles is the psycho-technological role, which involves the use of technological tools to enhance communication and collaboration among participants. Another crucial role is that of facilitator and moderator, which is essential in ensuring that democratic peer feedback is achieved due to the unique challenges that online group supervision can present, as described in the previous sub-section. Additionally, if shifting to the apprenticeship supervision model described, the supervisor will also need to act as the apprenticeship supervisor. Therefore, it is critical to adopt a co-supervision approach in online group supervision to ensure that all the necessary roles are fulfilled, promoting a more effective and comprehensive learning experience for all participants.

Managing Group Processes

One of the key roles of the group supervisor is to conduct and monitor group dynamics, including the supervisee experience with group cohesion, safety, conflict, and competition. This involves being aware of individual personalities and facilitating a positive, safe, and respectful environment for all participants to contribute openly and honestly.

While online group supervision is certainly a viable alternative to face-to-face sessions, it does pose challenges. Non-verbal communication cues, which are important in facilitating positive group dynamics and safety, may be limited or even absent in online sessions. We believe that this places even greater importance to ensure that group dynamics are beneficial and that participants feel safe and respected.

It is our suggestion that the group supervisor(s) should take proactive measures to cultivate cohesion in online groups by utilizing various tools available in the online environment. The contributors to this book have presented several innovative techniques, such as psychodrama, art therapy, and Somatic Experiencing, to name but a few. We strongly advise the group supervisor to dedicate group time to promote cohesion actively and directly, using these techniques or others that may be suitable for the group's specific needs and characteristics.

Parallel Processes

Using the parallel processes between the dynamics in the supervision group and the discussed case can become a powerful tool to bring the case alive, especially in the online setting since the screen barrier might limit the immediate experience of the participants in the supervision group. Parallel processes were first described by Ekstein and Wallerstein (1963). They refer to the unconscious repetition within supervision of the dynamics of the presented case. In the group analytic approach, they are referred to as equivalence. Equivalence is based on projective and intro-jective identifications in the service of attack, expulsion, control and above all on non-verbal communication, primarily in an effort to produce a narrative of unspeakable pain and suffering (Hopper, 2003).

Parallel processes can greatly enrich the supervisory process by bring-ing the emotional experience into the session. In online supervision, it can maintain the interest and involvement of the group participants and help them to stay focused despite the many distractions existing online. The group members can experience boredom, anxiety, irritation, or even excessive helpfulness, just as the presenting therapist experiences with their clients. To benefit from a parallel process, members must be willing to participate in the process rather than stay safely in a didactic role. Counselman and Gumpert (1993) described opportunities for learning from parallel processes, reducing professional isolation, and preventing clinician burnout.

One important equivalent aspect is manifested when the case brought for supervision is a case of online therapy. The processes and obstacles that are unique to online therapy can show themselves in the supervision group as well. For example, a supervisee may describe a patient from whom they feel disconnected, explaining how sessions feel bland when meeting online (a commonly reported experience by both therapists and patients during online sessions). The supervisor may choose to examine if a similar process is occurring in the supervision group. This parallel process provides a unique opportunity to experience what the patient feels and also to watch the reactions of the supervisor and the group to the same situation and learn from it.

Working with Supervisee Anxiety

Supervisee anxiety is a common issue in presenting cases and issues during online group therapy. While Mastoras and Andrews (2011) postulated that the group setting would reduce some of this anxiety, this hypothesis has yet to be fully investigated in online settings. The "online factor" may contribute to anxiety in participation, as well as the ease of multitasking that may lead to avoidance as a strategy for not sharing and being less engaged. Addressing not only anxiety in being evaluated by the supervisor but also specific aspects of the group supervision experience that may be anxiety-provoking can help supervisees to reflect more openly upon their own feelings, reactions, and behaviors. It can also normalize such experiences, thereby reducing feelings of isolation. Explicit discussions about concerns regarding the online platform can help to open discussions about the supervisees' experiences and emotions, which can expand to include concerns regarding the group and sharing. Such discussions can create greater openness and promote a more collaborative learning experience for all participants. It is important for the group supervisor to be attentive to supervisees' anxiety and provide support to minimize it, thereby fostering a more positive group supervision experience.

Embodiment

The partial absence of bodily reactions in remote therapy has been covered in all our books (Weinberg and Rolnick, 2019; Weinberg et al., 2022).

And, of course, it is discussed in the present book regarding online groups. How much more is it important in group supervision?

The first bodies that are absent in group supervision are the patient, the therapist, and the therapeutic dyad who are the subject of the case presentation. As mentioned above, working with parallel processes can overcome some of this absence. Utilizing recordings also enables us to overcome this absence to some extent, as we will discuss further in this chapter.

In their book about embodiment in supervision, Bownas and Fredman (2017) suggest paying attention to the unintentional (pre-reflective) and intentional expressions and constructions of the physical body. They describe many incidences where bodily reactions contribute to the supervision process. However, a closer examination reveals that the focus is on the subjective bodily reactions of the supervisor and the supervisee as they appear in their self-report. They can, of course, be very well used in online group supervision. It is true that in classical group supervision both the supervisor and the group can watch the bodily reactions of members of the group, while they cannot do so in remote group therapy. However, in online group supervision, both the supervisor and individual group members are able to see each other's facial expressions, which can be even clearer and more pronounced than during in-person supervision.

Who Do We View?

Another interesting advantage offered by online group supervision is the ability to view all the participants at the same time. This is in contrast to in-person group therapy where one would have to physically turn one's head to observe everyone in the group. This feature provides two benefits:

a   It gives supervisors (and participants) the unique opportunity to see the group as a whole and understand how each individual interacts with the others.
b   It is possible to focus on participants who are not speaking at the moment, instead of just focusing on the person who is talking. This is especially important in situations where the session is led by a single facilitator or supervisor, which is a common scenario in group supervision. This requires a conscious effort on behalf of the supervisor, as we naturally observe the speaker (frequently the supervisee/case presenter). From a psycho-technical aspect, this can be supported with the use of different views that video conferencing software offers, allowing whole group views (gallery view) or views focused on individual speakers (speaker/pinned view).

A New Supervision Paradigm

Live Observation of Therapy Sessions ("Virtual" One-Way Mirror)

We have discussed mutual observation, during which the supervisee sees how the supervisor works and the supervisor sees how the supervisee conducts treatment and gives them feedback.

A different approach is to use a one-way mirror, a technique which is more commonly used in family and couple therapy. It entails the use of a special set-up and is less frequently employed during supervision of individual therapists. Despite the potential benefits of this approach, it is not widely used partly due to the technical difficulties of setting up the necessary equipment for video recording. Sometimes the sound of the session is recorded (without video), which allows for a detailed understanding of the therapeutic interaction and the use of tones and timing; however, this method does not provide the information on non-verbal expressions.

The transition to online therapy has opened the opportunity for supervisors and therapists to observe therapy sessions in real time. Supervisors can provide immediate feedback and support to the therapist being supervised, which helps them to improve their skills more rapidly and provide better care to patients. Furthermore, when multiple therapists are able to observe a therapy session simultaneously, it enables them to collaborate more effectively, make decisions about a patient's care more swiftly, and provide greater continuity of care.

The benefits of utilizing video recordings are not restricted solely to therapeutic approaches that are skill-oriented. Despite some psychodynamic psychotherapists being hesitant to record therapy sessions on video, Kernberg (2010) argues that the act of watching video recordings can offer a wealth of information regarding the session's content and attitudes. This can facilitate the assessment of transference and countertransference by observing non-verbal behaviors exhibited by both the patient and therapist. Kernberg concludes that video recording may provide the most insightful means of evaluating a therapist's overall performance, as there may be significant discrepancies between what the therapist reports and what is actually observed on video (p. 622).

This opportunity does not come without drawbacks. Patients and therapists may feel uncomfortable with their therapy sessions being observed in real time, which could negatively impact their engagement with therapy. Additionally, patients may have concerns about the privacy of others discussed in the session, such as a spouse or parent. Furthermore, the therapist or supervisor observing the session can be distracted by trying to provide feedback or support while the session is ongoing, which may limit their understanding of the patient's history and context.

It is also important to note that watching a therapy session as it happens may not provide the supervisor or observing therapists a complete understanding of the patient's history and circumstances, as opposed to verbal debriefing.

Using the Session Recordings in an Online Supervision Session

As previously mentioned, reviewing recorded therapy sessions as an alternative to real-time observation provides an offline option while still adhering to the principles of the apprenticeship model. While recordings may not be as immersive as real-time observation, they do offer certain benefits such as the ability to revisit specific points as well the convenience of being able to review the session at a later time and focus on specific parts of the session, thus saving time.

The act of the supervisee reviewing the recording of his/her session with a client and choosing a specific moment, something he or she would like to work on is the essence of (or at least the beginning of) *deliberate practice* (Rousmaniere et al., 2017, p. 114). This is very different from the common approach of looking at how the group can help to solve a problem involving a specific client/situation, requiring the therapist to identify specific skills her or she would like to work on. The supervisor and group may also provide important insights for the supervisee, thereby highlighting potential areas for improvement.

In what follows we will outline the steps involved in conducting online group supervision. The process begins with the intake of new patients, during which the therapist should prepare them for the possibility of recording sessions. This can be done by saying something like, "I often bring recordings from meetings to supervision sessions with other therapists" (APA, n.d.). When the online sessions start, the therapist can ask the patient for permission to record the session, explaining that the recording will be kept on a secure server and that the patient can choose to have it erased and not used at the end of the session.

After the session, the therapist selects a 5–10-minute clip from the recording to share in the group supervision session. It is important that the therapist and supervisor discuss the purpose of sharing the recording and choose it accordingly. The goals may be formative or normative and may be as varied as the approaches to group therapy. The supervisor/supervisee may choose to use the recording to explore the therapist's response to a specific issue, providing the group with a sense of the patient so they can provide insights and feedback, or examining the use of a specific technique. The recording could also be an aid in examining issues of countertransference using the group.

An experiential technique described by Altfeld (1999), p. 273 describes how material presented to the group (verbally)

> stimulates conscious and unconscious parallel processes in group members. Through here-and-now responses, associations, and inter-actions among the supervisory members, countertransference issues that have eluded the presenter can make themselves known and be worked through on emotional as well as cognitive levels.

The use of recorded materials as opposed to verbal descriptions allows therapists and supervisors to experience non-verbal communication seen in the recording in addition to the verbal content. We suggest that this greatly enhances the processes described by Altfeld.

During the group supervision session, the therapist will briefly describe the case and then the group will watch the recording without stopping. After this stage, the group can discuss the issues that the therapist brought up and, if requested, go back to specific sections of the recording. Therefore, it is recommended that the therapist bringing the case should start and stop the video playback.

Using recorded materials in group supervision also carries certain dangers. Participants may falsely believe that they have a complete grasp of both the session and the patient, leading them to give advice or criticism to super-visees. Attention can easily be drawn away from the desired supervisory approach and group processes, focusing instead solely on the content. The supervisor may opt to remind the participants of the recorded presentation's purpose, keeping in mind the group's objectives and techniques.

In sum, remote treatment enables a change in how therapy is con-ducted, and how it is trained and observed. Furthermore, it enables a joint therapy experience and allows relatively straightforward recording and viewing of therapy and supervision sessions.

Privacy, Confidentiality and Allaying Concerns of Those Involved

The privacy and confidentiality of patients during therapy sessions and supervision are important considerations. The American Psychological Association's *Record Keeping Guidelines* emphasize the need to protect patients' security, integrity, confidentiality, and appropriate access, while complying with legal and ethical documentation procedures. Informed consent is the first requirement, and steps should be taken to maintain the recordings' security, integrity, and confidentiality. Patient identifying information should be removed, such as their name, voice, and face, to protect their confidentiality. However, this can be challenging, and there are no perfect solutions yet. For more information see the Appendix at the end of this chapter.

It is imperative to recognize that attending to these concerns is not solely a matter of meeting ethical and legal obligations. Instead, it is essential for effectively allaying the concerns of the recorded patient, the therapist/supervisee, the supervisor, and other members of the group.

Patients' and Therapists' Stance on Recording Sessions

The question of patients' willingness for therapy sessions to be recorded has been a topic of concern, as it is assumed that patients may not be willing to record the session due to privacy concerns. However, this assumption is not always true, and from our experience some patients may even request to record the session.

A 2016 study by Al Briggie et al. titled *Patient Comfort with Audio or Video Recording of Their Psychotherapy Sessions* primarily surveys the differences in knowledge acquired in this field since the 1950 and includes 390 participants who were in the process of referral to public clinics. It is important to note that the participants were informed that their stance on recording would not affect their acceptance for treatment in the same clinic. The results were clear: more than 70 percent of the patients did not object to recording the session and in some cases even requested it. Furthermore, many researchers have reported that both patients and therapists usually forget that recording is soon forgotten (e.g., Brown et al., 2013).

Our experience suggests that therapists are often reluctant to have their therapy sessions recorded on video, but according to a 2009 study by Shepherd et al., therapists generally have a positive view of audio recordings of sessions. The difference in attitudes towards audio and video recordings could explain this discrepancy, or it could be because our observations are based solely on anecdotal evidence. Clearly, further research is needed to better understand therapists' attitudes towards recording sessions and to find ways to alleviate their concerns.

Conclusion

This chapter has explored the advantages of transitioning to remote therapy for supervision purposes, in line with our recognition of the shortcomings of conventional group supervision methods. We believe that adopting online therapy will significantly enhance the utilization and efficacy of group supervision in the digital realm. However, we note that there is a lack of sufficient research on this particular form of supervision, and we encourage further investigation into online group supervision as outlined above.

Appendix: Issues of Privacy and Confidentiality in Session Recordings

As discussed in this chapter and in the Introduction to the book, issues of privacy and confidentiality are more complex when working with groups as opposed to individuals. Recording either patient sessions or supervision sessions can raise additional privacy concerns which need to be addressed. We suggest that session recordings should be treated as clinical records, which have ample preventative guidelines to ensure protection of patients' privacy. The APA Record Keeping Guidelines (APA, n.d.) state the responsibility to protect the security, integrity, confidentiality, and appropriate access, as well as compliance with applicable legal and ethical requirements for documentation procedures when conducting couple, family, or group therapy in order to respect the privacy and confidentiality of all parties.

The first requirement is the informed consent of the patient and/or therapists participating in the supervision.

In order to maintain the security, integrity, and confidentiality of recordings we suggest that the following steps should be taken. These must be in accordance to the legal (e.g., Health Insurance Portability and Accountability Act) and ethical frameworks to which the therapist/supervisor is subject to.

a   Recording is maintained on a secure server with access control, preventing the risk of unauthorized access to recordings.
b   In order to protect patient confidentiality, patient identifying information should be removed when possible. This can be complex and at present, is subject to technical challenges. We can separate between recording identifying information (similar to any other electronic patient record) and the sharing/display of the details during group supervision sessions.

Identifying information can include:

•   Content (name of patient, specific details, e.g. place of work).
•   Name of patient as displayed in the video conferencing window.
•   Patient's voice.
•   Patient's face.

Identifying content details are relatively easier to protect when presenting a recording to the group, and require the therapist's awareness when choosing which clip to share.

The name of the patient can be removed in various ways. Some video conferencing platforms allow the session to be recorded without the displayed names. Alternatively, the therapist can suggest that the patient uses a different name.

The patient's voice can theoretically be distorted. However, this comes at a price, requiring technical knowledge, suitable software, and time. Furthermore, distorting the voice can cause valuable information regarding the patient's intonation to be lost.

The patient's face is even more challenging as faces allow instantaneous recognition by participants in the group supervision setting. There are a number of workarounds, but none provide a perfect solution at present. One option is to edit the recording using video editing software to change lighting, blur or pixelate faces and identifying features. Another option, at the cost of losing much non-verbal information, is the use of avatars. A third option is the use of a second camera, focused below the patient's face, thus removing facial information but allowing other body gestures, such as hand gestures, to be seen. This solution requires a relatively high level of familiarity with the video conferencing software, enabling the therapist to see both of the patient's cameras, but recording only the therapist's camera and the patient's second camera, which is focused on their lower torso. This can technically be achieved using the Zoom platform and selecting the "Advanced share, content from 2nd camera" option.

It is worth noting that there are no perfect solutions yet; however, the complexity is justified by the potential for improving the care delivered to our patients.

Leak Risk Reduction

The recordings of these sessions may contain sensitive patient information. Sharing recordings (the files) with other people such as the supervisor or supervision group participants can increase the risk of privacy breaches and could potentially discourage participants from recording sessions. To mitigate this risk, we suggest using video conferencing platforms that allow viewing of recorded sessions without the option to download them. This solution decreases the chances of recordings being accessed by unauthorized parties, either intentionally or unintentionally.

References

Abbass, A., Arthey, S., Elliott, J., Fedak, T., Nowoweiski, D., Markovski, J., & Nowoweiski, S. (2011). Web-conference supervision for advanced psychotherapy training: A practical guide. *Psychotherapy*, 48(2), 109–118. https://doi.org/10.1037/a0022427.

Altfeld, D. A. (1999) An Experiential Group Model for Psychotherapy Supervision. *International Journal of Group Psychotherapy*, 49(2), 237–254. http://dx.doi.org/10.1080/00207284.1999.11491583.

American Psychological Association (APA) (n.d.). *Record keeping guidelines.* http s://www.apa.org/practice/guidelines/record-keeping.

Bernard, H. S. (1999). Introduction to special issue on group supervision of group psychotherapy. *International Journal of Group Psychotherapy*, 49(2), 153–157. https://doi.org/10.1080/00207284.1999.11491578.

Beutler, L. E., Machado, P. P. P., & Neufeldt, S. A. (1994). Therapist variables. In A. E. Bergin & S. L. Garfield (Eds.), *Handbook of psychotherapy and behavior change* (pp. 229–269). John Wiley & Sons.

Borges, J. L. (1962). The garden of forking paths. *Collected Fictions*, 119.

Bownas, J., & Fredman, G. (Eds.) (2017). *Working with embodiment in supervision: A systemic approach.* Routledge.

Brattland, H., Holgersen, K. H., Vogel, P. A., Anderson, T., & Ryum, T. (2022). An apprenticeship model in the training of psychotherapy students. Study protocol for a randomized controlled trial and qualitative investigation. *PLOS ONE*, 17(8), e0272164. https://doi.org/10.1371/journal.pone.0272164.

Briggie, A. M., Hilsenroth, M. J., Conway, F., Muran, J. C., & Jackson, J. M. (2016). Patient comfort with audio or video recording of their psychotherapy sessions: Relation to symptomatology, treatment refusal, duration, and out-come. *Professional Psychology: Research and Practice*, 47(1), 66–76. https://doi.org/10.1037/a0040063.

Brown, E., Moller, N., & Ramsey-Wade, C. (2013) Recording therapy sessions: What do clients and therapists really think? *Counselling and Psychotherapy Research*, 13(4), 254–262. doi:10.1080/14733145.2013.768286.

Butler, C., & Fredman, G. (2017). Supervision of arousal and disgust. In J. Bownas & G. Fredman (Eds.), *Working with embodiment in supervision: A systemic approach.* Routledge.

Collins (n.d.). Supervise. In *Collins English Dictionary.* https://www.collinsdictiona ry.com/dictionary/english/supervise.

Counselman, E. F., & Gumpert, P. (1993). Psychotherapy supervision in small leader-led groups. *Group, 17*, 25–32. https://doi.org/10.1007/BF01419603.

Ekstein, R., & Wallerstein, R. S. (1963). *The teaching and learning of psychotherapy.* Basic Books.

Elliott, J., Abbass, A., & Cooper, J. (2016). International group supervision using videoconferencing technology. In T. Rousmaniere & E. Renfro-Michel (Eds.), *Using technology to enhance clinical supervision* (pp. 191–202). John Wiley & Sons. https://doi.org/10.1002/9781119268499.ch12.

Falender, C. A., & Shafranske, E. P. (2014). Clinical supervision: The state of the art. *Journal of Clinical Psychology*, 70(11), 1030–1041. https://doi.org/10.1002/jclp.22124.

Geller, S., Hanetz-Gamliel, K., & Levy, S. (2023). Online group supervision in graduate psychology training during the COVID-19 pandemic. *Online Learning*, 27(1), 1–18.

Halpern, H. (2009). Supervision and the Johari Window: A framework for asking questions. *Education for Primary Care*, 20(1), 10–14. https://doi.org/10.1080/14739879.2009.11493757.

Hopper, E. (2003). *The Social Unconscious: Selected Papers.* Jessica Kingsley Publishers.

Inskipp, F., & Proctor, B. (2009). *The art, craft & tasks of counselling supervision. Part 1, Making the most of supervision: A workbook and digitalised CD* (2nd ed., rev). Cascade.

Kernberg O. F. (2010). Psychoanalytic supervision: The supervisor's tasks. *The Psychoanalytic Quarterly*, 79(3), 603–627. https://doi.org/10.1002/j.2167-4086. 2010.tb00459.x.

Klein, R. H., Bernard, H. S., & Schermer, V. L. (2010). *On becoming a psychotherapist*. Oxford University Press. https://doi.org/10.1093/acprof:oso/9780199736393.001.0001.

Mastoras, S. M., & Andrews, J. J. W. (2011). The supervisee experience of group supervision: Implications for research and practice. *Training and Education in Professional Psychology*, 5(2), 102–111. https://doi.org/10.1037/a0023567.

Morton, J. R., Jr. (2017). *Supervisors' experience of resistance during online group supervision: A phenomenological case study.* Southern Illinois University at Carbondale.

Nadan, Y., Shachar, R., Cramer, D., Leshem, T., Levenbach, D., Rozen, R., Salton, N., & Cramer, S. (2020). Behind the (virtual) mirror: online live supervision in couple and family therapy. *Family Process*, 59(3), 997–1006. https://doi.org/10.1111/famp.12573.

Pennington, M., Patton, R., & Katafiasz, H. (2020). Cybersupervision in psychotherapy. In H. Weinberg & A. Rolnick (Eds.), *Theory and practice of online therapy* (pp. 79–95). Routledge.

Proctor, B. (2008). *Group supervision: A guide to creative practice.* SAGE.

Rothwell, C., Kehoe, A., Farook, S. F., & Illing, J. (2021). Enablers and barriers to effective clinical supervision in the workplace: A rapid evidence review. *BMJ Open*, 11(9), e052929. https://doi.org/10.1136/bmjopen-2021-052929.

Rousmaniere, T., Goodyear, R. K., Miller, S. D., & Wampold, B. E. (Eds.) (2017). *The cycle of excellence: Using deliberate practice to improve supervision and training.* Wiley-Blackwell. https://doi.org/10.1002/9781119165590.

Shepherd, L., Salkovskis, P. M., & Morris, M. (2009). Recording therapy sessions: An evaluation of patient and therapist reported behaviours, attitudes and preferences. *Behavioural and Cognitive Psychotherapy*, 37(2), 141. doi:10.1017/s1352465809005190.

Thompson, B. L., Luoma, J. B., Terry, C. M., LeJeune, J. T., Guinther, P. M., & Robb, H. (2015). Creating a peer-led acceptance and commitment therapy consultation group: The Portland model. *Journal of Contextual Behavioral Science*, 4(3), 144–150.

Traube, D. E., Cederbaum, J. A., Taylor, A., Naish, L., & Rau, A. (2021). Telehealth training and provider experience of delivering behavioral health services. *The Journal of Behavioral Health Services & Research*, 48(1), 93–102. https://doi.org/10.1007/s11414-020-09718-0.

Watkins, C. E., Jr. (2011). Does psychotherapy supervision contribute to patient outcomes? Considering thirty years of research. *The Clinical Supervisor*, 30(2), 235–256. https://doi.org/10.1080/07325223.2011.619417.

Weinberg, H., & Rolnick, A. (2020). *Theory and practice of online therapy: Internet-delivered interventions for individuals, groups, families, and organizations* (1st ed.). Routledge. https://doi.org/10.4324/9781315545530.

Weinberg, H., Rolnick, A., & Leighton, A. (Eds.) (2022). *Advances in online therapy: Emergence of a new paradigm.* Taylor & Francis.

Chapter 27

Epilogue

Beyond Group Psychotherapy: Online Groups as the Modern Agora for Enhancing Democracy and Cohesion

Arnon Rolnick

As we conclude this book, it becomes evident that online groups can be a highly effective form of psychotherapy. During our exploration of various types of group therapy in this book, it has become apparent that transferring them to the online platform requires a conscious awareness of the differences and that it is certainly a unique experience compared to in-person groups. However, this adaptation does not detract from their effectiveness.

In this short epilogue, we propose that online groups have the potential to serve a greater purpose beyond psychotherapy. They can serve as a means of connection, fostering cohesion and resolving conflicts. Drawing inspiration from the Greek agora and tribal campfires, we posit that online groups can be utilized to reduce conflicts among nations, races, and political groups. In the group therapy literature, the large group modality is considered as a kind of socio-therapy (Weinberg and Schneider, 2003). Edelson (1970) applied large group theory and principles to understand how sociotherapy can deal with inter- and intra-group tensions. De Maré (1975) writes: "The large group ... offers us a context and a possible tool for exploring the interface between the polarised and split areas of psychotherapy and sociotherapy. This is the area of the inter-group and of the transdisciplinary" (p. 146). Chapters 8, 11 and 12 in this volume are examples of the use of online large groups for sociotherapy.

Online Groups as the Successor to Tribal Campfires, Public Squares, the Agora, and the Town Hall Meeting

The tribal campfire functioned as a hub where community members could congregate, interact, and exchange stories. Likewise, online groups offer a virtual hub where individuals can meet and connect with one another.

The tribal campfire provided a communal experience that fostered a sense of unity and belonging among all participants. Similarly, online groups can facilitate a shared experience, such as attending a virtual town hall or joining a digital book club, which can also engender feelings of community and connection.

DOI: 10.4324/9781003248606-32

In a similar vein, the Greek agora, or public square, served as a central gathering place where people could socialize, conduct business, and participate in politics. It played a pivotal role in shaping the culture and democracy of ancient Greece. In modern times, with technological advancements and the COVID-19 pandemic, online groups can effectively serve as replacements for tribal campfires and Greek agora gatherings. In fact, virtual video-based meetings offer several advantages:

Accessibility: The tribal campfire and agora meetings were limited to those physically present, whereas online groups can be accessed from anywhere with an internet connection. This allows individuals who are unable to attend in-person events, such as those who live far away or have disabilities, to still participate. In contrast to the Greek agora, which required physical presence, online groups offer accessibility to almost anyone with an adequate internet connection. This allows individuals who live far away or have physical limitations to engage in discussions and debates. Furthermore, it enables those who cannot travel due to financial or personal reasons to connect with others from the comfort of their own homes. Although online group accessibility is not universal, it still represents a significant improvement.

Flexibility: The tribal campfire often took place at a specific time and place, while online groups can be scheduled at any time and location that is convenient for participants. This flexibility allows a wider range of people to participate. Online groups provide a flexible way of communication that was not available in ancient Greece. People can schedule meetings at their convenience, and participants can join the conversation from any location at any time. This allows for a wider range of topics to be discussed and more people to participate.

Efficiency: online groups can save time and resources that would have been spent on transportation to the Greek agora. Participants can engage in discussions without worrying about the time or distance it takes to travel. It also allows for multiple discussions to happen simultaneously, thereby increasing productivity.

Diversity: Online groups can connect people from different cultures, countries, and backgrounds, providing a diverse range of perspectives. This can lead to a richer and more informed discussion, which is essential for a healthy democracy. In addition, advancing technologies have the potential to break down language barriers by enabling real-time translation and communication between individuals who do not share a common language, thereby reducing the "Tower of Babel" effect.

Safety: In situations in which physical gatherings may pose a risk to public health, such as during disease outbreaks or wartime, online groups offer a safe alternative that allows for discussions to still take place. Moreover, online groups can be moderated to ensure that conversations remain respectful and productive.

One significant difference between online groups and traditional gathering places like the campfire and the Greek agora is the initial incentive for attending. The campfire provided warmth and often food, while the agora was a central location that people would visit regardless of any social gathering. Communication platforms such as WhatsApp, WeChat, and Facebook Messenger that are prevalent in our daily lives can be seen as analogous to the Greek agora. Many of us frequently visit these platforms, which presents a potential alternative, albeit one that lacks the crucial visual aspect of in-person gatherings.

In order to fully leverage the potential of online groups as a social tool, we must contemplate ways to create an initial incentive that attracts a diverse range of individuals, not solely those who are already enthusiastic about the idea.

Online Groups for Reducing Conflicts Between Nations and Races

The Introduction to this book contains a citation from Carl Rogers (1968), who said that groups will be "the most significant social invention of the century" (p. 16). This assertion was part of a zeitgeist and a hope about the power of human potential and the importance of empathy and understanding in promoting personal growth. Rogers was known for his optimistic view of human nature and his belief that people have an innate desire to reach their full potential.

The reader may observe throughout the book a shared belief that groups can help individuals to gain insight into their own behavior and emotions by observing and reflecting on their interactions with others. Groups encourage members to be honest and open with each other, share their feelings, and provide feedback to one another. Large groups and approaches like sociodrama and sociometry can offer insight into how groups and society behave and interact internally and externally.

Over the past few decades, it seems that the world has shifted from a period of optimism and idealism about the possibility of achieving peace and mutual understanding among nations and people, as was characteristic of the 1960s, to a more pessimistic and skeptical view that such goals are increasingly difficult to attain. In recent years, many countries have seen a resurgence of nationalist and populist movements, which often emphasize divisions between nations and promote an "us versus them" mentality. This has made it harder to achieve international cooperation and understanding. Despite efforts to prevent or resolve conflicts, violence continues to be a major problem around the world. From ongoing conflicts in the Middle East to rising tensions between major powers, there seems to be little progress towards resolving conflicts peacefully.

We believe that groups with managed processes can play a valuable role in bridging conflicts by providing a space for individuals with different perspectives and experiences to come together and engage in constructive dialogue. The following are some ways in which groups can be beneficial:

Encouraging open communication: One of the biggest benefits of groups is that they can provide a safe space for individuals to express their thoughts and feelings without fear of judgment. By encouraging open communication and active listening, groups can help participants to understand each other's perspectives and work towards finding common ground.
Fostering empathy: When individuals are able to listen and understand each other's experiences, it can lead to increased empathy and understanding. By creating opportunities for individuals to share their stories and perspectives, groups can help to bridge divides and reduce misunderstandings.
Building trust: Conflict often arises from a lack of trust between individuals or groups. By creating a space for individuals to engage in open and honest communication, groups can help to build trust and establish a foundation for working together towards a common goal.
Providing a forum for collaboration: Groups can be a powerful tool for collaboration, as they bring together individuals with different strengths and experiences. By working together towards a shared goal, individuals can build relationships and find solutions that are mutually beneficial.

Overall, groups can be an effective tool for bridging conflicts by providing a safe space for open communication, fostering empathy, building trust, promoting collaboration, and encouraging accountability. By bringing individuals together in a structured and supportive environment, groups can help to promote understanding and create opportunities for positive change. The advantages of online groups may be precisely what is necessary to facilitate the expansion of online group therapy and as a result enhance its potential benefits for humanity.

References

De Maré, P. (1975). The politics of large groups. In L. Kreeger (Ed.), *The large group: Dynamics and therapy* (pp. 145–158). Constable.
Edelson, M. (1970). *The practice of sociotherapy*. Yale University Press.
Rogers, C. R. (1968). Interpersonal relationships: U.S.A. 2000. *The Journal of Applied Behavioral Science*, 4(3), 265–280. https://doi.org/10.1177/002188636800400301.
Weinberg, H., & Schneider, S. (2003). Introduction: Background, structure and dynamics of the large group. In S. Schneider & H. Weinberg (Eds.), *The large group revisited: The herd, primal horde, crowds and masses* (pp. 13–26). Jessica Kingsley Publishers.

Index